ROUTLEDGE LIBRARY EDITIONS: AMERICA – REVOLUTION & CIVIL WAR

Volume 7

EBENEZER HAZARD, JEREMY BELKNAP AND THE AMERICAN REVOLUTION

EBENEZER HAZARD, JEREMY BELKNAP AND THE AMERICAN REVOLUTION

RUSSELL M. LAWSON

LONDON AND NEW YORK

First published in 2011 by Pickering & Chatto (Publishers) Ltd

This edition first published in 2021
by Routledge
2 Park Square, Milton Park, Abingdon, Oxon OX14 4RN

and by Routledge
52 Vanderbilt Avenue, New York, NY 10017

Routledge is an imprint of the Taylor & Francis Group, an informa business

© 2011 Russell M. Lawson, Taylor & Francis Ltd

All rights reserved. No part of this book may be reprinted or reproduced or utilised in any form or by any electronic, mechanical, or other means, now known or hereafter invented, including photocopying and recording, or in any information storage or retrieval system, without permission in writing from the publishers.

Trademark notice: Product or corporate names may be trademarks or registered trademarks, and are used only for identification and explanation without intent to infringe.

British Library Cataloguing in Publication Data
A catalogue record for this book is available from the British Library

ISBN: 978-0-367-54033-3 (Set)
ISBN: 978-1-00-312459-7 (Set) (ebk)
ISBN: 978-0-367-64341-6 (Volume 7) (hbk)
ISBN: 978-1-00-312415-3 (Volume 7) (ebk)

Publisher's Note
The publisher has gone to great lengths to ensure the quality of this reprint but points out that some imperfections in the original copies may be apparent.

Disclaimer
The publisher has made every effort to trace copyright holders and would welcome correspondence from those they have been unable to trace.

EBENEZER HAZARD, JEREMY BELKNAP AND THE AMERICAN REVOLUTION

BY

Russell M. Lawson

LONDON AND NEW YORK

First published 2011 by Pickering & Chatto (Publishers) Limited

Published 2016 by Routledge
2 Park Square, Milton Park, Abingdon, Oxon OX14 4RN
711 Third Avenue, New York, NY 10017, USA

Routledge is an imprint of the Taylor & Francis Group, an informa business

© Taylor & Francis 2011
© Russell M. Lawson 2011

All rights reserved, including those of translation into foreign languages. No part of this book may be reprinted or reproduced or utilised in any form or by any electronic, mechanical, or other means, now known or hereafter invented, including photocopying and recording, or in any information storage or retrieval system, without permission in writing from the publisher

Notice:
Product or corporate names may be trademarks or registered trademarks, and are used only for identification and explanation without intent to infringe.

BRITISH LIBRARY CATALOGUING IN PUBLICATION DATA

Lawson, Russell M., 1957–
Ebenezer Hazard, Jeremy Belknap and the American Revolution. – (The Enlightenment world)
1. Hazard, Ebenezer, 1744–1817 – Correspondence. 2. Belknap, Jeremy, 1744–1798 – Correspondence. 3. Postmasters general – United States – Correspondence. 4. Historians – United States – Correspondence. 5. United States – History – Revolution, 1775–1783 –Sources.
I. Title II. Series III. Hazard, Ebenezer, 1744–1817.
IV. Belknap, Jeremy, 1744–1798.
973.3'0922-dc22

ISBN-13: 978-1-84893-045-2 (hbk)

Typeset by Pickering & Chatto (Publishers) Limited

CONTENTS

Acknowledgements ix
Prologue: Epistlers of the Revolution 1
1 Commencement of a Civil War 7
2 Melted Majesty 27
3 Barren as a Pitch-Pine Plain 55
4 Life of a Cabbage 63
5 Hurried through Life on Horseback 79
6 Touch and Go is a Good Pilot 101
7 War and *GREET Brittain* 117
8 Keeping the Belly and Back from Grumbling, and the Kitchen-Fire
  from Going Out 137
9 The Mysteries of Lucina 169
10 Patience and Flannel 193
Epilogue: Let *Passion* be Restrain'd within thy Soul 207

Notes 213
Works Cited 229
Index 233

ACKNOWLEDGEMENTS

Many institutions provided support and assistance in the writing of this book. I wish to thank the administration of Bacone College for unwavering support of my research and publications. The Professional Development Fund of Bacone College has been most helpful. The staffs of the libraries at Bacone College, the Oklahoma School of Science and Mathematics, Oklahoma State University, the New Hampshire Historical Society, Historical Society of Pennsylvania and American Philosophical Society have also provided much assistance. I particularly wish to thank the library staff at the Massachusetts Historical Society for their help during my visits. Unpublished materials from the Belknap Papers are reprinted by permission of the Massachusetts Historical Society where they are held.

For Dave

PROLOGUE: EPISTLERS OF THE REVOLUTION

Upon being appointed postmaster general of the United States of America in 1782, Ebenezer Hazard designed a seal for the burgeoning postal service. Hazard, a classicist and a Greek scholar, chose as the symbol of the post office the Roman god Mercury, the messenger of the gods and patron of commerce and travel. Mercury stood for the activities and characteristics that Hazard and his contemporaries, the Americans attempting to win independence from Great Britain, most cherished. Hazard's role during the War of American Independence was that of a messenger. When the war began he was appointed postmaster for New York; when New York fell to the British in 1776 he earned the job of surveyor of post roads. He succeeded so well as surveyor – planning, maintaining, and securing post roads – that he was appointed postmaster general. Throughout this conflict Hazard, constantly 'hurried through life on horseback', anchored himself in the written word. He was, like all of his friends and contemporaries of culture and learning, a master of the epistle. His favourite correspondent, Jeremy Belknap, was also devoted to the epistler's art. The two men lived in different parts of the country, but being hungry to know all that was happening in war and government, took upon themselves the onus of being messengers to one-another, sending news and commentary – their own and that of others as well – whenever the post presented the opportunity. The letters of Hazard and Belknap are filled with attempts to understand and to impart intelligence to others.[1]

Mercury was the god of thieves and deception, which was not lost on Postmaster Hazard when designing the seal for the nascent post office. His years as surveyor general of post roads during the War for Independence taught Hazard that subterfuge and the ability to escape detection were qualities enabling the post rider to evade capture, like a thief in the night. Communications during wartime were hazardous and unreliable; the careful correspondent used guarded wording or more direct forms of deception. Letters were sealed with wax and delivered often by anyone who happened to be available. Belknap's friend and cousin by marriage the Boston clergyman John Eliot wrote of the irregularity of his correspondence with Belknap in a letter dated 4 July 1776, complaining of the fate of one [of] your former letters, which pass'd thro' several towns & fifty or an hundred hands in every place, each one altering & emending the superscription till it was so variated & filled up as rendered it difficult to know the meaning & took me longer to read it *by odds* than the contents of the letter.

Hazard, as a postal official in a rebellion against the most powerful empire in the world, had to be particularly careful. It was already the habit of eighteenth-century letter-writers to use only the initials of the names of important or noteworthy people. Hazard and his friend Belknap went further, inventing a code to describe the subjects of their correspondence and to deceive anyone who read their letters by chance or wilfulness. John Eliot, who shared in the jocularity of their puns, was the *Freemason*, indicative of his political and social leanings. Eliot was Belknap's wife Ruth's cousin and his long-time correspondent who lived through the British occupation and subsequent poverty and disorder of Boston during the war. He was perceptive and witty, and enjoyed contributing to Belknap and Hazard's game of pseudonyms. Dr William Gordon, clergyman and historian, author of the *History of the Rise, Progress, and Establishment of the Independence of the United States* (1788) and Hazard's friend, was the *Plain Doctor*, as he lived at Jamaica Plain (Roxbury), outside of Boston. Hazard stayed with Gordon whenever his postal work took him to New England. Joseph Buckminster, a Portsmouth, New Hampshire clergyman, was the *Metropolitan*, a tongue-in-cheek reference to the actual size of Portsmouth compared to its importance in the estimation of its populace. Local pastors were frequently designated *bishops*, which of course the New England congregational scheme of independent churches eschewed. But that did not keep Belknap, Hazard and other correspondents from having fun at the expense of such humble pastors as Joseph Adams of Newington, New Hampshire, called the *Bishop of Newington*, and Joseph Haven of Rochester, New Hampshire, the *Bishop of Rochester*. Peter Thacher, a devoted servant of Christ and clergyman of Malden, Massachusetts, was *Cephas*: the rock. Isaac Mansfield, a clergyman of Exeter, New Hampshire, was *Democritus* in honour of his cynical wit. The Connecticut lexicographer Noah Webster was nicknamed the *Monarch* to evoke his formality and arrogance. Dr Geraldus Clarkson, physician of Philadelphia and Hazard's friend, was labelled *Ulysses*, the great-grandson of Mercury, while Philip Freneau, the American poet, when a young clerk in Hazard's office, was *Telemachus*, mercurial descendant and youth of promise. Hazard, a newlywed in 1783, referred to his wife as *Miranda* (wonderful); Belknap, married since 1767, was not so prosaic.[2]

Objects and ideas had pseudonyms as well in the correspondence of Belknap, Hazard and friends. After Belknap published a satirical piece designating the New Hampshire state constitutional convention a *hen* and the imperfect constitution of their creation the *egg*, neither man could refrain from designating any state constitutional convention as a hen producing eggs of various merit.

When Charles Chauncy, the venerable Old Light Boston pastor and theologian, penned a long manuscript on the subject of universal salvation, he nicknamed the subject, so objectionable to mainstream and conservative Protestants of his day, the *Pudding*. 'The *pudding*,' explained John Eliot to Jeremy Belknap in 1781, 'is a word which he uses when persons are nigh not acquainted with our sentiments' which, should it be known that less renowned clergymen such as Belknap and Eliot were universalists, could destroy their careers.[3]

Although there existed a variety of sources during the early years of the Revolution by which to gain information on political, military, social, economic, cultural and intellectual affairs, the epistle was nevertheless the chief means by which revolutionaries divided by long distances shared news and experimented with new ideas that were the *sine qua non* of revolution. The period from the 1770s to the 1790s was a mercurial age. During this time the United States of America was warring against England, establishing new governments, building a national identity, exploring the hinterland, and refining an American identity in both prose and verse. American patriots such as Ebenezer Hazard and Jeremy Belknap believed their role was to be involved in and be cognizant of the important changes in America. The letters of Belknap and Hazard encompassed twenty years, beginning in January of 1779 and extending until 1798, when Belknap unexpectedly died. During these years Belknap and Hazard were busily involved in all that was going on – the pitfalls as well as the promise. Their correspondence traced the course of the war and its aftermath from several different perspectives, as Belknap lived in northern New England until 1787 and Boston thereafter until his death, while Hazard, as a postal official, travelled throughout the thirteen states, making his headquarters (and home) variously at Philadelphia, Boston and New York. Belknap, raised in Boston but accepting the call of the first parish of Dover, New Hampshire, in 1767, was during the time of their initial correspondence thoughtful and lonely, wondering about his life's work, using quill and paper to ask questions and seek answers, to seek consolation and advice, to wonder aloud and invite comments and suggestions. Belknap envied Hazard, who was from 1776 to 1782 the surveyor of post roads for the United States of America, always on the road, seeing new places and enjoying (or enduring) a variety of different experiences. Hazard, thoughtful and lonely in a different way from Belknap, was always on the pad but wishing for the quiet moment next to the fireplace to examine some new find to go into his travelling 'museum' of historical and natural curiosities. Hazard was a bachelor unwilling to entertain the idea of marriage or family during a time of revolution, while Belknap was planted 'like a cabbage' at his parsonage at Dover on a fixed income dwindling in significance because of wartime inflation, trying to keep 'the belly from grumbling and the kitchen-fire from going out', challenged with rearing a family of six children during difficult times when money was scarce, schooling nonexistent, and his wife yearning for family, friends, culture and society in Boston. The War for Independence was not kind to the Belknap family: Ruth Eliot Belknap, wife of the pastor, showed signs of nervous exhaustion; and Rev. Belknap's income, which arrived sporadically and sometimes not at all from his financially-challenged parish, was never sufficient. Added to this was a crisis in belief brought on by the war, which engendered in Belknap doubts about his own self, spirituality and chosen career. He found mental and emotional release by means of historical and scientific inquiry.[4]

The mutual fascination in the questions of natural and human experience formed the foundation for the friendship of Belknap and Hazard. Belknap referred to their friendship as that of 'fellow travelers' into the human and natural past. The two men referred to themselves as antiquarians and collectors, researchers into 'antiquity'. Hazard's existence centred upon the written word. He was during his long life a bookseller, postal official, translator, editor and entrepreneur. Even as he served as surveyor of post roads and postmaster general, he transcribed, edited, produced, wrote and sold books, notably his friend Belknap's *History of New-Hampshire*. In 1794 Hazard published the results of his antiquarian labours, *Historical Collections*, and eventually collaborated with Charles Thomson to produce a translation of the Holy Bible (1808). Hazard's activities as a scientist were less empirical than literary. His friendships were with literary men with whom he engaged in extensive correspondence over countless pages and many years. A Presbyterian elder, Hazard recorded the details of his life for his own reflection and for the benefit of his posterity. As so many of his contemporaries did during the years of the American Enlightenment, Hazard used paper and quill to keep track of his experiences, journeys, thoughts and actions.[5]

Belknap, likewise, spent most days crouched at his writer's desk for long hours, scribbling memoranda, narratives, letters, transcriptions, verse and sermons. Belknap, raised in Boston and educated at Harvard, became well known for his three-volume *History of New-Hampshire* (1784, 1791, 1792), lauded by critics since its publication as the finest contemporary example of historical scholarship as well as a model of the narrative art. Belknap also wrote the two-volume *American Biography* (1794, 1798), one of the first attempts at a broad historical approach to understanding the American experience; the *Foresters* (1792), a political satire about early America; and *Sacred Poetry* (1795), a psalter modelled after Isaac Watts. Belknap was the founder of the Massachusetts Historical Society (1791), and the finest naturalist of northern New England. His accounts of the White Mountains of New Hampshire are some of the best natural histories of the late eighteenth century.[6]

In addition to their other literary interests, Hazard and Belknap were epistlers of note. The eighteenth-century Enlightenment was a time when the epistle was, along with the essay, narrative and verse, an art form reflective of a culture focused on beauty, grace and wit. English novelists such as Samuel Richardson and Americans such as Hannah Webster Foster used the epistolary form. So, too, did essayists – one thinks of Hector St John de Crevecoeur's *Letters from an American Farmer* (1782). The English poet Alexander Pope published a volume of personal letters, making the letter an accepted form of literary expression. The more mundane letter-writers of the eighteenth century sought to convey by means of their letters, their experiences, observations, thoughts, feelings and the news of their own times and places. The correspondence of Hazard and Belknap included letters to statesmen and soldiers such as Thomas Jefferson and George Washington, letters dealing with postal and governmental affairs, letters about the Articles of Confederation, state constitutions, and the Federal Constitution; letters about religion; and especially letters to friends and colleagues who shared with the two men a love of science in all its forms: history, geography, natural philosophy and medicine. Noteworthy 'sons of science' with whom Hazard and Belknap corresponded included the physician Benjamin Rush, the geographer Jedidiah Morse, the German geographer Christoph Ebeling, the lexicographer Noah Webster and the botanist Manasseh Cutler. But it is their letters to each other that is one of the great monuments to the eighteenth-century epistle.

The letters of Hazard and Belknap tell of an age when science and religion had not yet divorced owing to irreconcilable differences, when the most profound philosophy nestled comfortably next to a childlike fascination with the remarkable. The two men filled their letters with inquisitive attempts to know, to understand, and to express. The accomplished epistler is fascinated by the grand and trivial, the universal intersection of truth and self. The two friends explored in their epistles the nature of love, death and piety; the best way for humans to govern themselves; matters of religious and scientific truth and the best means to arrive at it; the methods and writing of history; human credulity; and the wonders of nature. If they were fascinated by the grand schemes and ideas of history and philosophy, they were at the same time fascinated by the momentary, the spontaneous and the banal: the alterations in the daily weather, the changes of nature, the slow movement of time and the daily happenings of the community. In this interest in the *remarkable* occurrences met with every day, we find American thinkers similar to Benjamin Franklin; minds as content with the yearly American almanac as with Locke's essays, as fascinated by fireflies in the night as by the transit of Venus across the disk of the sun.

The Belknap–Hazard correspondence provides a record of human events and natural history in late eighteenth-century America. The clergyman and the elder discussed the religious issues of the time, such as predestination and universalism; both surprisingly accepted the idea of a just God and universal salvation. The scientists discussed geology and geography, botany and biology;

they particularly enjoyed discoursing on their personal discoveries during journeys through forests and among mountains. The historians were on a joint quest to discover the American past, to build a national history, and hence a national identity of the American people. Patriots and citizens, both took a deep interest in the Revolution, the establishment of state governments and writing of state constitutions; the two friends were conservatives who criticized the Confederation and supported the Constitution. They examined contemporary culture and society and praised or criticized according to the apparent degree of human folly. Sometimes the correspondence was mundane and newsy, at other times profound. The letters are a journal of the lives of two Enlightenment thinkers in late eighteenth-century America, their personal almanac, a register of private, local, regional and national occurrences. Hazard, in one 1784 letter to Belknap, referred to his friend's epistolary meanderings as 'Essays on Man', suggesting that they were equal to the writings of the great eighteenth-century poet Alexander Pope. Indeed, the letters of Belknap and Hazard are inquisitive trials, spontaneous inquiries and experiments seeking to understand the nature of human experience. The Belknap–Hazard epistles, if they are not objective and disinterested, concrete in their knowledge and secure in their wisdom, are at least honest attempts to know.[7]

The English letter-writer Horace Walpole told a correspondent in 1784 that 'familiar letters written by eye-witnesses, and that, without design, disclose circumstances that let us more intimately into important events, are genuine history; and as far as they go, more satisfactory than formal premeditated narratives'. Walpole's comment is particularly apropos of the Belknap-Hazard correspondence. Historians, because of their perspective on time, make excellent critics. Hazard and Belknap possessed a unique ability to perceive and to assess society and culture in light of their own lives. If their published writings were significant, their private, informal letters, because of their forthrightness and penetrating observations and criticism, yield more important information about the nature of life, society, culture, government, religion, science and humanity during an age when Americans had won their independence and were attempting, in the words of Noah Webster's 1830 dictionary, to form, 'under the influence of Mercury', something 'active; sprightly; full of fire or vigour; as a mercurial youth; a mercurial nation'.[8]

1 COMMENCEMENT OF A CIVIL WAR

Travellers aboard Knight's Ferry felt the reluctance of spring to command winter in the icy breeze skimming the cold water of the Piscataqua River. Knight operated his ferry year-round, even during the coldest months of winter, courtesy of the rapid, fluctuating currents of the river, which rarely froze. The waters of half a dozen rivers of New Hampshire and Maine meet off Dover Point, which divides the currents flowing from the Squamscot, Lamprey, Back and Oyster rivers, which mingle in the estuaries known as the Great Bay and Little Bay, from the Piscataqua, formed from the Cocheco and Salmon Falls rivers. Added to the churning mix is the tidal brine of the Atlantic, which inexorably rises and falls through the maze of islands and narrows that mark the Piscataqua between Dover Point and the mouth of the river. Twenty years in the future the Piscataqua Bridge would make the ferry obsolete, but until then Knight's Ferry was the only way for the traveller to cross the river from the southern shores of Newington by way of Bloody Point to Dover Point. This year, 1775, was the seventieth that the Knight family had operated the ferry, the right to which Captain John Knight obtained in 1705.[1]

Belknap was frequently at Knight's Ferry coming or going, as he was on Thursday 20 April. Belknap regularly travelled by horseback or on foot to Portsmouth from his home built near the Cocheco Falls; the road led through Dover Point to the confluence of the Piscataqua and waters of the Great Bay, across which was Bloody Point, reached only by means of the ferry. The pastor had many friends and colleagues in Portsmouth and the neighbouring towns of Greenland, Kittery and Newington, having lived in Portsmouth and outlying towns since 1764, initially teaching primary school and studying for his Master's degree under two local ministers, Samuel Haven of Portsmouth and Samuel MacClintock of Greenland. He was influenced by other divines as well, such as Samuel Langdon, pastor of Portsmouth's North Parish, later president of Harvard College. Belknap became pastor of the First Parish of Dover in 1767. Once established in Piscataqua society, Belknap became friends with local leaders such as Captain Thomas Waldron of Dover, Theodore Atkinson of Portsmouth, and most notably, Governor John Wentworth. The governor and pastor shared an interest in natural and human history. When in 1773 Belknap had deposed on the Governor's behalf with the statement that New Hampshirans were 'equally loyal to their King and jealous of encroachments on their rights and priviledges [sic]', he doubtless thought that Wentworth would agree. The two had conversed at length over the natural and political history of New Hampshire, and Governor Wentworth had assisted Belknap in acquiring sources for the latter's work-in-progress, the *History of New-Hampshire*; indeed, Wentworth had recently read with a critical eye initial chapters of the manuscript, and had sent it back to the minister with his complements.[2]

On his many visits to Portsmouth, the conservative Belknap sensed the tension felt by the inhabitants brought about by the political debate raging for over a decade regarding the role of the colonies in the British Empire. Townspeople believed that the attack upon Fort William and Mary during the winter of 1774 by local militia not only presaged the beginning of conflict but also provided an apt motive for revenge. The fort, situated on the northern extreme of Newcastle Island overlooking the entrance to Portsmouth Harbor, had been fortified by the British for decades going back to the initial wars with the French for control of North America. In the wake of protests to British policies (such as the Stamp Act in 1765) among the populace and non-importation agreements enforced by Piscataqua merchants directed particularly against the British Tea Act of 1773, the British had determined to reinforce Fort William and Mary and had sent the frigate *Scarborough* to patrol the mouth of the river and Portsmouth Harbor. Patriots led by John Sullivan and John Langdon had anticipated the renewed British presence by attacking the fort in mid-December, confiscating the guns and ammo and disarming the garrison. Belknap considered the aggressive action too hasty and provocative, and had sympathized with his friend Governor Wentworth who had branded the action treasonous and demanded the arrest of the perpetrators – to no avail. Instead, a revolutionary assembly met at Exeter upriver from Portsmouth on the Squamscot River to determine what to do next to agitate for freedom. Belknap feared what war would bring to the colonies, and that the sometimes misguided order of British authority would give way to the misguided disorder of a rebellious rabble. Belknap considered John Wentworth a worthy man and governor, and could hardly imagine a revolutionary committee equal to his friend's discretion and benevolence.[3]

More dangerous to the cause of peace were the activities occurring in Massachusetts, especially during recent years – the Tea Party and the harsh British response, the Coercive Acts (Port Bill). The Boston native Belknap had many friends in Boston with whom he corresponded about recent occurrences. Likewise his father and mother and only sibling, a sister Nabby, lived in the city. The Boston Port Bill, which led to martial law, the arrival of the military governor General Gage, the fortification of the only land entrance and exit to and from the city – the Neck – 'occasioned', Belknap wrote, 'a melancholy prospect of the total ruin of the Town'. One of Belknap's favourite Boston correspondents was John Eliot. Clever and witty, wearing his heart on his sleeve in his letters and among his friends and family, Eliot tried to keep Belknap abreast of happenings in Boston during the months of growing conflict in the wake of the Tea Party. Eliot shared with Belknap foreboding over the disorderly acts of the inhabitants and overly forceful response of the British ministry. Well informed of political news coming from London, Eliot believed that King George had the Lords and Commons in his pocket, and that a new Parliament in late 1774 meant nothing. Neither Eliot nor Belknap considered independence a worthy alternative to repairing the relationship of the colonies to the Empire. Eliot had met and been entertained by Governor Wentworth during a visit to New Hampshire and, like Belknap, respected and honoured the man. During the early months of 1775, writing either from his father Andrew Eliot's home in Boston or from Cambridge across the Charles River from Boston, where he was working on his Master's degree at Harvard, Eliot informed Belknap of the disturbing happenings in Boston and surrounding communities. Eliot, like most residents of Massachusetts, felt uneasy with the presence of the British regular army patrolling the streets. The soldiery and populace were on edge, and sporadic disagreements and conflicts frequently erupted. Eliot befriended a British Lieutenant, Henry Barry, who had entered the pamphlet war over the dispute between the colonies and Empire. Barry argued that the colonies should be glad in their relationship with England; Eliot thought he had some good points, and passed his pamphlets on to Belknap, who responded more critically. Other Americans, less moderate, were vehemently opposed to any kind of economic or political advantages to be gained from membership in the Empire. Arguments and counter-arguments in an atmosphere of intransigence on both sides, the shortage of cool heads of moderation and conciliation, the lack of a disinterested moderator among the powers of Europe, pointed to an ultimate decision by 'the supreme arbiter of nations'. Even so, the friends of order awaited the arrival of ships from London in early spring bringing words of encouragement. These came and went, with some positive news from the Crown, only to be replaced by further demands from Parliament. Eliot encouraged Belknap to continue behaving as a 'good politician, gliding between the shoals of Scylla & Carybdis', working for a peaceful solution in New Hampshire.[4]

The fatigue of late winter in New England added to the situation in Boston that, John Eliot believed, as he wrote Belknap, presaged war. Bloodshed was coming and little could be done to stop it. The resolutions of the Continental Congress demanding that Parliament restore American rights to their pre-1763 state, denying parliamentary sovereignty in American affairs, were a declaration of war against Britain, according to disillusioned and angry Redcoats such as

Lieutenant Barry. Likewise, the hesitant arrival of spring in the Piscataqua Valley did not dispel the gloom that Belknap felt during the first months of 1775. It had become almost certain that a clash between the Redcoats and Patriots much more serious than the attack on Fort William and Mary was shortly to occur. General and Governor of Massachusetts Thomas Gage had convinced himself that the Americans would not respond to British imposition of order. Indeed, Gage wrote to friends in January indicating that American opposition to coercive measures was fading. Meanwhile committees of correspondence were establishing logistics of communication and storing black powder and balls so that the colonials could react to British aggression with a defiant response.[5]

Like many Bostonians who stayed in the city during the undisguised military occupation, Eliot read with interest the newspaper dialogue between Massachusettensis and Novanglus. With his moderate political views, Eliot suspended judgment on which of the two anonymous debaters carried the day. Massachusettensis ably contended that there could be but one sovereign power in America, and that for rational and historical reasons the colonial legislatures must respect the superiority of Parliament. Although the distance from America to the British Isles forbade actual representations of Americans in the British Parliament, nevertheless Americans were as ably represented by the broad-minded members of Parliament as English subjects in other parts of the empire. How besides, if the American colonies were independently sovereign, could the sovereignty of the British Crown be maintained? Should each colony have its own king? Novanglus responded that the sovereignty of king and Parliament in America had merely been assumed, never agreed upon, especially since the Glorious Revolution of 1689 and its fundamental alteration of the British Constitution. Historical experience and the logic of time and place had led the provincial assemblies to assume sovereignty in domestic affairs, though the Americans, as appendages of empire, respected the authority of the Crown to direct military and commercial affairs. The Americans had been and continued to welcome a relationship with Britain as separate but equal members of a worldwide commonwealth. But that Parliament and the King proclaim themselves sovereign and back it with armed force was absurd, inviting revolution.[6]

These arguments, along with Lieutenant Barry's, as relayed by Eliot to Belknap, led the Dover minister to contemplate a possible solution. He thought he had a temporary fix that could stave off war in the suggestion that the colonies agree to help pay England's war debt from the French-Indian War. But by the time Belknap sent Eliot his idea the latter responded that political and military events were taking over all rational plans and benevolent ideas. Although by the spring of 1775 Belknap realized the apparent imminence of war, he was like other moderate Congregational ministers wavering as to whether or not Americans should strive to be independent from the British. John Eliot, although still a student and younger than Belknap by ten years, similarly felt uncertain about the best course for Americans to take. Eliot was perhaps mirroring the attitude of his father, the Rev. Andrew Eliot, pastor of the New-North Church, to whom Belknap also looked up to. Reading liberal Whig thinkers of the early 1700s especially inspired Andrew Eliot to believe that the British were rejecting their own traditions of liberty and the rule of law; at the same time he could barely contemplate the logical consequence of Whig thought: American independence. Similarly, as late as 1774, Belknap had written a letter to the elder Eliot that included a prayer in which he asked blessings upon 'the British Nation & all its Dependencies' as well as 'the king', and to 'give wisdom to his ministry & Parliament & may they seek and pursue the true Interests of the whole Empire'. Belknap prayed that God

> let not those dreadful Judgments come upon them which thou has in thy holy word denounced against the throne of Iniquity which frameth mischief by a Law & against those who decree unrighteous decrees.

May the British 'act with moderation & peace toward all their Subjects that they may not bring the guilt of inocent [sic] blood upon their heads.

Further, 'mercifully regard this American Continent in our present Distress & Difficulty & pity thy people in the Capital of a neighbouring Province who are suffering oppression and affliction'. Belknap prayed that the people of Boston 'may … be inclined to comply with what is reasonably required of them'. Although Belknap as early as 1770 had branded the reign of George III as 'despotic', he had continued to believe that a 'divorce' from England was not the best way for Americans. By 1775 Belknap was a reluctant revolutionary, but not so wishy-washy and paralyzed by fear as his friend Andrew Eliot.[7]

The events of 19 April 1775 made largely irrelevant the learned arguments and counterarguments on sovereignty, laws and rule. Those who knew the situation in Massachusetts anticipated that the Americans and British would ultimately come to blows; only the questions when and where remained. The morning of 20 April, at Knight's Ferry, on his way to Portsmouth on horseback Belknap met an express rider crossing the Piscataqua towards Dover who had the news 'of the commencement of a Civil War'. Belknap knew where his duty lay; Boston was at the centre of war, in a stage of siege, and his parents and sister Nabby were certainly trapped in the city; he must go to them to help and if possible arrange their escape from the city, if it was not yet already 'in ashes'. Whether or not Belknap had time to learn from the express rider of all the events that had transpired on 19 April is uncertain. If not, no doubt in the coming days as he rushed south he heard scattered reports of the British movement west towards Concord the night of 18 April; the stand by the militia at Lexington and subsequent battle; the movement of the victorious Redcoats towards neighbouring Concord; the preparations of the Concord minutemen to defend their town and the military stores hidden there; the pitched battle; the return march of the British troops to Boston under attack of arriving armed militia from surrounding towns and provinces; the arrival of the troops to Boston and closure of the city as thousands of colonial militia closed in.[8]

Upon reaching Bloody Point, Belknap quickly scribbled a letter to Ruth, asking Knight to find a reliable traveller on his way to Dover to take the note 'with the utmost speed', which read:

> At Mr Knight's, 9 Ho.
>
> My Dear,
>
> Before you receive this, you will hear the awful news by the Express I met just now at the ferry, of the devastation the troops have made at Concord, and the commencement of a civil war; which makes it absolutely necessary that I should proceed immediately to Boston (if it is not in ashes before I get there). I shall try to get a chaise at Greenland. As necessity has no laws, the people must excuse my absence next Sabbath, if I should not return before it.
>
> Your affectionate husband,
> J.B.
>
> N.B. The Dragoons have arrived at Boston.[9]

Meanwhile Belknap urged his horse towards Newington where his friend the Rev. Joseph Adams served as pastor of the first parish. He proceeded along the old Newington Road, with the Great Bay nearby if mostly out of sight to his right. The soil was wet from recently melted snow. The road towards Greenland seemed particularly long as Belknap journeyed south, thinking of what he would find in the town of his birth. Belknap had been a frequent visitor at Greenland during the ten years he had resided in New Hampshire. He recalled cold winter days when he taught grammar school at Greenland in 1765. He frequently stopped at John Folsom's Tavern in Greenland for refreshment and the news, which he undoubtedly did this April day as well. Folsom's was the best place to borrow a chaise, if there was one to be had, to quicken his pace and prepare to retrieve family members from Boston. Unable to borrow and unwilling to tarry, he continued along the post road from Greenland to North Hampton, riding by farms cut from the New Hampshire pine forest. Farmers would be on their land ploughing and preparing the soil for seeding when May arrived in a few weeks. The post road turned due south at North Hampton, taking the traveller through the towns of Hampton, Hampton Falls and Seabrook in New Hampshire. These towns hugged the sea, which if not always visible could be sensed through the pungent sea air and the rank smell of the marshes, of which Hampton in particular had plenty. Hampton was an old town, 137 years old, founded by Stephen Batchellor at the site of the Algonquian village of Winnacunnet. Fatigued but hurried, Belknap eschewed lodging at his friend Ebenezer

Thayer's and continued on to Massachusetts. At Newburyport, Belknap crossed the broad Merrimack River by ferry at the terminus of State Street (the post road) in the centre of town. Newburyport was a growing port city, recently detached from the town of Newbury to the south; it featured a broad harbour at the mouth of the river, secured by a large sandbar. The road continued south to Newbury, where when Belknap arrived the town was in an uproar because of a rumour, soon found to be false, which had been spread that an enemy force was marching on the town; in such trying circumstances Belknap found lodging, perhaps at Lent's Tavern. Rising early the next morning, 21 April, Belknap proceeded through Rowley and Ipswich, which were forested, near the sea, but not harbour towns. Soon the road came to the port towns of Beverly and Salem, lying southwest of Cape Ann. Salem was one of the oldest towns on the Massachusetts coast, settled even before Boston. Salem had served as the chief port of Massachusetts during the months after the inauguration of the Boston Port Bill. The road turned south-west from Salem, mirroring the coast. Belknap crossed several small rivers on his way through Lynn to Malden, where he stopped to visit with his friend Peter Thacher, who informed Belknap of recent events, and offered his hospitality. At Malden, as on the previous day, rumour indicated that the town was under attack, which caused quite a fluster before events proved it was a false alarm. On 22 April Belknap set out early; as he got closer to Charleston, and crossed the Mystic River on the Penny Ferry, he encountered more and more men on horseback or on the march, as the word had been spread and the militia were on the move to besiege beleaguered Boston. He arrived at Cambridge where he saw a haphazard and motley gathering of troops bivouacking restlessly. The College was closed and the house of Jonathan Hastings, the college steward, had become the ad hoc headquarters for the American militia. The road and ferries into Boston were closed to any who wished to exit or enter, save those to whom the Redcoats granted a pass. Belknap sought word of his family through friends and acquaintances, such as Samuel Langdon, previously minister of Portsmouth's North Parish, now President of Harvard, and an old friend and mentor to Belknap. Langdon suggested that Belknap tarry in Cambridge as he awaited word of his parents, and that meanwhile Belknap preach to the assembled troops the following day, 23 April, the Sabbath. That morning, Belknap sent a letter to Ruth

Cambridge, Lord's Day morning, 23 April 1775.

My Dear,

I am arrived here, but cannot hear any news of my parents since this day week, when they were in Boston, where I suppose they are now, and must partake of the fate of the place. I think it best, and am advised by Dr. Landgon, to tarry in some of the neighboring towns a few days longer to see whether any way is opened for their escape. It is talked that an assault will be made upon the entrenchments at the Neck, by pressing large bundles of wet-screwed hay forward to shelter our men from the cannon-balls. Dr. Warren, who is one of the Committee of Safety, told me the town must be cleared, and would be soon. General Gage has made such a proposal to the Bostonians as the Romans to the Carthaginians, that if they would deliver up their arms they should be safe. But they were not such fools as to comply. The army here is pretty well regulated. Don't let my gun and ammunition get out of the house, if you can help it. The posts are stopt, and the mails opened by the Committee of War sitting here, so 't is in vain to write by post. Don't be frighted at my situation, for well am I guarded by at least ten thousand men. There are here more men than they want. You will doubtless have many false alarms. The tories have given out that they would keep us in alarm all about the country, to divert and distract us. I have been in two already; one at Newbury, and another at Malden. Couriers are established between here and Newbury; it would be well if our people took some care of that kind. I add no more, but that all our trust and confidence must be in God, and not in an arm of flesh.

Yours affectionately,
J.B.

He duly preached to the New Hampshire troops, then in the afternoon rode to Newton.[10]

Hearing nothing about his family at Cambridge or Newton, Belknap decided on 24 April to journey back to the Mystic River and the Penny Ferry to see if he could find out any information coming out of Boston through Charleston; no word. The next day, 25 April, he journeyed again to Charleston and then to Malden to see again his old friend Thacher. Pastor of Malden's First Parish and a member of the town's revolutionary Committee of Correspondence, Peter Thacher was devoted to his friend, who had once been his teacher at Milton. The two had formed a close teacher–student relationship that lasted in the following years when Peter lost his father in 1765 (his mother having died the year before) and attended Harvard in his early to mid-teen years. After Thacher had been ordained to the Malden parish, when he was only eighteen years old in 1770, Belknap had made a point to visit his friend when visiting Boston. Belknap had nicknamed his friend Cephas, *the rock*, because of Thacher's extremely serious nature in all matters, religious and otherwise, which was the complete opposite of the playful and witty John Eliot. Malden was just across from Charleston, separated by the Mystic River, which locals crossed by means of the Penny Ferry just below the confluence of the Malden River with the Mystic. Malden was busy and crowded in the few days after Lexington and Concord; refugees from Boston and Charleston, as well as militia returning from the initial conflict on the road from Cambridge to Lexington, filled the small town with people anxious and frightened. One of the many was Belknap, hoping, with the aid of his connections, to discover the whereabouts of his parents and sister and to help them escape Boston.[11]

Joseph and Sarah Byles Belknap and their daughter Nabby were meanwhile packing goods and ordering affairs the best they could in preparation to escape the occupied city. All of their friends and neighbours were doing likewise. The

Belknaps lived on Ann Street in residential quarters attached to Joseph Belknap's shop, nicely situated near the wharves on the harbour and only a block away from Faneuil Hall. The smells of the sea, fish and the goods of the market surrounded the Belknap family during good times. The Long Wharf jutted into the harbour nearby; masts of tall ships were a constant sight. The New-North Church was up the lane on Fish Street, while South Church, where the Belknap's were communicants, was down the lane just beyond the State House. At Old South under the guidance of pastors Thomas Prince and Joseph Sewall, Belknap had grown religiously and become a communicant of the parish. Thomas Prince had been a leading historian of New England, and Belknap followed in his footsteps. The Belknap family had migrated from England during the Great Migration of the 1630s. Jeremy's great-grandfather established the family at South Church; his grandfather owned land throughout the city, giving his name to Belknap's Lane (since called Joy Street); his father had a thriving business dealing with furs and skins. Joseph Belknap had been wealthy enough to send his only son to Harvard College. He was a sturdy, successful and law-abiding craftsman, not one to challenge tradition or rock the boat. He was a stalwart member of the Old South. He had witnessed the Boston Massacre in March, 1770, and testified in court. He doubtless knew where such troubles were leading Boston and New England. Business must be done notwithstanding politics. But the British occupation of the city and cessation of commercial activity required action for the sake of survival.[12]

Suffering brought about by war united the inhabitants of Boston during the British occupation, which lasted until March 1776. 'It is impossable [sic] for me to describe', wrote a Tory observer, Henry Pelham, preparing to leave Boston for England,

> The unhappy tran[s]actions of that fatal day [19 April] and the consequent Misery to which it has reduced [the] Inhabitants [of] this once flourishing and happy Town. Consternation is pictured in every face, every Cheek grows Pale, every lip trembles at the Recital of the Horrid tale.

Stating in a letter feelings that Patriots and Tories alike felt, those who lived in Boston and those who contemplated the proceedings of civil war, Pelham condemned those on both sides who allowed conflict to reach such a point of despair and desperation. The previous ten years, he wrote,

> has been productive of mutual je[a]lo[u]sy and mistrust, unnatural heartburn'g, hatred and Malice, among those whose Duty and interest it was to dwell together in Peace, mutually love'g and Cherishing each other. A Conduct which would be infinitely more agreable [sic] to the design of Providenc[e] in forming us Social Beings, and mak'g us dependant [sic] on those around us more consonant to the dictates of that boasted Reason which so eminently distinguishes Man from all the other Works

of Creation, and unquestionably more agreable [*sic*] to the express Commands of that Prince of Peace, whose Holy Religion we all profess to make the Rule of our Lives and Conduct. But alas! The last ten years is but an additional Confirmation of that Mallencholly [*sic*] truth taught us by the experienc[e] of ages that neither the light of Natural Religion, the dictates of Reason, the positive Commands of Christianity, nor even a Regard to present Happyness are effectual to curb the licentious Ambition, the Pride and Averice [*sic*] of man, or smoth [*sic*] those aspiraties [*sic*] of the Mind which too frequently break the ties of benevolence and Virtue, and render Man his own greatest Enemy. Whatever disagrement [*sic*] there may be respecting a parlimentary [*sic*] Right to tax us, or about American opposition, we must all agree in this that a Civill [*sic*] War is the most dreadful Evill [*sic*] that can befall a People, as it is subversive of that friendly intercourse that can so greatly heighten our Joys, gives such a cha[r]m to our innocent pleasu[res], and aleviates [*sic*] the Sorrows of Life.[13]

Identical were the feelings of the Reverend Andrew Eliot, who allowed the events to so overwhelm and confuse him as to drive away any thoughts of politics, whether rebellious or loyal. Letters reveal that he was beside himself with grief:

> The last week I thought myself in comfortable circumstances, had a convenient dwelling, well furnished; a fine library ... attended by a large, affectionate, and generous congregation; happy in a consort, one of the best of women; and surrounded by a large number of desirable children. Now, I am by cruel necessity turned out of my house; must leave my books and all I possess, perhaps to be destroyed by a licentious soldiery; my beloved congregation dispersed, my dear wife retreating to a distant part of the country, my children wandering, not knowing whither to go, perhaps left to perish for want; myself soon to leave this devoted capital, happy if I can find some obscure corner which will afford me a bare subsistence. I wish to God the authors of our misery could be witnesses of it.

Notwithstanding his lament, Eliot did not leave the city, his wife and daughters were cared for by his oldest son, Reverend Andrew Eliot, Jr, of Fairfield, Connecticut, and he was never forced to watch his library succumb to the ignorance of the British Redcoat. He remained in the 'poor garrison town', initially by choice, because he could not quite decide what to do, where to go or how to live. So he stayed in Boston to minister to a dispersed and motley congregation made up of refugees from other congregations whose ministers had fled. New-North Church was less the stalwart backbone of the influential Bostonian, and more a mission church for the sufferer of the whims of war. Those who departed were allowed a pass out of the city, by order of General Gage, if they gave up their firearms and most of their possessions. 'The most are obliged', wrote Eliot, 'to leave their furniture and effects of every kind, and indeed their all, to the uncertain chance of war, or rather to certain ruin and destruction'.[14]

While staying at Malden with his friend Cephas, Belknap received word from an unnamed source that his father had contrived to have trunks sent out of Boston destined for New Hampshire, the town of Exeter to be exact. As Boston appeared to be closed, no one coming or going, at least for the time being, Belknap decided to depart for New Hampshire, to see whether or not he could intercept the trunk. He departed 26 April, lodged at Newburyport, then on 27 April he reached Exeter, where he caught up with the trunks. He conveyed them to Dover, and home, on 28 April, where he found his family well.[15]

General Thomas Gage, after the initial conflict on 19 April and British retreat to Boston, encouraged inhabitants of the city to turn in their arms, which would gain them an easier occupation and more freedom of movement. Joseph Belknap, hearing that General Gage was allowing unarmed comers and goers with a pass, requested his wife and daughter depart for Charleston, then Malden, where perchance they would find friends or family to help them; there was news that Jeremy had been or was to be there, waiting. Joseph would stay behind to continue getting their affairs in order, as he had determined to leave his shop and home, never to return. Wife and daughter bade farewell to husband and father, and set out from Ann Street on the morning of Saturday 29 April, following Fish Street along the narrowest part of uptown between the Mill Cove and the harbour. In 1775 Boston was still the 'tadpole shaped' peninsula of Shawmut, so called by the local Massachusetts Indians before the arrival of the English, led by John Winthrop, in 1630. Its south-western edge, the Neck, connected to the mainland by a mere strip of land that the tide sometimes covered, making Shawmut a temporary island. The north-eastern extreme of the island, the North End, jutted between the sea, the Mill Cove, enclosed by an artificial breakwater, and the mouth of the Charles River, across which lay Charleston. Mother and daughter, one imagines, passed by the New-North Church in North Square, where Rev. Eliot still reluctantly officiated; perhaps they stopped to visit with the pastor, a family friend and relative since he married his niece Ruth to Jeremy in 1767. Andrew Eliot lived in the house of those early ministers of the New-North, notably Increase and Cotton Mather, which was near the church and across the street from Governor Thomas Hutchinson's old house, at the corner of Hanover and Bennett streets. Eliot had saved Hutchinson's papers from the mob when in 1774 they descended upon his house and the Governor fled, never to return. Eliot had been under suspicion then, before, and since, as he was friendly to this most famous of his parishioners. One imagines that Sarah and Nabby roused the reverend from the ruminations afforded by his library of great works, some acquired during the Mather years, others recently sent by the liberal thinker Thomas Hollis, of whom Eliot had been an obsequious friend. Perhaps Rev. Eliot offered tea, or some other beverage, and asked the Belknap women to sit awhile. With most of his family gone and the remainder, including his wife, preparing to go any day, he was quite lonely, or preparing to be so. Loquacious and pitiful, Eliot reflected on the calamity that the three knew all too well.

Poor Boston! May God sanctify our distresses ... Such a Sabbath of melancholy and darkness I never knew. Most of the meeting-houses shut up, the ministers gone, our congregation crowded with strangers ... This town a garrison; every face gathering paleness; all hurry and confusion; one going this way, and another that; others not knowing where to go.

The Belknap women had an idea where to go, as they expected Jeremy to be at Malden, so took leave of Rev. Eliot and hurried on towards the extreme of the North End, past the Anglican Old North Church, lately used by Paul Revere and his cohorts, skirting Copp's Hill to their right, from which the British would fire their cannons upon American troops in six weeks at Charleston, towards the ferry that took mother and daughter to Charleston. Nabby would return one day, years later, in the company of her brother, who moved back to Boston after almost two decades living in New Hampshire; she would not stay, however, finding the city so changed, and soon returned to Dover to live out her days. Sarah never returned, spending her remaining nine years in exile in Dover. Sarah and Nabby obtained a permit from an officer at the ferry (if they had not already obtained one earlier) which they filled out, which stated: 'PERMIT Sarah Byles Belknap and Abigail Belknap ... together with their Effects, to pass' by ferry 'between Sunrise and Sunset. By Order of His Excellency the Governor. No arms nor ammunition is allowed to pass'. They carried little with them, and certainly not of a volatile nature. Sarah and Nabby were more fortunate than they knew, as within weeks General Gage would rethink his policy of allowing so many Boston women and family possessions to leave the city, and clamp down with greater restrictions. The ferry crossed to Charleston through waters guarded by the British navy; the 74-gun *Somerset* was the chief threat. Charleston was built on an oddly shaped peninsula jutting out into the mingling waters of the sea, the Mystic River and the Charles River. The road from the ferry passed through the town and winded along the west shore of the peninsula, skirting the hills, Breeds and Bunker, to the right. British troops were present in Charleston, and there was great foreboding among the inhabitants that their town would follow in the path of military occupation like their neighbour. The Belknap women proceeded to the Penny Ferry along with so many others fleeing Charleston, which took them across the Mystic River.[16]

It was afternoon when they arrived at Malden; a young man, Samuel Sewall, met them there. Sewall had been in communication with Joseph Belknap ever since the beginning of war. Sewall had been christened at South Church, where his father, Deacon Samuel Sewall, and mother, Elizabeth Quincy, had been friends with Joseph and Sarah Belknap. He was grandson to the venerable pastor of Old South, Joseph Sewall. After his mother Elizabeth died in February 1770, and his father Deacon Samuel about a year later, largely penniless after several financial reverses, the Belknap's took under their wing the thirteen-year-old boy.

He appears to have lived with the Belknap's for at least part of the next several years, so that he considered himself part of the family; Mrs Belknap, he wrote a few years later, 'has been a mother to me'. Hints in the Belknap correspondence suggest that Joseph sponsored the boy at Harvard, paying for at least some of his schooling. Samuel, but seventeen years old in May 1775, assisted the Belknap's in any way he could. He informed Madam and Nabby that Jeremy had been there, but had gone north in pursuit of the supposed trunk; he wrote to Joseph of the safe arrival of his wife and daughter. After a day or two, waiting in Malden with the Belknap women, Samuel received a letter from Jeremy at Dover, who informed his family that 'as soon as he hears of Boston's being open he will bring or send his horse & chaise'. Mrs Belknap immediately dictated a letter to Jeremy not to delay, but to come as soon as possible with a cart. Meanwhile, she dictated another to her husband, requesting 'you would get every thing over the Ferry that you can; more especially the trunks, barrels, &c., that were packed up. You may send them safely without coming yourself, if you provide some person to receive them on this side the Ferry', meaning in Charleston, where, she had been assured on her own journey through the peninsula, 'any person of your acquaintance will receive them into their house'. Meanwhile Jeremy arrived on 2 May and reunited with his mother and sister. He contrived to take the ferry to Charleston to see about the trunks and barrels, but could not get across. So he and his mother and sister set out for Dover. On 14 May, Joseph Belknap and, one assumes, the remainder of the family's goods, arrived at Dover. Samuel Sewall stayed at Cambridge where he continued to receive aid and attention from Joseph and Jeremy, who solicited help from others, such as the philanthropist John Phillips, on the young man's behalf.[17]

During the ensuing summer months, Belknap and his family learned of events in Boston and vicinity by means of the Eliots – father and son. Belknap heard of a raging fire in Boston on 17 May, and of the fight at Noddle's Island in Boston Harbor on 27 May, when American and British troops skirmished over the livestock and hay on the island. Andrew Eliot remained in Boston throughout the entire siege; his son John was in and out of the city visiting his father, searching for a means of a living in surrounding towns, temporarily staying with various friends. Belknap contrived to interest a sufficient number of Dover families in Eliot's abilities as a teacher to arrange for his friend to hold a grammar school for several months during the spring and summer, 1775; while in Dover he stayed with the Belknap family. With his wife and five children, mother and father, sister Nabby, and cousin John Eliot, the Belknap family filled the two-story white clapboard to the brim. The elder Eliot periodically wrote Belknap melancholy letters of his endless experiences in the occupied city. In the first week in June, a fortnight before the Battle of Bunker Hill, Eliot wrote to Belknap that 'could you see Boston, it would break your heart'. The occupied city was by this time surrounded by thousands of provincial troops from Massachusetts, Connecticut, Rhode Island and New Hampshire. American soldiers were busy building entrenchments and other fortifications, competing with the British for control of the many islands in Boston Harbor, jostling among themselves for authority in an inherently disorderly situation of lack of central control, and awaiting anticipated moves by the British to break out of Boston and conquer surrounding towns. Throughout New England enterprising local leaders were raising companies of citizen-soldiers to march to Charleston, Cambridge or Roxbury to participate in the siege of Boston. Captain Benjamin Titcomb of Dover raised such a band of patriots in May and June; preparing to march south, they gathered on the Sabbath, 14 June, to hear the words of their pastor, who spoke to them of conscience. Belknap preached:

> You are accountable to a higher tribunal than any earthly power, and you have a right to examine and it is your duty to examine whether the cause in which you are engaged is just, and if you find that it is so, you can fight with a good conscience, and with a hope in the Divine Providence for liberty and success.

These men were preparing to engage British troops that throughout May and June were receiving reinforcements led by generals Burgoyne, Howe and Clinton. The British, realizing that they could not break the siege until the heights of Charleston peninsula and Dorchester Neck were taken, began to plan accordingly. The Americans, meanwhile, built fortifications on these heights. The British, spying from Boston the works thrown up on Charleston peninsula during the early morning hours of 17 June, mobilized their forces, bombarded the American fortifications and landed men on the southern and eastern shores of the peninsula, which began the Battle of Bunker Hill.[18]

The British won the battle but at a great cost of men. News of the Pyrrhic victory hurried quickly north, which disturbed and excited inhabitants in Dover as well as other towns throughout New Hampshire. As thousands of men congregated around Boston, physical as well as spiritual illnesses broke out, requiring physicians of the body and soul. In July, the New Hampshire Committee of Safety directed one of its members, Samuel Webster, to apply to Belknap to encourage him to serve as a chaplain to the New Hampshire militia forces besieging Boston. Webster wrote to Belknap:

> I am sensible that it will be in many respects a self-denying work, but I trust this will not discourage you. It is surely very important that our many friends & brethren in the army, engaged in a cause which we trust God approves, surrounded with deaths & temptations, should not want the advantages of social worship, & the more private instructions, cautions, & encouragements which may be afforded by a faithful chaplain.

Belknap was, however, previously engaged with a parish, family, numerous children, and a very worried wife who could not bear to be separated from her husband for extensive periods. The family experienced numerous trials during the month of July that convinced Belknap he made the right decision. His mother had been very ill, and Ruth had fallen and broken her hand and a local apothecary had tried setting it without success. Belknap sent for Dr Hall Jackson from Portsmouth, who stayed with the Belknap's several days re-setting Ruth's hand and, strangely, operating on Sarah Belknap's hand as well. In the larger public matters of war, Belknap was willing to help, but not to be given full responsibility. Meanwhile, in late July, Belknap, probably at Cousin John's suggestion, wrote to Andrew Eliot to encourage him to leave the city for a visit to New Hampshire; perhaps he would find peace and tranquillity. But Eliot declined, telling Belknap,

> I can do but little for God & his people, but hope my tarrying here has been of use. I am continually employed in visiting the sick, who are numerous, in attending the prisoners, tho' it has not been tho't proper I should see them of late.[19]

Throughout the summer the inhabitants of the Piscataqua Valley continued to be concerned of a British attack; the British man-of-war *Scarborough* patrolled the outer harbour, taking whatever private vessels it could intercept. A 'Rumpus at Portsmouth and Newcastle about [the] Man of War' on 13 August compelled Belknap and John Eliot to journey downriver to Kittery Point, on 21 August, to spy, as it were, on the man-of-war. And they saw not one but two! Having performed their surreptitious deed, the two men returned to Dover. Two days later they heard that Governor Wentworth and family departed New Hampshire for good aboard the *Scarborough*; as soon as the two ships departed, the inhabitants occupied Fort William and Mary, setting 'about building batteries'. The enthusiasm for such works spread to Dover; some of Belknap's parishioners volunteered to go to Portsmouth and build such fortifications on other islands of the Piscataqua in case of the return of the man-of-wars. On 20 August Belknap heard that his old friend Governor Wentworth was temporarily residing at the Isles of Shoals, several miles off the New Hampshire coast.[20]

In October, Belknap took his turn condoling with the distressed inhabitants of the towns surrounding Boston and preaching to and counselling the New England militia laying siege to the city. He set out from Dover on 16 October, arriving at Haverhill, where he lodged for the night. The next day he arrived at Cambridge, having first passed through Medford and seeing the troops encamped about Winter Hill. He learned more about a brief battle that had taken place on the hill a few months before. During the next few days he journeyed north, west and south of Boston. At Malden he visited his friend Thacher, who informed Belknap of all that his Dover friend had not heard about the

Battle of Bunker Hill, of which Thacher served as the official historian of the Massachusetts Committee of Safety. The absence of inhabitants in the towns of Malden and Cambridge amazed Belknap. That night at Cambridge, 17 October, he witnessed an armed barge, or 'floating battery', being launched by the rebels; the barge had several cannon, from which they hoped to lob balls into Boston Common, where Redcoats were camped. Unfortunately one of the cannon split apart, causing a disaster for the men manning it, and a failed result to a flimsy effort. Belknap found the American troops stationed at Cambridge as well as the local inhabitants, to be 'much more healthy than I supposed', especially after having heard of the many negative reports of the ragtag, sick American army put out by Tory sympathizers. He wrote to Ruth that the Dover militia were generally in good health, notwithstanding the disorderly situation they found themselves in, trying to maintain military order in an inherently chaotic situation. Rainy weather on 19 October dashed his hopes to visit the front siege lines in Cambridge to see, across the Charles, the layout of British troops defending Boston and what appeared to be the state of the besieged city. Instead, Belknap journeyed across the Charles west of Boston, south to 'Brooklyne' on the Muddy River, then east to Roxbury on the south shore, where he hoped to gain a similar vantage point. Roxbury lay down the road from Boston, connected to the city by the narrow Neck that kept Boston from becoming an island, and which separated the sea from the Charles River. Belknap spent the night at the tavern run by Robert Pierpoint, where General Artemas Ward, who at that time commanded the New Hampshire and Connecticut militia, the right wing of the American army, also stayed. Belknap met and spoke with the General's aide-de-camp, Joshua Ward, who filled the pastor in on the current activities of the Continental Congress. The Congress had been busy petitioning King George for redress of their concerns and to discover a way to still salvage peace; meanwhile, preparing for the contingency of continued war and independence, they had planned a temporary government in which an itinerant Congress would travel from province to province, each equally independent and enjoying complete self-government. Belknap understood that the American generals favoured an outright declaration of independence.[21]

Isaac Mansfield, who later became Belknap's friend and neighbour when in 1776 he became pastor of the First Parish of Exeter, New Hampshire, currently served as chaplain to militia troops under General John Thomas; on 20 October he asked Belknap to pray with the troops. Afterward, accompanying 'an officer of the picquet guard', Belknap journeyed to the forward lines at Roxbury neck, where he could see what had happened to the town, and view the Redcoats, if at a distance. He recorded in his diary:

> Nothing struck me with more horror than the present condition of Roxbury: that once busy, crowded street is now occupied only by a picquet guard. The houses are deserted; the windows taken out, and many shot-holes visible; some have been burnt, and other pulled down, to make room for the fortifications. A wall of earth is carried across the street where there is a formidable fort mounted with cannon.

Belknap toured the fortifications, and could see the Redcoat sentries across the Neck, which was a no-man's land. Belknap also made the rounds with the generals, joining General Ward for dinner and, back in Cambridge, enjoying an audience with General Israel Putnam, whom Belknap tabbed as 'a rough, fiery genius'. General Ward, who was methodical and studious, like Belknap, gave the pastor his version of the events at Bunker Hill, including an account of the tragic death of Dr Joseph Warren and the lack of respect to the hero's body, which was exhumed and re-buried again and again to satisfy the curiosity of Tories who crossed from Boston and Charleston and back to view the scenes of the infamous battle.[22]

The morning of 21 October again greeted the people of Cambridge with rain, which prevented Belknap from viewing the American and British lines, and kept him indoors in conversation with friends and new acquaintances. One of the latter was General John Sullivan of Durham, New Hampshire, who in time Belknap would come to know quite well. On this day General Sullivan informed the pastor that, in response to the dastardly attack three days earlier on Falmouth, Maine by H.M.S. *Canceau,* Henry Mowat, captain, he was to amass New Hampshire militia at Cambridge and quickly march to Portsmouth to protect the city from a similar attack in which the British would seek to terrorize more innocent civilians. Belknap spoke with General Thomas Mifflin, former delegate to the Continental Congress from Pennsylvania and current Quartermaster General, who invited Belknap to dinner, which turned out to be quite an extensive banquet featuring many leaders of the American forces. Included at the table were General Charles Lee, whose manners and language fascinated and offended most of his audience, including Belknap; a committee from 'the Grand Congress' sent to meet with the generals that included Benjamin Franklin of Philadelphia, Colonel Benjamin Harrison of Virginia (later Governor), and Thomas Lynch, Jr, of South Carolina; Adjutant General Horatio Gates of Virginia; Colonel Joseph Reed and George Baylor, aide-de-camps to General Washington (who unfortunately was not present at the dinner); Connecticut Lieutenant-Governor Matthew Griswold; and chaplain to Connecticut forces Abiel Leonard. The diners discussed which countries produced the best soldiers, and what should be the ongoing strategy to force the British from Boston; one view, to which Belknap vehemently disagreed, was to burn the city.[23]

On the Sabbath, 22 October, as was the custom in New England, ministers such as Belknap preached the entire day to hearers. There were numerous tightropes that American ministers had to walk in their sermons during these years of war. Although Christ taught the doctrine of turning the other cheek to enemies, at the same time the Old Testament taught that God had instilled the instinct of self-preservation in humans, which necessitated the urge to repulse attacks on life and liberty. As early as 1772 Belknap, preaching *A Sermon on Military Duty* before Governor John Wentworth and New Hampshire militia troops, had noted that self-preservation resulted in 'martial spirit' and 'natural courage'. 'And can it be supposed that we must make no use of these gifts of nature, even after providence points out the necessity? Do we guard our fields from devouring beasts, our houses and our bodies from the injuries of weather? And shall we not have the privilege of defending our lives, our liberties, our property, our families, our civil government from hostile invaders? Must we tamely yield to every lawless usurper, and suffer tyrants to sport with the lives and estates of mankind?' When Belknap made these remarks in 1772, he hardly thought that the 'hostile invaders' and 'tyrants' would be the English people and King! Like many thoughtful colonists, Belknap enthusiastically received the news in 1762 of the ascension of George III to the throne, believing that the young King was enlightened and would rule the realm with patience and wisdom. Subsequent events having indicated the contrary, Belknap had over the years continued to hope that the British would see the errors of their ways and relent in their oppression of their loyal provincial countrymen. He had welcomed the Fast Days ordered by provincial governments and the Continental Congress to pray with humility for peace and unity. Even after witnessing the apparent break between the provincials and the king, and seeing the destruction done to such communities as Roxbury, Belknap was unwilling to abandon hope that reconciliation might still be brought about, if not by men then by God's will. He was therefore at ease in continuing to pray for the health and well-being of George III in sermons like those of 22 October. Although he was informed afterward that the American officers did not approve of praying for the King, Belknap refused to back down, proclaiming that 'the same authority which appointed the generals had ordered the king to be prayed for at the late Continental fast' of 20 June 1775; 'and, till that was revoked, I should think it my duty to do it'. Belknap concluded that 'it is too assuming in the generals to find fault with it'. Belknap ended the Sabbath visiting the sick among the troops.[24]

The following day, 23 October, Belknap prepared to return home to New Hampshire. He spoke to General Mifflin about when the siege might become an offensive attack; Mifflin replied that, though preparations continued for such a purpose, he doubted that it would be soon. This gratified Belknap, who did not wish Boston to end up like Charleston; and, as he told his wife in a letter of 18 October, were the Patriots to attempt an assault using such methods as the failed floating battery of 17 October, they would surely not succeed. Belknap walked over to Prospect Hill, which lay along the road from Cambridge to Charleston, from which he could see the Charles River, Boston, the remains of the burnt town of Charleston and the British positions at Bunker Hill. The presence of the British in his home town of Boston, the horrible stories arriving from the north of the savagery of the attack on the seacoast town of Falmouth, and fears of similar attacks at other seacoast towns, convinced Belknap that for his return journey to Dover he should keep inland.[25]

Accordingly, when he departed Cambridge on the afternoon of 23 October he took the Andover Road going due north towards Medford. Along the way he halted at Winter Hill, from which he could gain a good look of the Mystic River and Charleston peninsula. From Medford, the road proceeded north through Woburn and Wilmington to Andover, where the road jogged to the east, paralleling the descending Merrimack River. The river blocked Belknap's route to Bradford and Haverhill; compared to the Charles to the south and the Piscataqua to the north, the Merrimack typically had a narrow stream. However, unusually plentiful October rains had swelled the river on its descent from the White Mountains of New Hampshire. The flood was great enough to furnish the inhabitants of Bradford and Haverhill with plentiful drift wood, but was not too great to prevent the ferryman from taking his passenger north across the river to Haverhill. This Belknap did after having spent the night on the southern side, crossing in the morning to the northern side; from here it was a short distance to New Hampshire at Plaistow, from which he continued from one small town to another: Kingston, Exeter, Stratham, Newington. After crossing the Piscataqua from Bloody Point to Dover Point, it was a quick ride home to Dover. The town was strangely crowded with refugees from Portsmouth who had fled the city in expectation of a visit from Captain Mowat and the *Canceau* (which never occurred).[26]

The anxiety of Jeremy Belknap and his extended family over British attacks of the Piscataqua Valley and the continued occupation of Boston continued through the autumn and winter. As soon as Belknap returned to Dover he set about 'making Cartridges' and 'casting bulletts [*sic*]' just in case the fears of Piscataqua residents were realized. Andrew Eliot periodically sent word of his and other Bostonians' experiences of deprivation and fear. 'You cannot conceive the anxiety I am in', Eliot wrote to Belknap in November. Eliot, like other inhabitants of Boston, was afraid that the rasher would prevail over the cooler, more patient, heads among American generals, and that Boston would be put to the torch or suffer a direct attack, or both, with innocent civilians caught in between angry and vengeful men on both sides. Fortunately for the people of Boston, General Washington did not feel that his army was strong enough to force the issue, the British entrenchments at Boston Neck and at Charleston being too formidable to attack 'without great slaughter on our side'. Belknap heard of scattered skirmishes and failed strategies throughout the winter. The longer the siege dragged on, the greater the scarcity of food and wood, and the greater the general privation and suffering of the inhabitants. The Redcoats were caged up in the city, restless, cold and hungry, and often released their anxiety and boredom on the inhabitants. The Americans finally forced the issue when in the first week of March 1776, they fortified Dorchester heights, which lay south of Boston, artillery from which could harass British warships and bombard the city. General Howe realized how insecure the British position had become, and resolved to quit the town. News reached Dover daily of the 'cannonading' of Boston. On 17 March the American army occupied Charleston peninsula and Boston, and the long siege was over. The fires in Boston spurred by the American siege and British evacuation lit the night sky, and could be seen for miles around. Belknap could see the light on the southern horizon on 20 March. The inhabitants of Boston, meanwhile, watched as 'the whole fleet and army' sailed from Boston Harbor 'to the universal joy of its Inhabitants'. The destination of the tall ships was unknown.[27]

2 MELTED MAJESTY

When in March 1776 fast-riding couriers brought word to cities and towns up and down the American coast that the British had evacuated Boston, joy over the American success mixed with consternation over the whereabouts of the British fleet. Initial fears that the fleet had gone to attack another American port were allayed when news arrived that Halifax, Nova Scotia, was the destination. However, the Americans knew that the brothers Howe, General William and Admiral Richard, were not giving up, but rather licking their wounds and gathering strength before again descending upon the American coast.

A former bookseller and stationer, since the summer of 1775 Postmaster of New York, Ebenezer Hazard, was one of the first of Manhattan's inhabitants to hear the news of Boston's salvation and the British retreat to Halifax. For almost a year Hazard had been responsible for sending and receiving letters of the 'eastern' post that departed from and returned to New York City to and from the eastern colonies of Connecticut, Rhode Island, Massachusetts and New Hampshire. In the wake of the battles of Lexington and Concord in April 1775, accompanying the confusion that had erupted in the streets of New York between Whigs and Tories there had been a chaotic battle for control of the post; letters sent between New York and New England had been intercepted by different revolutionary committees along the way; thoughtful people had realized the necessity of a system to ensure the regular delivery of mail even in wartime. A few weeks after Lexington and Concord the New York Committee of Safety had brought about order by dismissing the previous postmaster, and appointing Hazard, along with William Goddard and John Holt, to send and receive the colonial, Whig mails sent by those who refused to use or did not trust the parliamentary, Tory post. Goddard had christened the operation the 'constitutional Post Office'. Later, in July, the New York Provincial Congress had recommended Hazard to Postmaster General Benjamin Franklin as the best person to run the New York office. Hazard had been selected over his counterpart Holt, who had hitherto used his printing office as a post office. Hazard had the right qualities to be entrusted with the secretive communications of the fledgling New York Provincial Congress as well as the Continental Congress and Continental Army.[1]

New York's postmaster was a native of Philadelphia; his father, Samuel, and mother, Catherine Clarkson, were natives of New York who had relocated to Philadelphia, where Ebenezer was born in 1744. He was baptized by the New Light preacher Gilbert Tennent, his grandfather, and was educated at New Light evangelist and his uncle Samuel Finley's West Nottingham Academy in Maryland; he matriculated at the College of New Jersey, where Uncle Finley had become president, earning the Bachelors degree in 1762. After having spent some time at sea, Hazard moved to New York in 1765 to engage in book-selling, eventually becoming a partner with Garret Noel. Noel and Hazard was a Manhattan firm for several years in the early 1770s, advertising in Rivington's *New-York Gazetteer* that they were selling books on history and political philosophy. Hazard travelled to England in 1772, partly for business reasons. For a short time he was part of Benedict & Hazard, Booksellers. New York's postmaster wore his brown hair long over the collar, as was the style; his eyes, which dominated his face, were particularly piercing. His face was full and round, which matched his muscular, if fleshy, physique. Hazard possessed the Calvinist viewpoint that life involves work well done.[2]

Hazard was formal and conservative, his Presbyterian stock engendering a dignified bearing that matched his aloof emotions. He was brought up to believe in and live his life in conformity to a rigid formal Presbyterianism. Hazard's father had been an elder and one of the founders, along with George Whitefield and Gilbert Tennent, of the Second Presbyterian Church of Philadelphia, where his grandfather Tennent was the first preacher. His education under Samuel Finley and upbringing in the eighteenth-century New Light Presbyterian community nurtured in Hazard a methodical mindset that neatly categorized life and learning, human experience and the natural and the supernatural, into mental folders organizing history, religion, politics, morality and business into precise subjects of information. These intellectual characteristics combined with habits of hard work and devotion to tradition and duty enabled Hazard to be successful in most of his life's callings, public and private. His profound understanding of what is right and his unyielding sense of duty carried him through the chaotic months of the fall of New York, while his methodical habits of business resulted in an efficiency in organizing postal routes and managing post riders that helped the Americans carry the day, at least in communications.[3]

On 4 July 1776, while the Continental Congress signed the Declaration of Independence the British fleet of seventy ships out of Nova Scotia sailed under Long Island, reaching Staten Island and the Narrows, the inlet between the two islands now crossed by the Verrazano Bridge. Hazard learned of these events at the coffee house near the southern tip of lower Manhattan frequented by himself and other New Yorkers seeking news and conversation. Reports at the coffee house indicated that these were the troops from Nova Scotia commanded by

Lord William Howe, that companies of men were seeking supplies of food and water on Staten Island, and that the inhabitants were friendly towards them and providing whatever assistance they could render. Americans on the Jersey shore, across the narrow inlets, or kills, from Staten Island, were not so friendly, as British troops soon discovered when men in small boats, trying to pursue the advantage gained by the occupation of Staten Island, came under attack. Hazard, as Postmaster of New York, had a wide range of correspondents, some of whom had become epistler-friends who provided him with news of events outside of New York, to which he responded with news from the city. One of these friends was the Rev. William Gordon, the Roxbury pastor, who had been informing Hazard during the past twelve plus months of affairs in Boston. Hazard and Gordon had a mutual friend in General Horatio Gates, who relied on Gordon to inform him about military and other matters in Massachusetts, and on Hazard to provide him with news about New York. One assumes without positive knowledge that Gates met Gordon during the siege of Boston and Hazard during the aftermath, when General Gates marched south with Washington's army to New York. In the late spring of 1776, Congress appointed Gates to the command of the Canadian Department, to reinforce and defend Fort Ticonderoga and the northern approaches to Canada, namely Lake George and Lake Champlain. Accordingly Hazard wrote successive letters to Gates over the course of July, informing the General of the British arrival at New York Harbor and their movements as they sought to invest their forces beyond Staten Island to Brooklyn, Manhattan, the East River and the Hudson River. On 5 July, Hazard wrote to Gates that

> it was last night reported at the coffee-house, (and I believe the report may be depended on,) that the Congress had determined on a Declaration of Independence, and that the vote was unanimous, except *New York*, whose Delegates, not being instructed, could not vote.

A week later, Hazard wrote that General Howe commanded eight thousand troops, that they had 'taken possession of Staten Island', and that American forces intended to attack before Admiral Howe arrived with reinforcements. 'Desertions are frequent among them: almost every night some men make their escape'. Hazard sent Gates a copy of the Declaration, which had been 'proclaimed ... in the Army here, and received, as might naturally be expected, with great joy'. An equestrian statue of King George III dressed in the garb of Marcus Aurelius, erected after the Stamp Act Crisis in a square in southern Manhattan called Bowling Green, surrounded by a wrought iron fence to keep away vandals, succumbed to the spirit and wrath of the Whigs in the wake of the reading of the Declaration of Independence. The lead statue was pulled down and taken apart. Hazard, who either witnessed the action of the crowd or heard about it, remarked that the lead of the statue was to be melted and recast into thousands of musket balls; the King's troops as a result will 'have melted Majesty fired at them'. All mirth aside, the American hold on New York was tenuous at best; even the most ideal success in recruiting would scarcely result in equal odds with the British troops already in possession of Staten Island, and there were many more yet to come. Admiral Howe would surely bring more, and King George was negotiating with German princes to send mercenaries to America. The Americans were to be greatly outnumbered by late summer; in July, however, inhabitants of Manhattan could still cling to the fading fantasy that they would not have to abandon their homes to the Loyalists and Redcoats. With each week, however, more Redcoats arrived. When July gave way to August, over 30,000 armed troops at Staten Island awaited the order to attack. Reports at the coffee shop, based on figures provided by deserters, were more optimistic. Hazard wrote Gates on 9 August that 'Howe musters now about thirteen thousand men in all, and affects to hold the "Rebel Army" in contempt. One would have thought experience had taught him better'. The Battle of Long Island was not, however, to be a repeat of the Battle of Bunker Hill.[4]

General Washington had determined after arriving at New York in the spring that the best defence of the city was in fortifying western Long Island, particularly Brooklyn Heights, which lay across the East River from Manhattan. By August he had committed 8,000 men to the defence of Long Island, though in doing so he had divided his forces between Manhattan and Long Island without securing control of the East River separating them. The British Navy dominated the waters of the Upper Bay and Lower Bay, but could not risk an attack on Manhattan with the Americans entrenched on Brooklyn Heights. General Howe therefore resolved on a frontal attack of the American forces on Long Island, and crossed 15,000 troops on 22 August. The Americans, under General John Sullivan and Lord Stirling, were vastly outnumbered – and outgeneralled as well. The Battle of Long Island quickly became an American debacle, forcing retreat across the East River to Manhattan. Fortunately for the Americans, General Howe and Admiral Howe were slow to respond to success, and allowed the Americans to execute a quick and neat crossing from Brooklyn to Manhattan during the early morning hours of 29 August. Meanwhile, New York citizens did what they could to prepare for an attack. Hazard worked with the local militia leader Captain Samuel Broome to locate the ingredients for black powder for small arms if and when the British attacked Manhattan. He wrote a letter to New York Congressional delegate Robert Livingston on 29 August, the same day that the American forces retreated across the East River, asking that Congress keep in mind those patriotic citizens who wished to fight, such as the group Hazard was a member of, the Independent Company of Free Citizens. At the same time, Hazard had to consider how best to preserve communications with Manhattan under siege; he appeared on 30 August before a committee of the

New York Congress, called now the Committee of Safety, meeting at White Plains, north of Manhattan, to request their advice on where to keep the post office, 'as an invasion of the City of *New-York* is hourly expected'.[5]

During the waning days of August 1776, the number of refugees fleeing New York increased as families fled before the coming storm of war and Whigs departed in the face of British invasion and occupation of the city. The Continental Congress rejected calls by hard-hearted military strategists for the burning of the city to make it useless to the Tories. Hazard, in charge of communications for the city, delayed the inevitable until the end of August, when the New York Committee of Safety ordered him to relocate the post office to a location near Dobb's Ferry on the eastern banks of the Hudson River, above Manhattan. In shaking the dust from his feet he gave up his part in a privateering scheme, selling his interest in a sloop – for the waters in and about New York Harbor would not be accommodating for Whigs and rebels in the coming years. In the early days of September, Hazard packed his trunks and moved north, coming to Dobb's Ferry, named after the family who operated the ferry service in the eighteenth century. He found quarters a little farther to the north, staying at the house of Major Abraham Storm and keeping a temporary office next door at the residence of Hercules Cronk, where he performed his duties of receiving and forwarding the mail even as chaos in civil and military affairs reigned. Postmaster General Benjamin Franklin, however, believed that the postmaster of New York, whose primary role was to send and receive communications from General Washington and his staff, should form his office at the headquarters of the army. Hazard duly relocated again during the month of September, attaching himself to the Continental Army at Harlem Heights, trying to make the best of his life as an itinerant postmaster. Hazard was constantly called upon to absorb the cost of mail, the necessity of war increasing the use of the franking privilege, whereby letters were sent at no cost to the sender or receiver. Post riders to and from New York complained of danger and insufficient and non-existent remuneration. Hazard repeatedly wrote to the New York Committee of Safety for payment of his own and his rider's expenses. Although he was not required to keep a horse when he lived in Manhattan, this changed when Hazard moved; to fulfil his duties running a post office out of a trunk, and following the army wherever it might deploy, required a horse; but neither the Committee of Safety nor the quartermaster of the army accommodated his request. The Committee of Safety added to his duties in October, requiring that the Postmaster obtain for them copies of newspapers from all of the principle cities up and down the coast; the Postmaster must pay for them up front, though he was promised compensation in time.[6]

On 11 October Hazard wrote to General Horatio Gates at Ticonderoga that General Washington intended to make his stand at Harlem Heights, and that the British 'appear rather shy since a drubbing they got some weeks ago' – an apparent reference to the American retreat across the East River. Meanwhile, General Howe again put his troops on the move. Hoping to encircle the American army, the British moved up the East River during the second week in October, landing at Throg's Neck, where they encountered stiff resistance. Howe moved further east to New Rochelle, which forced Washington to abandon Harlem Heights; the army retreated to White Plains, then at the end of the month, to North Castle. Hazard followed, dragging his trunk. General Howe at this point realized that the Americans had left in their rear a strong garrison at Fort Washington, on the eastern banks of the Hudson in upper Manhattan. He immediately marched south in mid-November to take the fort. Washington responded by dividing his forces, leaving half under General Charles Lee at North Castle, while he led the other half across the Hudson and down its west side to Fort Lee, opposite Fort Washington. By the time he arrived at Fort Lee, however, the British had already laid siege to Fort Washington, which they quickly overran.[7]

Although Hazard was at the centre of communications, rumour and miscommunication still had its way in wartime; he, and no doubt many others, misinterpreted the British march towards Dobb's Ferry as a retreat rather than an attack. Anticipating that Lee's army would follow Washington's west across the Hudson any day, dreading that he must 'follow the Army' on foot 'like a sutler', Hazard allowed his frustration to take hold over duty and purpose. He therefore penned a long 'Memorial', or petition, to the Continental Congress, in which he discussed the small commission that he earned from his office that could hardly pay for his expenses, especially since prices for food, lodging, clothing and washing necessarily increased wherever the army bivouacked. Hazard concluded his petition with the appeal:

> that he apprehends it to have been the design of Congress that the Postmaster of so important and capital a district as that of *New-York*, should not diminish his private property by his assiduity in serving the publick, but that he should receive a decent maintenance from his office.

Hazard also wrote separately to a friend who served in Congress, the Presbyterian minister John Witherspoon, President of Princeton College, hoping to have an insider working on his behalf. He told Witherspoon that the majority of the mail that he handled was correspondence to and from General Washington. Congress responded in recognition that, with the fall of New York, Hazard was no longer postmaster of a city under occupation, yet at the same time he had been assuming the role as the unofficial postmaster of the Continental Army. Hazard was clearly indispensable. In November 1776, the Postmaster received word that he had been promoted to a new position of responsibility and commensurate danger, surveyor of post roads. For the next six years, Hazard's would be a mercurial life on the road.[8]

Military communications not to mention public and private correspondence came to a near standstill with the Declaration of Independence and the aggressive pursuit of war. Field commanders complained that dispatches from Congress or General Washington took weeks and months rather than days. Jumbled postal routes, incompetent or disloyal post riders and local postmasters, and enemy action ensured that the post was irregular at best. Congress, knowing that victory was built upon adequate communications, required in 1776 that postmasters engage riders who would travel non-stop, day or night, for thirty miles at a time. The post should move from stop to stop, the mail pass from rider to rider, at least three times a week. It was up to Ebenezer Hazard to determine the best routes for travel, to find postmasters with experience and connections who could be trusted to handle the mail and recruit trustworthy young men who had the will and courage to evade the enemy and bring the mail from place to place. In each place Hazard had to judge the attitude of the locals towards the rebels. A civilian working for the rebel government, his own life was in peril should he be captured. British proclamations warned that such civilian rebels would be summarily executed for their treasonous activities.

To this end Hazard, upon his appointment as surveyor of post roads, journeyed to Philadelphia to meet with Congress and the new Postmaster General Richard Bache to learn about the precise nature of his duties. Hazard's initial task as the surveyor of post roads was to establish adequate communications between Philadelphia and New England. A coastal route was out of the question because of the superiority of the British Navy and the British occupation of New York City, the Connecticut coast, and Rhode Island. Logically, a post rider would leave Philadelphia riding due north paralleling the descending Delaware River, crossing the river at Trenton, proceeding north to Princeton, then to New Brunswick and Newark. Washington's victory in late 1776 ensured that the post could cross the river at Trenton, although the road north to New Brunswick remained closed, forcing Hazard to establish communications on an arc going from Princeton to Kingston to Morristown then east to Chatham, Springfield, Elizabeth and Newark. Newark and the surrounding vicinity had seen sporadic fighting during the first few years of the war. There was a frequent presence of British troops in the area, and Loyalist sympathies continued to run strong. Hazard had to be on his guard no matter where he was in New Jersey. From Newark, the post road necessarily veered north-west towards the town of Pompton on the Ramapo River, passing the Passaic Falls. From here the road proceeded north between the Ramapo Mountains and the Hudson Valley towards Bear Mountain. South of Bear Mountain the Hudson broadened into the so-called Tappan Sea; the high cliffs of the western shores of the Hudson River were known as the Palisades, from which an observer had an extensive view of the lower Hudson and Manhattan Island. This part of the Hudson Valley was dangerous for the surveyor of post roads. The British had taken Fort Washington on the New York side and Fort Lee on the New Jersey side of the Hudson. British troops patrolled the region north of Fort Lee to Stony Point. North of Bear Mountain, the post road was more secure. Scattered American fortifications included Fort Clinton on Bear Mountain, which loomed above the Hudson, and Fort Montgomery. Further north was West Point, where Washington would make his headquarters in the summer of 1777 and where a great iron link chain would be stretched across the Hudson in 1778 to prevent British control of the upper Hudson. The post road north of Bear Mountain towards West Point and on to Newburgh paralleled the Hudson in the same fashion as Route 9W does today. Notwithstanding that the post was put on a firm basis, the entire Hudson Valley was dangerous to travel, as the British saw the region as the key to victory. Control of the Hudson would allow the British to divide and conquer, to separate New England from the states to the south.

In 1777 the only American ferry across the Hudson was between New Windsor and Fishkill. There was an American troop presence in these two towns, where Hazard heard the conversations and stories of citizens and soldiers regarding all of the happenings of war. For centuries Fishkill, an old Dutch settlement, had been a northern terminus on the route of peoples, Native Americans and Colonials, moving north or south along the Hudson. Logically, the best route along the Hudson was from Fishkill south to Peekskill, Tarrytown, Philipsburg, and past Dobb's Ferry to Manhattan Island. But, since the British held the eastern side of the Hudson from the Croton River south, this was out of the question.

Fishkill served as a headquarters and supply depot for American troops; several thousand American troops were frequently stationed there. When the British took New York City during the previous summer, the provincial congress of New York retreated to Fishkill, where they held emergency meetings at the old Dutch Reformed Church. Hazard remembered frequenting the church, meeting with state officials, receiving orders respecting roads and postal routes, and living out of a trunk. The nearby Anglican Trinity Church was converted to a military hospital for the sick and wounded. Hazard's old school friend Benjamin Rush called such hospitals 'sinks of human life', referring to the terrible mortality of soldiers who died more often from disease than battle casualty. The most prevalent diseases were typhoid fever and dysentery. Rush and other surgeons, bound still to the ancient belief in humours, bled patients, which weakened the sick and contributed to a greater number of fatalities. Eighteenth-century physicians did not yet understand the role of micro-organisms in the cause and effect of disease. Rush thought that confinement in makeshift hospitals such as Fishkill's Trinity Church 'robbed the United States of more citizens than the sword'. He believed in fresh air rather than four walls. But his was a minority opinion of the time.[9]

From Fishkill, Hazard moved across the forested, hilly lands of New York into Connecticut. This region of western Connecticut between the Hudson and the Connecticut River was home to sturdy, hardworking farm men and women who eschewed enthusiastic pipe dreams of renewal and reform and were conservative in their political sympathies and religious beliefs. After a brief stop at Danbury, Hazard followed the Housatonic downriver to the ford at Newtown, then east, fording the Naugatuck River to Derby. From Derby the road went east to New Haven, the home of Yale College, on the Quinnipiac River. From New Haven he travelled to Middletown, then paralleled the Connecticut River on its western shores north to Hartford, where he forded the river. The Connecticut was the historic route that for decades adventurous settlers from Connecticut journeyed upon north to discover and settle the fertile intervales of the upper Connecticut valley in Vermont and New Hampshire. From Hartford, the road east passed through a forested region of conifers, pines and hemlocks, their branches weighed down with snow. The road intersected with numerous small streams descending from the hilly north falling to the sea. Small rivers and streams connected one pond to another, all of them frozen in the deep winter. The goal of horse and rider was to stay warm. Otherwise winter offered a relative ease of travel free from mud and spring's constant challenge of fording rushing streams and swollen rivulets. The land of eastern Connecticut still bore the marks of wilderness. Snow covered rocky, hard soil that made farming difficult. Walls of granite stone dug from the soil documented the labour of the inhabitants. This had once been the land of the Nipmuck and Narragansett tribes. Small snow-covered mountains dotted the region of Pomfret and Ashford. Horse and rider crossed numerous rivulets, such as the Mashamoquet, flowing south, eventually to form the Thames River. The post road proceeded north-east into the hilly country of north-eastern Connecticut, crossing the frozen Quinebaug River in the township of Thompson. The region had been settled decades before primarily by men from Roxbury, Massachusetts. The tavern of John Jacobs offered the traveller respite from the cold. Eschewing Rhode Island, under British control, Hazard proceeded into southern Massachusetts through rolling, forested land crossing rivers such as the Charles and Blackstone. He passed through the town of Mendon and perchance stopped at Clark Tavern on the way to Dedham; the tavern was halfway between the two towns. The road from Dedham brought Hazard to Roxbury and the home of his friend the Rev. William Gordon.[10]

Gordon, the minister of the Third Parish at Jamaica Plain, was, like many New England clergymen, at the same time a historian, philosopher, scientist and divine. Recognizing the revolutionary nature of the conflict between the colonies and mother country, Gordon diligently began work on a history of the War for Independence; he frequently discussed his work with his comrade in historical inquiry Hazard. Gordon saw in Ebenezer Hazard someone of his type and inclination. Both men were thoroughgoing Protestants, Patriots, and passionate about history. The two discussed their respective interests: Gordon in penning a narrative of the conflict, Hazard in creating a documentary history of the war. Gordon invited Hazard to use his parsonage as a way-station while he established the postal service in Boston and northern locations.[11]

Boston and the vicinity were still recovering from the British occupation that had lasted from the beginning of the war when Lexington and Concord were invaded in April 1775 to the British evacuation of Boston in March 1776. By means of Gordon's account Hazard could picture the battles that raged in the region, at Bunker Hill and Breeds Hill and in and about Roxbury. The Roxbury native and local hero Dr Joseph Warren had died at the Battle of Bunker Hill. The situation of the citizenry at Boston had been dire ever since the Coercive Acts of 1774 closed Boston Harbour to trade and imposed martial law on the colony. Even after General Washington had forced the retreat of the British from Boston in March 1776, the city and region had scarcely recovered from the occupation. Trade had not yet recovered, money was scarce and inflation rampant. Inflation could destroy the personal finances of those on fixed salaries – civil servants such as Hazard and clergymen such as Gordon. Rev. Gordon and his wife and children made ends meet by working the land outside of the parsonage, growing Siberian wheat and other crops for consumption and sale. The postmaster of Boston and surrounding towns was Jonathan Hastings, who for a few years served as the steward of Harvard College before he opened a shop in Boston. For years Hastings involved himself in the post, expanding his activities (during the 1780s) to the upper Merrimack River. He also served as a bookseller, active in the acquisition of subscriptions for such books as Belknap's *History of New-Hampshire*.

From Boston the post road travelled north along the coast. Today's Route 1 mirrors the route Hazard took during the winter of 1777, going through Danvers, Topsfield and Newburyport, from which the road crossed the Merrimack River on the road to New Hampshire. The snow was heavy and privation great between stops at taverns along the road. At least the Surveyor of Post Roads Hazard had a horse, which had not been the case during the bleak summer and autumn months in New York. The region north of Boston had little strategic value for the British, hence Hazard felt relatively secure from capture along this north-easterly route. When Hazard saw Newburyport it was a lively port city of about 3,000 inhabitants engaged in all sorts of activities involving the sea: trade, fishing, shipbuilding, rope-making, barrel-making and sail-making. Hazard the Presbyterian saw the spire of the First Presbyterian a short distance to the east as he travelled on State Street north to the frozen river.[12]

After negotiating the frozen Merrimack, Hazard travelled the remaining five miles in Massachusetts, passing through Salisbury before reaching the state of New Hampshire. Hazard rode the snowy road through Seabrook, Hampton

Falls, Hampton and Greenland before reaching Portsmouth. Even in the cold the smell of the salt sea, icy tidal pools and marshes of New Hampshire's marine environment, invigorated and invited the traveller. Hampton had a small port but plentiful marshes that produced abundant hay for livestock. Hay-cocks dotted the broad expanses of the marshland. At the small town of North Hampton the post road took a westerly turn towards the pastoral community of Greenland. The farmland was rich though snow-covered and the salt-box homes snug with smoke billowing from their numerous fireplaces. Along the way Hazard probably stopped at taverns such as Wells at Hampton Falls and the Globe at the plains on the southern fringes of the town of Portsmouth.

Portsmouth was the dominant city north of Boston, built along the southern shores of the Piscataqua River, the shipbuilding and mercantile centre of eighteenth-century northern New England; it was the natural hub of communications for coastal and inland New Hampshire and Maine. The broad Piscataqua River, which divides Portsmouth from Kittery Maine, is a rapid, undulating river of competing currents amid the rise and fall of the tide. Fresh and salt water compete for dominance. The river current between Portsmouth and Kittery is impeded and distorted by numerous islands in the river. Some of these were uninhabited when Hazard saw Portsmouth in 1777; others hosted shipbuilding operations; a few had wooden structures – stages, for drying fish. The large island at the mouth of the Piscataqua, known as Great Island, was the location of the town of Newcastle. At the eastern extreme of the island was a lighthouse and fort that guarded the entrance to the harbour. Fort William and Mary had protected Portsmouth Harbor for scores of years. Portsmouth Harbor itself was a deep, still pool that provided anchorage for the largest ships. The hub of trade was at Puddle Dock, where the most lively mercantile and shipbuilding interests were located.[13]

Hazard entered a town still talking of the British burning of neighbouring Falmouth the year before. Doors were bolted with more determination; window-shutters remained closed even on fair days. Fishermen, unwilling to risk their boats on a chance run-in with British cruisers in coastal waters, contributed to the scarcity of food, and the rising prices. The economic privation of Portsmouth was not unusual among American port cities. Humans tend to think their lot worse than their neighbour's. Few people gained Hazard's perspective, derived from his varied journeys, of the widespread and universal suffering of Americans.

In the coming five years Hazard would make half-a-dozen forays north from Boston to the Piscataqua River and beyond to Maine. His journeys would be pleasantly interrupted by the rows of brightly-painted salt-box cottages, jumbled shops and wharves, and rich smells of grain on Ceres Street, fish at Strawbery Banke and ale at Market Square. Indeed, Hazard made Portsmouth his headquarters, as it were, for northern New England; he operated out of the office/home of Jeremiah Libbey, a shopkeeper and overseer of the poor who became the local postmaster. Besides Libbey, Hazard came to enjoy the company of the physician and town notable Dr Joshua Brackett of Portsmouth. Hazard hired Captain Thomas Barnard to deliver the mail about the Piscataqua Valley north all the way to Falmouth, and south to Boston. Captain Barnard served as a post rider and stage driver for over a decade. Belknap, who relied on Barnard to deliver books, wrote to Hazard years later that Bernard, 'is a clever fellow, and does not charge me any freight, but says that he will take it out in preaching'.[14]

The turbulent waters of the Piscataqua at Portsmouth would not be bridged for decades. In the meantime travellers and postal officials such as Hazard relied on ferries to cross the river. On the northern side of the Piscataqua was the Maine town of Kittery, a lesser seaport than Portsmouth, though just as picturesque. Here Hazard came to know the Reverend Benjamin Stevens, who lived at Kittery Point, and through him the Rev. Stevens' daughter Elizabeth. Miss Elizabeth Stevens was delicate and beautiful; she dazzled all potential suitors, including Hazard. But Hazard's heart could not be won easily; he was serious, formal, living according to a personal moral code that brooked no dissent from the kind of irregular, disordered feelings inspired by love.

From Kittery the post road proceeded to York, Maine, which was in the shadow of Mount Agamenticus, a small hill that was an important seamark along the Maine coast. York Harbor and Kennebunkport were minor inlets along the way that hosted a few schooners and barks. Hazard stopped for rest and refreshment, perhaps, at Woodbridge's Tavern in Old York. Nathaniel Kimball kept a tavern and was postmaster at Kennebunkport, which was a small, picturesque coastal town at the edge of the Maine forest. The white clapboard meetinghouse with black shutters to keep out the cold north wind on the winter Sabbath day was staffed by Rev. Daniel Little, pastor of the First Parish. Little was energetic and eccentric, and at the same time a botanist, inventor, theologian and missionary. Belknap optimistically believed Little to be a chemist, and would in time recommend that Hazard seek an acquaintance with the pious scientist. During and after the war, Little went on numerous journeys to the Penobscot Valley to bring Protestant Christianity to the Abenaki tribes, former allies of the French in the wars of the sixteenth and seventeenth centuries and converts to Roman Catholicism.[15]

The post road from Kennebunkport took the traveller north along the coast to the fine seaport of Falmouth (Portland). There were stops along the way at Arundel, Saco and Scarborough, at any of which Hazard could have stopped for refreshment. The Falmouth postmaster was Samuel Freeman, who during his life was variously a register and judge of probate and a church deacon. Falmouth was the northern terminus of the post road during Hazard's tenure as surveyor of post roads. On those few occasions when Hazard journeyed to Falmouth he saw the broad harbour, Casco Bay, dotted with islands; the picturesque opening of the harbour brings the cool sea breeze, allowing the pensive observer to spy the blue Atlantic in the distance. Locals recurrently referred to the autumn day in 1775 when a British flotilla commanded by Captain Henry Mowat disturbed the beauty and solemnity of the harbour. Mowat, captain of the frigate *Canceau*, sought revenge for having been briefly imprisoned by the citizens of Falmouth a few months earlier. In the morning of 18 October, the *Canceau* and several other British warships opened fire on the town. One townsmen recalled that 'all the vessels in the harbor' shot 'balls from three to nine pounds weight, bombs, carcasses, shells, grape shot, and musket balls'. The British supplemented the bombardment by sending parties of sailors into the town to fire public buildings and residences. A large portion of the town lay in ruins by the end of the day. Hazard, eighteen months later, understood the continuing fury of the people of Falmouth against the British; they turned to privateering in great numbers to wreak havoc on British shipping.[16]

After Hazard ordered the post road from Philadelphia to Falmouth, he turned his attention southward. His efforts earned the respect of many observers and inspired hope that not everything was doomed to failure during the winter and spring of 1777. John Adams wrote to his friend Thomas Jefferson in May that 'Mr. Hazard has now gone southward in the character of surveyor of the post office, and I hope will have as good success as he lately had, eastward, where he put the office into very good order'.[17]

Hazard set forth from Philadelphia in May to fulfil Adams' expectations. He paralleled the Delaware River passing through Chester, Pennsylvania, and Wilmington and Newark, Delaware, coming to Maryland at the 'Head of Elk', Elkton, where the Big Elk Creek begins its brief journey to the Chesapeake. Hazard came to Elkton on 16 May, three months before British troops under Lord Howe used the mouth of the Elk to begin the march north in the invasion of Pennsylvania. The road continued south, crossing the Northeast River, where an iron works was situated, then on to Charlestown, at the northernmost extreme of Chesapeake Bay. Hazard found the town old and decayed, though its situation on a highland provided a beautiful prospect of the Bay. The surrounding land of shrubs and forest was not as cultivated as the traveller expected. Nearing the Susquehanna River, the land was swampy. One mile above the mouth of the Susquehanna was the ferry, where Hazard crossed the river, which was 'about a Mile & a quarter wide; the Depth at low Water about 5 Fathoms'. The landscape thereabouts 'is a wild, bleak Place within about a Mile of Chesapeake Bay'. Water fowl soared above, squawking noisily. This was a place that for centuries had been the destination of explorers – the most famous was Captain John Smith 170 years before. At the ferry Hazard met and spoke briefly with a 'Company of Virginians', militia on their way to Philadelphia. They told Hazard they had recently been inoculated for smallpox, a natural precaution for those going to a strange city during wartime. Across the river the post road turned abruptly to the south-west. Hazard stopped at Rodgers' Tavern at Havre de Grace. The tavern, he wrote in his journal, was 'a very good House'.[18]

The road from Havre de Grace to Baltimore was good, with only one 'dangerous Ford' of the several rivers and creeks along the way. Hazard found Harford on the Bush River to be 'a very small shabby Place'. Hazard stopped for refreshment at the Red Lion Inn owned 'by a man who has the singular Name of Godsgrace'. Such were the needs of a company of Maryland militia that greeted the Surveyor General on their way to Philadelphia. They were smartly outfitted in the regimental uniform of knickers, coat, and vest. Baltimore was at this time 'a very small Town, situate upon Patapsco River'. Baltimore had a fortified harbour protected by the American naval frigate *Virginia*, the product of Baltimore shipyards located at Fell's Point. The Congress had lately been in Baltimore while Philadelphia seemed under threat from British arms. In March they had returned to Philadelphia. Hazard stayed at the Fountain Inn, made of brick (as were most structures in Baltimore).[19]

The surrounding countryside sponsored iron works, grist mills and tobacco production, although grain was currently outpacing tobacco among farmers. Otherwise the landscape was of shrubs and pines in sandy soil. The beauties of nature provided diversion for the traveller. Hazard was traversing the piny landscape of Maryland and Virginia at the height of the wildflower season. Not a botanist, Hazard could nevertheless appreciate the beauty of the delicate pink azalea (*Rhododenron nudiflorum*), its perfume infiltrating the air; the blue phlox (*Phlox divaricata*), known colloquially as Wild Sweet William; columbine (*Aquilegia canadensis*), with its lovely drooping red-orange petals, yet poisonous for man and beast; trout lily (*Erythronium americanum*) decorating the roadside, which the American Indians used in tea for fevers, as an emetic, and as a poultice for skin conditions; and bloodroot (*Sanguinaria canadensis*), also used by American Indians as an antiseptic, analgesic, emetic and love potion.[20]

Hazard, incredulous about such Indian folk medicine, proceeded to Annapolis at the mouth of the Severn River. Annapolis was an old city of brick; the large State House dominated the centre of town. Hazard, allowing himself to act the tourist while he stayed in Annapolis ordering the local post, toured the building and commented on its elegance. A large portrait of William Pitt by Charles Wilson Peale drew his attention. Notwithstanding the age of the city, Hazard thought it singular that there was no church, although an Episcopal building was planned. The city was, however, well-fortified with batteries on which cannon pointed ominously towards the harbour and bay.[21]

On 20 May Hazard departed Annapolis on the road to Alexandria, Virginia. He crossed the South River by ferry, refreshed himself at Rawling's Tavern, and then crossed the upper Patuxent by a ferry that was little more than a rowboat navigated by two young women. Hazard gallantly rowed the three across. Proceeding south in the rain on sandy soil, the road passed through tobacco country. Large plantations and gangs of African labourers drew Hazard's attention, his empathy and his anger:

> It is astonishing that Men who feel the Value and Importance of Liberty as much as the Inhabitants of the southern States do that of their own, should keep such Numbers of the human Species in a State of so absolute Vassalage. Every Argument which can be urged in Favor of our own Liberties will certainly operate with equal Force in Favor of that of the Negroes: nor can we with any Propriety contend for the one while we withhold the other.[22]

Hazard spent the night at a tavern in Upper Marlboro situated on a small brook flowing into the Patuxent River. The inhabitants of Upper Marlboro were racked with fear because of the presence of smallpox. Hazard learned that great numbers of soldiers who were not kept properly quarantined while they experienced the sickness, which is a consequence of inoculation, had spread the disease to the general public, most of whom were not inoculated. Hazard, having been inoculated years before and hence immune to the disease, was unafraid.[23]

The post road through this region of Maryland was strangely not the same as the main road that passed directly from Annapolis through Bladensburg to Alexandria. The reason for this departure from the norm was that Hazard's precursors had found in Stephen West, who owned a large plantation called Woodyard off the beaten path, a reliable postmaster. After meeting West Hazard was equally reluctant to find a replacement and relocate the post road. West was a charming, hospitable host. He showed Hazard his manufacturing interests, featuring a distillery, brewery and a small factory for spinning flax, hemp, wool and cotton. 'Among his machines for manufacturing is one for spinning cotton in which one Wheel turns 22 Spindles & as many Threads are spun at once'.[24]

On 22 May 1777 Hazard crossed the Potomac River into Virginia. He was impressed by the width and power of the river; the wind, blowing through the valley, was such as to prevent passage on the ferry until the more peaceful zephyrs of evening. General Washington's home at Mt Vernon was several miles downstream. Hazard was tempted to go see it, but duty kept him to his business. Of utmost importance was the postal situation at Alexandria, a small town of several thousand souls with orderly streets, wood homes and two brick churches. Alexandria was the central tobacco and wheat port, as large vessels could navigate the Potomac upstream to the town's wharves. Hazard heard that several Tories had concocted a plan to burn the town, kill the people and make their escape in a flat-bottomed gundalow – 'but their Plan was discovered, & they are now in Gaol here'. Alexandria was busy with troop movements – soldiers from Virginia and North Carolina, many awaiting the symptoms of smallpox brought on by inoculation before proceeding north.[25]

The post road departed from the Potomac south to Colchester on the Occaquam River and Dumfries on the Quantico. Hazard found the road from Alexandria to Dumfries to be 'very muddy' and hilly, 'thinly settled', with intermittent plantations. At Dumfries Hazard met two such plantation owners and local leaders, William Grayson and George Mason. Post riders travelling through this area would find few accommodations, the best being Seton's Tavern, a dirty place – 'very little in or about it for either Man or Beast; I could not get even clean Sheets to sleep in, & the dirty ones were very ragged'. Dumfries was at the foothills of a small range of mountains to the west that begot the short-lived rivers and streams that flowed into the Potomac. The town had a few eminences from which the surrounding countryside could be seen with pleasure. Dumfries itself was a small town of 600 people, the county seat of Prince William County. It had a lively trade and was busy with passing troops, activity at the small courthouse (which Hazard described as 'neat' and 'tasty'), and a gaol holding prisoners of war, including Hessians captured at the surprise attack on Trenton during Christmas, 1776.[26]

Hazard continued south on 25 May, the road taking him through a forested, hilly landscape with numerous streams that he could easily ford – but he learned that with sufficient rain these streams became 'impassable' torrents that delayed the post for several days. He eventually crossed the Rappahannoc to Fredericksburg, a small town situated just below the falls and 150 miles from Chesapeake Bay. Fredericksburg was busy with boats loaded with grain and tobacco preparing to journey downriver to the Chesapeake. The houses were of brick and wood; Smith's Tavern was clean and restful. Hazard learned of a house 'entirely devoted to Dissipation' – dancing, cards and 'retirement': 'proof' that 'even this small Town' can sponsor 'Luxury & Extravagance' belied by its size. Hazard kept to a more sober and respectable society, men such as Charles Dick and James Mercer: the former a farmer and gun manufacturer, the latter operating a 'Manufactory' that produced cotton thread. Dick's factory employed sixty people and produced about twenty muskets and bayonets per week. Mercer's mechanical looms produced high quality cotton. Hazard noted that cotton production was increasing in this region, in part because of the introduction of 'an Instrument called a Gin', which helped separate the fibre from the seed.[27]

Hazard departed Fredericksburg on 28 May following the descending Rappahannoc to Port Royal, from which he proceeded south, the post road traversing forested, largely uninhabited land. The warm weather felt good after several cool, rainy days. Numerous laurels, such as the mountain laurel (*Kalmia latifolia*) and great laurel (*Rhododendron maximum*) were in bloom. The road was sandy. Hazard had to ford several creeks and rivers, notably Tuckahoe Creek and Mattaponi River. He lodged at a tavern on the road to King William county courthouse.[28]

The next morning he awoke to a cold fog, which dissipated during the morning's ride as it turned sunny and hot. Hazard relaxed on the journey and observed typically undisturbed wildlife – squirrels, rabbits and lizards – fleeing the noise of the horse's hoofs. Forest and meadows abounded with locusts. He stopped briefly at King William courthouse to view the brick building and the outlying structures, several of which were gaols. Hazard noted that the cattle and horses of Virginians were not as large or healthy as those of Pennsylvania, a phenomenon that he explained according to the feed given the livestock – corn rather than hay.[29]

After spending the night at Cartwright's Tavern, Hazard rode sixteen miles to Williamsburg, the capitol of Virginia situated near the James River and the original settlement of the colony at Jamestown. Besides checking on the status of the post and postmaster at Williamsburg, Hazard also wished to address the state assembly requesting that postal personnel, who ensured safe and confidential military and political communications, deserved to be exempt from service in the state militia. Hazard had also conceived the idea to transcribe, preserve and eventually publish the public records of the thirteen states. He had requested from the Continental Congress letters of support directed to public officials of each state. When appearing before state legislatures, he added this request for access to, and help transcribing, records, to his list of petitions. On his return journey two weeks later he found that the assembly concurred with his varied requests. He found the town smaller than he expected, yet orderly and pleasant. The College of William and Mary was not impressive, the chief hall being 'badly contrived, and the Inside ... shabby'. Adjoining the hall was the President's house and a building that housed Indian students. Like many colleges, Dartmouth for example, William and Mary opened its doors to the education of Native Americans. Hazard found the college grounds pleasant and well-ordered. The school of divinity was suspended because of war; indeed the college, Hazard wrote, 'has been on the Decline for some Years'. Another prominent building in the town was the 'Mad-House', which Hazard avoided. He also saw and met with Cherokee Indians who were apparently trying to patch up relations with the Virginians in the wake of their aggression at the beginning of the war. Hazard briefly spoke with several Cherokees, 'Little Carpenter' and 'the Pidgeon', and smoked the calumet, or peace pipe, with them. He saw in the distance Colonel William Christian, who defeated the Cherokees the previous year.[30]

On 1 June – Lord's Day – Hazard attended the Episcopal parish at Williamsburg. He found the church attractive, and the organ music delightful. However, he noted that 'the Ladies here are not handsome', and Patrick Henry, Governor of Virginia, who was in attendance, appeared aged and weather-beaten. The capitol building was made of brick with marble added inside to add to the elegance of the porticoes, columns, courtyard, paintings and statues. The building continued to bear the marks of royalty and extravagance. For example, the hall where the House of Burgesses sat had two portraits at each end, one of George II and the other of Queen Caroline. The grandeur of the capitol encouraged in the burgesses 'great Decorum in their Conduct'.[31]

The capitol building hosted a concert and dance the evening of 4 June. The homeliness of the ladies of a week earlier was reversed at the ball, as 'the Ladies made a brilliant Appearance'. A trio sang to the accompaniment of the harpsichord. Later, dancing and gaiety prevailed upstairs, partly due to the terrible quality of the water, which induced the inhabitants to rely on hard spirits. The James and York rivers were both three miles away from Williamsburg, one to the south, the other to the north. The town sat atop a watershed between the two rivers. Fortunately it rained for several days starting 8 June, which refreshed animals, plants, crops and humans. Among the latter were those held in bondage. Hazard, vehemently opposed to slavery, wrote:

> The Virginians, even in the city, do not pay proper Attention to Decency in the Appearance of their Negroes; I have seen Boys of 10 & 12 Years of Age going through the Streets quite naked, & others with only Part of a Shirt hanging Part of the Way down their Backs. This is so common a sight that even the Ladies do not appear to be shocked at it.

The phenomenon of the 'peculiar institution' tempered Hazard's appreciation for Williamsburg, about which he laconically commented, upon leaving on 10 June, that it was 'in a few Words ... a small, regular, sandy, dusty, wooden, unpaved City'.[32]

Hazard, who had never been so far south, found his Presbyterian worldview of rigid code of conduct and devotion to duty continually challenged by what he experienced. He rode to Jamestown where the ferry was located, and found the famous site of English beginnings in America 'a very small, deserted Village, in a ruinous state'. The crossing of the James River, here three miles wide, was treacherous with the winds and current. Arriving at the opposite shore he found himself at Cobham, 'a paltry shabby Village'. The road from Cobham to Smithfield paralleled the descending James and required several creek crossings, one by means of a well-constructed wooden bridge, another by means of wit and luck. The heat was oppressive. Hazard lunched at one 'Nelson's Ordinary (a good House)', where he learned that the principal activity of locals during wartime was the upcoming cock fight between the people of Surry County (where Cobham was located) and those of Isle of Wight County (where Smithfield was found). Horse-racing was a close second in gaining the attention of the populace. Hazard travelled through Smithfield, then Suffolk, where he stopped at Howel's Tavern; here he found coarse fare, 'but the People are remarkably civil'. The road traversed low-lying, swampy land dominated by grain production and pine forests. Hazard's way included one river crossing on a narrow bridge; the incredible

June humidity gave way to a heavy thunderstorm. At Suffolk, Hazard lodged at Langston's, a 'tolerable House'. Here he had the ill fortune to be thrust into the company of a besotted Episcopal priest, Patrick Lunan, who was not only drunk but had a filthy mouth and seemed as irreligious as possible. Apparently he was rarely sober. Hazard wondered why a drunk would be allowed to remain in his position as a priest of the church, and was told that there was no authority to remove him. Virginia was a colony where an established, state-supported religion – the Anglican Church – prevailed. The people were at least cognizant of this contradiction, and in desperation to remove the priest from his parish paid him to relinquish control. 'An irreligious Clergyman', Hazard concluded, 'is the most contemptible of all Characters'.[33]

Rev. Lunan added to Hazard's overall negative assessment of the people of Virginia. He found them similar to the people of Connecticut in that the better sort of people 'are in general sensible, polite, hospitable, & of an independent Spirit'. All Virginians, even the 'ignorant & abject' poor, 'are of an inquisitive turn'. The difference between southerners and northerners, Hazard believed, was in their respective morals. The Virginians are 'much addicted to Gaming, drinking, swearing, horse-racing, Cockfighting, & most Kinds of Dissipation'. And the disparity between the wealthy and the poor, including slaves, was beyond what Hazard had ever experienced in the north.[34]

The next morning, 12 June, Hazard awoke to find the Rev. Lunan 'as drunk as ever'. Told that the heavy rain would have made the post road impassable, Hazard determined to stay another night at Suffolk. Fortunately he met Colonel Wills Riddick, who invited the traveller to his home for the night. The next morning Hazard set out in company with several other men; the travellers' path took them through swampy land on the border between Virginia and North Carolina that included a massive track of land (about 750 square miles by Hazard's reckoning) called the Great Dismal Swamp. The post road was in many places covered with several feet of water; fortunately the sandy base of the road provided a firm foundation for the horses. Hazard thought it 'a scandalous Thing that the Legislature do not order Bridges to be built' to facilitate the passing of people and goods, as well as the post, through this region. Hazard's companions told him the turpentine and tar were the chief productions of the region, the pitch pine trees (*Pinus rigida*) being notched to allow the turpentine to flow. By late afternoon the travellers came to Sumner's Tavern in the midst of a cedar swamp. They supped and decided to pursue the road to Edenton. But Hazard, whose head ached terribly and who could not fathom an evening ride of another twenty miles through swampy land of uncertain roads, decided to let his companions pursue the journey, while he stayed the night. The fare at Sumner's, like at most taverns in Virginia and North Carolina, centred on bacon.[35]

The ride to Edenton was a brief morning jaunt in extremely hot weather, 'the ticks, Gnats & Horse Flies ... very troublesome'. The air was still, which on such a hot, humid day made it oppressive. Hazard decided that he had had enough of the southern summer and determined to began the return journey north as soon as his business was completed. He found Edenton unimpressive, though Albemarle Sound was astonishingly beautiful, the water still and fresh from the Roanoke and Chowan rivers. The winds and currents were, however, treacherous, as Hazard saw exhibited the night of 16 June, when a day hotter than could be recalled was countered at dusk by a huge 'Squall of wind' that 'drove a Brig & Schooner on Shore in the Sound directly opposite to Edenton; it was accompanied with as heavy a Rain as ever I saw; red Lightnings [sic] flashed almost incessantly, and Peals of dreadful Thunder followed each other in terrible Succession'. The oaths brought forth from the mouths of the old salts and other mariners astonished and offended Hazard. The Surveyor General made note that the ferry across the sound was dangerous on untrustworthy boats. An alternate (and safer) post road was across the Chowan River and up the Roanoke River to Halifax.

Hazard grew increasingly offended at the behaviour of southerners towards their slaves. He found that North Carolinians, like Virginians, dressed their slaves in rags such that they often appeared half-naked. Worse, when some benevolent Quakers emancipated some slaves the state assembly determined that because they might prove a threat to society they must be captured, enslaved again, and auctioned off to new masters. Hazard spent several days at the assembly listening to the absurd proceedings of the legislators regarding the slave issue, as well as hearing justices of the state court demand that Tories be required to give an oath to the state or depart. He found the court to be completely without 'Dignity'. The town itself he branded as 'a dull disagreeable Place'. He was not loathe to depart for more familiar northern places.[36]

Hazard was as committed a Patriot as could be found. During his return journey through Virginia in June he recorded with interest the case of several Tories who tried to flee Virginia in a ship, and were detained by a British Man-of-War and their vessel confiscated. Forced to return to Virginia, the state authorities demanded that they depart since they had refused to take the Oath of Loyalty. The men again tried to gain quarter with the British Navy, but were refused and forced back to Virginia. Hazard had little sympathy for 'these unhappy Men', who had themselves to blame for their 'foolish Attachment to the Tyranny' of Great Britain'.[37]

As Hazard crossed the Potomac River into Maryland news arrived of the fighting over the previous winter and spring in New Jersey, and the British retreat from most of New Jersey during the spring. Hazard returned to Philadelphia in July, and then made an excursion to New Jersey in August. He set out on 5 August following the same post road as he took the previous winter to the northern states, going from Philadelphia up the Delaware, crossing at Trenton the following day and proceeding to Princeton, passing through the Quaker hamlet of Maidenhead. The signs of the ravages of war in Princeton shocked Hazard, who despondently toured his *alma mater*. The meetinghouse where he used to attend divine service had been almost destroyed. 'The College', he wrote,

> is in a very ruinous Situation, but this suffered more from the Licentiousness of our own Troops than from the ravages of the Enemy; The latter knocked down a Study in each Room, but the former destroyed the Library, damaged the Orrery, broke down the Pews and Rostrum in the Hall, cut the Pillars which supported the Gallery, stole all the Pipes of the Organ, destroyed an elegant whole Length Picture of George 2d & defaced that of Govr. Belcher. All the Windows of the College are broken, & every room in it looks like a Stable.

The British continued to maintain a presence around Amboy, across from Staten Island, so the post road, and Hazard, proceeded from Princeton north-west to Morristown. Along the route was Somerset (Millsborough), where 'the Dutch & Presbyterian Churches (framed Buildings) were stripped of their Pulpits & Pews, their Doors & Windows were broken, & the Boards torn off the Outside, so as to leave the Frames bare'. The remains of the British encampment were still visible, as were American fortifications in the mountainous region (the Watchung range) towards Morristown. Nine miles out from Morristown Hazard stopped briefly at Mrs White's Tavern, where General Charles Lee had been captured by a British patrol in December 1776. Hazard was baffled as to how the General had put himself in such a silly situation, open and unprotected.[38]

Morristown was sufficiently secluded from scenes of battle to provide security for the Continental Army, which encamped there the previous winter. Hazard declared Morristown 'a very pleasant village, surrounded with Hills; it is situated partly on a Hill, & partly in a Valley'. The town had defensive fortifications – 'a Breast Work and a Guard House'. Hazard had been to the Guard House, situated on an eminence in the town –'from thence, there is a beautiful & extensive Prospect'. Hazard attended worship services at the First Presbyterian Church whenever he spent the Sabbath at Morristown. He lodged at Mrs Bleecker's, a relative of the deceased Garret Noel, Hazard's former partner in the book trade. Hazard reported that 'the Licenciousness [*sic*] of our Troops had damaged the Town a great Deal'.[39]

From Morristown, Hazard rode east through Chatham, a small hamlet on the Passaic River, followed by Springfield and Connecticut Farms, which were now at peace. Hazard arrived at Elizabeth on 11 August. Elizabeth, which looked out upon Staten Island, held by the British, was the scene of much action during the war. Hazard heard numerous stories of Tory deprecations upon the inhabitants; the Hessians in particular had plundered the town. Hazard stayed at the Widow Noel's, whose husband Garret had died the previous September. Elizabeth was a pleasant town with tall church spires; Hazard's favourite, the First Presbyterian Church, had been remarkably spared, owing, Hazard believed, to the piety of the Hessians, who performed their own Sabbath services in it. The parsonage connected to the church had been damaged; the church itself would unfortunately in a few years lie in rubble, destroyed by a Hessian attack. On his ride through what had been until just a few months before a battle ground, Hazard was amazed that crops and pastureland had generally escaped destruction. 'Thus Heaven', he wrote, 'provides for the Support & Comfort of those who have suffered so much by the War, & had every Reason to expect a Famine amongst them!' From Elizabeth, Hazard journeyed the few miles north to Newark, where he found that the town had emerged from the recent conflicts with little damage. Hazard stayed the night at the home of the pastor of Newark's First Presbyterian Church, Alexander McWhorter. He travelled north-west to Orange, then called Newark Mountains or Wardsessing, a strongly Presbyterian country, where he visited a house at which his property had been stored the previous year while he had operated the New York post office on the run and journeyed north and south as surveyor of post roads. He felt blessed to find that his property had been 'remarkably preserved'. On a clear day, 13 August, he spied Manhattan from Newark Mountains, which made him think of lines from Oliver Goldsmith's *A Deserted Village*:

> The blazing Sun now pours a downward Ray,
> And fiercely sheds intolerable Day.

These lines fitted exactly Hazard's state of mind: shocked by the horrors of war while at the same time certain that God's benevolent design was at work.[40]

The following October, Hazard set forth once again on a journey to order the post roads, hire and organize local postmasters, and petition state assemblies for support of the nascent United States postal service. He would be gone for six months, travelling from Philadelphia to Savannah and back. His decision to leave Philadelphia at the end of September and the course of his journey south-west towards Lancaster, eschewing the Delaware River route, was made for him, as it were, by the British, because of General Howe's advance up the Chesapeake in August and disembarkment of troops at Head of Elk and march towards Philadelphia in September. After the Battle of Brandywine on 11 September and Washington's move north, crossing the Schuykill River at the time of the autumnal equinox, Howe moved east and occupied Philadelphia on 26 September. The Americans had been unsure about Howe's movements during the late summer, which emphasized all the more the importance of good post roads to ensure efficient intelligence. Hazard at some point during the summer had attached himself to Washington's army, because he departed for the south on 8 October from Parker Ford on the Schuykill, west of Philadelphia. His route took him to Lancaster, and after that, York, following in the wake of the Continental Congress, which had scattered from Philadelphia in September, met briefly in Lancaster, then settled upon York as its temporary home and the location of the United States government. York was a small town, its buildings 'generally small & shabby, framed, & the Interstices filled with Clay stiffened with Straw'. Hazard wrote on 16 October, 'the Congress sits here at present: the Town is much crowded, & every Thing extravagantly dear'. Lancaster was apparently the medium place of communication between Washington's army and the Congress, and Hazard was for several weeks forced to travel to and fro. At Lancaster on 21 October, the town's people held a patriotic party in which guns were fired, toasts were drank, and houses illuminated. Rains at the end of October so swelled the Susquehanna that although Hazard sought to cross the river on his way to York, the rising water forced his return to Lancaster. When he again tried to cross the river the first few days of November, he was repeatedly delayed by the large numbers of troops headed from Maryland into Pennsylvania to join Washington's army. Eventually, on 3 November he made it across, went to York, lodged there for two nights, and prepared to continue his journey to the South.[41]

Hazard's long and tiresome journey over the next five months involved treading, riding, paddling and sailing upon land and water routes that were centuries' old. The Algonquians had first carved paths marking old animal traces and found by means of dug-out and birch-bark canoes the shortest ways up and down rivers and streams and across bays from point to point. Rivers and streams were the initial routes of settlement, hosting the movement of goods and people, during past centuries. Modern highways follow these old paths, and still tend to parallel waterways as the most efficient way to travel the region. The roads that Hazard travelled were little more than foot- and cart-paths, clearings in the forest following routes of least obstruction; they wound about, traversing lowlands dotted with moist bog and swamp land over which causeways and bridges had to be built.

Hazard's journey from York, Pennsylvania, towards the south included intermittent rain and sometimes 'vile' taverns; the hills and valleys were numerous over the road that was perhaps 'the worst [he] ever travelled'. Hazard sometimes lost his way. At York, Virginia, to which he arrived on 23 November, he was astonished to find that the 'Town has been much damaged by the Licentiousness of our own Soldiers'. At the same time the state assembly had decided to raise 5,000 troops to be sent north. The assembly also passed a bill for 'impressing Necessaries for the Army'. There were a few precious diversions provided by natural phenomena. The best was an aurora borealis that Hazard witnessed on 27 November. He had to stay at Williamsburg for a fortnight because of the weather and consequent badness of the road. During this time he heard that the assembly despaired of raising 5,000 troops voluntarily, so decided upon a draft of bachelors and widowers. To impress goods the bill was passed and printed in secret. Some citizens awoke on the morning of 2 December to find the consequence of the bill upon their own property. Hazard attended the assembly meeting as a spectator on 4 December, but was bored by the proceedings. Eventually on 8 December he set out for North Carolina, only to be halted at the James River by high water and forced to return to Williamsburg. For another week Hazard entertained himself observing the habits of the Virginians. He found the people addicted to gambling, even the legislators, though they passed a law against said 'Gaming'. Hazard wondered about the leaders of the state, and was informed of a 'great Uneasiness' that people had for their leaders. To raise money, the College of William and Mary had to sell thirty of its slaves and rent some of its lands. Finally on 15 December notwithstanding gloomy weather Hazard made it to and across the James River. Along the road to North Carolina, Hazard stayed in one tavern where he was unwanted, and had to 'coax' the proprietor to let him stay, and in another he wrote that the mistress 'was so drunk that she would not cook me any Dinner, & I was forced to go without'. At Edenton, North Carolina, on 18 December, Hazard enjoyed a spectacle of ships' guns being 'fired at Noon' in celebration of the news of the fall of Saratoga. He heard about rising taxes on the citizens and fleeing loyalists, saw another aurora borealis, and had to stay at Edenton for several days because 'the Ferryman', who would take him across the mouth of the Chowan River flowing into Ablemarle Sound, had 'run away'. Forced to spend Christmas at Edenton, Hazard made the best of it, attending the Anglican parish that included hymns composed by the New Light George Whitefield. Hazard drank 'arrack Punch' and joined in the 'frolic', which included the firing of guns from the Sound. Before Hazard set out from Edenton the day after Christmas, he solicited Charles Bondfield, a local leader and patriot, to be postmaster. Hazard had a time of it, 'a Kind of Fatality' that 'seemed to attend [him]', in trying to cross the Sound. Errant ferrymen, having to cross without a horse, being rowed in a large pirogue, and taking the longest way, were the happenstances of the day. Locals informed Hazard of hurricanes in recent years that destroyed property. The tavern at which Hazard stayed on 27 December, perhaps because of the hurricanes, had 'not a Pane of Glass belonging to it'. This region was swampy, filled with rivers and low-lying areas giving way to the sea – a nightmare for the lone surveyor of post roads. Hazard found himself at the mercy of ferrymen and masters generous with their slaves to convey him down one river to the next. After traversing the 'mostly low, sunken Land' of the region from Ablemarle Sound to Pamlico River, Hazard stayed at Bath with the local postmaster, William Brown, a militia officer and political leader. The first day of the year, 1778, Hazard 'appointed' Richard Stephens, formerly of New York, as 'Surveyor of the Post Office in the Southern District'; when Stephens took over in April he would relieve Hazard of a huge region for which he had hitherto been responsible. Stephens accompanied Hazard across Pamlico River through a generally 'barren Neck of Land' to New Bern on the Neuse River; New Bern was the capital of North Carolina and Hazard toured the Governor's residence, called 'The Palace'. The end of the first week of January, notwithstanding the sometimes cold weather, Hazard 'met with a Number of Negro children of both sexes, entirely naked: I suppose they have never had Clothes on them'. Hazard passed his time strolling through the churchyard cemetery, recording the epitaphs on the stones.[42]

At New Bern Hazard and Stephens split and Hazard proceeded south towards Wilmington. The route was through the same low-lying tidewater, barren swamps; one stretch of eight miles on the road was over wooden causeways. Hazard continued to be dismayed to see so many slave children without any clothes at all during winter. Although the path was often sandy and root-strewn, difficult riding for horse and rider, Hazard still considered it better than the route further inland. Hazard reached Wilmington on 11 January. While he stayed in Wilmington for a few days, Hazard heard much about the late governor, William Tryon. He heard of his arrogance and expensive habits, his cruelty in suppressing the Regulators, farmers of western Carolina who opposed rising taxes. Hazard departed Wilmington on 16 January, following the road southwest, paralleling the coast, riding through swamps and crossing rivers. Someone informed Hazard of a 'short cut', which he took, then wrote himself a 'Memorandum. Take no more short Cuts in North Carolina'. The way saved him twelve miles but cost him hard riding of 'great Difficulty' through a 'Cypress Swamp', in which he lost his way. After a tiring day he halted at a 'rascally House' where his horse was fed 'mouldy' corn, which he would not eat, and the water set before Hazard to drink was yellow. Unwilling to lodge here, Hazard rode on another twelve miles through a deserted region, where 'the Road is nothing more than a Foot Path … In one of the Swamps the Water came up to my Saddle Skirts'. The swamp was so daunting that Hazard would not have ventured through it had he not happened upon a riding companion who knew the way. Thankfully, Hazard must have thought, he would not be the surveyor of post roads for the southern district for much longer.[43]

Hazard's introduction to South Carolina was hardly better. The coastal route was uninhabited and he and his horse did not eat the entire day of 18 January. The next day, Hazard rode along what is called Myrtle Beach today, then called 'Long Bay, a sandy beach of 15 miles in length. On the left is the open sea from which the surf comes rolling in with great noise, and often frightens the traveller's horse unless he is very gentle. On the right is a disagreeable sand bank'. He found it difficult to find lodgings for the night. The next day the road again was rough and fatiguing. Finally he arrived at Georgetown, and stayed in a nice house, owned by Peter Lesesne, who sufficiently impressed Hazard that the Surveyor General offered him the job of local postmaster. Georgetown was a pleasant town situated on a creek just above the bay; 'a fort of 9 or 10 guns' defended the harbour against enemy encroachments. It continued to annoy Hazard how many slaves there were in the south, and how dismally they were treated. He attended the Presbyterian church on Sunday, and heard the minister preach again a few days later, as the weather prevented him from leaving Georgetown for several days. Finally on 27 January there was 'exceeding fine weather', and Hazard 'set out for Charles Town'. The road that traversed the low-lying land between North Santee River and the South Santee was badly constructed, and Hazard could well imagine that both horse and rider could sometimes be 'swamped'. On 29 January, Hazard reached Charleston by ferry; the town was situated on a peninsula between two rivers jutting into the bay; a fire had just a few days before destroyed a large part of the commercial district. Charleston was the capitol of the state, and the assembly was meeting in the State House when Hazard visited. They were considering the Confederation lately drawn up in Pennsylvania. Hazard believed 'they are very jealous of the northern, especially, the New England states'. Naturally Hazard sought out and visited the physician and historian David Ramsay, whom he had known at Princeton in the 1760s when they were both students. Like Hazard, Ramsay was a native of Philadelphia. Hazard drank tea with and spent several evenings with Ramsay. He spent a fortnight in South Carolina, petitioning the legislature regarding the delivery of the post and exemptions for postmasters. The legislature was not agreeable, and Hazard had to canvas varied members to try to make his point. He departed on 12 February with matters still unresolved. He found that,

> the poor people of South Carolina are proud, and the rich haughty and insolent, and all of them remarkably indolent. They understand rules of politeness but reduce them to practice only upon particular occasions. They appear to pay more attention to dress than any thing else.

On his journey to Savannah, Hazard travelled a road that was sand and dirt, messy when wet. His route was the same as that of American General Benjamin Lincoln and British General Augustine Prevost a year later during the contest for Georgia and South Carolina. He lodged at a house where bedbugs and a sow feeding her piglets kept him up half the night. On the road he came upon an escaped slave just being recaptured; the looks of terror on his face 'from terrible apprehensions of future punishment', affected Hazard, who declared in his journal: 'Heaven will avenge the cause of the Negroes'. Ten days later, on his return trip through South Carolina, Hazard was more critical of the slave owners of the South, declaring South Carolinians to be by their own account 'all-sufficient' and 'self-sufficient', though in reality 'insufficient'. They are both vain and ignorant, he wrote. Those who own the most slaves are considered the best men. 'It is strange that men should value themselves most upon what they ought to be most ashamed of'. Hazard's Presbyterian principles informed him that this was clear evidence of 'the depravity of human nature'. Ministers among the rest showed their foolishness. One Moses Allen, the 'fighting parson', who dressed like a true Christian soldier, was 'preposterous': 'an ambassador from the prince of peace' who aped 'the appearance of a butcher of mankind'. Hazard recorded the views of South Carolina's slave owners thus: they believe that their slaves were destined from birth for such a role; that whites could not do the work a slave can do; that they must be treated harshly to prevent insurrection. Hazard cleverly surmised, 'that man can enjoy but little happiness who is under continual apprehensions from his slaves'. On 16 February Hazard was rowed down the Savannah River to the town of the same name. Savannah was built 'on the top of a sand hill'. While there he addressed the legislature about his concerns for the post, achieving a more satisfactory response than he had in Charleston. Hazard also recruited and appointed William Hornby as postmaster of Savannah. False rumour in Georgia had it, that General Washington had driven General Howe from Philadelphia. Perhaps Hazard's labours to put the post office in good order would work to prevent the spread of unsubstantiated rumour.[44]

3 BARREN AS A PITCH-PINE PLAIN

Signs of normalcy returned to Boston in the wake of the British exodus in March 1776, including the resumption of Election Day, when inhabitants voted for town officers. This was always an occasion for one of Boston's native sons, Jeremy Belknap, to return to the city to experience the annual expression of the spirit of liberty, which was expressed more vociferously this year than usual. Belknap arrived on 1 June and stayed for 'almost a week. He preached for Andrew Eliot, dined with friends, and saw the sights, which meant, of course, the signs of battle. He journeyed to Fort Hill, the eminence in Roxbury that looked out upon the Neck, to Dorchester Heights, and to Cambridge. After a week of catching up, feeling a sense of relief that Boston still stood with very few scars, Belknap returned to Dover. Summer in Dover involved household chores, such as gardening, to supplement the salt pork that typically dominated the family dinners. Belknap was constantly engaged in visiting the sick and widowed and presiding over burials, baptisms and marriages. He kept up with any war news coming out of Portsmouth, such as the launch a few weeks earlier of the '32 Gun frigate', *Raleigh*. On 25 June and again a fortnight later he watched men train on the town green in preparation of joining an expedition to Canada. The Canadian campaign was not going well for the Americans, though they were not yet ready to give it up; many still hoped that Canada would become the fourteenth state. But so much blood had been spilled there during the past century; John Eliot wrote to Belknap on 4 July that 'that country has ... been a sink of men's lives'. Eliot ruefully told Belknap that Boston men were volunteering in droves to work on fortifications if it would forestall being recruited for a Canadian campaign. British ships continued to threaten the coast, so that such fortifications seemed of great importance anyway. On 18 July word came that the Continental Congress had declared independence, which caused Belknap to write in his almanac, under 4 July: the 'Era of Independence'. On 22 July he journeyed to Newcastle to view the fortifications at Fort William and Mary; a week later he returned to Portsmouth to view and tour the *Raleigh*, which was commissioned by Congress and constructed by Portsmouth master shipbuilders.[1]

Such activity, however, could not mask a growing dissatisfaction that Belknap felt about his position in life. Having once been enthusiastic about his commission to spread the Gospel to the simple woodsmen and women of Dover, he felt intellectually stifled and economically straitened by his life in Dover. Inflation made his salary insufficient, but such were Dover's problems that the townspeople struggled even to pay their pastor, whose family was large and growing larger – John, Jeremy and Ruth's fifth child, was born on 30 December 1776. For weeks after the birth, Ruth was in 'much weakness and pain'. Besides caring for his wife, Belknap was forced to scrape, practice greater domestic economy, and borrow from friends; he grew increasingly frustrated. Historical inquiry, once his great passion, was becoming more of a burden as well. He felt that clergymen were called to be historians, to render for their contemporaries a didactic account of God's will in human affairs, but the process of inquiring for and accumulating scattered documents seemed almost too much during a time when the future was so uncertain, both for his family and his country. The course of the conflict with Britain also weighed upon him. 'I often ruminate', he wrote to Samuel Cooper of Boston on 14 January 1777, 'on the present state of America & its future prospects with an anxiety which I wish disipated [*sic*] by some brighter beams than have ever yet penetrated the gloom of my mind'.[2]

Fortunately Belknap had the periodic letters of John Eliot to make him smile and think. Eliot wrote to Belknap in January, 1777, that word had arrived in Boston on the wings of rumour from the south 'that the whole British army was cut off in a late *general action* at Princeton'. Eliot wrote that he was becoming as incredulous as Doubting Thomas about such rumours, which rarely had a legitimate source, being carried by word of mouth.

> Little less than the evidence of my own senses will persuade me to believe the daily reports which are current among all orders of people, and which, as fast as the succession of moments, cause them to wear the face of joy & knit the brow of sorrow.

But to show reasonable doubt was to have others suspect your loyalty; one man told Eliot that because Tories are cowards, and because Scripture condemns cowards, that all Tories are damned for all eternity. Such stories gave Eliot pause, as he still had his doubts that America's cause was the right one, and he wondered in his letter to Belknap (after requesting that his friend show due candour) whether or not it was right to declare independence; that it would actually unite Great Britain, those who once supported America and those who had always been enemies to America; that trade would suffer so as to impoverish America; that France would not willingly come to the aid of a people who less than twenty years before hated the French in Canada. Perhaps to help his friend, pining for the delights of Boston, to set him straight that Dover was not so bad, Eliot caricatured his townsmen as closed-minded, arrogant men who constantly paraded their own merit with military titles: 'Colonel A., Major B., Captain C., denominates every puppy that "bays the moon"'. And those without military titles were not content to be normal citizens; rather,

> to suppose a person a mechanic is an affront. Everyone belongs to some Committee of Correspondence, or Safety, or Supply, or else holds a seat under some gentlemen who fill these important places, & therefore must be treated with such complaisance that we must learn all the twistings of the body which is necessary for a *valet de chambre* before we can receive a token of cognisance. We are all obliged to go barefoot & ragged, for you may as well fish for pearls in Oyster River, or look for the planet Venus at midday, as seek for some creatures in Boston as a taylor [*sic*] or shoemaker.

As a further comment to make his friend appreciate his rural situation, Eliot wrote, 'I have my health much better than I had before I visited your region of salubrity'. Eliot sent Belknap another newsy letter in March, in which he described religious affairs in Boston, his own activities preaching, how horrible was the British bombardment of Fairfield, Connecticut, where his brother and family lived, and how his father, Andrew Eliot, was convinced that the British were soon to return to Boston. John asked his friend Jeremy, with a little tongue and cheek but also to spur the mind and senses, 'Has any light penetrated the chinks of the dark cottage lately?'[3]

The chinks of the cottage were increasingly wearing away, in part because of the apparent apathy that Belknap's parishioners displayed towards the economic stability of their pastor. Belknap finally decided that waiting around for them to act was not going to happen, so he penned them a diplomatic yet forceful letter. He wrote in March,

> It is at all times very disagreeable to me to make complaints; but that confidence which I have in the candor and kindness of the people of this parish encourages me, tho' with extreme reluctance, to desire them to consider the increase of my family & the dearness of some of the necessaries of life, both of which have rendered it impossible for me to live on the salary which both they & myself at first expected would be sufficient.

He realized that war constrained every person's purse, and he could hardly expect not to suffer some, nevertheless it was even more painful for a clergyman to have to focus so much on the material concerns of life, when his 'attention ought to be chiefly directed to matters of more importance'. Unfortunately, the parish selectmen responded with a token gift of twenty pounds, called a meeting to discuss the matter, but postponed the meeting throughout the spring, summer and autumn, not deigning to join together to deal with the issue until the following year.[4]

In the spring letters arrived from John Eliot to help dispel the gloom of Dover. Eliot began with a disclaimer:

> It is no fault that so few letters have passed between us the year agone; for many letters of mine (which you would have answered), tho' written, have never reached you. To mention particularly one instance: a packett [*sic*] containing a letter to you ... is now, and has lain in your brother's drawer near four months. I wish opportunities were more immediate. 'Tis true I could send to Portsmouth often, but it then remains uncertain whether you will ever receive them. John Clarke [the local postmaster] is a careless case, (which with my compliments you may tell him, if you please,) and perhaps they would not even get to him.

Eliot again entertained Belknap with the arrogance and superficiality of Boston's civic leaders, each of whom decried the times, the decline of morality, the evils of the Tories, and the sins of everyone else but himself. No one took responsibility for their particular actions that had resulted in Boston's malaise. He wrote,

> Was you at Boston, my dear Sir, you would be affected with the calamitous moan of every individual, while you would be struck with indignation at our behaviour. We often hear excellent discourses on patriotism & on the moral virtues, which are as the morning cloud & early dew.

It dissipates quickly. Boston's speech-makers paint Patriotism,

> in the most elegant colours, as a child of Heaven whom most nations have cast out as a deformed bantling, unworthy their protection, but whom the Genius of America has nourished at her breast, fostered & supported, & who has spread a spirit of liberality & benevolence thro'out this land.

At the same time the hypocritical spirit of mob rule controlled Boston politics, and anyone suspected of being a Tory paid a dear price. 'If we are in a state of anarchy', Eliot demanded, 'let us not have the credit or be at the expense of maintaining a Legislature'. The Boston Tories were paying for the crimes of the Connecticut Tories, whose actions in western Connecticut made a regicide seem good by comparison. The Eliot family, John's brother Andrew, suffered much from British attacks on Fairfield, Connecticut. Poor Andrew Eliot Sr feared so much another attack on Boston that he bought a farm in Concord and would go there to retire – and soon to die. As Belknap's father Joseph made recurring trips to Boston to visit old friends and deal with old business, John Eliot grabbed him and hoisted a number of letters he had written to Joseph's son, so that in mid-May Jeremy received an epistolary cornucopia. In one letter Eliot asked Belknap pointedly 'how is it with the *soul's dark cottage?*', a reference to Belknap's growing despondency over his situation. Was Jeremy allowing the 'balsamic' air of the country to beat back those thoughts?[5]

A good balsam for Belknap's moods were Eliot's letters, which were newsy, poignant and humorous, all at the same time. His letter of 17 June told Belknap of the Boston inquisition, in which Tories were tried and condemned (not to death, rather humiliation and sometimes exile). The most notorious was Belknap's great-uncle Mather Byles, the poet and wit, who was an unabashed Tory who spit in the eyes of his accusers with his absurd puns. Eliot despised him, and Belknap, who once loved him, tended to forget those old feelings for what the times demanded. Eliot paraded Byles before Belknap in his letters, encouraging his disparagement as well as his laughter. Then there was Eliot himself, who was as apt to make fun of himself as anyone else. He told Belknap of his lameness, brought about by a borrowed horse who was so hard to ride as to injure the delicate Bostonian, who sought to hide his lameness by tying a handkerchief tight around his leg, which led to a sore that lamed him further. About the time he recovered, he tripped and sprained his knee. He told Belknap honestly, 'it would divert you to see me'. More seriously, he said that such was Boston's domestic economy that 'we are all starving here'.[6]

All the while during the spring and summer of 1777 Belknap wrote to Eliot what the latter called brilliant, insightful letters – letters that the recipient failed to preserve, so they are lost to us. Two that survive in manuscript in Belknap's Letterbook include one of 17 September 1777, in which Belknap explained that he had not been a punctual correspondent during the summer because 'my "souls dark cottage" has been very much "batter'd and decay'd" by a nervous disorder' that plagued him 'for some weeks'. It forced Belknap 'to lay aside the Pen & betake myself to my horse'. The summer had been hot, the Belknap household noisy with children and domestic activity, which brought Belknap to a melancholy state that only rides through New Hampshire forests could dispel. 'I have had a touch of it', he told Eliot,

> but if travelling in the woods – alone –up and down mountains, over rivers, broken bridges, rocks, and mire be sufficient to cure it I am cured for such a Journey I never made before ... My spirits were alternately in every form of agitation that they could possibly be in – sometimes I went almost perpendicularly up & sometimes as nearly so Down.

According to Belknap, the constant exercise finally helped his nerves to be made finally 'right again & I hope will keep so at least till I finish this Letter'. Three weeks passed and the letter lay unfinished in Belknap's study. Eventually he learned that his father was travelling to Boston on 6 October, so on 5 October Belknap determined to fill up the remaining paper for Eliot notwithstanding that 'my mind is as barren as a Pitch-pine plain'. Nevertheless Belknap roused himself to speak of some of his late reading. He had perused John Wynne's *A General History of the British Empire in America*, published in 1770, and found him but 'an indifferent Compiler'. Better was John Winthrop's Journal, the manuscript of which was sent to Belknap by Ezra Stiles. Winthrop's comment that '*the best part is always the least*, & of that best part *the wiser part is always the lesser*', gratified Belknap, who like Eliot felt that contemporary statesmen were far from the wisest men. In November, Belknap took to his horse for a trip to Boston. He attended the Dudleian Lecture at Harvard, an annual occasion devoted to exploring the intersection of science and religion, on 5 November; two days later saw the defeated British regulars from the Battle of Saratoga arriving as prisoners to Boston; a day later he saw General Burgoyne himself; and the following day, the Sabbath, he preached for both Andrew Eliot and Charles Chauncy. Even so he told his diary upon his return to Dover that the trip had been a 'tedious journey'.[7]

However, during the waning months of 1777 such exercise worked to help Belknap recover from despondency to approach his situation with confidence and hope. The arrival of French warships to Portsmouth in December, providing concrete evidence of long-anticipated French support for the American cause, lifted his spirits. Although his parish was evasive about putting his finances on better footing, and he gradually came to accept the fact that they were not ever to do anything more on his behalf; even though he felt lonely and out of place in the 'wooden world' of Dover; and though news of the war was not good, and the American cause seemed almost to falter, Belknap acquired a renewed spirit during the months of spring, summer and autumn of 1777. He received support from two avenues: his 'hobby horse', historical inquiry, and the *word*, namely, prophecy from the Old Testament.[8]

The war had imposed itself on Belknap's self-imposed goal of writing a history of New Hampshire. The political disputations of 1774 and 1775, the initial outbreak of war and contest over Boston, and the financial disruption that descended upon the Piscataqua Valley, combined to make his research and writing slow and not as frequent as he would have liked. It went on, though, and he at times received encouragement from friends to proceed, that such a history would be well-received and useful. An example was letter written by the Portsmouth physician, Joshua Brackett, in 1778, in which the doctor informed Belknap that some of New Hampshire's leading statesmen, such as the Langdons, John and Woodbury, encouraged the pastor to continue his efforts, and expected that the New Hampshire legislature would provide financial encouragement. Belknap believed anyway that historical inquiry was not just an avocation. Because it was incumbent upon ministers to be historians, to trace providential history, Belknap felt compelled not to give up his task. Helping in this determination was an answer he received to prayer. His anxiety over the future of America was stilled somewhat during the spring and summer of 1777 by a close reading of Scripture, especially the prophecies of Daniel in the Old Testament. The great king Nebuchadnezzar dreamed of a huge figure made of a gold head, silver arms, bronze torso and thighs, iron legs, and feet with a mixture of iron and clay. A huge stone smashed the feet, which caused the entire figure to fall apart. Daniel interpreted the dream thus: Nebuchadnezzar's kingdom was of gold; it would be followed by another of silver, another of bronze, and finally another of iron. But the iron kingdom, because it was mixed with clay, would be divided. Eventually a great kingdom, like the stone, would crush the kingdom of iron and clay and rule forever. But then Daniel had his own dream of four terrible beasts, the last of which had ten horns. Soon a horn that took shape like a *Messiah* destroyed the beast with ten horns. Belknap combined the two dreams into one general interpretation. He believed the four beasts were the kingdoms of Nebuchadnezzar's Chaldean Empire, the Persian Empire, Alexander's Hellenistic Empire, and the Roman Empire. The latter empire was a mixture of republican virtue like iron and despotic tyranny like clay, which because iron and clay do not mix, the empire finally collapsed. Its ten toes, like the ten horns of the fourth beast, represented ten kingdoms that emerged from the collapse of the Roman Empire. But these were like Rome a mixture of iron and clay, of virtuous republican ideas and tyrannical despotic habits. Great Britain was the tenth kingdom, and it was collapsing because iron and clay, republicanism and despotism, do not mix. Its iron component was America, which had all of the republican virtue that England lacked. Belknap's interpretation of Biblical prophecy provided 'encouragement to rest my *hope*, that the formidable power ... at war with us, would not prevail'. With such thoughts Belknap found 'sufficient ground for consolation in the height of our', and his own personal, 'distress'. The divine will, revealed in the Book of Daniel, was that America would be free and independent.[9]

Such ideas strengthened the pastor's determination to continue on with his historical work. He received another spur of support when he met Ebenezer Hazard in late 1778. Hazard had arrived at Portsmouth around Christmas, having made the journey north from Boston in mid-December. They had heard of each other through a mutual acquaintance in Portsmouth – perhaps Dr Joseph Brackett or the Rev. Benjamin Stevens. The antiquarian spirit of historical inquiry was the mutual interest that had initially drawn the two men together. Both were collectors of ancient things; they both had personal *museums* that included fossils and other wonders of nature, artefacts of colonial America, heirlooms and historical documents. Belknap invited Hazard to stay with him for a few days, and the latter arrived on 28 December. During the waning days of December, 1778, Hazard and Belknap investigated the needs and requirements of postal roads in the upper Piscataqua valley and examined Belknap's many historical papers; of particular interest were those written more than a century earlier. On 29 December, the two men crossed the shallow, frozen Salmon Falls River to Berwick, perhaps because Belknap wanted to show Hazard a likely postal route to the Saco Valley, and also to meet Belknap's friend William Chadborne.[10]

After this brief visit, Hazard departed downriver to Portsmouth and then across the Piscataqua north to Falmouth on business; he had promised on his return to drop by Belknap's home again. During the third week in January, finishing his business with Postmaster Freeman in Falmouth, Hazard returned south on the icy post road again to Portsmouth, whence he intended to return to Belknap's hearth to enjoy the warmth of friendship. His aim was to follow the slow route by horseback paralleling the descending Piscataqua to Newington, where he would take Knight's Ferry from Bloody Point across the Piscataqua to Dover Point, from which he would ride along the frozen Cocheco River to the falls, where Belknap lived. Although Hazard was prevented from returning, both men knew that they had found a mutual friend with whom to share historical interests and knowledge. Their friendship was based on their similar political views, religious proclivity towards a more liberal interpretation of the scripture than their conservative Calvinist upbringing would otherwise indicate, disposition towards investigation and inquiry, and interest in all things literary.

4 LIFE OF A CABBAGE

Ebenezer Hazard to Jeremy Belknap

Portsmouth, Jan. 29, 1779.

Reverend Sir, – Some advices received by last post rendering it necessary for me to proceed as expeditiously as possible to Philadelphia, I am deprived of the pleasure of paying you a second visit as I intended, and laid under the necessity of sending Gorge's History to you, instead of delivering it in person, which, I doubt not, the necessity of the case will induce you to excuse.[1]

Belknap did not receive the hastily sent message of his new friend Hazard until four days had passed, notwithstanding that Portsmouth was but ten miles downstream from Dover by boat – less as the crow flies. But it was winter, and there was war; nothing was in order, nothing passed for normal, and the letter received was like everything else – one's salary, a break in the weather, peace – much too late. And now Hazard was gone, riding slowly along post roads to the south, to Boston and beyond, to warmer regions than the deep woods of New Hampshire – though warmer not by much.

Upon Hazard's return to Portsmouth after his lengthy journey to Maine, he had found arrived at Postmaster Libbey's an express from Philadelphia calling the Surveyor of Post Roads south. Hazard and Belknap postponed discussing pages of Gorges's *History*; first there were effective communications to establish and a war to win. In a rush, Hazard quickly concluded his letter to Belknap at Postmaster Libbey's; he hoped to make quick time on the post road so to get to Hampton Falls, and Wells's Tavern, before nightfall.

> The papers you were kind enough to promise me, I must beg you to send to the post-office in this place, directed to me at Boston, to the care of the Reverend Dr. Gordon, who will carefully forward them. Please to mention on each paper the *authority* or book from which it was taken, and please favour me with a line informing me whether they were transcribed *literatim*. With compliments to Mrs. Belknap, I am, reverend sir,
> Your very humble servant,
> Eben. Hazard[2]

Hazard, beginning his third year as surveyor of post roads, was still unmarried and practically homeless; he spent his time on the road, securing the post to ensure adequate communication, especially of military documents and correspondence. Fortunately in 1778 two more surveyors of post roads had been added, one for the southern and one for the middle states, leaving Hazard responsible for the northern states alone.

Meanwhile at the Dover parsonage, on the morning of 2 February, Belknap, looking over Hazard's letter written from Portsmouth, realized that in his friend's hurry he had misconstrued the meaning of Belknap's offer to allow Hazard the chance to peruse some manuscripts Belknap had in his possession. Belknap had no wish to *give* them to Hazard, so wrote his friend:

> I am favoured with yours of 29th ult[imo], and the return of Gorge's History. I know not how you mistook my meaning with regard to the papers which you desire. Those which I mentioned to you are some records and files which I have made use of in compiling my History, and from which I have made some transcripts to be annexed to it either as authorities or as curiosities.

Belknap had offered only to *loan* them. However, he continued, 'as you have placed some dependence on my sending you some, I here subjoin the titles of sundry papers which are among those in my possession, and which I do not desire to swell my appendix with'. Belknap offered to engage in the onerous task of transcribing by pen those documents of which Hazard would desire a copy, explaining his 'desire ... to do whatever is in my power to forward any undertaking for the public good'. Belknap, like Hazard, was convinced that the freedom of a young republic depended upon public knowledge of the past. Belknap's offer was also in response to Hazard's generous inclusion (in his letter) of a pamphlet directed towards leading Quakers to recognition of the error of their ways. Belknap distrusted Quakers because of their Antinomian beliefs, that each person's *inner light* was sufficient to guide their religious journey, but was afraid to confront them directly in his parish, which had sufficient troubles already. Belknap spoke for himself and his wife Ruth in assuring Hazard, 'we were much disappointed in not seeing you again. Perhaps your business will lead you into these parts some other time, when I shall be happy in welcoming you to my house'.[3]

Mrs Ruth Eliot Belknap kept as tidy a home as she could in such an environment as Dover, a lumber mill and fur-trading town of several thousand inhabitants. Living on the frontier was not her desire; but she had willingly agreed to marry her friend and confidant Jeremy Belknap in 1767 upon his answering the call of the Dover parish. She did her duty as a pastor's companion and farmer's wife; she was pregnant for the last time with their sixth child – it would be her fourth boy to add to two girls. The boredom of farm life was rarely interrupted with the kind of excitement she had known as a girl growing up in Boston. Mr Hazard of Philadelphia, the cultural capital of America, brought his wit and charm, and his stories of *civilized life* and current fashions, when he visited; he would always be welcome.[4]

The parsonage occupied a favourable location overlooking the Cocheco River, where the rising inland elevation formed Cocheco Falls, which attracted nearby mills – an important reason for the existence of the town. Besides the typical gristmills there were plentiful sawmills, which droned from sunrise to sunset. Belknap and Ruth, being products of cultured city life, were among the few who objected to the noisy mills and their human contingent. A frontier mill town hosts few balls and banquets, has few libraries and cultural centres – indeed none at all. Hence the delicate Mrs Belknap and her portly scholar of a husband felt singularly out of place and very lonely at Dover. Pastor and wife countered such objectionable feelings with excursions south to Boston to see friends and family, and, in the case of the reverend, journeys into the northern forests in search of peace and knowledge. Ruth, and Jeremy too, made frequent use of pen and paper; scribbling newsy, loquacious letters to correspondents far and wide. For said purpose Mrs Belknap retreated to her letter-desk; Rev. Belknap found solace in his study. There he kept his books on theology, history and philosophy – Plutarch, Virgil, Pope, Watts, Hume, Locke, and his many papers – notes for and drafts of sermons; notes for and drafts of works of history; scientific observations, measurements and drawings; memorandum books; in short, partial and complete manuscripts from his own pen and those of many others. The parsonage was two-story, of white clapboard offset by black shutters, with eight rooms and as many hearths surrounding a central flue and chimney. The parson was short, obese, dark-haired and not terribly handsome. He was given to passivity and contemplation, judgment and reserve, shyness and scepticism, served by a delightfully caustic wit that frequently exuded from his many epistles to Hazard.[5]

Besides Ruth's compliments Belknap added to the letter a proposal that Hazard undertake as part of his 'researches into antiquity' the task of compiling information about some of the great figures of America's past: 'Might not a collection of these in the form of a biographical dictionary be an useful work?', he asked. The application of knowledge was always on Belknap's mind – perhaps too often. He had so many ideas of books and pamphlets and other intellectual projects that he would never be able to accomplish them no matter how long he lived. Hazard's travels would allow him easier access to the documents and traditions that are the bases of collective biography. Belknap had made a feeble beginning, but would willingly yield the task to his friend.[6]

As Belknap proposed that his travelling friend take on one more task, Hazard was on his way south from Boston to Philadelphia. Belknap's letter made its way south, slowly. The disruptions of war, muddy roads, bumbling postmasters and the like ensured that spring was on its way when Hazard, now in Philadelphia, opened it. Upon reading Belknap's letter and becoming aware of the mistake he had made in assuming that Belknap would *give* him a collection of manuscripts, Hazard, afraid that his friend might think it was a '*design*', wrote:

'I assure you that was not the case, and have no doubt your candour will give due credit to the assertion'. Hazard wondered whether or not he had made a similar mistake regarding the manuscript copy of Indian treaties recorded by Captain John Gyles that Belknap had presented to him – was this too merely a *loan*? He wrote, 'If so, please to let me know, for it is not too late to return them, notwithstanding I have wrote my name in them'. He assured Belknap of his desire to visit Dover again: 'Should our lives be spared, it is not improbable that I may have the pleasure of seeing you at Dover, either this summer or fall'. Hazard was 'charmed' with Belknap's idea of a biographical dictionary, but he had as many intended projects as Belknap – to add one more to the list was out of the question. Do you not recall, he asked his friend, that 'I am forming an American Geography'? Hazard was one of the most travelled Americans of his time: who else was as qualified to engage in geographical treatises? Biographies, which focus on human personality, fit better with the proclivities of a clergyman, who was forced to know human nature. Belknap should do it. 'It is unjust, and would argue based ingratitude, that the characters of worthy men should be buried with their dust'. Hazard ended his letter: 'We have no news'.[7]

One May afternoon three weeks later Belknap, who was much engaged in sermon-writing, historical research and gardening, received Hazard's letter. The idea of a biographical dictionary still intrigued him, though he protested his inability to produce it, and continued to prod his friend to take the burden off of his literary shoulders. Ruth was due at any time; money was scarce, and with inflation and his parish's disinclination to pay him, growing scarcer. If enemy troops were not an immediate threat, since coastal New Hampshire held very little strategic value, nevertheless the war was unsettling, and thrust most people into a cautious, conservative mode. Belknap's parishioners hoarded their money and were unwilling to part with it. Religion was declining at a time when it was most needed. Belknap felt tied to the soil, tied to his duty, tied to toil. Seeking to describe his situation, he recalled the words of one of his favourite authors, Alexander Pope, who claimed with Belknap's enthusiastic approval that the life of the poet and writer is often 'the life of a cabbage'. Belknap envied Hazard's life of travel: carefree, alone, with no family to support. Ironically, Hazard envied Belknap's life of study, of the warm hearth, the laughter of children, the companion of the cold nights. Each man thought the other best able to undertake literary tasks. Belknap hoped Hazard would accept the unofficial title of American Biographer; perhaps as he travelled the varied states of America he could engage the support of gentlemen of learning and science. If it were up to Belknap, the project would doubtless 'come to nothing'. Belknap chided his friend:

> I shall expect to see you again before winter, and will keep the papers whose titles I mentioned till you come, unless they be sooner called for. They will find you employment for a few days, which I shall be happy if you will spend at my house.

Thoughts of family – of growing sons and daughters – intervened as Belknap closed the letter; he requested that Hazard pick up 'a copy of Lord Chesterfield's "Principles of Politeness", reprinted at Philadelphia, which I will pay you for.' Dover schools were closed due to war and apathy. Belknap acted as tutor to his children, the girls as well as the boys. Though the many distractions of the clergy, his literary hobbies and farm life ensured that his heart was not quite in it, duty and filial affection required him to try.

> P.S. I should be heartily ashamed of this paper, in any other circumstances. But it is an exact picture of the times; for even this rascally sheet is three dollars per quire.
> To Ebenezer Hazard, Esq.[8]

The summer was long and hot. Belknap hungered for news. The struggle between the British and the American forces under General Washington increasingly focused upon the South; not that New England was free from conflict. While England controlled the seas, coastal communities, such as those along the Piscataqua River, Great Bay and tributaries (such as the Cocheco) had to be on constant guard against British warships. Portsmouth in particular, where the ship *America* was being built, was on the defensive. Belknap thought of such regional concerns even as his focus this summer was on the exhausting and nerve-racking events of fatherhood. The baby, Andrew Eliot, namesake of the lately deceased Rev. Andrew Eliot, Ruth's uncle, was born on 4 June, an odd and wonderful birthday present [Old Style dating] for the thirty-five-year-old Belknap. Somehow Belknap found time for spells of writing his *History of New Hampshire*. He was also busy filling in for other local clergymen, who would in turn share his pulpit. Farm life was sufficiently monotonous that the entertainment of Sunday sermons had to be spiced up with visitors, news and interesting sermons. Belknap delivered one such sermon at Hampton Falls, a little village thirty-some-odd miles south of Dover, in June. The congregation liked it enough to encourage that it be published – 'and may the divine blessing accompany it into the world' – and soon after Daniel Fowle, a well-known Portsmouth publisher, undertook the task. Belknap also busied himself with various shorter literary efforts. He loved nothing better than to toss off a brief sample of wit, particularly on local or national politics. New Hampshire's many attempts at forming a viable government gave him much fodder to engage in this singular amusement; he took full advantage of it.[9]

When a letter from Belknap found him at the end of June, 1779, Hazard was in Philadelphia preparing to journey north. A month later, on 4 August, he was at Jamaica Plain, staying with his friend Gordon, relaxing and working on his hobbyhorse, collecting and transcribing America's ancient documents. He had been much engaged in transcribing the five-hundred-page manuscript volume of the 'Records of the United Colonies of New England'. The so-called New England Confederation existed from the 1640s to the 1680s, uniting the nascent colonies of Connecticut, New Haven, Massachusetts Bay and Plymouth, against foreign, particularly Indian, threats. Few copies were in existence, and Hazard wanted to ensure that, through multiple copies, such important records of early American would never be lost. Yet, he wrote to Belknap, 'had I known at first what I was undertaking, I would not have enrolled my name in the list of American Antiquarians'. Hazard sought personal evidence of the validity of the Roman poet Horace's assertion; *nothing is too difficult that cannot be conquered by habit*. Hazard's interest in Belknap's biographical project continued. He was himself a biographer of his uncle Dr Samuel Finley, former president of Princeton College. As a young man in his early twenties Hazard had tried to get his biography of Finley published, without success. But he made himself into something of an expert on the history of Princeton, his *Alma Mater*. He informed Belknap that besides Finley, the lives of two other Princeton presidents 'have been published: that of the former will need pruning; uncouth excrescences abound in it. It is of no importance to the world to know that his grandmother's great-grandmother helped to make a ruff for Queen Elizabeth'. History is not the stuff of triviality.[10]

Hazard promised to do his best to return to New England and to visit his new friend Belknap – but as to *when* he was uncertain. Before closing the letter, Hazard briefly mentioned 'an odd affair' that 'has happened lately, which I must tell you of, though I am in a hurry':

> Somebody wrote an account of a Cock and a Hen, and a strange kind of an Egg which was laid, or to be laid, at Pennycook; and imprudently added, as a postscript, that 'the ingenious Mr. Hazard would probably be glad to have the Egg'. Some of Mr. H.'s friends, by a concatenation of ideas which was not unnatural, were led to think he was intended by the Cock; that he had either led the Hen astray, or been led astray by her; and there was danger of introducing a spurious breed among the poultry. Mr. H., being accused of worse that 'filthy handling', and in a newspaper too, was forced to take measures for the vindication of his moral character. He called upon the printer, and got, as he thought, the name of the *author*, and sat down and wrote him such a letter as the feelings of an innocent man, thus injured, dictated. An *éclaircissement* took place, the genuine writer's name was given, the transaction alluded to proved to be not *natural* but *political*, an apology agreed upon, and the point settled. But two (I believe) very honest men had very disagreeable feelings on the occasion, as I doubt not a third will (though unnecessarily), and even the printer did not escape without a severe admonition to 'take heed'.

Having dropped a significant bombshell into the lap of his friend, Hazard ended the letter light-heartedly, responding to Belknap's complaint of paper: 'P. S. If this paper is not good, it is large, and therefore I make no apology for it'.[11]

Fortunately the aforementioned *éclaircissement*, or airing of feelings, did not involve a duel, as it often did at this time, or Belknap would have been crushed and not merely embarrassed. The letter took twelve days to travel the seventy miles north to Dover; Belknap opened it on 16 August. Little had he known in July that his witty story, printed in the Boston *Independent Ledger*, about the new Constitution (*Egg*) of the New Hampshire state convention (*Cock* and *Hen*) drawn up at the capitol, Concord (Pennycook), would do more than raise a few legislative eyebrows. He immediately wrote by way of confession to Hazard:

> Had I entertained the least suspicion that any honest man, though ever so great a stranger to me, could have conceived himself injured or offended, or been put to one moment's uneasiness by any passage of my political fable, that part of it should immediately have been suppressed. But that my worthy friend Hazard should so *toto cœlo* mistake the design of the postscript as to imagine it contained a reflexion of his moral character, I never could have believed, had I been told it from any lesser authority than his own. You were mentioned only in your public character as a collector of curiosities, and it was hinted as the wish of the writer that the production alluded to might exist nowhere but in a collection such as you are making, in which I dare engage you have got many political monsters besides this'.[12]

In the strange world of wartime politics and untrustworthy newspapers, the association of Hazard with the *egg* led to innuendos about a possible 'intrigue' involving a 'British officer'. Hazard sought out the supposed writer, John Eliot (who had sent it to the *Independent Ledger* on Belknap's behalf). The *éclaircissement* between Eliot and Hazard led to Hazard realizing his own gullibility. Eliot himself was 'somewhat happy at what has taken place', he wrote to Belknap, 'since it has [brought] me to the acquaintance and encreasing [*sic*] intimacy of a gentleman [Hazard] h[igh] in my esteem'.[13]

Belknap's incredulity that Hazard could have been so mistaken mixed with utter guilt. But it had been weeks since the incident took place. Belknap read his friend's mind: 'I am sure you must now view it in a very harmless light, so that I need not make any further apology'. He now moved on to politics: the Constitution 'has been rejected by a very large majority', so 'it will depend on you to be transmitted to posterity as a monument, among many others, of the *wisdom*, *learning*, and *consistency* of the present age'.[14]

Belknap relaxed his tongue from his cheek to discuss antiquarian issues. He thanked Hazard for 'Dr. Finley's Life and Character', and repeated his wish that writers (such as Hazard) other than himself would engage in the biographical project. A snail would sooner leave its shell and fly like an eagle than that Belknap would compile such a dictionary:

> I do think that something very clever might be done. There have been some very worthy characters, some very bad, and some very odd, and all of them together would form such a group as would afford both instruction and amusement.

Belknap continued on in this vein, describing in detail the layout and content of such a project at the same time as he protested his inability to engage it.

There are many now living characters who must in time be admitted into the collection: it would be of use to keep a memorandum for such hints concerning them as may be of use hereafter. Some have already fallen in the course of this war, who must be remembered with honour. When you come here, which I have been long wishing for, I will give you a list of names which I have collected; and, if you can furnish hints respecting the characters and actions of any of them, I shall be obliged to you. But you have business enough on hand. I shall therefore beg your patience no longer than while I assure you that I am, with great esteem and regard,
    Your obliged friend and obedient servant,
    Jeremy Belknap[15]

Hazard knew how upset Belknap would be when he wrote to his friend of the incident:

'Knowing your benevolence and sensibility, I was afraid to write to you about the Pennycook Egg, lest I should hurt your feelings; but, upon second thoughts, it appeared best, for, as I was confident you would hear of what had happened, I supposed my silence would hurt them more; but, though I wrote, I hoped I had done it in such a way as to convince you that any apology on your part was unnecessary, I find, however, by your favour of the 16th inst. [in statu quo], that I was mistaken. Let this matter rest for the present. When we meet, we will revive it for the sake of an *hearty laugh*, which I know you enjoy as much as I do.'[16]

Regarding the biographical dictionary, Hazard had done his duty: he had spoken to men such as his friend Dr Gordon, the historian, and Dr Ezra Stiles of Yale College, and all approved the design and offered their help. But Hazard was suspicious and doubtful. His work transcribing colonial and state papers convinced him that most people speak of action without doing it: 'I have been repeatedly served so with respect to my collection, and even public bodies act in the same manner with individuals'. Hazard experienced first-hand the weakness of the Congress to enforce its will upon the states. He complained that though Congress had recommended it to the several states

to furnish me with copies of such parts of their records as I may want, they have not yet done it in any one instance, except where they had printed copies of them, but I have been obliged to transcribe all that I have yet collected with my own hand. I feel, at times, almost discouraged, and half resolve to drop the design, notwithstanding all that I have done. A conviction of the utility of it alone prevents.

His comments were by way of a preface to convince Belknap to engage in his biographical undertaking and not to lose heart. 'But I have already exceeded the little time I could allot for this letter, and must, after due respects to Mrs. Belknap, bid you adieu. Eben. Hazard'.[17]

The arrival of Hazard's letter in early October found Belknap steeped in composing his *History of New Hampshire*. The two friends had reunited in mid-

September upon Hazard's journey to the north; Belknap had promised to send some papers to Hazard and appended the documents to the letter he composed. One was a copy of depositions by Walter Barefoote, Lieutenant Governor of New Hampshire, and Robert Mason, Proprietor of New Hampshire, against rebellious New Hampshirans who in the 1680s wanted freedom more than order. The depositions described, Belknap wrote, 'the assault and battery committed on their venerable persons, coats, periwigs, and cravats, which all suffered in the struggle'. Thinking about the current revolutionary struggle, Belknap reflected: 'it appears that the enemies of this country have been playing at the same game from the beginning; viz., first, to provoke the people to acts of violence, and then make those acts of violence a pretext for further violences upon them'. The events of a century past so intrigued Belknap that he yearned to engage in an exhaustive study, to write 'something in the form of Prince's Chronology' to 'give a just picture of the temper and manners of the times'. Thomas Prince, formerly pastor of South Church in Boston, where Belknap had grown up and at which he had been a communicant, was like Belknap a clergyman who engaged in the writing of history; he had made quite an impression on Belknap, who hoped to model Prince.[18]

Belknap's literary interests were, like Hazard's, ubiquitous. A given week would find the parson engaged reading the religious pamphlets of Doddridge, histories like that of Hume, such verse as Virgil or Watts, the biographies of Plutarch, and such scientific treatises as could be mustered from the bookshelves of rural Dover. In early October 1779 Belknap had been reading Andrew Burnaby's *Travels* (1775), which compared the soil of New Jersey to that of the Holy Land. Hazard, familiar with New Jersey, would certainly want to see this! Belknap transcribed a few lines, which argued that the soil of both places was 'exceedingly mellow, and ... fertile to the highest degree'. Belknap knew he was writing to a sympathetic listener when he told Hazard that such a 'remark ... may serve to obviate the objection which has sometimes been made by infidels against the truth of the Scripture History', arguing that the 'apparent barrenness of the Holy Land' could not have supported the armies and numbers of people described in the Old Testament. But the 'laborious husbandman of Israel' of the past is not the same as 'the indolent Turk' of the present. What the latter abandoned the former turned to wonderful gardens of fruits and vegetables. 'But this is not the only instance of inattention which the half-reasoning adversaries of religion are chargeable with'. Hazard had come and gone on a recent visit to northern New England; Belknap recalled their conversations with pleasure, only wishing that Hazard's visit could have been longer. Then, he could have been at Belknap's at the same time as Ruth's cousin John Eliot: 'we should then have been an happy triumvirate'.[19]

Belknap moved on to recent news of the *Egg*: 'its perambulation round the country was unfavourable to its fecundity, for at the last sitting of the Hen' the convention in Concord, the capitol, 'proved rotten, having been rejected by

1700 and odd against 1100 and odd; so that now the ingenious Mr. Hazard is the sole proprietor of it, as it will exist nowhere except he gives it a place in his Museum'. One act by the convention was singular, 'a *trap* for the honest to fall into, and a *ladder* for rogues to climb to gain and greatness'. Traps and ladders do not mix, as Belknap realized as soon as his pen was still. 'What a jumble of metaphors! Were Pope and Swift alive, this paragraph would certainly be admitted into the *Art of Sinking*. I am ashamed of it, but cannot copy the whole letter again for the sake of leaving it out, so you must be as candid in reading as I am careless in writing'.[20]

During his visit to Dover Hazard had apologized for the length of his letters, to which Belknap replied again: 'I beg you would not make any more apologies for the length of your letters: were they as long as *Caryl on Job*, they would need none'. Belknap sprinkled the end of his epistle with like sentiments and requests, such as one for copies of Philadelphia and other newspapers to help Belknap keep up with the events of the war in the South, and another to know when Hazard would go to Plymouth, Massachusetts – Belknap had some questions for 'old Mr. Cotton'. When would Hazard be back this way? Would he attend John Eliot's upcoming ordination? There the friends would be reunited again. Belknap for his part would surely 'be present at the solemnity'.[21]

Hazard, staying at Jamaica Plain, received Belknap's letter a fortnight later but his reply was delayed because the messenger delivered it towards evening and had to return the five miles to town, that is Boston, and so could not await Hazard's reply. Apologizing for the delay Hazard wrote to Belknap,

> My situation here often subjects me to this inconvenience; and therefore, should I appear, as in this instance, to neglect you in future, I must beg you to apologize for it as I now do, for you may be assured that nothing but necessity shall ever prevent my treating your letters with due respect.

Hazard thanked Belknap for the 'depositions' by the Tories Barefoote and Mason, which 'are worthy a place in the museum of every *virtuoso*'. He agreed with Belknap that England had been trying to 'shackle' the colonies from the beginning, particularly 'when she found that, through the smiles of Heaven, they were rising fast into importance'. Always interested in geography and geology, Hazard responded to Belknap's excerpts and comments from Burnaby's *Travels* with pleasure. He doubted Burnaby's claim that the red clay of New Jersey turned to marl. 'However, in consequence of the hint, I will either make experiments myself to prove the truth of the assertion, or get others to do it'. He continued,

> The circumstance of the soil of the Holy Land being similar to that of New Jersey is worth attending to, not for the conviction of those whose faith is not more extensive than their sight, but for the confirmation of the faith of such as can believe the Word of God, even in things which reason itself cannot comprehend. I never could

conceive why fuller and clearer evidence should be required to prove the truth of Scripture than of any other history; nor is it easy to account for infidels withholding their assent, even when this evidence is afforded. Though they pretend to honour Reason, they degrade it by their infidelity; for she certainly would be satisfied either by the internal marks of authenticity contained in Scripture, or by the fulfilment of the Prophecies, or by the miracles which we daily see.[22]

Meanwhile, Hazard reported that he had not seen their mutual friend John Eliot notwithstanding his intention: 'Our playing hide-and-seek upon the road was really curious'. But then Hazard was always on the road. He had journeyed north to Portsmouth and would have visited Belknap but discovered something amiss back in Boston which, he wrote, 'made me think it adviseable to come directly home'. Picking up on Belknap's delightful metaphor, Hazard reported that the *hen*, also known as the Massachusetts state convention, 'lays plentifully, but seldom hatches; almost all her eggs are essentially defective, and I believe she is of the same breed with yours'. Connecticut's hen was similarly '*speckled*', proposing acts to impose order on a disorderly, revolutionary situation. Hazard wrote,

> I wish it may answer the end proposed, but doubt it very much. There are too many amongst us whose *interest* it is to oppose it, and men will ever be governed by their *interest*; besides, such regulations are directly contrary to the very nature of trade, which will never, like Christianity, flourish most when most oppressed, but must be left perfectly free.

Having expressed his conservative political philosophy, Hazard invited Belknap to Dr Gordon's at Jamaica Plain where, he wrote, Belknap would find 'something wholesome for you to eat ... either cider or grog to drink', and 'some excellent hay for your horse'. He had not forgotten Belknap's biographical project, and continued to pressure Belknap to take on the task himself. He sent Belknap several epitaphs of Massachusetts pioneers from Dorchester tombstones, because 'their Lives will doubtless be in the Biography'. His most immediate concern, however, was a journey south to New York: 'I must go there to establish a post-office, and change the post-road, and to help drive off the Tories'.[23]

New York was still in the hands of the British, and would be till the end of the war. There had been hot action in the past few years, especially east of New York in Connecticut, where in 1777 frigates of the Royal Navy had bombarded Fairfield unceasingly, at least according to the perspective of residents such as John Eliot's brother Andrew, who reported in March 1777 that women and children had fled the town, which was partially sacked by British regulars and colonial loyalists. When Hazard saw Danbury, Connecticut, in the winter of 1779, the town was still recovering from the violent British attack of April 1777, when Major-General William Tryon ordered the burning and sack of the town. When Hazard travelled from Danbury to Fishkill and New Windsor, then south along the west side of the Hudson to West Point, and saw the powerful American troop presence, he felt confident that the British would never achieve their goal of controlling the Hudson Valley. West Point was a bastion to prevent British incursions up the Hudson. The fort had at times served as Washington's headquarters, and whenever Hazard passed through he saw military barracks and heard the sounds of camp life pervading the place. In 1778 a great iron link chain had been stretched across the river to Constitution Island to prevent British warships from entering the upper Hudson. The British strategy increasingly was to turn attention to the southern states, where they thought that they could most effectively counter the American strategy of controlling the most territory and isolating British forces. Travelling through Connecticut, New York, and New Jersey was still dangerous for Hazard, but not as dangerous as in former years.[24]

'Now for all the news we have': Hazard's news was, like most news during wartime, based on rumour: a nameless 'gentleman who came up from Boston last night says they have an account there, which they credit, that the whole British army in Georgia had surrendered to General Lincoln'. After Hazard had departed from the south in the winter of 1778, the British had mounted an invasion, capturing Georgia in the early winter of 1779. Places that Hazard had seen the year before, such as Savannah, had fallen to the British the following year. General Benjamin Lincoln had come to the aid of beleaguered southerners, but had himself been caught at Charleston in May 1779. Hazard himself speculated that Rhode Island would soon fall to the Americans, upon which the British, 'in point of territory on this continent', would be 'just where they were in October, 1776. What rapid progress they make!'[25]

One of the countless misfortunes of the past is the loss of a record of life, which is important in itself as well as to those who in time seek to discover what happened. Belknap wrote Hazard a letter in mid-October that the latter subsequently lost; but we can reconstruct the letter from Hazard's response of October 30. The two had planned a rendezvous at Jamaica Plain; Hazard reported, however, that

> what I feared has come to pass. I am obliged to go to Philadelphia, and propose setting out on Monday next. It is hard, very hard, my friend, to be kicked about the world at this rate, but I am "*under* authority", and must submit.

Hazard particularly missed the prospect of joining his two friends Belknap and Gordon in historical merriment. Gordon, with whom Hazard stayed when in New England, was respecting historical research 'as rapacious as a wolf'. Belknap had expressed concern in his letter to Hazard that Gordon, with whom Hazard apparently shared Belknap's draft of his history, would steal some of his ideas and research, if not his manuscript. Hazard assured his friend that Gordon 'has no design to injure others, or deprive them of any part of the laurels which they merit'. Belknap had inquired after Hazard's health, to which the latter responded that 'the pumpkin-shell has not become so *dry* yet as to be in any great danger of cracking, and I hope it will be even strengthened by the present journey'. Hazard had the pleasure of passing on to his friend the wonderful news of victories in Georgia; his source based on rumour, he could not have known that American and French attempts to retake Georgia from the British had failed. Nevertheless Hazard took tremendous enjoyment from what he thought he knew. He also informed Belknap of a real American success, the British abandonment of Newport, Rhode Island. 'It is said the enemy did not go from Rhode Island towards New York, but directly out to sea'. Hazard's prediction of the imminent fall of New York appeared to be coming true, as the British abandoned sites along the Hudson River; 'so that they possess now no greater a part of the United States than they did in September, 1776, excepting Penobscot', Maine. 'How foolishly have they expended both their money and their blood!'

Other news: 'A brig from Holland arrived last night at Boston, but I have not heard either what passage she had, or what intelligence she brings'. On a more mundane note, but of extreme importance to Belknap, Hazard reported that John Eliot 'is to be ordained the next' week. 'Dr. Gordon joins me in cordial salutations'.[26]

Perhaps we should be amazed just how many of Belknap's letters have survived considering Hazard's hectic lifestyle. His journey to Philadelphia ensured, however, that several Belknap letters were forgotten, dropped, or otherwise lost along the way. Hazard never reached Philadelphia because he received news along the way, apparently at Fishkill, New York, that it was 'unnecessary to go farther'. He spent the night at a Fishkill tavern, conveniently located on a branch of the post road that ran from Boston to New York. Hazard's wayward journey to New York back to Jamaica Plain of almost 400 miles took almost the entire month of November. The exhausted Hazard wrote on the last day of November 1779 to report his return to New England and to send to Belknap some much desired newspapers from the South. He found awaiting him at Jamaica Plain, on loan from Belknap, Burnaby's *Travels*, from which Hazard made 'large extracts'. He liked Burnaby well enough, though criticized the author for not making 'that allowance for Divine interposition which a clergyman ought to have done'. Hazard closed the brief epistle asking Belknap's opinion 'of the New York law for preventing robberies'.[27]

Belknap had written on 4 November, sending it to Philadelphia as per Hazard's request. The letter journeyed to Philadelphia and back to New England over the course of six weeks before Hazard received it. Belknap's letter did not survive; but in it he wrote at large respecting the epistolary accounts by General John Sullivan of his victories over western Indian tribes, the Six Nations of the Iroquois of upstate New York. Belknap condemned them as 'simple narratives', and apparently criticized them in other ways as well, possibly regarding the

General's vanity. Sullivan was not unknown to Belknap; they were neighbours, Sullivan owning a nice farm on the banks of the Oyster River down the road from Dover. In time President Sullivan of New Hampshire would be a supporter of Belknap's historical efforts and would gain the admiration of the Dover pastor for his willingness to counter disorder with force. Belknap, feeling perhaps a little guilty over his criticism of a victorious American general, apologized at length. Hazard replied, however, that 'there was not the least need of any part of all the apologies contained in' Belknap's letter; indeed Hazard believed that Belknap did not go nearly far enough in his criticism of Sullivan's personality or his narrative. Hazard disagreed with Belknap; Sullivan's letters were not '"simple narratives", but rather pompous accounts of simple transactions'. Hazard considered Sullivan's account of a grand military victory to be the result of 'lively fancy'.

> Besides, it is not to be expected that a *General* would tell a story in the way that you and I and other common folks would. What advantage would arise from *being a General*, if, after all, he must be like other people? To be serious, I suppose the account contains, after stripping it of figure, nothing more than this, that forty Indian towns were destroyed, and the country in their vicinity desolated in such a manner as to cut off the Indians' hopes of subsistence by the fruit of their labours in the field.

Odd as this was for an eighteenth-century Patriot to be sympathetic to the enemy, even a native American enemy, Hazard was not alone; Belknap joined him in his sympathies, and feelings of responsibility, for much of what Indians suffered at the hands of their white counterparts. Even so, as this was war, Hazard was glad of Sullivan's overall victory, which would pacify at least part of the frontier. Notwithstanding Sullivan's pomposity, Hazard concluded that the 'expedition was of importance; and it seems to be the general opinion that the conductor managed it judiciously'. This written, Hazard quickly ended the letter, as 'I expect the post every minute'.[28]

Neither man wrote to the other until late December when, ironically, they both wrote the other simultaneously, on 28 December. Hazard's note was quick and hurried, explaining his silence as due to 'the bad weather, which has occasioned some irregularity in the posts of late'. He reported 'no news'.[29]

Belknap, on the other hand, made efficient use of his paper, filling it with comments, questions, observations and stories. He began by thanking Hazard for the southern newspapers, which included delightful excerpts of the Vermonter Colonel Ethan Allen's narrative of his war experiences. 'From what I have read, and from a short casual interview which I had with him at Boston, I think him an original in his way, but as rough and boisterous as the scenes he has passed through'. Responding to Hazard's request for his 'opinion of the N. Y. Law of Robbery', Belknap confessed he knew little of it except that it 'seems to be constructed on the old maxim, "Set a rogue to catch a rogue"'. As a New

Englander and a scientist, Belknap declared it impossible 'to judge *a priori* of the expediency of the law, the experiment must be tried'. Expressing his desire to help in any way possible Hazard in his geographical inquiries, Belknap pointed out 'a very curious account of Niagara Falls, with an adventure of two Indians who were driven by the current on an island which impends the Falls in the middle of the stream'. He also promised to extract long portions from 'An Essay on the Agitations of the Sea, and other Remarkables attending the Earthquakes of the year 1755'. For information on the Spanish territory of Louisiana he recommended that Hazard read the history written by Page Du Pratz; better yet, he suggested Father Louis Hennepin's exciting narrative description of the upper Mississippi River.[30]

'As to my biographical project, I find by experience that the execution of it in my hands grows daily more impracticable'. Hopefully John Eliot could be induced 'to undertake it' if he continued practising the 'virtue of celibacy, of which another of my very good friends [Hazard] is possessed *pro tempore*', for the time being. 'I wish you would urge it on him (by *it* I do not mean the *virtue* above mentioned, but the work, possibly he may make it consistent with the *opposite virtue of matrimony*)'. If Hazard was not yet sufficiently confused by his friend's 'immethodical letter', Belknap added, 'an anecdote handed to me as a fact by a gentlemen of credit who was on the spot'. The story was of a New Hampshire legislator who picked up a joiner's hammer 'and pawned it for a *jill of rum*'. 'This is a specimen of the little villainy of the *cattle* by whom we *are*, I should say *have been*, governed; for, as that assembly is dissolved, 't is no blasphemy to tell the truth'.[31]

Belknap closed his letter, and with it the year – one satisfying on the whole for both men, notwithstanding the many frustrations of the war and its consequences. Merely carrying on responsibly, doing one's duty at a time of crisis, when disorder and anarchy threaten, was a sufficient accomplishment. But always in the minds of the two men, often revealed in their letters, was the desire for more: for order, for a thriving republic, for peace, and for the fruits of peace, and in particular the opportunity to engage more fully in pursuing the works of God in natural and human history.

5 HURRIED THROUGH LIFE ON HORSEBACK

By time honoured tradition, not to mention force of necessity, military affairs come to rest during winter, the truth of which in January 1780 allowed Surveyor of Post Roads Hazard the opportunity to rest comfortably and compose largely when he sat to write an epistle in response to Belknap's of the '28th ult.', 28 December 1779.[1]

Whereas Belknap had merely a vague, fleeting acquaintance with Ethan Allen of Vermont, Hazard knew him, and outlined his character in detail:

> Allen is really an original; at least, I never met with a genius like him. Had his natural talents been cultivated by a liberal education, he would have made no bad figure among the sons of science; but perhaps his want of such an education is not to be lamented, as, unless he had more grace, it would make him a dangerous member of society.

A more succinct and accurate picture of Allen could not be drawn. To be sure, Allen's attempt at Deist philosophy and activities as a Vermont patriot indicated the potential yet inconsistency of his character. A 'son of science' as Hazard meant it required diligence, patience, caution, erudition and curiosity. Hazard found the progeny of science to rest firmly in Belknap's character and behaviour. Hazard had asked his friend for an opinion about a New York Law about which he himself was quite decided. It was a law enforced by Patriot militias to intimidate those who harboured Tories (and others) who plundered innocent farmers.

> I think it will answer the end. The Tories are too weak in point of numbers to form combinations, and have been so frequently detected, and so many hanged, that the remainder would not dare to do it, were their numbers greater.

Hazard thanked Belknap for his assistance furnishing hints of good literary sources of information for his proposed Geography, but admitted that 'though books may assist me in my enquiries, my principal sources of information will be gentlemen of learning and abilities in the several States' – men such as Belknap – 'to whom I intend to write upon the subject'.[2]

Would John Eliot be able to pursue the biographical dictionary should he attain 'the virtue of celibacy?' Hazard was doubtful:

for his situation as a city minister [in Boston] will oblige him to make and receive many visits; and, if he attends to these … all his remaining time will be little enough to prepare for the Sabbath; and, besides this, you know he must study to add to his stock of knowledge in divinity, or his sermons will soon become 'a tale that has been told', and he will sink in the opinion of his people.

Hazard declared that Belknap's 'anecdote' regarding the 'thievish rascal of a representative', who 'ought to have been knocked on the head with the hammer as soon as it was found' increased the *'miscellanea curiosa'* of his *museum*.[3]

Although Hazard had promised the return of Burnaby's *Travels* a week before, and promised it now again, he was not sure when Belknap would receive Hazard's packet of correspondence, for, he wrote,

the depth of the snow is so great that I think the post cannot come in for a day or two yet. I do not remember having ever seen so much snow on the ground at once before. It is extremely favourable for the winter grain, and promises us plentiful crops.[4]

In closing the letter Hazard thanked Belknap for a copy of one of his published sermons, and passed along Dr Gordon's request for a copy as well. William Gordon experienced the same difficulties that all ministers had during wartime (Belknap included), that is, the inability to get paid regularly and fully their contracted (peacetime) salary. War and inflation made contracts of ten or twenty years earlier essentially void. Gordon tried to get around the difficulty of inflation by requesting of his parish 'his salary (the *peace sum*) *in produce*, at peace price'. Hazard wondered whether or not such a plan would work for Belknap as well.[5]

Hazard's prediction that his letter would be long in coming to Belknap proved accurate. Belknap briefly wrote to his friend on 1 February to indicate the receipt of the letter and its contents, which included one of Dr Gordon's sermons in trade for one of Belknap's. The reverend sent Hazard a recently published sermon, *Jesus Christ, the Only Foundation*, the message and eloquence of which the author hoped would differ greatly from 'the meanness of the paper', which 'can only be apologized for by the wretchedness of the times'. Such paper as the printer, Daniel Fowle, had was insufficient to produce very many, so that Belknap could spare only a few, and requested that Dr Gordon accept a substitute. This scarcity of a published sermon was a rarity in New England, and a clear sign of the times; typically, sermons were the chief products of New England presses. It was a recalcitrant, inarticulate pastor indeed who did not have at least one product of his eloquence published.[6]

Belknap was hurried, and had to close the letter, but not before telling Hazard of the past Friday night, when his evangelical side got the best of him and he journeyed inland to a distant mountain, called Moose Mountain by the locals, 'to visit and preach to the new settlers'. The experience impressed Belknap that 'there is not a colder situation in North America' – but then, he had yet to journey to the White Mountains of New Hampshire. The settlers declared it the coldest winter in memory; 'but what is remarkable the snow is not so deep back in the woods as it is here', at Dover. Belknap added, 'The spring and better travelling will be very acceptable'.[7]

Three days later Belknap had a chance to write at large. The winter months forced him indoors, where letter-writing was a welcome relief from family and parish matters. Belknap transcribed for Hazard's benefit long portions of an 'Essay on the Agitations of the Sea' which tried to explain the causes and consequence of earthquakes, to which Belknap appended his own geologic account, based on a childhood memory, of Gay Head 'at the west end of Martha's Vineyard'. 'I was there once when very young and not capable of making the most accurate observations', he confessed. Yet the detail with which Belknap recollected the island after twenty-four years was remarkable. He discussed the soil and specimens of petrified wood, which upon collecting he unfortunately 'gave ... to a person who was making a collection of curiosities, which is now scattered and lost by his death'. Belknap recalled in detail the apparent effects on the land of the great earthquake of 1755. 'Now I have got into this track', he continued, 'I will mention a discovery ... of that species of *talc* vulgarly called ising-glass', also known as '*Specularis Lapis*'. Belknap continued, 'There is a quarry of it at Boscawen, a town lying above Penicook (so famous for *Eggs*) on Merrimack River'. Many people used it to replace the now scarce 'window-glass'. 'There is a stream about six miles from hence, known by the name of Ising-glass River, where specimens of the same substance have been observed. I intend in the spring to make a particular examination of the ground thereabout'.[8]

Like Hazard, Belknap was familiar with the common theory of European scientists that America, as a *newer* continent emerging from the universal flood later, being peopled later, produced *newer*, hence smaller and of lower quality creations than those of the Old World. But Belknap's investigations convinced him that 'this part of the globe is as well stored with useful minerals, fossils, and earths as any other quarter, it being equally the product of infinite wisdom, power, and benevolence'. He yearned to be part of the larger effort of the sons of science, engaged in exploration, research, experimentation, communication and acquisition of knowledge. He anticipated the activities of modern scientific and humanistic societies in promoting inquiries into human and natural history. He wished for a 'republic of letters' in the same way that he supported a republic of free citizens. He asked why the war could not be about freedom of inquiry as well as political freedom; 'Why may there not be a Congress of Philosophers as well as of Statesmen?'; 'I am so far an enthusiast in the cause of America as to wish she may shine Mistress of the Sciences, as well as the Asylum of Liberty'. Belknap closed with an assurance that whatever information or knowledge should fall into his lap would be communicated for Hazard's 'use or amusement'.[9]

Hazard received the letter a mere fortnight later. He wrote a charming response. He thanked Belknap for the 'Essay on the Agitation of the Sea' which, if it was 'too much learned ... for the unenlightened mind of a tyro ... may, at least, be ... entertainment' for 'the literati'. Having never visited the eastern extreme of Long Island, Hazard now longed to go. He wrote,

> Should my life be spared, it is not improbable I may have an opportunity of visiting both, and the hints you have favoured me with will serve to direct my enquiries; and I don't know but your account of the Gay Head may tempt me to go there when it may be *comfortably*, *conveniently*, and *safely* practicable [after the war]. I never knew any thing about it before, except that there was such a place. How strangely thoughts pop into one's head! I was just going to wish that you had 'attained to the virtue of celibacy', and that things were so ordered that we could be fellow travellers in quest of knowledge'.[10]

Belknap's description of the geology of Gay Head reminded Hazard of a stone he held in his 'little museum', which he had discovered during one of his excursions in Pennsylvania. Fascinated with the stone, he had performed simple experiments on it:

> I put one into a shovel, and placing it over the fire, increased the heat by blowing. The stone emitted a very strong sulphureous smell; and, upon being cooled, I easily reduced it to powder by rubbing its contents between my finger and thumb.

He promised to send Belknap a sample 'for the gratification of your curiosity'.[11]

Hazard was just getting started. He described in detail the '*Lapis calaminaris*, which' contains 'almost *pure* zink, or spelter'; he described a 'soft and pliable' slate found in Massachusetts with which some people use to cover their houses, and 'stands both the heat of summer and the frost of winter exceeding well. Query: Might not this, in its soft state, be used as a cement, or for rough-casting the outsides of houses, or for plastering cellars to keep the frost out, &c'. A friend whom Hazard often visited on his journeys to Maine 'informed [him] of *copperas* found in New Hampshire'. Hazard knew of '*petrefactions*' found in the Ohio and Mississippi river valleys; of 'several kinds of paints, jalap, and rhubarb ... found in Virginia and North Carolina'; of 'brilliant stones ... resembling ... garnets' found throughout the several states. Hazard recalled his journey through Virginia in 1777. He wrote that the post road 'crossed a valley, in which was a small rivulet. The hill on each side of the valley was divided by the road, and each hill was filled with strata ... of scallop shells.' He added, 'The summits of the hills were, I suppose, fifteen or twenty feet above the road, and covered with a growth of timber. Some of the trees were large. Is not this a proof of an universal deluge' as described in the Book of Genesis? Hazard, always on the road, wished he could visit the ising-glass streams of New Hampshire. 'I have no doubt that America furnishes every necessary, as well as many conveniences, for its inhabitants. Nothing is wanting but men of genius, of a proper cast, with suitable encouragement, to bring to light these *present* secrets of Nature'. Hazard agreed with Belknap that organizations to promote science were necessary. He wrote:

> I have made such remarks as my abilities and opportunities would admit, and have endeavoured to stimulate others to it; but one-half of mankind seem to think it sinful to know more than their grandfathers, and seven-eighths of the other half are too lazy to trouble their heads about knowing any thing ... 'A Congress of Philosophers' is a pretty thought; but I question whether it could be carried into effect, for genius is envious, and you will meet with but here and there a choice spirit who is willing to communicate his discoveries. Carry your enthusiasm in favour of America as far as you please, I will most cordially join you. I will join you as far as I am able in making useful discoveries, and I will join you in publishing them for the common good.

Let us by guided by 'Lord [Francis] Bacon's philosophical works'.[12] Hazard's pen followed his mind quickly from Bacon's *Essays* and *Novum Organum* to 'what dyes are used with you, how they are prepared, and with what the colour is set'; to the means by which rabbit fur may be 'mixed with cotton' to 'make a strong warm stocking', like he saw on his journey to Maryland in 1777. While in Virginia on the same journey in November he recalled,

> a gentleman ... gave me a spirit of his own distilling to taste, which had the flavour of the best Nantes brandy ... Why would not the bark of the root of sassafras, dried and powdered, make a good substitute for some kinds of spice?[13]

Having spent over an hour ruminating by means of the words on the page, Hazard recalled his intended haste, so quickly closed. He sent Belknap several newspapers that he playfully 'stole' from Boston Postmaster Jonathan Hastings when Hazard was 'in Boston t'other day'; 'though the receiver of stolen goods is as bad as the thief, there will be no danger of your suffering by taking them'. 'Affectionate regards to Mrs. Belknap from Your friend, Eben. Hazard'.[14]

It was not until early March that Hazard received Belknap's two epistles written on 1 and 4 February; strangely, he received the last one first – about which he wrote, 'I cannot account for it, unless by supposing some neglect in the person who was to carry it from Dover to Portsmouth'. Hazard gladly received and read Belknap's *Jesus Christ, the Only Foundation*. He was 'much pleased' with it because Belknap appeared to be the exception to the rule that '*modern* divinity, in general, does not appear to me to be scriptural'. Indeed Hazard thought it 'a just remark, with respect to many modern divines, that a man may sit very comfortably under their ministry for almost half a century, and go to the Devil when he has done'. All laughter aside, Hazard was a fine *New Testament* scholar whose criticism matched his wit.

You meet now with little of that keen, searching, discriminating preaching, – you meet with little of that ardent yet rational zeal, – which formerly did so much honour, and made so many converts, to the religion of Jesus; and this is undoubtedly one cause, and a very great one too, of the present awful decay of vital piety. Let us, my dear sir, be incessant in fervent addresses to the Throne of Grace for speedy and plentiful effusions of the Spirit in his quickening and sanctifying influences.[15]

Hazard agreed with Belknap that the winter was severe, perhaps more severe than that of 1777. A recent letter from his friend the Reverend William Tennent of Connecticut commented particularly on the harsh weather and also included an interesting account from the Western explorer John Evans. Evans, a Boston clergyman, had accompanied the 'Western Expedition' that had pacified the Appalachian frontier; Hazard wrote of him as 'a sensible, judicious man, and a good preacher'.

Hazard then moved on to news of British defeats. He reported the Spanish capture of 'forty-two sail of vessels' headed for British-held Gibraltar and a similar disaster to the British fleet caught in a storm off the Carolinas. With no more time for leisure, Hazard closed. The next day, however, 11 March, he picked up his pen again to finish writing upon those topics clear in his mind. With all his travel, and headaches over maintaining the post roads, and his work transcribing historical documents as well as his intended Geography, Hazard had a new idea: 'What would you think of an American Chronology?'

Hazard had been at work, off and on, recording events and dates for several years. Lately, 'as the roads were so bad', and with time on his hands, he worked feverishly, abridging Thomas Prince's chronological history, which began with the Creation and ended in America – Hazard sensibly left out 'the "Creation, Adam, Noah", and some other things which did not peculiarly belong to America'. He added more information from Cotton Mather's ecclesiastical history of America and other historians to produce quite a corpus. 'Upon reviewing it, I find I was rather inattentive to this part of my plan while in your State [New Hampshire], and must beg your assistance to complete it ... My plan is to include every remarkable event'– charters of towns, institutions, Indian relics, governors, et cetera. 'To prevent the work's being a dull, heavy, unentertaining thing, I now and then introduce a *ludicrous* matter, where it can be done with propriety'. Hazard intended to include events of nature as well. He added, 'I have been told there was some years ago a remarkable whirlwind, or something of that kind, which tore a vessel off the stocks at Portsmouth. Pray, can you tell when it happened?'[16]

On other matters, Hazard wondered whether what the English scientists and essayist Francis Bacon wrote was true, that if good English housewives 'put their candles in flour or bran, one by one', it would 'make them last half as long again as they otherwise do'. He continued, 'If this is a fact, it is worth knowing, especially in these times, when candles are so dear'. Not a farmer, Hazard had no bran, so asked Belknap to try the experiment. He asked about dye being made from 'shrub oaks', and whether or not Belknap had seen a stone like one at Roxbury, Massachusetts, that combined pebbles and 'petrified mud' into a 'blueish color'. Jumping on to Scriptural matters, Belknap's sermon had inspired Hazard to recall how Anglican theologian Archbishop Tillotson had interpreted the text, 'The foundation of God standeth sure, having this seal', where the Archbishop believed the literal translation of *seal* would be *inscription*. Hazard wondered whether or not Belknap agreed, and then closed the letter, 'Adieu'.[17]

Hazard's two letters upon receipt required an extensive reply from Belknap, who had on his mind several topics that not surprisingly coincided with those in Hazard's letters. Consulting dictionaries, Belknap discovered that ising-glass 'is found in great quantities in Siberia, and is used all over that country, as well as in all parts of Russia, for window lights. It was known and used by the ancient Romans as such'. Likewise the English had used it, even for 'ships' windows'. He concluded, 'I think therefore that it must be a valuable discovery'. Responding to Hazard's offer of joint exploration, Belknap enthusiastically requested the approximate dates of Hazard's hypothetical arrival to go in search of the precious talc; 'Nothing would please me better than to be your fellow-traveller, in quest of natural curiosities'. Unfortunately Belknap did not possess a 'good system of Natural History', and wrote, 'I can command nothing of this kind but "Nature Displayed", which is an entertaining epitome, and gives a relish to an inquisitive mind for further enquiries'. In his letter, Hazard had inquired about dyes. Belknap, consulting his wife, contrived a suitable response, describing the intricacies of dying. 'I rejoice to hear of a Philosophical Society being *thought of* in the Massachusetts'. Belknap hoped no rivalry would develop with Philadelphia's American Philosophical Society. Moving on , 'Old [Louis] Hennepin has afforded me considerable entertainment this winter, and there are some things in him worthy of your notice'. Father Hennepin's *Description of Louisiana*, written a century before, described the Great Lakes and upper Mississippi valley. In particular,

> he gives a most frightful, marvellous, and romantic account of Niagara Fall, which his imagination made 600 feet in height, though by admeasurement it falls short of 140. But he makes ample amends for such an imposition, by the very sensible remarks he makes on the propagation of the Gospel among the Indians, of which, though a Franciscan fryar [*sic*], and pretty zealous too in some things, he entertains no very sanguine expectations.

Belknap, the frustrated missionary who had often felt called upon to bring the message but doubted his ability and the prospects of success, agreed with Hennepin. Appended to his praise of Hennepin, however, was criticism; Belknap could not resist a direct cut to the 'superstition' of the 'Romish churches', such as 'their useless treasures', their 'wooden saints', and their proclivity to enshrine 'rotten bones'.[18]

Fortunately, Belknap joked, New Hampshire 'abounds with geniuses, and our legislature is made up of a number of the brightest of them'. The speeches of one New Hampshire Solon, recorded by the Reverend Isaac Mansfield of Exeter, whom Belknap referred to as the *Democritus* of Exeter, 'richly deserve a place in your *miscel. curiosa*'. Belknap provided a few samples from one speech:

> Our men behaved with great *turpitude* at the *vacation* of Ti—, for General Burgoyne shot *language* at them with a view to *intimate* them, but it only served to *astimate* them, for they picked up the *dientical* language, and shot it back so as to do great *persecution*, for the weather was so hot that their wounds *purified* immediately.

Belknap joked that with such nonsense 'the said Democritus ... has greatly augmented his vocabulary and other curious collections this winter. I think he takes a good method to preserve himself from the spleen', that is, melancholy. Belknap signed and closed the letter, slipped in a sample of *Lapis Specularis*, but before mailing added another sheet with:

> I don't know whether you will think me a good or bad correspondent, for filling up every grain of paper. My only apology for being so prolix this time is, that when I get into a fit of writing, and am not interrupted by other matters, I am apt to disgorge plentifully. If I do not nauseate you, I shall be thankful.
> My respects to Dr. G. Mrs. B. joins in compliments.
> Yours affectionately,
> Jeremy Belknap[19]

Hazard, in his epistle of 1 April, responded methodically to Belknap's letter, following the order of the sequence of topics; in this case Hazard responded to three Belknap letters all written during the month of March. Experimenting upon the talc that Belknap sent, Hazard discovered that heat 'destroys its transparency entirely, and its elasticity in some measure'. He thought it might have dozens of uses ranging from a coating on 'phials used in electrical experiments' to use as a 'good substitute for tinfoil'. Hazard begged off a visit to New Hampshire for scientific exploring, explaining that he must journey to Philadelphia on postal business; besides, he would be very busy over the next few months wrapping up his work in Massachusetts, at which he had achieved success; for example, postal service to and from Philadelphia and Boston would be doubled to twice rather than once weekly. Hazard regretted that his 'present vagabond mode of life' prevented him from extensive investigation into natural history, an object of inquiry that otherwise 'would suit my taste exactly'. In response to Belknap's abstracts from the *Description of Louisiana*, Hazard agreed that Father Hennepin's comments on the native Americans were just.

> What the designs of Heaven respecting those poor creatures may be, none can tell; but their present mode of living and their education are much against their conversion, and past experience has too plainly shewn the futility of attempting to alter either.

As for the Catholics, Hazard was similarly disparaging. He thought many Catholics in New York had been 'converted ... to Churchmen' over 'a pot of cider'; 'a new blanket would make the best of them *Mahometans*!' Regarding *Democritus*, Hazard intended to claim all of his humorous recollections by right of his being 'Continental Collector-General of Curiosities'. Speaking of curiosities and bombastic speeches, Hazard noted that Pennsylvania had 'dignified' its college 'with the title of university', and Harvard threatened to do the same. 'As your G[eneral] C[ourt] copy all laudable examples, no doubt Dartmouth will be thought of, too'.[20]

Hazard apparently took a break from writing to split 'a "mortal great" log for the sake of exercise'; upon returning to the writing desk he could hardly write from his hand shaking, and the urgency he felt in finishing the letter: 'I am obliged to write in such haste that I hardly know what I do write'. He was leaving for Philadelphia in three days and was trying to get all of his affairs in order – including his letters written – before the journey. As for news of Boston, the city 'affords nothing new but complaints upon complaints'. Boston had been reeling ever since the start of the war. The British evacuated in 1776, to be sure, but the Boston Port Bill, which halted trade in 1774, and the declaration of martial law in 1775, continued to haunt the city.

> I have been credibly informed that a person, who used to live *well*, has been obliged to take the feathers out of his bed, and sell them to an upholsterer, to get money to buy bread. Many, doubtless, are exceedingly distressed; and yet, such is the infatuation of the day, that the rich, regardless of the necessities of the poor, are more luxurious and extravagant than formerly.

According to Hazard, 'Boston exceeds even Tyre' the ancient Phoenician city infamous for wealth and gluttony, 'for not only are her merchants princes, but even her tavern-keepers are gentlemen ... There can be no surer sign of a decay of morals in a large city than the tavern-keepers growing rich fast' or the clergy 'trifling with serious things'. As an example, Hazard passed on to Belknap a comment from the pulpit of a local clergyman, who prayed that 'heaven would, of its infinite mercy, be pleased to restore' Massachusetts paper currency 'to its former value'.[21]

Belknap the same day wrote from Dover in response to Hazard's two March letters. Still on Belknap's mind was the *Lapis specularis*, 'which I think must be ranked among the most curious as well as useful works of Nature, and the discovery of which at this day is a very singular blessing'. Belknap tried the same experiment as Hazard of applying heat to the talc, but with a far different, happy result: 'it will bear a considerable degree of *heat* ... without the least injury'. In response to Hazard's praise for the sermon *Jesus Christ, the Only Foundation*, Belknap wrote: 'It is a plain practical performance directed *to the heart*, which is the seat of true religion. It was desired for the press by a number of honest, sensible country-people', of Hampton Falls, New Hampshire, 'and I took more pleasure in gratifying *them* than if a *General Court* had made a similar request. That preaching which commends itself to the taste of people of common sense and honesty has in general a good claim to the character of *useful*'. Belknap had good news as well: after several years of cajoling, his parish at Dover had pledged 'five hundred bushels of corn for the year ensuing'. Should it happen, Belknap assumed that it would force the differentiation between those who truly wanted to support the parish and its pastor and those who did not; these latter, Belknap supposed, would 'turn Baptists, but those who remain will be the more closely united and zealously engaged; and I had rather have a few solid firm friends than a collection of people round me who are governed by no fixed principle of action'. Belknap, who continued to look to the Protestant Reformation to do great things in the spiritual world, was not as intent on saving souls as before the war, when his aggressive evangelism caused division in the parish. The war tempered his *New Light* proclivities; he grew more conservative, concerned less with spiritual awakening than moral reform, the need for which accelerated as the war approached its sixth year.[22]

Hazard continued to assume that Belknap was pursuing the biographical project; rather it should be Hazard's responsibility! 'I have, as you know, from the beginning, spoken of such a performance rather as a thing that I wish for than one which I shall ever execute; and every day convinces me that my diffidence is well founded'. Rather, Hazard should add this to his growing list of tasks: 'as you have already two sprouts growing out of your main stem, viz., a Geographical and a Chronological, you would let a third, viz., a Biographical, vegetate along with them'. To tantalize Hazard, Belknap offered his collection of newspapers from 1727 to 1753 and 1756 to the current year.[23]

The 'whirlwind' about which Hazard inquired 'was at *Amesbury* about seven or eight years ago ... It was very remarkable'. Mrs Belknap was agreeable to assisting with Hazard's 'proposed experiment on candles in bran'. Neither she nor her husband thought it would effect a lengthier burning candle. Ruth Belknap added her 'compliments' to her husband's, to end the letter. Later, Belknap added a humorous postscript.

> I met with 'an odd quotation' in Hervey's Letters, No. 183, the reading of which made me think of you. And, as it may afford you some *consolation* in your present state of 'virtuous celibacy', I will transcribe it. 'I cannot but admire the wisdom of Nature in denying to men and women that foresight when they are young, which they acquire at a greater age; for, without that, I believe the world could not subsist above fourscore years, and a *new creation* of men would be wanted once every hundred years at

least; since the inconveniences of marriage are experimentally known to overbalance the conveniences. This young folks will not believe, and thus the world is peopled'.[24]

Belknap's letter travelled to Boston and then on to Philadelphia in pursuit of its intended; it took over a month for Hazard to receive it. When he did, in early May, postal business so occupied Hazard that he had to hurry a brief response. Belknap's reconciliation with his parish delighted Hazard, who thought 'it ought to have been done sooner. The secession of the malcontents will be beneficial, as it will remove a dangerous leaven, which might frequently be troublesome'. Hazard refused 'to increase' his 'number of 'sprouts': the 'main stem' would be injured by it'. Hazard also informed Belknap that David Rittenhouse of the American Philosophical Society was glad to receive a fragment of the *Lapis specularis* from Hazard. What of news of the war in the South? – Nothing yet on the battle over Charleston, South Carolina. Hazard did hear that in the West Indies 'the French at Martinique have been strongly reinforced lately, and are said to be much superior to the English'.[25]

Belknap was as meticulous as a squirrel in storing papers and documents among the books and other accoutrements of his study. It is thus hard to explain how Hazard's letter of 12 May disappeared. When Belknap wrote to Hazard it was early June, two months since his last – a cornucopia of information spread from pen to paper. Still on Belknap's mind was a remarkable phenomenon of nature witnessed a fortnight earlier:

> I mean *the darkness* which overspread almost the whole of New England on the 19th of May. As I am no theorist, I shall not trouble you with any conjectures, but shall rather give you a detail of such *facts* as either fell under my own observation or are creditably evidenced by others.

The darkness caused amazement, consternation and fascination throughout the states of New England. Some people thought it a supernatural event; Belknap examined it in typical American scientific fashion. He relied chiefly on his own observations, supplemented with the observations and anecdotes of others, the validity of which he sifted through his own common-sense judgment.[26]

It was a typical sunny spring day until noon, when darkness spread sufficiently that by early afternoon candles were lit and kept burning the remainder of the day. 'It was not the darkness of a thunder-cloud, but a vapour like the smoke of a malt-house or a coal-kiln, and there was a strong smell of smoke the whole day, as there had been for some days before'. There had been little recent rain, and it was the time of year 'for burning the woods to plant corn on the new lands'. In recent days the air was smoky, it was often difficult to see, and sunlight disappeared a 'half an hour before setting'. Several days before the event,

> I well remember that ... every part of our house was full of smoke, as well as all the surrounding air, and I examined to see if it proceeded from our own fire, but was satisfied it was the same vapour that the air was full of.²⁷

Notwithstanding the fantastic accounts of others, Belknap studied the matter enough to know that the cause of the darkness was simply smoke. He provided Hazard with a brief detailing of the evidence upon which his conclusion was based. For example, 'Colonel Hazzen, of the Continental troops, was riding in the woods somewhere about Pennicook, and in the *low grounds* the vapour was so thick that it was difficult to fetch his breath'. Also, 'small birds, such as sparrows and yellow-birds, were found dead in divers places; and some flew into the houses, very probably to avoid the suffocating vapour'. As for the extent of the damage, Belknap wrote to acquaintances to discover just how far the smoke spread.²⁸

Belknap asked, 'Shall I now entertain you with the whims and apprehensions of mankind upon this unusual appearance? It is not surprising that the vulgar should turn it all into prodigy and miracle; but what would you think of men of sense, and of a liberal education', who said, as did one local clergyman, 'that it was the fulfilling of Joel's prophecy of a "pillar of smoke"' found in the Old Testament? 'Another wondered at me for not placing this phenomenon in the same rank with [the ancient historian] Josephus's signs of the destruction of Jerusalem' in 70 AD. One drew from it inspiration to explain the mysteries of the Book of Revelation. 'Another ... called his congregation together during the darkness, and prayed that the sun might shine again'. Those with fewer religious proclivities thought to explain it as the 'earth ... passing through the tail of a comet'.

> How many more extravagant conceptions have been formed by men, whose minds one would think had been enlarged by reason and philosophy, I know not. Doubtless you will hear enough on your return to make you stand amazed at the power which fear and superstition have over the minds of men.

Belknap was particularly interested in what Hazard could find out from Philadelphians, New Yorkers and gentlemen of southern New England.²⁹

Turning to other scientific matters, Belknap related his journey of the past week to a nearby site where he located and examined specimens of the talc *Lapis specularis*. He provided Hazard with a newspaper account of the whirlwind or tornado that struck towns in northern Massachusetts some years back. 'You see, my dear sir, that I have some inclination to look into the works of Nature'. If only Belknap had the equipment and leisure to engage his inclination. He added, 'I want a friend *near* me too, who would join in the search' – a search that continues long after death.

> It is ... a pleasing idea, which I often indulge, that in the *future state* there will be sufficient *leisure*, and the greatest *advantages*, for searching the boundless variety of the

works of God; and I don't know that it is at all out of point to suppose that persons will pursue different branches of improvement suited to their respective geniuses, in the other state as well as in this, ascending in a rational line through second cause to *the First*, and turning all their knowledge into matter of divine love and praise. The surest way then to arrive at the highest state of improvement in natural knowledge is by aiming at that *character* to which the promise of eternal life is made, by faith in Him whose creating, upholding, reconciling, and renovating power is equally extensive, and whose boundless perfections are unceasingly employed in administering the moral government, and in bringing the universal plan of God into effect. How pleasing to think that though we are but mere atoms in the Universe, yet the Universe is composed of atoms, and none of them will be lost, but all answer in some degree the important purpose for which the Universe was brought into being. Let our improvements then, in the present state, be of such a nature *as not to be discontinued* (except for a short intermission by death), but pursued with greater ardour and to vastly better purpose, when at the resurrection we shall be 'clothed upon' with our 'house from heaven', and 'mortality shall be swallowed up of life'. Adieu!'[30]

Postscript: does Hazard know of 'Siberian wheat in Pennsylvania?' It works well in New Hampshire. Also, would Hazard kindly purchase a copy of the 'Maxims, or Principles, or Elements (I forget which) of *Politeness*, collected from the Earl of Chesterfield, and I will pay you for it when I see you. I want it for my children, who are under no great advantages for learning *it* any other way.'[31]

Belknap's letter found Hazard not at Philadelphia but returned to Massachusetts. Hazard replied on 27 June that 'I can add but very little to your present stock of ideas about the darkness, &c., of the 19th May, for as it was not so remarkable at Philadelphia, but little attention was paid to it'. Hazard did, however, pick up some titbits on his journey north: 'A lady at Middletown upper houses (in Connecticut) told me she was ironing on that day, and was very much mortified to find her clothes look so yellow'. It was sufficiently dark in Massachusetts for 'our friends ... to dine by candle-light, and the night was "darkness visible". Some people who were going home from a public meeting could hardly get their horses to stir. From this circumstance it appears as if every thing like light had been absolutely banished'.[32]

Hazard recalled travelling through the type of landscape where one might find *Lapis specularis*; 'but, having no idea at those times of any thing so capital as has been since discovered, I gave them barely a superficial glance, and left them. This will not be the case in future'. Belknap's account of his frustration in pursuit of science, Hazard felt also, as, he wrote,

> it recalled a number of very disagreeable ideas I had had on thinking of my own situation with reference to the same subject. Equally unprovided with books and instruments, and hurried through life on horseback, it is impossible for me to make any great proficiency in this useful branch of science. However, let us not be discouraged. We *can* do something; more than we can is not expected from us; and perhaps

our feeble attempts may be useful to others. They will, at least, be pleasing to ourselves; and, I trust, not unprofitable either.

Hazard had in mind the kind of *profit* that comes from uncovering the wisdom inherent in the works of the Creator:

> I never critically contemplate any of the works of Nature without such views of the wisdom, the power, and the majesty of God, as are rapturous and transporting. These views often carry me quite beyond the creature. I get lost in the Creator; come back to earth, and despise myself.[33]

Siberian wheat was a topic of which Hazard was well informed, though not from his experience in Philadelphia; rather his host at Jamaica Plain, Dr Gordon, had a little over an acre of land, right outside Hazard's window, sewn with New Hampshire Siberian wheat. It was not nearly as luxuriant, nor did it promise so great a harvest as a grain grown by Germans in Pennsylvania, called *spelts*, which makes a 'very white' flour and very good bread.[34]

Moving on to entertainment: On his journey south Hazard had visited a place he had passed by many times before without stopping to explore: the New Jersey 'Falls of Pasaic', which were a mere 'hundred yards' from the post road. Hazard described the lay of the land, the river and the 'craggy rocks' upon which he tread to see the falls. 'Near the cleft into which the river falls, and cross-wise of the stream, is another so narrow that I stepped across it, and yet, as near as I could judge, a hundred feet deep' – 'The sight is grand,' he wrote, 'and the scene amazingly romantic'. While in Philadelphia the man who seemingly was always on a horse 'took [his] horse and went to see' the 'diamond rock (so called) about twenty-four miles from Philadelphia'. Hazard also, while in Philadelphia, journeyed down the street to 'a Popish church' to watch a mass dedicated to the soul of 'a Spanish gentleman of eminence'. The Presbyterian Hazard 'had never seen even the inside of a Popish Church', and he expected the worst. He was pleasantly surprised, however, that with the exception of various signs of 'bigotry' and 'delusions', 'the behaviour of the Papists in time of worship was very decent and solemn, vastly more so than among the generality of Protestants', some of whom 'behaved irreverently'. A beautifully wrought 'picture of a crucifixion' found 'above the altar' was 'a very fine piece of painting', which reminded Hazard of the work of Charles Wilson Peale, a collection of whose portraits Hazard went to see.[35]

On other matters, David Rittenhouse the famous Philadelphia scientist was not impressed with the *Lapis specularis*, but presented Hazard instead with a sample of asbestos, shreds of which when recently drawn from the earth could be pulled from it; Rittenhouse 'made' a 'wick for a lamp with some of it'. Hazard wrote, 'During my absence [from Massachusetts] the General Court has instituted the "American Academy of Arts and Sciences"', of which 'the title is neither modest nor proper'. As for politics, 'martial law is proclaimed in Philadelphia', recently liberated from the British. Connecticut, meanwhile, had 'invested the Governour and Council of Safety with dictatorial authority'. Other bad news included that Charleston, South Carolina, was in British hands – 'What the consequences of all this will be, Time, the grand tell-tale, must determine'.[36]

> From reading the foregoing, you will see the *state of my ideas,* – jumbled all together by my journey, like the blanks and prizes in a lottery-wheel. You know how to sort them. Remember me affectionately to Mrs. Belknap, and be assured of the warmest esteem of Your friend, Eben. Hazard.[37]

Hazard 'expected to have been in New Hampshire ere this time' (early July) when he penned Belknap a brief letter, but he had been 'unavoidably detained' by postal business. In the mean time, until his expected visit, Hazard provided material 'to amuse' his friend. The newspapers Hazard sent to Belknap included one from British held Charleston, which contained a printed British proclamation that hinted that the Patriots still resisted, which Hazard applauded, considering that the long and difficult Patriot challenge to British-held Pennsylvania in time paid off. Meanwhile, he added, 'New York and New Jersey have been unaccountably neglected. For four years they have had to encounter all the horrors and difficulties of the war'. Hazard knew from first-hand experience. 'Their towns are burned and their inhabitants murdered, and other States with indifference behold the flames, and are unaffected by the sight of even the reeking blood of their fellow-citizens'. A downside of travelling throughout states torn by warfare is that scenes of war rarely evade one's view. A mere three years earlier on his journey to New Jersey Hazard witnessed and heard about the destruction, hardship, murder and rape resulting from the British occupation of such towns as Elizabeth. And it still haunted him.[38]

Three weeks passed, and although Belknap received Hazard's letter of late June the follow up of 11 July had yet to arrive – nor had Hazard. In the first week of August, Belknap wrote,

> Ever since your return from Philadelphia I have delayed writing to you, expecting every week to see you in person, and acknowledge *viva voce* the receipt of your very curious and entertaining letter on natural subjects ... This expectation was so strong that I endeavoured as much as possible to keep myself disengaged, especially on the Sabbath.

Belknap knew that his friend was coming, but when? Then on Friday 28 July Belknap was strolling with a fellow scientist – 'to whom I accidentally mentioned your name, when I was wishing for a pocket microscope to examine more accurately some vegetables which we met with in our walk' – who recalled seeing Hazard several days earlier. 'I then imagined you might be at Falmouth on your post business, and would call upon me in your way back, and I looked with particular eagerness for you on Saturday night'. Unknown to Belknap, Hazard arrived back at Portsmouth on Monday the last day of July. He intended to visit Belknap and went so far as to proceed to Knight's Ferry to take him across the Piscataqua River to Dover Point, 'but was disappointed of an horse'. Belknap received a message from his friend Dr Langdon to this effect at 1 p.m. on Monday afternoon. Belknap's horse being 'at pasture two miles off', he:

> immediately borrowed one, mounted my chaise, and leaving my business, in which I was much engaged, rode express to the ferry, indulging the pleasing hope of seeing you, and if possible detaching you from the company with whom I imagined you were there spending the afternoon, that I might bring you home for *at least* one night. You may judge of my feelings when on my arrival I learnt that you had been there on a morning's ride, and was gone three hours before.

Belknap was disappointed, the more so because such a failed rendezvous had occurred several times. He wrote of 'last November, when you set out from Roxberry [*sic*] for the southward, the day before my coming to Boston'. 'I have been examining myself to see if there has been any thing in my conduct that could possibly lead you to a suspicion that I should not have been glad to see you, and I cannot find the shadow of any thing'. At least by means of the Reverend Joseph Buckminster of Portsmouth Belknap heard that Hazard's visit there was agreeable. He wrote to Hazard,

> your visit there was so very agreeable to several gentlemen of my acquaintance, particularly Mr. Stevens of Kittery, who speaks of you with much respect. I shall always rejoice in every thing that advances your reputation or increases your satisfaction and pleasure, and shall endeavour by every means in my power to forward your usefulness. By the way, Mrs. B. was much disappointed as well.[39]

As soon as Hazard returned home to Jamaica Plain, long before he received Belknap's lamentations of 5 August, he sent Belknap a long letter explaining his intended plan while in New Hampshire of journeying to Belknap's at Dover, the two friends proceeding from there on a geological survey of the area in search of 'copperas, grindstone, and *Lapis specularis*'. 'But I was mortified by being disappointed in every part' of the design. Once again Congress requested that Surveyor General Hazard return to Philadelphia at once; Hazard was even now preparing to go. 'I leave you to judge of my feelings', he wrote to his friend, 'under such a disappointment'.

On to other matters, he was sending along newspapers. Also enclosed was a book by Dr John Gregory, *A Father's Legacy to his Daughters*, in lieu of Chesterfield's *Principles of Politeness*, the cost of which was prohibitive (especially for a clergyman). Hazard warned Belknap that the book might be too advanced for his daughters, the oldest of whom was twelve; 'but this difficulty may be removed by your explanations; or, if the pamphlet will not do to put into their hands at all at present, it may at least furnish hints for you to descant upon'. 'The *amusements* the Doctor recommends' will perhaps be thought 'improper for a clergyman's daughter'. 'Dancing', on the other hand, 'is not only innocent, but, properly practiced, is salutary exercise'. The theatre, likewise, is theoretically harmless, 'but it is so extremely difficult to keep them within due limits, that I think our legislatures have acted wisely in prohibiting them. They ought never to be admitted into a young country'. That the book countenanced 'gaming' shocked Hazard. Nevertheless Hazard suggested that Belknap pass the book around his parish for the edification of parents and their daughters, especially those 'whose beauty could not fail to attract attention'.[40]

Hazard now set 'upon the begging plan', requesting of Belknap an additional specimen of the talc that they both admired as well as a copy of a satirical hymn composed at the expense of Belknap's rhyming uncle Mather Byles. Hazard expected to be in Philadelphia all winter, 'but as to this, I must be governed by circumstances'. The Congress has 'been such of late as to keep me almost constantly upon the trot, and I now wish for a little rest'. At least while in Philadelphia Hazard could transcribe whatever significant documents from the 'Philadelphia papers' that he could find. 'Adieu, my dear sir'.[41]

Belknap was delighted to receive Hazard's letter 'of the 9th inst.', for it fully explained Hazard's absence and his similar disappointment: 'This is nearly the language of my last to you, so that it seems we have had *mutual feelings* on the occasion, and these you know are in many cases the best criterion of truth'. But alas, 'you are now gone to Philadelphia! To tarry there till spring!' If only Belknap could be there, too. 'If I was as unfettered as you are, I should think it a great happiness to visit for such a space of time the *centre* of science in America, and rub off the rust contracted in this obscurity' living in Dover.

> But – but I won't plague you with the antithesis! There are some who think even *my* situation preferable to theirs. Happiness in this world is altogether comparative. If we make a proper use of the advantages which we have, it will turn to better account than to complain for want of more.

Belknap thanked Hazard for the book by Dr Gregory. Chesterfield's *Principles of Politeness*, with which Belknap had lately grown more acquainted, is valuable only for adding ornament to a well-cultivated character; 'yet I think the ornamental part is not of so much consequence as to risque the morals'. Belknap enclosed the requested *Lapis specularis* and told Hazard of 'a piece of the asbestos', given to him by Daniel Little of Wells, Maine, who got it at Newburyport, Massachusetts; it 'is capable of being spun with the finger into threads'.[42]

Hazard requested Joseph Greene's parody of Mather Byles's hymn, *Upon the Objects then in View*, which Byles composed decades earlier when in the company of Governor Jonathan Belcher on a voyage to Maine 'to treat with the Indians'. Byles, as the chaplain of the voyage, performed 'Divine Service on Shipboard'; however, he 'had forgot his psalm-book, and the ship did not furnish one, so his ingenuity was set to work to supply the defect', which became one of his most famous hymns, published as *Hymn at Sea*, in *Poems on Several Occasions*.

> See the broad sun forsake the skies,
> Glow on the waves, and downward slide;
> Anon! Heaven opens all its eyes,
> And starbeams tremble in the tide.[43]

'The singing of this hymn', Belknap continued, 'furnished Jo. Greene with the hint for the following piece of satire', which Greene dubbed the '151st Psalm'.

> With vast amazement we survey
> The wonders of the deep,
> Where mackrel swim, and porpoise play,
> And crabs and lobsters creep.[44]

The laughter at Byles's expense from Belknap's pen was all in fun, yet enhanced by the cool relations then prevailing between uncle and nephew after years of very close ties. Byles's allegiance was still to the King, to Belknap's amazement and horror. Byles was a spectacle in Boston and the butt of constant jokes. Byles had once been Belknap's mentor and spiritual adviser; Belknap still loved the old man but was utterly embarrassed by him.

Embarrassment extended to Belknap's own situation in life. 'While you are at Philadelphia', he cajoled his friend,

> revelling in the full luxury of scientific entertainment, you must think sometimes of your poor friend starving in these forlorn regions, and let him have now and them a crum [*sic*] from your table. Pray tell me if any thing new arises, or has arisen, in the world of literature.

Belknap was constantly searching his part of the world (usually in vain) for scientific or literary titbits of which Hazard was perhaps ignorant. Had he heard of this? The account Belknap got by means of 'a prize', a captured British ship 'lately come into Cape Ann, on board of which are some new books'. In one was the story 'of a prodigy in the musical way', '*a child of 2 years and 3 months old*', who plays, if 'imperfectly', 'God save the king' from ear quite well, according to one of the British prisoners who accompanied the prize ship into port.[45]

Hazard, at Philadelphia in early October, recovering from 'an epidemic fever which has for some time raged here, and laid violent hands upon me as well as others', received Belknap's lamentations on the missed visit penned in early August.

Hazard warned, 'from the variety and uncertainty of calls upon me, such an accident may happen again'. When it did, he suggested to Belknap to say to himself:

> Mr. H. would have called upon me, but something or other rendered it impracticable: I shall hear from him soon, and know the reason. He has had no cause to doubt my friendship, and I have had none to doubt his. Some unforeseen accident must therefore have prevented.

This bit of counselling concluded, Hazard engaged in his own lamentations about the necessity to be on the road back to Massachusetts:

> I now expect to dig snow again out of the roads at the Plain this winter. Did you ever know a man kept in such constant uncertainty? Which is worst, to be fettered as you are, or to be a vagabond like myself? But why should we complain? Why expect happiness in a world which was never intended to contain it?

'The grand secret' the Postmaster harangued the pastor,

> 'which will bring us as near it as any thing here is, "in whatever station we are, to be therewith content", and by "patient continuance in well doing" to gain the approbation of our own consciences, and thence derive a rational hope of "glory, honour, and immortality" hereafter'.[46]

Hazard agreed that Chesterfield's 'honey is mixed with poison'. The 'musical genius' Belknap mentioned reminded Hazard of a similar prodigy he had seen on his travels in 1777. The 'child' was '22 months old', and 'could not' yet 'talk', and yet he could 'beat upon a drum' in perfect accompaniment with 'army fifers'. The child

> kept time with great exactness, and made no mistakes in other respects. When the fifer was going to change a tune, he gave the child no warning, but played on without stopping, as if he was continuing the former tune. The child immediately perceived the change, and beat the tune the fifer played. Of all this I was an eye and ear witness.[47]

More astonishing was the tale of Benedict Arnold's treasonous design to turn over West Point to the enemy. Fortunately his accomplice, the British officer Major André, was 'apprehended as a spy'. Arnold escaped, 'but I think vengeance will overtake him yet. Divine justice cannot suffer crimes of such enormity to pass unpunished'. Even so, West Point was safe, which was

> another striking proof of the interposition of Heaven in favour of our just cause, – and, I am sorry to add, of human depravity too. It is mortifying that such rascals should have any claim to humanity, and that better men should be obliged to belong to the same genus of creatures'. Patriots in Philadelphia 'burned in effigy' the traitor along with 'the Devil'.[48]

Belknap responded three weeks later that he took Hazard's silence to be a possible indication of illness, which turned out to be true by 'yours of the 2d inst., which came to hand Saturday night last'. Rejoicing at the recovery, Belknap called upon 'heaven' to 'grant you a confirmed state of health, that you may be able to complete the important plans you have entered upon'. Belknap still remembered the missed visit with severe 'disappointment' notwithstanding his attempt to think upon it as a 'Stoic'. He expected new supplies of *Lapis specularis* any day; 'The grand magazine of it is at a mountain in the Township of Grafton', in western New Hampshire, 'not far from Dartmouth College'. Apparently a 'hunter' who 'took shelter from an approaching storm in a cavern' discovered 'in the morning ... his lodging-place surrounded with a shining substance'. Belknap himself, continually driven by wanderlust and frustration, journeyed to Lebanon, Maine, to examine 'a bluish, shelly stone' that 'emits a blue flame' and 'the smell of sulphur'. Belknap sent 'some specimens ... to our newly established academy' at Exeter – Phillips Exeter Academy – by the hand of Daniel Little, his 'worthy friend', 'a sensible, ingenious man, well versed in natural history and chimistry [*sic*]', whom Hazard ought to meet. Little, who was actively involved in the affairs of the new academy, also deposited in their new 'museum' '*an idol*' from the native American past recently unearthed at his parish at Wells, Maine. He had informed Belknap of many records of Maine's early history deposited at Saco on the coast – perhaps Hazard should journey this way to transcribe them as well as to visit 'your sincere and obliged friend, Jeremy Belknap'.[49]

Delays and the Congress got the better of Hazard during the late autumn and early winter of 1780. Throughout the month of November he was continually '*setting out* for New Hampshire' but never left Philadelphia – some duty or person prevented the departure. Hence he refrained until 2 December from answering Belknap's letter of late October. 'Next Wednesday is now the time fixed on for my departure'. He had looming over him a full '*month on the road*' in winter during war – not an enviable position in which to be. Hazard's brief letter centred upon his continuing interest in American geological specimens, of which asbestos (more than *Lapis specularis*) intrigued him most. Hazard had been in correspondence with Daniel Little, who 'obliged me very much by sending me some of the asbestos'. Little had a series of questions about asbestos that he put to Hazard, who did not know the answers, which he passed on to other, better informed men (of the Philosophical Society). But 'those who possess' the information 'will not communicate it: they sacrifice public good to their own interest'. Little's discovery of the pagan idol of the Indians, with a drawing of a serpent upon it, reminded Hazard of similar artefacts he had seen in England before the war. 'They are very numerous on stones with which the houses in a country town (through which I rode, but forget the name) are built, and are considered as a natural curiosity'. Hazard, typically busy, wrote cryptically of 'a new employment' that kept him so 'immersed' that he had 'visited the post-office but once a week for some time past'.⁵⁰

Belknap meanwhile, having not heard from Hazard for almost three months, understandably asked in his December letter, a week before Christmas, 'what is the matter with my friend Hazard?' Was his friend ill or had the Tories robbed the post of his letter? Belknap was not sure where to send his letter; indeed the uncertainty of whether or not Hazard would receive it explains the brevity with which Belknap wrote. Belknap decided the best course would be to send it to the Boston Postmaster Jonathan Hastings and let him decide where to send it – to Jamaica Plain or Philadelphia, or somewhere on the road.

> After having been so long favoured with your correspondence, you may well think an abstinence of above two months is extremely disagreeable. I beg to be relieved of my anxious apprehensions as speedily as possible, for I am really afraid you have got a relapse.

Belknap had yet to receive a new supply of his favourite talc, *Lapis specularis*; the source was Grafton County, New Hampshire, a territory near the upper Connecticut River, which had recently been on the defensive thanks to an Indian attack on the community of Royalton, Vermont. In the meantime a nearby mountain in Maine called Bonabeag furnished Belknap with some specimens of a 'very fine free-stone', which 'has been made into grindstones, and is capable of being sawed into hearths, chimney backs, &c'. Notwithstanding the condescending remarks about America of French and British philosophers, Belknap proclaimed with pride and confidence: 'The treasures which Nature has deposited in America come daily into view, and I doubt not we shall find the New World as well stored with all useful materials as the Old'.⁵¹

Hazard was on the road in December, and spent Christmas at a nameless tavern. Belknap's Christmas was a bit warmer thanks to the arrival of Hazard's letter of 2 December, which explained his delay as caused not by sickness but by business. Belknap spent part of Christmas day writing a response to Hazard, which has since been lost. In it Belknap hoped his friend, heading towards northern New England, would spend New Year's at the Belknap homestead. Belknap wondered whether or not Hazard's 'new employment' was in fact an employment of the heart. Hazard was thirty-six, never married, yet viral and amiable – with the war nearing a close, perhaps Hazard was preparing to put a close to his heretofore 'virtue of celibacy'.⁵²

Hazard's engagement, rather, was of a more practical nature, involved with contributing to putting an end to a war that, with the surrender of Cornwallis in the coming months, was slowly drawing to a close, as was the year 1780, a year of frustration for Hazard, always on the road, and Belknap, always at home. Notwithstanding this and all the other differences that separated the friends by physical distance as well as by private matters of home and hearth, the epistles of 1780 carved a niche in the hearts and minds of these two men, bringing them together in a firm and lasting friendship that would only be terminated by death.

6 TOUCH AND GO IS A GOOD PILOT

The new year, 1781, found Hazard on the road and Belknap in bed. Indeed so sick was Belknap with rheumatism that after his letter of Christmas Day, 1780, he was not able to write for over two months. Hazard, meanwhile, was travelling towards Jamaica Plain and Dr Gordon's home when the New Year arrived. Such was his attention to business, however, that he was unable to write to Belknap until early February.

Hazard wrote from Portsmouth, ten miles downriver from Dover; he apologized for not being able to visit his friend: 'for however great my friendship for you is, as well as my anxiety for an interview with you, I cannot reconcile it with my conscience to go to Dover now'. Hazard was trying to drum up takers of tickets for a lottery sponsored by unnamed persons from the south involved in an unnamed scheme that Hazard was willing to term simply (and vaguely) 'admiralty business'. Belknap (and others since then) had hardly a clue to what Hazard was referring; Belknap left well enough alone, and so shall we.[1]

No, Hazard wrote, he was not in the business of 'either love or matrimony'. Nor would he be for some time, so that 'Mrs. B ... will hardly be able to salute Mrs. H. before the war is over'. Until then, Hazard's love was history and science. As evidence, Hazard sent Belknap 'two small glasses' that have little use

> but to startle people with a sudden smart explosion. You see there is water in them. Scrape the ashes [of the hearth] on one side, and lay one of them before and pretty close to the fire; the heat will make the water evaporate, and burst the glass. If you put it *in* the ashes, or among the coals, it will make them fly about the house.[2]

As February dragged on, Hazard received a letter from Joseph Buckminster of Portsmouth, the *Metropolitan*, that Belknap had been very ill. Hazard wrote on 1 March to check on his friend: 'How do you do now? I sympathize with all the afflicted, but more specially with my friends. If the pain is not very violent, perhaps your attention may be diverted from it for awhile by the enclosed papers'. Hazard had more to say to encourage Belknap to continue his 'history'. He also wished to discuss 'the good news which has been crowding upon us of late' about the war, such as the Patriot victory at Cowpens in South Carolina in January. But he was called to breakfast at the Gordon's table, so had to quickly close.

'I expect to set out for Plymouth to-morrow, to copy the second volume of the Records of the United Colonies'. Even when Hazard had time to relax he was off on some new mission. 'Your letters direct to Boston will find their way to me. Respects to Mrs. B. Adieu.[3]

Belknap was finally well enough to write in early March. He told Hazard about his rheumatism, which was

> accompanied by an inflammation, which, after pervading every limb in rotation, went off about the end of January, leaving me very weak. I was for three Sabbaths unable to preach at all, and two more I preached at my own house. I have now so far recovered as to ride (chiefly) abroad, not caring to walk much on the snow, which by its dampness causes a weakness and pain in my knees and feet.

At least the sickness was not as severe as that experienced seven years before. This time it was different also in that Belknap had such wonderful sensations reflecting

> upon the wisdom and benevolence of the Deity, who having first secured our eternal salvation by the most astonishing of all means, which being entirely out of our power to accomplish, was never required of us, but was the work of His own Son, has so established the order of his moral kingdom as to make our personal improvement in virtue absolutely necessary to our enjoying the blessedness thus provided for us, and has even made our enduring suffering one of the intermediate steps to our arrival at supreme happiness.

For many years the inconsistencies of the Puritan, Calvinist tradition plagued Belknap, who could not reconcile eternal punishment with the eternal goodness of God. This period of sickness was a turning point for Belknap in his movement towards a more liberal theological viewpoint. Astonishing also, to him, was that his soul seemed to soar above the pains of the flesh: never had he been able to think so intensely, so clearly, upon divine topics. Had the pains been more intense, he could have born them easily. Yet, he wrote, 'At the same time I was really not so capable of attending to or managing any domestic or worldly concerns as I ordinarily am in a time of health'. So great was the break from corporeal feelings and concerns that Belknap had a brief flashing sense of the experience of eternity. To Belknap, this was

> plain proof that spiritual and heavenly things are properly the soul's element, and the more she is abstracted from the material world the more exalted and congenial are her enjoyments. Let us therefore look and long and pray for the coming of that glorious state, in which all the bubbles which are so apt now to amuse and employ us, shall vanish into their native nothing, and where we shall contemplate and enjoy substantial good. But I am preaching instead of writing a letter. I will descend to other matters.[4]

Belknap occupied his less sublime moments in bed reading the newspapers sent by Hazard. One especially caught his attention for its inclusion of George

Washington's 'Tour to the Ohio in 1753'. Throughout his life Belknap, more than Hazard, was a constant secular worshiper at the throne of Washington: 'As I have a regard for that character little short of *veneration*, every particle of intelligence concerning his life and actions, and every shred of his writings, is peculiarly pleasing to me'. Belknap had read other of Washington's writings, including some purported letters 'found in Philadelphia when the enemy had possession of it'. Belknap was 'charmed beyond measure with the spirit and sentiments' of Washington's writings. 'If he should (as God grant he may) preserve the same character through life in which he now appears, at least to me, he will certainly merit the highest place in the Roll of Worthies'. Belknap was particularly impressed by such men 'that think justly, and acknowledge the agency of Divine Providence in matters wherein they have a concern. A man is never more truly noble than when he is sensible that he is only a secondary instrument of bringing to pass God's great designs'.[5]

Yet more spilled from Belknap's pen: The victory at the Battle of Cowpens and the heroism of the Patriot commander Daniel Morgan thrilled him. He thought Morgan was like Washington, a modest conqueror. Hazard's 'glass bubbles' worked perfectly well in Belknap's fireplace – they reminded Belknap of his days as a student taking Professor John Winthrop IV's 'Experimental Philosophy' course at Harvard. One experiment was to place such a glass ball 'on a lighted candle' – it 'exploded with a report equal to a pocket pistol'. Such experiments evinced 'the elasticity of the air'. Belknap hoped that while Hazard was at Plymouth copying records he would visit 'Father Cotton', the Rev. John Cotton. He wrote to Hazard that if in discussing issues with the Reverence or others 'you meet with any thing new in the natural way, don't fail to let me partake of the pleasure'. The grapevine passed along a report to Belknap of 'some red and yellow oker [ocher] which have been discovered in this and the next town. When the snow goes off, I hope to visit the spots and examine them'. Belknap congratulated Hazard on his election to the American Academy of Arts and Sciences in Boston: 'You will have opportunity to serve the cause of science thereby'. Belknap thought membership in such societies should be open to all, even 'intelligent' and observant 'tradesmen' and 'masters of ships', who could

> prove useful members by communicating experiments and observations in their respective occupations, wherein all the active powers and many of the productions of nature are constantly employed, and by furnishing specimens of what is curious from abroad.
> P. S. How long shall you be at Plymouth?[6]

Not for six weeks did Hazard respond, and then he did so late at night, 'by candle-light' – a true 'lucubration'. Hazard laughed that he treated his eyes unjustly, for 'if my eyes serve me faithfully in the day-time, as they usually do, and have done to-day, I think it a piece of justice to give them what an Irishman might call a *holiday at night*. Hazard wrote from Jamaica Plain, where he 'returned last night from Plymouth'. He wrote,

> Although I am so old a traveller, my bones are so sore, and my joints so stiff, that I move very clumsily and in great pain. This I attribute to my confining myself closely to writing for above five weeks, and not using any exercise in that time.

Meanwhile Hazard was glad of Belknap's recovery, but warned him 'not to expose yourself unnecessarily, and be especially upon your guard against a damp air for fear of a relapse'. Regarding Belknap's supposed proof of the immateriality of the soul released from the prison of the body, Hazard thought it was possible in Belknap's case; but one could hardly make a universal theory of it. Otherwise the vigour of the mind 'would be in exact proportion to the decay of the body, but observation teaches us it is not so'. 'Pain and retirement' naturally 'concentrate the thoughts, and, by bringing them to a focus, make them more intense'. What is more important, however, are the images and ideas upon which Belknap's mind ruminated. These, Hazard wrote, have

> often engaged my attention and excited my astonishment. Even a superficial view of the Christian scheme, and the outlines of the plan of Divine government, are sufficient to fill the soul with admiration of the wisdom and benevolence of God; but a more accurate examination of them cannot fail of producing rapturous adoration. No other system *makes it a man's interest to do his duty*, and therefore no other system contains so much wisdom and bids so fair for success.

Why then, Hazard asked, are there so many unbelievers?

> The doctrine of *original sin* will not, in my opinion, sufficiently account for the strange and absurd conduct of mankind in this respect. The guilt descending from that source appears to me but trifling compared with *artificial depravity*. *Unbelief* must be the root of the evil. Men are governed principally by their senses, and these are not so much affected by things future and invisible as by present and sensible objects. Were the former to make as deep an impression as the latter, and did men really believe it to be their interest to be virtuous, a principle of self-love would drive them to it. But it was not my intention when I began to attempt a discussion of theological questions. I shall therefore proceed to other subjects to which I am more equal.[7]

Hazard, too, enjoyed reading Washington's journal, but the letters to which Belknap referred he believed 'were nothing more than well-executed *counterfeits*'. Hazard agreed that Daniel Morgan indeed showed 'magnanimity' in 'victory'. Of the glass bubbles he sent to Belknap: 'a pretty contrivance for shewing the elasticity of the air. I had no small diversion with them'. Hazard's visit to Plymouth was successful: he transcribed 399 pages of 'the Records of the United Colonies of New England; viz., Plymouth, Massachusetts, Connecticut, and Newhaven', documents that cover the years 1643, when the Confederation of colonies formed, to 1679. 'Only two' copies of the records 'remain, and, lest these should be lost or destroyed, I took the trouble of transcribing the whole, as I think them important'. That this Confederation of the seventeenth century and the present Confederation of the United States had many similarities particularly intrigued Hazard. He knew Belknap would want to see them, so offered it 'if it can be done consistently with the safety of the manuscript, which I confess I value very highly, as the fruit of great labor and expence'. Hazard would send the manuscript under the careful attention of a friend to Portsmouth, where Belknap would have to 'contrive a plan for its security between Dover and Portsmouth'.[8]

Hazard also described his particular success in locating 'a valuable acquisition' to his personal museum.

> It is a circular picture of about five inches diameter, emblematical of January. The device is two men and two women sitting drinking, and on the background is a door through which you see people scating [skating] ... Round it, on the maple, is this inscription: 'Janus loves good drincks, warme cloathes convenient bee: and sporting on the ice affordeth passing glee'.

The item 'is one of twelve (The Months) which belonged to Gover[nor] Edward Winslow' of Plymouth Colony, 'and was brought over by him in 1620'. Hazard also picked up 'a French copper coined in 1646' as well as a sermon from 1620. Hazard was surprised at his election to the American Academy: 'it was a mark of polite attention I had no right to expect, and I am happy in it, as it will give me an opportunity of serving the cause of science'.[9]

Belknap, in response, was astonished that Hazard should even offer to lend the Records of the United Colonies: 'I should not have dared to ask such a favour, and even now I am extremely scrupulous about accepting the offer, lest any accident might befall them, in their progress here and back again'. Belknap had recently been searching for colonial records in Portsmouth that would tell about the Wentworth family, and had applied to Michael Wentworth, but found that Hazard had anticipated him: 'Be so kind as to let me know what papers you had from him, and whether they will be of service to me or not'. Belknap was well enough to walk the ten miles from Portsmouth to Dover, 'though my feet were very wet'.[10]

'I am quite willing' Belknap continued, 'to allow that the 'natural tendency of pain and confinement is to concentrate the thoughts'. 'I a little suspected my theory before you furnished me with this hint, from recollecting the decay of the mental powers by *age*. We are not without need of correction from one another, and we often find occasion to correct ourselves'.

Belknap then moved on to Hazard's more important discussion regarding sin, guilt and divine benevolence. 'By what law' is 'guilt' transferred from the Fall of Man in the Garden of Eden to those humans of the present? 'Is it by an establishment of the Creator? Where is that establishment to be found?' 'Universal depravity' is not the result of a mysterious inheritance from antiquity, rather from the *universal* fact that 'the senses and appetites are *sooner* in exercise' than reason, 'and thereby get the man in subjection before reason is mature enough to operate'. *Unbelief* was 'the original root of evil', which the descendants of Adam have inherited. Human sin is not inherent materially, rather spiritually, because of doubt and self-interest. He continued,

> for this reason I apprehend the Gospel must appear Divine, because it is fitted to the state man is in. It does not require him to be abstracted from himself, and to pursue virtue for virtue's sake *only*, but because it is conducive to his own happiness. So far from endeavouring to eradicate this natural principle, the Gospel is *grafted* upon it.[11]

Hence Belknap speculated and challenged the tradition of his fathers in response to Hazard's thoughts and questions. 'If you and I should not think in one channel', Belknap told his friend,

> we need only propose our thoughts one to the other; and, as I am persuaded we both aim at the truth, if our enquiry be conducted with that openness of mind which the importance of the object demands, we shall be in the ready way to come at it.

Belknap himself found 'it a thing *extremely difficult* to disengage myself from early prejudices and the force of human authority'. Such was the ironic heritage of the Protestant Reformation. 'I have been labouring to do it for many years, but dare not say I have wholly overcome, though it is my sincere desire to do it'.[12]

Hazard responded in mid-May from Portsmouth, where he had gone on postal business – though he took the time to visit Dover briefly. On his way back to Roxbury, passing through Portsmouth, he had dinner at Little Harbour, the site of one of the earliest settlements on the Piscataqua River. There he 'obtained a promise of *certain papers*' that 'were worth waiting for', so he spent the night. Upon arrival home Hazard would examine the score of documents he just received; 'you shall have the use of all that can be serviceable to you'. During his visit at Dover Hazard had cajoled Belknap to rise above 'a *small constitutional infirmity*' of hesitancy when approaching others for historical documents. Hazard believed in action and perseverance in all of life's matters, even in the search for historical documents. Belknap's disillusionment about his position in life and lack of literary accomplishments tempted him to abandon his projected *History of New Hampshire*. Hazard disagreed; Belknap should continue: 'It is necessary to prevent the loss of all the time and labour what you have already done has cost you' – a full ten years of time and labour. Hazard promised Belknap, 'you may rely on every assistance I can give you either personally or through the instrumentality of others'. Hazard upon examining this sentence felt it too immodest, so added: 'By the odd connection of the parts of the last sentence, I have placed myself in a more important light than I intended, or is proper: excuse it. It was perfectly extemporaneous.'[13]

Hazard threw out the names of several men who held important colonial papers: George Jaffrey and David Jeffries. Hazard strongly urged Belknap to approach these men by letter or in person, and apply to them for their papers and assistance. 'Don't forget *suaviter in modo* and *fortiter in re*' – grace, action, fortitude – 'and should new ideas, rising in the mind, divert the conversation from a good hint, then comes in *perseverando*' – perseverance. 'Repeat the hint', he added.[14]

Belknap two weeks later at Portsmouth, preaching, took 'the opportunity of writing by this post'. He thanked Hazard for various documents as well as his friend's transcription of the Records of the United Colonies, of which Belknap would take good care. He was sorry to hear that Hazard was off to Philadelphia again; it might cancel a planned rendezvous in Boston. 'However', wrote Belknap, 'I will, if I can, contrive to put off my going there till your return; and, so strange a creature am I, it is not certain that I shall go there at all'. Belknap feared,

> I shall not be able to learn your Chesterfieldian lesson of *suaviter in modo*. I feel my own incapacity in that respect, but am happy sometimes in having the defect supplied by the kindness of my friends, and particularly Mr. Hazard, who has much of the affections and regard of his much obliged, though at present hurried (as you'll see by the scrawl), Jeremy Belknap.[15]

Letter-writing in the eighteenth century had this risk: that the many people conveying letters from friend to friend might break the wax seal and look within. During wartime, of course, there was the special risk that the enemy might capture post riders and the letters in their care. Hence Belknap and Hazard were *careful* – sometimes too careful. They developed a code of their own in reference to certain events and particular people – especially the famous. As we look over the shoulders of these letter-writers and peer into the contents of their lives and thoughts, some of what we read was so personal, so familiar to them, that it is difficult to decipher to what people or events they referred. For example, Hazard kindly sent to his eager friend some of the documents he had lately acquired through his antiquarian industry. Belknap was especially interested in letters involving the period of King George's War and the capture of Louisbourg (in 1745). He wrote to Hazard,

> I trust it will be no breach of the confidence you have reposed in me, if I shew some of them to an intimate friend of mine, who is able to explain something in them from his personal knowledge of the transactions and events therein referred to, especially as I conceal your having any concern in procuring them.

It is unclear to whom Belknap was referring. Nevertheless, the recollections of such actors in past events were important sources for Belknap in the writing of his history. Belknap knew Deacon David Jeffries of Boston, and informed Hazard,

> I have applied to him by letter some time since, and engaged a friend of mine to speak to him besides; but, like many other persons with whom both you and I have been concerned in the same way, he either forgets it or has not leisure, or something else, so that I expect nothing from that quarter without a personal rummaging of his garrett.[16]

One *garret* promised a letter from General John Sullivan to François Marbois, the secretary to the French ambassador to the United States, describing the natural environment of New England, in particular the White Mountains. Belknap promised Hazard a look at the letter and 'some of his flights' of imagination. Belknap read Hazard's transcription of the Records of the United Colonies with mixed feelings, at once inherently fascinated by proceedings of the past yet disappointed that they contained very little useful to his own research about New Hampshire. One item caught his attention: 'In one place, I observe that the Sagamore of Agawam had a coarse coat given him, to induce him to "learn to know God". Query: Whether, if this be good policy', that is, if it leads to conversion to Christianity, 'we can blame the Jesuits for giving the Indians a shirt as a reward for coming to baptism?' Meanwhile the 'Hen sits this week, in order to "lay" ... a Plan of Government. What she will produce, time will discover'.[17]

Hazard at Philadelphia received 'your favours of May 28th and June' on 1 July. The delay in receiving them was a product of war, 'in consequence of a little irregularity occasioned by a rider's being taken [by the enemy] some time ago'. Notwithstanding Hazard's efforts the dangers of carrying the mail were still great. Mail-carriers were typically rugged individuals not afraid to play fast and loose with the postal regulations; often they provided a personal mail service where they assumed responsibility for postal fees and delivery. One can hardly blame them. Notwithstanding the promises of Congress, salaries paid to postal employees (like all servants of the government, including soldiers) were usually late at best; inflation made the salary difficult to live on. So postal workers 'moonlighted', as it were, to make ends meet. Frugality and bachelorhood, more than other things, stretched Hazard's deflated salary. Hazard again insisted that Belknap practice '*perseverando*': 'you *must* learn the *lesson*. Should you not be able to do it perfectly, the impudence of your friend shall assist you as opportunity offers'.

Regarding news of the war: 'We are creditably informed that General [Nathaniel] Greene has taken Ninety-Six', a British fort in South Carolina, 'with 500 prisoners, 16 brass field-pieces, and a large quantity of ammunition and stores, and that Cornwallis is retreating from Virginia'. Hazard's informants were often erroneous, or overly optimistic. Greene's success was mixed, and British General

Lord Cornwallis was staying put in Virginia. In response to Belknap's indecision about going to Boston, expressed in his letter of 28 May, Hazard joked:

> I declare you have as much indetermination about you as if you were an old bachelor. You *will* go to Boston and you *won't* go, and you don't know whether you will or not.

Hazard signed the letter *Quercus*, adding a postscript: 'I *lend* you the enclosed.'[18]

The 'enclosed' was apparently a satirical essay on the misuse of language addressed to a '*Druid*', which sufficiently peaked Belknap's curiosity to set him in motion questioning who it could be, and got him off on the track of how people develop 'peculiarities' of speech by 'habit'. Belknap himself liked the various dialects of English:

> One advantage is the distinguishing people of different towns, counties, neighbourhoods, by their local barbarisms, or persons of different occupations by their use of technical terms. For instance, when a common person would say *Stop*, a military man would say *Halt*, a sailor *Avast*, a plough-jogger *Whoh*, or *Hush*, and a quoter of poetry, "Stick a pin there". But enough of this.

Belknap took *quercus* to imply Hazard's similarity to the stability or immobility of an *oak*: 'That is the stiffest thing in the world', he wrote in reply, 'and very unbecoming your character, or else you are greatly mistaken in supposing indetermination to be the characteristic of an old bachelor. A man that determines not to marry till the war is over can hardly charge himself with this defect!'[19]

Belknap had a 'budget' of other matters, some of which he now related. He proposed to send Hazard's Records of the United Colonies by means of Colonel Josiah Waters of Boston, who would convey them to Roxbury, and Dr Gordon's house. 'The *Hen* has sat once. She was not so large, nor so speckled as heretofore. There is a prospect of something being not only laid, but hatched, that will be clever in itself. Whether it will suit the taste of the people is uncertain. September or October will produce it'. Belknap enclosed 'some remarkable curiosities that had been handed to a certain Monsieur from a certain Major General. I am now favoured with the original, and for your entertainment, will select a few passages, the most romantic distinguished by a black *line*'. Lest the reader think Belknap enclosed the account of a romantic tryst, the document was neither seductive nor risqué. General John Sullivan, the object of so much fun at this time in Belknap's letters, penned a description of the White Mountains of New Hampshire to Monsieur Marbois. The description was, indeed, exaggerated and erroneous. Sullivan elevated the mountains to some of the most amazing on the globe, so difficult to approach as to have never been ascended, which was untrue – the most recent ascent had been in 1774. Sullivan wrote further that even in summer the summit of the highest feels like winter. The traveller ascending the highest, Mount Washington, journeys almost perpendicularly from the base. Along the way he sees waterfalls of up to 500 ft! Belknap knew Sullivan's description was nonsense, and wanted very much to replace such fantasies with scientific fact by visiting the mountains himself.[20]

Hazard had fooled Belknap and he revelled in it. 'Don't you know, my dear sir, why *Quercus* was used as a signature? It was because the piece was addressed to a Druid', often garlanded in leaves of oak. Hazard explained the satirical essay as the product of a 'comical fellow' who wished to point out Americanisms in language. Hazard assumed Belknap laughed long and hard over the essay. He thought Belknap's 'budget' included many more historical documents – 'aye, I must see that; for I am as wolfish as our friend at the Plain', Dr Gordon, in historical matters. Hazard planned to depart 'this city', Philadelphia, 'the day after to-morrow', accompanied by 'a very clever young gentleman ... who is to be my companion, and to whom I am to be *Mentor*', who guided Telemachus in Homer's *Odyssey*. The 'gentleman' who worked for Hazard was Philip Freneau. Hazard's immediate 'destination' was Jamaica Plain – 'but I have the White Hills [Mountains] in my eye. By the bye, don't you intend to go there?' Hazard was 'glad the Records of the U[nited] C[olonies] have afforded you both "instruction and amusement". That's *utile dulce*', simultaneously useful and pleasant. 'I love to contribute to the improvement of my friends'. 'News from the southward continues to be good'. The British were slowly losing South Carolina, though they retained Charleston. Ships were arriving of late to Philadelphia from Charleston; the stories that refugees told,

> confirm our opinion that the British are rascals, thieves, murderers, and every thing that's bad ... Only think of the rascals! They banished even the wives and children of what they call rebels. This year, I hope, will put an end to their tyranny. The post won't stay. So good bye. E. H.[21]

Four weeks later Hazard was back in Massachusetts when he received Belknap's letter of 25 August, which has not survived. In it Belknap discussed the private affairs of their mutual friend Joseph Buckminster, and his engagement to Miss Eliza Stevens of Kittery, Maine. Miss Stevens, a reputed beauty, had attracted the attention of Hazard as well, who responded:

> You have obliged me by the information respecting the Metropolitan [Joseph Buckminster]. It has come seasonably on one account, but would have been more so, had it arrived sooner. You shall know the reason when I see you. I find by it that my suspicions were rightly founded. No other damage will arise from the affair referred to than a small derangement of my plan of operations. In matters of this nature, circumstances must and will govern.[22]

Also in this letter Belknap complained bitterly to Hazard about his own inactivity and anonymity, as well as the amount of time he spent tutoring his children because of the lack of public schools in Dover. Hazard counselled:

> I don't believe you misspend time half as much as you seem to think. If you do as much good as you *can*, you do as much as you *ought* to do, and in this case you cannot justly censure yourself. We have different spheres of action allotted us. Providence has devolved the care of a large family upon you, which has confined your usefulness within narrower limits at present than perhaps you would wish; and this kind of usefulness does not make that *show* which some others do. Indeed a man in reviewing his day's account would hardly give himself credit for it, and yet all the time he has been attending to his family he has been actually doing his duty, and a very essential part of it too. But usefulness of this sort must not be calculated from *present* appearances. Look forward, – see your children become valuable members of society, and then judge of your services in qualifying them for being such.[23]

Belknap informed Hazard of one of the few incursions by the enemy into New Hampshire, which happened in July, 1781, when British-instigated Algonquian warriors descended on some of the frontier towns of the Androscoggin River, north of the White Mountains. Colonel Joseph Whipple owned a large *plantation* in Dartmouth (Jefferson) New Hampshire, which attracted the attackers; Whipple narrowly escaped. Hazard wondered of the complicity of the Republic of Vermont in such matters: 'there is reason to think . . . that they are too friendly to the British. I believe it may be relied on that Congress will admit them into the Union, upon their giving up the New Hampshire towns' along the Connecticut River 'and their claim to Hudson's River on the side of New York, which my information leads me to think they will do'. Hazard (based on his *sources*) was confident that the war was nearing a close; negotiations of peace were in earnest, and 'the principal European powers are undoubtedly in our favour, and fully convinced it is for their interest that we should be independent'. England could afford no further troops in America, and 'we expect a large reinforcement from France and Spain'. An unconfirmed account had it 'that a French and Spanish fleet of upwards of thirty sail of the line has got into Chesapeake' Bay. A fleet of 'thirteen [British] sail' arrived at New York; 'a British 50 gun-ship took' a 'French frigate' that recently convoyed a 'mast ship from Portsmouth', bound for Boston.[24]

Hazard, who knew Monsieur Marbois, intended to visit him while in Philadelphia but could not, which prevented Hazard from responding to Belknap's query about the Frenchman's 'collection' of curiosities. 'Yes', Hazard planned on a 'tour ... to the White Hills' but postponed it due to British-inspired raids: 'the mere gratification of curiosity is not a sufficient inducement to me to run the risk of either my life or my liberty'.[25]

Hazard made to conclude 'my story notwithstanding all the grease of the paper', which nevertheless did not prevent him from several postscripts, one of which respected New Hampshire's latest egg as it related to the question, inspired by the ancient Greek philosopher Plutarch, of 'which was first in the order of nature, the Egg or the Hen?'[26]

We could easily confirm the confusion and disorder of Hazard's life during the autumn of 1781 if by no other way than the number of Belknap letters he lost! Belknap was busy enough, writing twice in October. Hazard jotted down a response, scribbling: 'At present am much hurried'. No wonder – Hazard journeyed from Philadelphia to Boston to Portsmouth and back from August to November. Belknap was apparently hurried as well, for it took him a month to map out a plan of a proposed road from New Hampshire to Canada that Hazard had requested when they saw each other at Jamaica Plain in October. It appears that Hazard conceived of a post road from the Piscataqua Valley (if not farther north along the coast) directly north, which Belknap warned would 'pass through the St. Francis tribe of Indians', infamous for their aggression. Belknap proposed a better alternative, paralleling the Connecticut River then crossing Vermont to Montreal. Along with the map Belknap enclosed a large piece of *Lapis specularis*, which he received from a friend who was a 'pedlar' of the talc, getting as much as 'sixpence' for 'a square of 8 by 6'. Belknap concluded his letter of 16 November assuring Hazard of his friendship, that the Belknaps were well, and that 'the Metropolitan's marriage is not yet complete, but things are in a fair way'.[27]

Hazard in passing through Portsmouth in late September had left a packet of papers for Belknap, who did not receive them until mid-November. Contained in the packet were also several 'little books for my children', Belknap wrote, which 'are peculiarly pleasing. I beg you to accept of my thanks, and *theirs* in particular, for your condescending notice of them'. Hazard doubtless had begun to think of such matters as fatherhood through the agency of the *amour* he had lost to Joseph Buckminster. His amiable frustration was apparent in his brief letter to Belknap of 4 December, wherein he complained that 'the Metropolitan makes long work of it. I wish him happiness, but am not sure I shall not break the tenth commandment' – that is, prohibiting the coveting of a neighbour's wife! Hazard yearned for the felicity of domestic life yet was aware of the emotions that occur as a consequence thereof. On his mind as he closed the letter to Belknap was the melancholy incident of the murder in New Jersey of Rev. James Caldwell, whose wife, 'you remember, was killed when the British came to Springfield. By this cruel act nine children are made orphans; the youngest is but two years old. Except the care of Heaven, the cold hand of charity will be their principal dependence. Remember me to Mrs. B. Adieu'.[28]

The final correspondence of 1781 between the two friends occurred mid-December, when Hazard dashed off another hurried letter to his friend. He was fascinated to read New Hampshire's new state constitution, adding 'and think I could live very comfortably under it'. Clearly, the constitution 'of Massachusetts was evidently your pattern. In some parts you have improved upon it; in others, perhaps, you have not'. Hazard wondered about the clause that required the Governor of the state to be Protestant; Massachusetts was not so persnickety respecting religious qualifications. Nor was Hazard who, though a lifelong Presbyterian, considered theology the pursuit of the open-minded and religion a matter of pious devotion above politics. He took freedom of conscience literally within the overall obviousness of Christianity. His friend Belknap, a Protestant minister with more at stake, welcomed the proscription against Catholics. Would that it had included Quakers and Baptists as well![29]

Belknap was the first to write in the new year, 1782, but Hazard 'was so excessively hurried' that he 'could not answer it' – and then he lost it! When Hazard did respond it was mid-winter February and he was still overwhelmed with work. Hazard was playfully reticent in his letters, always keeping Belknap (and subsequent readers) guessing. Hence he vaguely blamed his tardiness on 'a late alteration in our department' – he would let Belknap discover what the 'alteration' was on his own. Meanwhile, Belknap in his letter of 5 January asked Hazard 'upon what terms Maryland acceded to the Confederation' – that is, officially became a part of the Confederation government organized under 'Articles' four years earlier in 1777. Hazard did not know but promised to find out. Belknap wondered about the war in Virginia as well as the situation in Vermont. Hazard thought, regarding the latter, '*something* is on the anvil, but the members of Congress keep it to themselves'. Belknap wondered as well whether or not his friend would make his permanent residence, upon the close of war, at Boston. Hazard replied in utter vagueness that the 'alteration' mentioned earlier meant that Philadelphia would be his home, 'which makes what has happened more disagreeable' – at least to Belknap and Hazard's other friends in New England. Mrs Belknap apparently added a postscript to her husband's letter wishing Hazard would live happily married in New England. Hazard responded: 'Remember me affectionately to Mrs. B. Tell her I hope *all* her good wishes will not be in vain. Adieu'.[30]

Belknap was suitably shocked when he found out from a different source that the 'alteration' was the selection of Hazard as postmaster general of the United States of America, replacing Richard Bache. He congratulated his friend in a letter of 17 February, but also expressed chagrin that it would no doubt force Hazard to reside where the Congress met, in Philadelphia. Belknap, meanwhile, was hard at work on his history: 'I am going on *rapidly* (for me) with my continuation, but the rapidity is scarce perceptible'. He hoped to produce another chapter by spring; 'after that, I do not foresee any great difficulty that will come in my way till I arrive at the negotiation with Mason in 1747, and then, I believe, I must take for my motto, *Touch and go is a good pilot*'. Current events were forming, as it were, future chapters of Belknap's history. He sent Hazard newspapers describing the 'revolt' of New Hampshire's westernmost towns along the

Connecticut River. Geographically as well as historically and emotionally they identified with the people of Vermont; they merely wanted an official political connection as part of the Republic of Vermont. Belknap joked about a New Hampshire 'proclamation out against the revolters, conceived in Jonah's style, – *Yet forty days*, &c'. New Hampshire prepared to send troops to make this modern day Ninevah experience doom if they did not come back into the fold. 'Their forty days will be out next week, and then – what? Why, General Sullivan is appointed to go up and reduce them, as he did the Senecas'.

> Adieu. Let me hear how much your new post will be to your advantage, for I feel interested in your welfare. Mrs. B. salutes and congratulates you with your affectionate friend,
> Jeremy Belknap.
>
> P.S. Our Hen has adjourned her sitting till next June. Be so kind as to enquire of some of your literary friends what is the best complete system of *natural history* now extant, whether it can be had, and at what price.[31]

Hazard responded briefly at the end of February, informing Belknap that Maryland's demand by which they would join the Confederation 'was that Virginia should cede to the United States a part of the enormous territory', stretching all the way to the Mississippi River, 'which she claimed: which was complied with'. Hazard sent Belknap a published sermon written by the Rev. Israel Evans: 'I don't know whether you are acquainted with the preacher; but, if you are, I think you must be pleased with him upon many accounts'. Hazard also requested the return of 'my Chronology per post, as I have frequent occasion to refer to it'. He concluded the letter telling Belknap of reports of naval engagements in the waters off Cuba.[32]

A fortnight later Hazard responded to Belknap's 'favour of 17th ult'. True, Hazard would not be travelling to New England as often, 'but you may rely upon the warmest friendly attachment'. He enclosed for Belknap a plan for the Merrimack River of central New Hampshire for use in the geographical sections of Belknap's book. Respecting the part of his book about which Belknap dreaded to write, 'the negotiation with Mason in 1747' – the controversy that lasted over a century between the descendants of the original proprietor John Mason and the towns and government of New Hampshire over ownership and jurisdiction – Hazard's advice was to assume a critical stance, taking the respective legal claims with a grain of salt. 'State it impartially, and leave the public to form their own judgment', which was precisely Hazard's motto respecting his proposed book of public documents. Hazard distrusted historians and their tendency to impose on the past opinions formed at a later time. Documents, at least, are straightforward respecting their temporal nature, contemporary rather than anachronistic.[33]

Before Hazard closed the letter he reported on a piece of 'intelligence' that 'comes by a vessel which arrived here yesterday from Grenada', respecting French victories in the Caribbean. Belknap wondered about Hazard's salary: '1250 dollars per annum'.[34]

In Belknap's letter of 20 March he included a commentary on the work of the seventeenth-century scientist and journalist John Josselyn, in particular his description of the White Mountains, a topic and pursuit that was largely upon Belknap's mind, because of the frequent research and reading he did upon the subject, and because he hoped 'to see them myself this fall, if there is no further irruption of the enemy in that quarter'. He invited Hazard to be his companion. Belknap returned Hazard's 'Chronology' as per his friend's request, appending to it a detailed account of New Hampshire's chronological history. Respecting chronology, Belknap pointed out to Hazard a difficulty his friend had run into regarding the years 1689–90. With the adoption of the Gregorian calendar by the British empire in 1752, which made the first of the year January (instead of March 25 according to the Julian calendar), dates in the Old Style constantly had to be changed to the New Style. 'I have been sometimes blundered by such dates', Belknap wrote, 'especially as different dates were used by different persons'. As an example Belknap described the letters of Massachusetts Governor William Shirley regarding the expedition to Louisbourg in 1745. Shirley's dating system was Old Style, 'beginning the year on Lady Day', the traditional date of the Annunciation, when Gabriel announced the coming birth of Christ to Mary; 'but the newspapers of that period are dated as we do now, beginning it on 1st January'.[35]

Speaking of Governor Shirley, Belknap wondered whether or not Hazard would like to possess Shirley's 'instructions ... to Sir William Pepperell, when he was going to Cape Breton in 1745' during King William's War'. He continued,

> The instructions are a curiosity. They are just such as you would imagine a lawyer would give to a merchant whom he had placed at the head of a band of farmers and fishermen, and sent to scale the walls of a regular fortress the very night of their arrival on an inhospitable shore, in a stormy season of the year!!!![36]

Belknap also had in his possession letters of a more recent time, those 'that passed between the Sons of Liberty in Portsmouth and their brethren in Boston, Providence, Connecticut, New York, &c., during the time of the Stamp Act'. Belknap thought it amazing with what 'affection and respect' they referred to King George III. How, Belknap asked, can we believe the claims of the British of the unwarranted and premature calls for independence among the Sons of Liberty 'when in these letters we find the warmest expressions of duty and loyalty to the King, his person, family, and constitutional authority, together with a determined resolution not to submit to the dangerous innovations then making'? These at least were Belknap's feelings about the Crown in 1765 – perhaps they were as well those of his counterparts the Sons of Liberty. Belknap hoped that war with England would not spawn war among Americans: 'the Vermont affair will, I hope, terminate without shedding any thing but ink'. Such would be the dictates of 'Common Sense', which 'I find, has got to work again. Pray does he [Thomas Paine] hold any office now under the States?'[37]

Belknap, like Hazard, surrounded himself with the ink of letters and documents.

> Do you not find that your work grows on your hands? State papers are multiplied as fast as insects in a summer day. I have heretofore recommended to you to begin your publication before you have completed your collection; and I must now add, as my opinion, that, if you do not, you will never begin at all.

Advice begets advice: 'I expect to hear very soon that your present settled way of life will not prove such an impediment to a matrimonial connexion as your *quondam* [former] roving one did'. Hazard could join the ranks of the married that now included the 'Metropolitan', whose intention 'is published, and I suppose you will soon see the consummatory paragraph in the papers'.[38]

Belknap himself wanted to be *published*. Hazard was the ideal person from whom to seek advice. His background as a bookseller and publisher in New York for ten years, first as the assistant to and then as the partner of Garrat Noel, as well as his years with the post office first of New York then of the Confederation, made him an expert on the process and cost of printing, and distributing and selling written materials. 'On what terms do you suppose the Philadelphia printers would undertake my History, what per sheet or per token, supposing it to contain from four to five hundred pages'. Or would it be best '(supposing peace)' to seek a publisher in London?[39]

Hazard sent Belknap documents concerning the rebellion of one Edward Gove in 1683, which helped Belknap to have 'a more precise understanding of the affair' than he had before. Gove was a drunkard who took up arms against the province of New Hampshire. Belknap added, 'I know one of his grandsons, who was a very warm brother in the time of the Stamp Act, and has been so ever since, and his courage is inflamed by liquor as well as his wit. I fancy he is a chip of the old block'.[40]

'But 't is time that I should have done writing,' Belknap concluded, 'to go to look out a conveyance for this long letter (with its *et ceteras*) to the post-office'.[41]

7 WAR AND *GREET BRITTAIN*

Having taken up residence in Philadelphia as postmaster general of the United States of America, Hazard, no longer on the road but twice as busy, decided it was best to write his letters in shifts. His plan was to begin the process of 'acknowledging the receipt' of Belknap's letters, such as 'your favour of 20th ult', days before the post was due to go. 'I should be glad to bear you company to the White Hills; but, from present appearances, am apprehensive I shall never see them'. There would be other opportunities to go, but indeed Hazard never found the time to journey to the most fascinating destination of the eighteenth-century American scientist, the White Mountains of New Hampshire, or as they were often called, as by Hazard, the White Hills. The summits Hazard now endeavoured to climb were Congressional, his dealings with which he told Belknap taught him 'the meaning of Anxiety'. Hazard agreed with Belknap that the British had long tried to spread the erroneous rumour 'that the Colonies were disaffected to the royal government, and thirsted after independence'. In consequence, Hazard considered it the 'duty incumbent on every American historian to use his endeavours to wipe off so unjust an aspersion' – he encouraged Belknap to publish the letters of the Sons of Liberty. Regarding Belknap's history, Hazard believed the best printer in Philadelphia was Robert Aitken, with whom Hazard discussed Belknap's manuscript. Aitken told Hazard about the type and cost of paper and how much he would charge to print it. 'Aitken binds books as neatly as he prints them. Should you have the work done here, I would wish you to employ him, as I know him to be an honest, conscientious man'. This plan, in Hazard's opinion, was preferable to publishing the book exclusively in London; rather, publish it in America but find a London publisher who will publish and distribute an edition in England for 'half the copyright'. 'By this means you will secure half the profits of the European sales, and prevent your being *printed upon*, as we booksellers call it'. Dr Gordon, Hazard's friend, had a 'brother-in-law, Mr. Field', in the publishing industry in England, whom Hazard asserted would be, 'a proper person to engage with'.[1]

Hazard was still *Mentor* to the young man Philip Freneau, dubbed now with the Homeric title of *Telemachus*. 'At the last Commencement here, a brother of my Telemachus delivered an Oration in *Praise* of *Knowledge*, of which I intend to send you a copy, but have not time now'. Hazard was once again being sly with the pen, as Belknap would soon discover. In all honesty Hazard responded to Belknap's query about marriage: 'the *settled* way of life makes me think of being more so; and, would time permit, that business should be seriously thought of. Till then, I must be content to pay the tax on single freemen. A *center of affection* does not yet appear'. At least, one not already engaged by another. The object of affection existed, if it was not yet apparent; she would be discovered soon.[2]

When Hazard's letter of 10 April reached Belknap at Dover, the latter was 'in a pretty good mood for copying'. Fortunately the weather cooperated with 'two foul days'. Belknap transcribed many of the letters of Governor William Shirley and William Pepperell respecting the conquest of Louisbourg during King William's War. Belknap told his friend that when he read them,

> you will think it had been necessary that General Pepperell should have had as much power over the night as Joshua once had over the day; besides being inspired with as much skill in war as other Generals gain by seven years' experience, and able to communicate the same to his men, and that they must have had the hearts of lions and the eyes of owls to carry that design into execution.

In return for this favour Belknap hoped Hazard would respond to

> some thoughts on the population of America, of which I desire your *critical* judgment; and, if you think proper to shew them to any of your literary friends for your judgment, I shall be obliged to you for their remarks ... I beg you to be extremely critical upon them, point out any defect, or suggest any amendment, and give me your opinion with that severe impartiality which a regard to truth ought to inspire.

Belknap had another favour Hazard had already begun to attend to, namely the making of inquiries among the Protestant congregations of Philadelphia for the sake of possible employment of one of Belknap's dear friends, and former students, Peter Thacher, *Cephas*, who was presently minister of Boston's Brattle Street Church, formerly minister at Malden at the outset of the war, but who experienced the same problems as Belknap of delayed and insufficient salary, and so was seeking a new flock to lead. Thatcher would, like 'Æneas', be shown the way by the divine will. 'I imagine he would have no objection to any place or business which would give him opportunity to be useful according to his capacity', wrote Belknap. Ironically, in four years he would be writing similar letters to Hazard about not a friend but himself.[3]

Hazard had in his last letter enclosed a letter and accompanying poem for Belknap's 'amusement', transcribed ergo:

> Dear Cousin, – It is now Thanksgiving Night, and I should be thankful indeed if I could call and spend the evening with you, or have some agreeable friend call in upon me, but as this cannot be, I must converse this way. I have had frequent opportunities to *Boston* this fall, but expect this will be the last for some time: therefore am willing

to improve it. And I think for your amusement I will send you 'The Pleasures of a Country Life', written when I had a true taste of them by having no *maid*.

Up in the morning I must rise
Before I've time to rub my eyes,
With half-pin'd gown, unbuckled shoe,
I haste to milk my lowing cow.
But, Oh! It makes my heart to ake,
I have no bread till I can bake,
And then, alas! It makes me sputter,
For I must churn or have no butter.
The hogs with swill too I must serve;
For hogs must eat or men will starve.
Besides, my spouse can get no cloaths
Unless I much offend my nose.
For all that try it know it's true
There is no smell like colouring blue.
Then round the parish I must ride
And make enquiry far and wide
To find some girl that is a spinner,
Then hurry home to get my dinner.
If with romantic steps I stray
Around the fields and meadows gay,
The grass, besprinkled with the dews,
Will wet my feet and rot my shoes.
If on a mossy bank I sleep
Pismires and crickets o'er me creep,
Or near the purling rill am seen
There dire musquitos pierce my skin.
Yet such delights I seldom see
Confind to house and family.
All summer long I toil & sweat,
Blister my hands, and scold & fret.
And when the summer's work is o'er,
New toils arise from Autumn's store.
Corn must be husk'd and pork be kill'd,
The house with all confusion fill'd.
O could you see the grand display
Upon our annual butchering day, –
See me look like ten thousand sluts,
My kitchen spread with grease & guts, –
You'd lift your hands surpris'd, & swear
That Mother Trisket's self were there.
Yet starch'd up folks that live in town,
That lounge upon your beds till noon,
That never tire yourselves with work,
Unless with handling knife & fork,
Come, see the sweets of country life,
Display'd in Parson B—'s wife.

Parson Belknap's wife wrote them, as Hazard well knew.

> You have much obliged Mrs. B. with a *very correct* copy of some verses which she wrote three or four years ago, descriptive of her own circumstances. She wonders how you came by them, as she did not give the copy to but *one* friend, though I must own it was a *female*. You need to wish for her opinion, when I assure you she says the one half was not told. She might now write *the second part of the same tune*, and entitle it the *Progress of Misery*. It is better, however, to laugh at our misfortunes than to sink under the pressure of them.[4]

Belknap looked forward to the promised 'copy of the Oration in Praise of Knowledge', by Hazard's protege *Telemachus*, whom Belknap thought 'an amiable youth'. Belknap closed the letter noting that his friend and relative the Rev. John Eliot, the *Freemason,* was visiting Philadelphia; no doubt he would also visit Hazard.[5]

That the office of postmaster general gave Hazard more time to write he would not admit; but in retrospect it was clearly true, as revealed in his letter of 14 May, which was 'a work of supererogation', initiated by him rather than in response to Belknap's correspondence. Hazard enclosed the 'Oration in Praise of Knowledge', requesting that Belknap share it with others, including Hazard's former *amour*, now 'the Metropolitan's lady'. Hazard briefly described the Oration as he assumed that such 'Dover folks' as Belknap 'are so "despert" plain that you will not be able to understand it'. Hence Hazard felt called upon to explain the fashion of elegant Philadelphia women who competed amongst themselves to imitate and to equal the latest styles of the French Rococo.

> It is the fashion here for ladies to wear on their heads an enormous *compages* of cushions, rolls, pads, and curls, besides an almost immeasurable quantity of gauze. Besides all this, when they go abroad they put on a *calash*, which may be called a kind of bonnet, composed of silk and whalebone, so large as to cover all the rest, and in capacity about equal to a half-bushel. It is tied round the neck, and so completely envelopes the head that even an anxious bachelor can hardly get a peep at a virgin's face, if she wears a calash. When thrown back, they fall in folds, like the top of a chaise. So much for the head. The breasts are almost as much exposed as the face, or, if any thing is between them and the eye of the spectator, it is only a flimsy gauze, which is hardly an apology for a covering. The ladies' shoe-heels are very high.[6]

War news included reports that Lord North, British Prime Minister, had resigned over the British defeat at Yorktown; a new government directed the war effort. 'But I cannot help thinking that peace is upon the anvil'. Meanwhile there was a 'parade' and a 'night' of 'elegant fireworks' in honour of the birth of the French royal heir, the 'Dauphin'. Hazard thought it was 'grand and pleasing', and believed 'this portends nothing favourable to Sir Guy Carleton', now the commander-in-chief of the British forces, charged with trying to restrict the growing friendship between France and America. He added that, 'Mr. Eliot was here some time since, and preached to good acceptance. I believe if all the clergy were single men, more young women would go to Heaven than do now'.[7]

Three weeks later in June Hazard responded to the latest Belknap letter: 'It was fortunate for me, my dear sir, that my last found you in so good a mood for copying'. He received many materials from Belknap, including Belknap's 'thoughts on the population of America', which he would consider and to which he would respond 'as soon as I can get leisure'. Hazard recommended that Belknap not publish in Boston because 'they print so badly'. He had been thinking about Belknap's friend Peter Thacher, and wondered about him keeping 'something like an *academy* in this city'. He continued,

> Why, did Mrs. B. write those verses? ... I did not think enough was said about the *children*, of which you know country clergymen generally have their share, but now I can account for that circumstance. 'Three or four years' make a material difference.

Hazard agreed with Belknap that they must 'laugh at our misfortunes', adding that 'our share must be very great indeed, if we cannot find many persons who have a much greater'. Accusingly, Hazard asked Belknap 'why did you not inform me that the Metropolitan was married? I have had a most rapturous letter from him upon the subject, which, were I as intimate with him as with you, would probably produce some laughable speculations'.[8]

Belknap, in Boston, 19 June, 'got Mr. Hastings', the Boston postmaster, 'to open the Portsmouth mail ... and by that means am possessed of yours of 5th inst'. Belknap was doubtless in Boston to help Thacher, who had a '*faint* expectation of things being settled upon the old foundation'. Yet he asked Hazard to continue his efforts to discover what options existed in Philadelphia, though to keep them 'hypothetical, that, in case of an accommodation on the old ground, there may be a decent and safe retreat, and yet a door opened in case of necessity'.[9]

Belknap had finally discovered 'the channel' by which Hazard obtained Ruth Belknap's verse, which Belknap admitted was humourous when written, but 'matters are now so serious that there is no disposition to merriment, besides I find that her health is impaired, and I tremble for the consequence'. Belknap requested Hazard not mention her health in letters, which she read – it was a nervous complaint. The Metropolitan and lady were married in March, and 'are now at housekeeping, and very happy'. Belknap enjoyed the 'Oration on Knowledge', which Hazard had claimed was written by *Telemachus* (Freneau); but Belknap detected the familiar style of a sly fox – 'by the way, did you not *write* it yourself?' Belknap agreed that Philadelphia printers were superior, but he had worked with a printer in Salem, Massachusetts, Samuel Hall, 'who shines in correctness, and I dare say, if he has good paper, will do very well'. Belknap would find out 'his terms', then 'form my judgment of the best way of executing, and shall pay a particular deference to your advice'. Belknap's only news was a political disorder in Hampshire County, Massachusetts, which led the General Court to 'suspend the *habeas corpus* for six months within that County, and order out the *posse comitatus* to bring the rioters to Boston. These convulsions do not augur well to a newly and hardly established republican government'. Belknap had to quickly close because of his hurry, 'but, whether here or elsewhere, or in whatever circumstances, I shall ever be your very much obliged and sincerely grateful friend and servant'.[10]

Eight days later Belknap followed with another letter, the chief intent of which was to ask the former New Yorker Hazard whether or not he knew of incidents described in the Anglican 'Abstracts of the Society for Propagating the Gospel', which '*if true*, are a great disgrace to this country, and if *not* (for those abstracts were not usually the asylum of truth), deserve to be contradicted and the matters set in a true light'. A particular incident involved the apparent Patriot invasion of an Anglican Church in New York before the state's occupation by the British in 1776. American troops marched into the church with all apparent intent to harm the worshipers, but God's will, according to the Abstracts, 'overruled their purpose, whatever it was'.[11]

Hazard responded on 1 July having thoughtfully considered Belknap's 'Thoughts on the Original Population of America', an essay written by Belknap that tried to reconcile the Great Commission of Jesus of Nazareth, as described in the Gospel of Mark and Gospel of Matthew, to spread the *word* to all nations, with the reality that the American Indians were ignorant of knowledge of Christ until the arrival of the Europeans. Belknap argued that it was simply that the migration of Indians to America occurred *after* the death of Christ – hence America was not a nation to be included in his commission. Hazard was suspicious of Belknap's conclusion, and recommended that he publish his 'Thoughts' only 'as a fugitive piece in a newspaper without any name annexed to them'. There were too many problems of history and logic with the theory. Perhaps by 'the whole world' Jesus meant simply the Roman Empire and not the entire globe. How could the apostles have preached to the whole world anyway? 'Had their lives been as long as Methuselah's, they would have been too short for such a business'. Perhaps the great commission includes 'all Gospel ministers to the end of time'.[12]

Respecting other matters, Hazard suggested that Peter Thacher consider keeping an 'academy ... in which the English, French, Latin, and Greek languages might be taught, together with Writing, Arithmetic, and the most useful branches of the Mathematics, Geography, Bookkeeping, &c. A plan of this kind you see might be enlarged almost *ad infinitum*'. Hazard claimed that he was 'glad the Metropolitan lives so comfortably. His letter to me informing of his marriage was very rapturous indeed. It might easily be known to have come from the pen of a young husband'. 'Yes, I *wrote* the oration', Hazard confessed. He did not *give* it, rather was in the audience, who was in 'good humour' throughout the speech, 'though some of them growled confoundedly about it when they got out of the hall'. In response to Belknap's earlier request for a suggested natural history Hazard 'lately met' with one by Oliver Goldsmith, and now recommended it to Belknap, although he realized it would not precisely suit Belknap, who 'would wish for something to direct ... enquiries, rather than an account of what others have observed'.[13]

Summer heat apparently drove Belknap indoors for a long day of writing on 26 July 1782: he produced two letters to Hazard during that one day. The first was solely concerned with responding to Hazard's comments about Belknap's ideas on the recent population of America. Belknap enjoyed the 'freedom' with which Americans amiably pursued the truth, which was the ultimate object of inquiry. Belknap wondered why anyone would doubt that when Jesus, 'the Lord of heaven and earth', said *whole world* he meant it literally. *He* knew what perhaps others did not know – that the Roman Empire was just a small part of the world. Even if Belknap did take a very literal point of view regarding the Gospels, he conceded that the process of spreading the *word* could have been gradual – but in the end all people would 'hear the sound of salvation'. Belknap discussed anecdotal evidence of the great travels of the Apostles throughout Europe and Asia; he had clearly done his homework regarding such ancient sources as Clement of Alexander and Eusebius of Caesarea.

> When Augustus Cæsar decrees, that 'all the world' shall be taxed, we must understand all the subjects of his empire. But when Jesus Christ commands 'all the world' to be discipled, we must understand every nation under heaven. For this purpose were the Apostles endowed with the gift of tongues, and the power of miracles.

Belknap hoped that Hazard would continue to consider the theory. He wrote,

> I do not wish to defend what I have wrote merely because it is the spawn of my own brain; but I wish to satisfy myself about it, and if I find upon the whole that it is indefensible, or that any other way of solving the difficulty is preferable, I shall not scruple to give up the point.[14]

Later the same day Belknap discussed natural history and other issues. He had a question for Hazard to ask among scientific circles in Philadelphia. Belknap knew from descriptions of the White Mountains of the existence of a bird 'called the *Cross-bill*'. 'I want to know whether it is a bird peculiar to America,' Belknap asked, 'and to this part of America, or whether it is found elsewhere and where?' With the same stroke of the pen Belknap asked an obvious corollary question: how could he get a copy of Count Buffon's 'Natural History'. Buffon was a great advocate for the idea of immature and weaker American natural productions, which implied distinct and unique American species, which related (in Belknap's mind) to the issue of the origin of life (and humans) in America. What Belknap sought in a natural historian was 'a guide, a systematical guide, such an one as Linnæus, and I understand Buffon has adopted his system. Excuse my giving you so much trouble. I know, however, that you will, when you consider how far removed I am here from the means of knowledge'.[15]

News of the war (according to anecdotal sources) included:

> I saw a Vermont man last week, who told me that a trade was opened by the way of Lake Champlain between their country and Canada ... He added that the whole country thereabouts, and even on this side Connecticut River [in New Hampshire], would go there [Vermont/Canadian border] next winter to market ... It seems to me that the new [British] ministry have adopted a plan which will drain us of our money and cut off our supplies, ruin our trade and set us a quarrelling among ourselves.

Frustrated, he asked his friend: 'Is there any hope of peace from abroad?'[16]

More bad news followed: 'We have here a three weeks' drought. Our wheat is mildewed, and mowed for fodder. The spring was so wet that they could not burn in the woods, so no corn is planted on the new lands'. The price of corn was so high that when 'two small vessels from Connecticut arrived at Portsmouth this week', and offered '500 bushels' of corn at a low price of '7 shillings', 'the people thronged on board so as to endanger the sinking of the vessels'.[17]

Hazard responded to Belknap's two letters – and another one besides from June – the first week in August. 'I believe really, my dear sir, that in the hurry of business I have omitted answering your favour of June 27th. It was long on the road, but came safely to hand at last'. Hazard had heard of the British claims of American depredations of Anglican churches, but most Patriots considered it 'a *lie* told for the good of the Church'. The explanation was this: in 1776 when New York was subject to contention American troops often went to church with 'their bayonets ... fixed ... in regular order'. It was entirely possible, therefore, for American troops to march to church in good military fashion; but they would enter its doors respectfully. Hazard remembered when he was in New York before it fell to the British: 'I recollect perfectly that my minister, finding the congregation were disturbed by the [martial] music's continuing so long, mentioned it to the commanding officer, and after that it was stopped at some distance from the church, so as to be no way inconvenient'. 'In short', Hazard concluded, 'I believe the truth of the matter to have been nothing more than that a number of our soldiers went to church to hear a sermon, behaved themselves very decently there, and after service very peaceably retired;' the Anglican priest 'thought he should recommend himself to his employers by exhibiting an instance of fortitude and perseverance in the midst of surrounding dangers, and therefore made the dreadful tale'. A last point: 'General Washington, who had the supreme command of the troops, and was then upon the spot, is a member of the Church of England, and most certainly would not suffer such an indignity to be offered to her'. The priest, Rev. Charles Inglis, had since been a leading Tory; 'his estate has been confiscated by the laws of the State'.[18]

Rumour had it and according to Hazard, 'we generally suppose not only Savannah, but Charlestown also, to be evacuated'. Hazard's information was accurate for Savannah but not for Charleston. He added as a postscript: 'The Metropolitan's raptures still continue'.[19]

Three weeks later Hazard followed up with a brief letter 'sent merely to let you see I have not forgot you, and to enclose you some newspapers and Mr. [Thomas] Paine's late publication', the *Crisis*. Belknap had earlier informed Hazard of his interest in subscribing to the series of poems being published by John Trumbull, 'McFingal'; 'you are the only subscriber ... that I have heard of', responded Hazard matter-of-factly.[20]

Belknap answered Hazard's letter of 7 August in the first week in September, 1782. Belknap received the letter on the road to Portsmouth, 'and the first chance I had to read it was in the ferry boat' that crossed the Piscataqua River. 'The Metropolitan's raptures had so taken hold of my imagination that I could not help complimenting him upon the subject, withal adding that he had reason to be in raptures' – hence Belknap confirmed her beauty and Hazard's obvious reason to *still be* attracted to her. 'I hope I have not transgressed the bounds of friendship in so doing. They seem at present to be very well pleased with each other'.[21]

'Inglis's affair turns out much as I suspected', which must serve 'to excite the pity of the good ladies, and others who annually contribute to the Society [for the Propagation of the Gospel]'. Belknap had seen an advertisement respecting Dr William Gordon, the *Plain Doctor*, Hazard's good friend from Jamaica Plain; his 'library' was 'for sale. Is he going to *England* again?' – Or, as Dr Gordon pronounced it, '*GREET Brittain?* – and will he carry off all the papers he has collected towards an History of the Revolution?'[22]

War news included that while Belknap was at Portsmouth he saw four French Men-of-War in the harbour. 'One of them ... was sadly mauled in the action with [Admiral George] Rodney. They are new masting her' – naturally, for New Hampshire, hence Portsmouth, was famous for its white pine masts, long treasured by the British navy. 'This is a most excellent harbour for such business, as masts are the natural produce of the country, and there happens to be a good number ready got into the river'. Cutting down the white pine, shearing it of branches and leaves and then transporting it from inland rivers to the primary channel for navigation, the Piscataqua, was a year-round task, made easier by the churning waters of the Piscataqua, which never froze. Dry-docked at Portsmouth Harbour was the pride of the Portsmouth shipbuilding community: a '74' gun ship awaited by the notorious and glamorous Captain John Paul Jones, who stayed in Portsmouth in the meantime. 'They talk of launching her this fall;

but, if the French should purchase her, as 't is said they will, in lieu of the *Magnifique*, which they have lost in Boston harbour, the Chevalier Jones's nose will be out of joint'. Belknap was glad to hear that Congress was thinking of building a United States Navy.[23]

'What think you of peace, shall we have it or not? Are not seven years a sufficient space of time to make experiments in?' Is not the American Revolution the most dramatic recent *experiment* in government? 'Cannot a nation tell within that time whether they are likely to win or lose?' Belknap's question was mostly rhetorical considering Lord Cornwallis' surrender to Washington at Yorktown in the autumn of 1781, which by and large halted the fighting, if not the negotiations for peace. The Belknap–Hazard correspondence is strangely silent about the surrender of Cornwallis, perhaps because its significance was so obvious, not at all *newsworthy*.[24]

'You see I am in a talking mood', Belknap continued, 'and you'll indulge me in asking a few more questions. Suppose we should have peace and independence, how are we to trade to the East Indies? Are we to purchase East India commodities in Europe, or erect [trading] factories for ourselves in India? I have wondered (and ignorant folks, you know, are very apt to wonder) why we could not get East India goods across the Pacific by the way of Acapulco, and purchase them at La Vera Cruz? It would be no more than a common West India voyage to go there, and our flour and fish would come to market among the Mexican Spaniards'.[25]

Belknap left the letter open until the next day, when he wrote a short postscript informing Hazard that the affairs of Peter Thacher had been settled amiably – he was re-established on good financial terms with his parish. Speaking of religious matters, Belknap enclosed 'a pamphlet, which is intended to set in a fair light a sentiment which has of late been much abused' – Belknap referred to the belief in *universal salvation*. He wanted Hazard's opinion on the topic.[26]

The same day at Philadelphia Hazard sat down to write at length to Belknap by way of catching up. Hazard's information on the cross-bill was that it was 'neither peculiar to New Hampshire nor America, but is found in Europe'. Hazard had not heard of an English translation of Buffon from the French, but since Goldsmith is 'a passionate admirer of Buffon', he 'will be your man' – 'he seems calculated to give a man who is not professedly devoted to the study of Natural History a general, entertaining, and useful view of it'. Hazard, who was a passionate admirer of the English jurist and writer Lord Edward Coke, believed Belknap's friend Thacher would be best served by Coke's advice to *hasten calmly*. As Belknap knew, 'public affairs must always have a great influence on the situation of individuals, and they are in such a state at present as cannot continue long, but must very soon receive important alterations'. Charleston, if not yet evacuated, would be soon. 'There is the greatest reason to expect the evacuation of New York, and, I think, peace in the course of the winter'.[27]

Pennsylvania's weather over the summer of 1782 was also 'very uncommonly dry ... the prospect of a second crop of hay is entirely blasted, and the Indian corn has suffered much'. Having fully considered Belknap's 'Thoughts on the Original Population of American' Hazard now confessed that 'they strike me more forceably than they did at first; nevertheless, I think some difficulty may arise from the *Gospel never having been preached*', in Belknap's words, not only in America before 1492 but in Sweden, Norway, and Russia until many centuries after the birth of Christ. 'If this is admitted as an argument in favour of the *youth* of America, may it not be inferred, by a parity of reason, that the peopling of those parts is of an equally recent date?' – which is absurd.[28]

Hazard, forever hurried, quickly closed and sealed the letter; later he recalled not even signing it, so scribbled on the outside: 'Since sealing this, have recollected that it is unfinished'.[29]

Belknap became smitten the autumn of 1782, as authors sometimes do when confronting the reality of seeing their years of hard work aglow with print. The object of Belknap's adoration was the Philadelphia printer Robert Aitken, whom Hazard suggested as Belknap's only real choice and who wrote Belknap a convincing letter advertising his talents. So convinced was Belknap that he told Hazard in a letter of 10 September, 'I am afraid [Aitken] is too good a man to get money by printing'. His work was clearly 'excellent', and Belknap now adopted him and his work – such as his English edition of the Bible – as objects of concern and support. The illusion of goodness would not wear off and be replaced by an altogether antithetical image for many years. In the meantime, unfortunately for sales of Aitken's Bible in New England, 'Bibles are now a drug in the shops of Portsmouth'.[30]

The drought in New England continued to the detriment of the poor and hungry. Belknap wrote that his wife Ruth 'is very poorly, and has been all summer at times'. He reminded Hazard that he 'sent you last week two pamphlets' discussing universal salvation,

> one by a disciple of M—y [the Rev. John Murray], the other by I know not who, but on a much more rational, though not less benevolent plan. I apprehend this latter is designed to open the way for a larger work, by some hints which have been given me.

The hints came from Boston, where the pamphlet itself originated, inspired, Belknap would soon discover, by an old acquaintance, the Rev. Charles Chauncy.[31]

Belknap added, 'P. S. If you can conveniently, I wish you would send me a few more of the glass bubbles inclosing a drop of water, which you once sent me'.[32]

Two weeks later Belknap received Hazard's two letters of late August and early September, enclosing among other things Thomas Paine's *Crisis*. Belknap was impressed: Paine 'has, I think, done himself and his country honour, though he certainly has not told the *whole* truth about the paper money'. The 'whole truth' for Belknap, a fiscal conservative, would be to rid the country of the stuff, an important cause of the inflation for which Belknap and his family had these past seven years paid dearly. 'Pray, are you acquainted with this gentleman? Is he accessible and free in private acquaintance?' Belknap asked because of Paine's apparent interest in 'literary property', for which there were no laws in the young America protecting 'the fraternity of writers' from 'printers and booksellers' who usually 'have the whole profit'. Belknap had thoughts of writing to Paine in a show of support.[33]

Belknap thanked Hazard for his criticism of Belknap's American population theory. 'I wish to have as many objections and difficulties as possible proposed, that I may see whether my subject is insuperably embarrassed before I venture it forth'. Belknap's idea, that America was uninhabited until sometime in the first millennium, A. D., was of course untenable but for the time understandable. Europeans had long wondered whence came the Indians: were they subject to the Fall of Man? Was America the mythical Elysian Fields, Paradise, Eden, Atlantis or the Antilles? Were the Indians early Britons or perhaps even direct descendants of the Hebrew patriarchs? Remember, too, that at this time the earth was still considered, even by the most sophisticated scientists, only about six or seven thousand years old. The idea that America was settled twelve or more thousand years ago, as anthropologists claim today, would be unthinkable to the eighteenth-century mind. So Belknap continued to try to make error work as truth. Perhaps the Apostles did not go to Scandinavia because,

> they might foresee by the spirit of prophecy that the inhabitants of those regions would in a few years emigrate, and by coming into the country where Christianity had been preached would learn it, and profess it; for this was the fact when the Goths and Vandals invaded the Roman Empire.

He added, 'These are only sudden thoughts' – indeed!'[34]

Belknap, as intellectual leader 'of the little world in which I move', was the inspiration behind a new 'social' library at Dover – such libraries operated according to paid membership; they were the precursors to modern public libraries. Belknap had seen an advertisement for the published journal of Captain James Cook's voyages; he asked Hazard to find out the price and availability.[35]

Now for a 'history of my little sphere, which I dare say you will think about equal to [Jonathan] Swift's news from the hen-roost'. Belknap, constantly endeavouring to find out the truth about America's natural productions as a counter to European fantasies, would whenever possible journey inland in pursuit of knowledge. Recently he journeyed 'thirty miles into the country, and in the course of my ramble visited a place called the Flume in Salmon Fall river ... From my own observation I will describe the place for you'. The river divided Maine and New

Hampshire. 'The water was very low, owing to long and severe drought, yet the descent was so great and the stream so rapid that it was with difficulty my companions and I could hear each other speak except when we were close together'. What attracted Belknap the most was a strange phenomenon of 'water whirling small stones and wearing deep holes, some in the form of a cylinder, others of a globe. I measured five of these cavities, and their dimensions are as follow:

Diameters.		Depth.	
Feet	Inches.	Feet	Inches.
7			
3		3	
1	3	4	
1		3	
	4	1	4

In one cavity Belknap 'found a large turtle and two frogs ... These cavities the country people call *mortars*', which 'put me in mind of the mortars which are bored in the rock at the Island of Malta, from which it is said they can fire a whole shower of shot and shells on shipping that attempt to approach them'. Another part of the journal was the ascent of 'a very high mountain called *The Moose*'. Mountains, more than any other of God's works, fascinated Belknap, who with difficulty reached the summit, there to be overwhelmed by the vastness of the forest, which obscured his view of the surrounding world.[36]

The drought made 'the pastures' as 'dry as in December'. Fires blazed out of control all over the region.

> Yesterday morning the smoke was as thick as the thickest fog I ever saw ... The air is sometimes almost suffocating. I heard one thing yesterday that is remarkable. In a swamp that is on fire at Barrington [New Hampshire] there is a small hillock which the fire surrounded, and on it was a collection of toads, frogs, and snakes, who had taken refuge there, and were all croaking and hissing at once in the utmost distress.

Such was Belknap's tale: 'If I had any larger and more important matters to entertain you with, you know they would be equally at your service'.[37]

Four days later he followed up with a brief request of Hazard that, 'if you are not tired of executing my commissions', should you come upon Garcilasso de la Vega's *History of the Incas* please send it as it 'may elucidate the subject of the antiquity and population of America'.[38]

Hazard was now, at the beginning of October, several letters 'in [Belknap's] debt', so penned two epistles, one at the start and another at the end of the month. 'I am glad *you* think the Metropolitan has reason to be rapturous, for the happiness of my friends always encreases [*sic*] mine'. If one would wonder of whose happiness Hazard was speaking, he clarified it further: 'It will always give me pleasure to hear that his continues'. Hazard unlike Belknap did not like the idea of Congress building a navy; 'we ought rather to pay our debts, in which we have been extremely deficient. With us, a navy ought to be the work of peace'. '*Greet Brittain*' was so strong, and had captured so many American '*frigates*' during the war, that a US Navy would serve to increase the power of England. 'You will know before this reaches you that Congress have given the 74' gun ship, the *America*, at Portsmouth Harbour intended for the command of John Paul Jones, 'to France. A good stroke! I think we shall have peace by spring. The Spaniards would hardly approve of your plan of East India trade'.[39]

Hazard did not know when he would journey north again; not for some time. He closed the letter, 'Aitken's Bible sells well here. He can hardly bind them fast enough to supply his own shop. Can you tell how many were brought into Portsmouth? ... Am sorry to hear of Mrs. B.'s indisposition. Remember me affectionately to her ... Excuse hast. Adieu'.[40]

Hazard's second letter began,

> Dear Sir, – I am again a letter in your debt, and I am sorry to add that you have a new proof that I am not as punctual a correspondent as formerly. Indeed, I *cannot* be, for my burden of business is much encreased [*sic*]. However, this you may rely on, that you shall never be *neglected*.

Hazard would communicate Belknap's interest in 'literary property' to Thomas Paine, whom Hazard knew. He assumed that Paine's ideas on the subject would 'be perfectly *English*; *i.e.*, that laws should pass in the several States, vesting literary property in authors and their assigns for a term of years'. Hazard used a bit of Aristotelian logic to show the absurdity of Belknap's proposition regarding the age of American and the age of Scandinavia:

> A country and its inhabitants may be of great antiquity, although the Gospel was not preached in it by the Apostles. The Gospel was not preached by them in Norway, Sweden, &c., which are known to be very ancient countries. *Ergo*, America may be such too.[41]

Hazard quickly responded to other issues addressed by Belknap. John Sparhawk, who marketed James Cook's voyages, 'is not the man for your purpose. No person buys of him who can find what he wants elsewhere. He knows it, and makes people pay accordingly'. Hazard enjoyed Belknap's brief natural history and thought he would pass it on to Monsieur Marbois who could compare it with the more 'romantic' information penned by General John Sullivan. Drought continued to plague Pennsylvania, though 'we have lately had refreshing rains, and I am in hopes that cleanness of teeth', due to famine, 'will not be our lot next year'.[42]

Belknap himself could not write until November, having been to Boston, 'where I was as much hurried as Dowling the lawyer in Tom Jones'. There Belknap made a discovery: 'Ah! Sir, I have found out one of your tricks! You was fully acquainted with the writer of the Country Parson's Wife's Poetry before you sent it to me. I know the channel in which it was conveyed to you!' The channel was John Eliot, Ruth's cousin, who visited Philadelphia in April and slipped Hazard a copy of the poem, and whispered the name of the true author of the poem. Touché to Hazard!⁴³

Belknap continued: 'Our Hen has laid again. I send you one of the Eggs. We have a Constitution as often as we have an almanac and the more we have the worse'. Belknap, himself very poor, but also very conservative, did not like the reducing of 'the pecuniary qualifications of the officers of government and of the voters'. ⁴⁴

News from Portsmouth, where a French ship of '84 guns', L'Auguste, 'was struck last Thursday night with lightning'. 'Her foremast ... split and broke, two of her beams broke, part of her forecastle fell in, two guns fell through the upper deck, and the whole mass of timber, rigging, and guns killed and wounded seven or eight of her men.' Belknap added, 'It was a terrible thunderstorm, indeed, in this neighbourhood', which usually did not have such violent storms. On a happier note, 'the America, after two attempts, is launched'. Portsmouth bookshops 'are full' of Aitken's Bibles; 'I am glad to hear that Mr. Aitken has so great a demand for his edition'. 'Adieu! I am yours'.⁴⁵

During November Hazard was hurried, as usual, but had enough time to read the two pamphlets sent to him by his friend, and to form an epistolary response. One pamphlet was by a female advocate of universalism. Of this Hazard wrote,

> There is nothing in the strength of argument contained in the *Deductions* to contradict the assertion in the preface that they were made by *a female*; but, were I to judge from her manner, I should suspect that she sometimes *claims the breeches* as her right. Her performance is a strange medley. The other [an anonymous pamphlet, written by the Rev. John Clarke of Boston] I think rational; if it is antiscriptural, I am too ignorant to be able to see it.

All this coming from a Greek scholar of the New Testament! He continued, 'I think, however, it does honour to the mercy of the Deity, without injury to Divine justice. I wish for your sentiments. Pray can you tell me who are the authors of those pamphlets?'⁴⁶

A week later Hazard received Belknap's of 10 September, *in statu quo*. 'So, my dear sir, you have found out one of my tricks. How fortunate for me that it was an innocent one! Tell the Freemason [John Eliot], when you see him, that revealing secrets is contrary to the rules of the craft'. Tory newspaperman James Rivington wrote that 'the America was damaged in launching'. Was this true?⁴⁷

Belknap wrote in the first week of December,

> My Dear Sir – You are certainly the last of all my friends that I should think of charging with neglect. I beg, therefore, you would not do yourself so much injustice as

to imagine that I entertain such a suspicion. Your present business, I know, requires constant attention; and, if I had no other proof of it, your not having been able to read the two pamphlets I sent you is sufficient.

Belknap, adopting Robert Aitken as a literary *cause*, wished 'he would undertake something on the plan of the *Annual Register*' – or, in today's parlance, a *world almanac*. 'I wish it were in my power to send you any thing from this quarter' for such a publication, 'but you know what a barren region this is. A weekly paper filled with thrice-told tales, a budget of Acts of Assembly after every session, and once a year a new Constitution, are the principal productions of our press'. Even so, Belknap did his literary best – a Congressional act protecting copyright would come just in time.[48]

Hazard sent Belknap pamphlets describing Presbyterianism to which Belknap had several questions. For example, he asked why is it that

> the 'principle of holding communion with all that are deemed *good* people' is branded with the epithet 'latitudinarian', and not only enumerated among the sins of the times, but loaded with the reproach of tending 'to subvert the whole system of Divine truth, and efface the very form of the visible Church'. This, I say appears *to me* very extraordinary; and the reason is that I have, for many years, thought it my duty to hold communion with all that I can charitably hope to be 'good people', let them belong to whatever denomination of Christians.

The alternative merely engenders 'a spirit of bigotry'. Belknap knew from personal experience, having practised such bigotry and exclusiveness in his own parish for several years before the War – but of late he had given up the cause of spiritual reformation, and now worked merely for goodness and charity. Bigotry and exclusiveness, he also discovered, derive from beliefs on the selectivity of the afterlife – in this, too, Belknap's attitudes had gone through a revolution.[49]

Still considering who should print his book, Belknap took Hazard's advice and wrote to a London publisher who was acquainted with his wife's brother Samuel Eliot.

> As to publishing here, I am at a loss, unless I could meet with a printer who was *able* to advance something, and *generous* enough to share the risque with me ... To advance so great a sum as £3 or 400 is out of *my* power. I wish I had you here to talk over the matter. I know of no person more capable of advising me. Mrs. B. begs to be remembered to you; she is much better than in the summer. The Metropolitan's lady advances fast towards blessing him with a boy [he hoped]![50]

Winter had come to New Hampshire: the snow was piling up, and small rivers (such as the Cocheco, just outside Belknap's door) were freezing. 'If my letters are not so regular as they ought to be,' Belknap wrote, 'you must impute it to my distance from the office, and the difficulty of communication at this season of the year, when the rivers are impassable.'[51]

Hazard sent Belknap two quick letters in succession within a week in mid-December. He found a copy of 'Vega's Royal Commentaries of Peru' and began to read, searching for evidence to support or to contradict Belknap's American population theory. A week later when he wrote, Hazard had discovered information to confirm Belknap's supposition that the legendary founder of the Peruvian empire, Manco Capac, ruled around the same time as King Henry II of England. Since it might take four or five hundred years for a people to form such a sophisticated society, there was still a gap of at least half a millennium when the first inhabitants could have arrived to America.[52]

Hazard enclosed more newspapers, but was sick and tired of them. He complained,

> The papers of this place have become the most indecent publications of the kind I ever met with. They are now the receptacles of obscenity and filth, the vehicles of scandal, and the instruments of the most infamous abuse ... If any character, public or private, however respectable, may not with impunity be attacked with the most indecent virulence, then the liberty of the press is in danger

At least such were the claims of newspaper editors. 'Our printers, with their present license, appear to me the most dangerous set of men amongst us' – Aitken excluded.[53]

Belknap's very long epistle of 19 December was the last that passed between the two friends in 1782. In it, he contradicted Rivington's assertion that 'the America was hurt in launching'. Belknap knew better, having been present during the first attempted launching from an island in Portsmouth Harbor.

> The reason of her not going off was, in the carpenter's phrase, that she was too *strait-laced* (as you are a bachelor, you'll doubtless understand *that*). They had taken so much care to keep her from falling, that she could not move but about twelve feet.

The second attempt, a few days later (when Belknap was in Boston – but he heard about it later), 'she went off as easily and gently as a canoe'.[54]

In other matters, 'the Freemason, John Eliot, is not to be blamed for revealing secrets. Your friend, the *Plain* Doctor', Dr William Gordon of Jamaica *Plain*, 'was the person from whom I had the information; and, by his own confession, he was the *primum mobile* of the whole *trick*', having convinced Eliot to carry the poem to Philadelphia, present it to Hazard, and hide from him the author's name.[55]

The Philadelphia newspapers *were* indecent!, Belknap exclaimed. 'Pray who are the "Skunk Association" and the "Priest of Cloacina"?' He also read about one 'Major Philip *Pancake*', and assumed it a joke until he realized it was the Major's actual name:

> The theory of English sirnames would be a curious object, and a proper appendix to the noble science of heraldry. I once began a collection of odd names, and ranged them under different heads, but other matters of more importance diverted me from pursuing the subject.[56]

General Charles Lee was dead, and Belknap wanted to know the 'circumstances' – 'can you pick up any anecdotes of his life worthy of being preserved? I know he was an odd character, and a remarkable one, and he must be noticed in the Biographia Americana', for which, Belknap's protests notwithstanding, he was actively engaged in collecting information.[57]

Now for the main thrust of Belknap's letter. Belknap wished to discuss the arguments of the two pamphlets on universal salvation that he (and Hazard) had read. Both were by New England theologians, who added their ideas into a pot simmering and overflowing with nonsense, mysticism and speculation – everything but scriptural authority. Clearly, 'the doctrine of universal restitution has long been kept as a secret among learned men'. The problem was that too many advocates of the idea denied 'any future state of punishment, and from thence take occasion to "continue in sin that grace may abound"', which was untenable. The best argument was that of Dr Charles Chauncy of Boston, 'who has had for some years prepared for the press a very laboured, judicious, and strongly argumentative, as well as deeply critical, treatise upon the subject', of which the pamphlet by John Clarke was a taste. But it had led to arguments and counter-arguments. Belknap wrote,

> All this I am sorry for: it does no good; it is only the skirmishing of light infantry, while the main body lies still, and nothing decisive will come of it. The passions of the contending parties will be embittered, and I am afraid that such prejudices will be raised against the doctrine that, if it should be properly published, it will not be so generally received.[58]

All of this bothered Belknap exceedingly, who was a convert: 'I frankly own to you that I have for several years been growing in my acquaintance with it and my regard to' the idea of universal salvation. Since 1780, at least, Belknap had repeatedly discussed the idea with John Eliot. He grew so fond of it that he forgot himself, temporarily, in a sermon before the New Hampshire Association of Ministers, who had to admonish him for heretical statements. War and ubiquitous suffering and death compelled the minister to wish 'it might be true, long before I saw any just reason to conclude it was so'. Inheriting the Calvinist idea of the elect, Belknap could only break from tradition through compelling evidence, which he found by a re-examination of what the apostle Paul wrote on the topic. Paul wrote that 'I have *hope* towards God that there shall be a resurrection of the dead, both just and *unjust*'. The implication was that even sinners will be saved. Confused, Belknap 'applied to one of the most celebrated divines in this eastern world, Mr. [Moses] Hemmenway of Wells, for a solution of the difficulty. He exhausted his ingenuity and learning for my satisfaction, but in vain'. When Charles Chauncy invited Belknap, on a visit to Boston in 1780, to examine his manuscript, Belknap found an argument and a writer 'which afforded me more satisfaction than any thing I had before seen'. Belknap liked the concept so well that he was long overdue in returning the manuscript to its owner, notwithstanding Chauncy's impatient calls for its return. Belknap tried to keep an open mind, 'but at present I do not see how the doctrine can be disproved, if the scripture be allowed to speak for itself'.

> I wish you was here at my elbow, instead of three or four hundred miles off: I would then talk with you till midnight upon the subject. Corresponding at this distance is a dull way of communicating ideas, especially when they flow so fast as mine do upon this darling theme ... In the mean time, rest assured that my attachment to you is increased by an apprehension which your last letter suggests, that you are a friend to the above doctrine.

But 'what will your high Presbyterian clergy say to it? If holding communion with all *good* people is reprobated by them, what would they say to a doctrine which sets mankind on such a level?' In ending the letter, Belknap added Ruth Belknap's regards: 'I may add that she is as well pleased as I am with finding you in favour of a certain doctrine!'[59]

8 KEEPING THE BELLY AND BACK FROM GRUMBLING, AND THE KITCHEN-FIRE FROM GOING OUT

Dear Sir, – This is the coldest day we have yet had, and, as I have no disposition to stir abroad, I shall devote part of it to you; though, as you tell me sometimes, I am not a letter in debt, excepting indeed the short script in which you told me you had found the Commentaries of De la Vega.[1]

The world outside seemed motionless, without life. The Cocheco was hard frozen; feet of snow covered the ground. Conifers drooped from the weight of the snow. Sunlight, such as it was, appeared perfunctory. Indoors, however, the crackling warmth of the fireplace bespoke life and movement, keeping time with the pen conjuring up ideas and images of time and place. Belknap, lonely for the companionship of a fellow 'son of science', spent the afternoon as best he could.

'We hear a talk of peace: doubtless you know more about it, for the news is said to come from your quarter'. Even in the depth of winter rumour and report went forth unimpeded. Belknap knew only of local, rather than national or international, political affairs. He found it simultaneously frustrating and entertaining that the New Hampshire legislature imposed a 'test oath', requiring conformity to Protestantism, upon office-holders; he viewed it 'as a species of persecution for conscience' sake'. His friend *Democritus* (Isaac Mansfield), asked to support the new law, responded that 'he would, if they would let him put a title to it, and that should be, "An Act to encourage Perjury and Profaneness"'. Belknap found it delightful that the constitutional convention should reject the oath at the same time that the legislature sought (unsuccessfully) to pass it. 'Don't you think we are in a curious situation, with two supreme dictatorial bodies subsisting, and independent of each other?' Less entertaining and more worrisome was that, according to rumour, the British offered Vermont's Governor Thomas Chittenden a commission as *Royal* Governor of Vermont. 'Thus what has long been suspect is reduced to a certainty', Belknap erroneously concluded.[2]

Just to show his friend that no, Belknap was not associating freedom of conscience with *acceptance* of the Society of Friends or Roman Catholicism, Belknap included the tale of 'a young gentleman who is lately returned from the Havanna', Cuba, where 'he became acquainted with a Spanish priest', who condescended to allow the young man to peer at a generally restricted portrait of the Virgin Mary. 'You may judge of his feelings when, on drawing up the veil, a *black* face appeared, shewing a set of fine *white* teeth'. In reply to the young man's astonishment, 'the priest very seriously told him that the negroes were the best friends the Church had in that part of the world now'. 'Upon the whole', Belknap concluded, 'it appeared that this smutty business is an instance of priestcraft, which knows how to accommodate itself to its interest in every shape and colour'.[3]

Belknap did not have a chance to mail the letter for another week, during which time he received an epistle from Hazard, which discussed evidence in support of Belknap's population theory; Belknap asked Hazard's opinion whether or not he advised prefacing his *History of New-Hampshire* with a theoretical discussion of the origin of population in America. 'Would it add a *decus* or a *dedecus* to it', that is, honour or disgrace?'[4]

Since he was on the topic of his history, Belknap had received a proposal from a Boston printer to publish the *History* in serial form. He wrote to his friend, 'I wish I had you here to talk about it'. Belknap listed a series of questions: How much would a typical four hundred page book cost the consumer? What percent of the revenue should the author request from the printer? Under what terms would Philadelphia printer Robert Aitken publish the book? What about printing one in Boston and one in Philadelphia? 'My dear sir, I know your friendship will excuse the trouble I give you. I am sure I would do you any service that is in my power, and I judge of your heart by my own'.[5]

Belknap agreed with Hazard about the worthlessness of some newspapers; but some provide 'European intelligence' and others 'a political piece which has some merit'. The proposed impost (tax on trade) to provide a revenue for the current Confederation government interested Belknap, and he was hungry to read as much as he could about it. 'Indeed, I am willing even to scrape a dunghill, if I may find a jewel at the bottom'. Belknap passed all the newspapers Hazard sent to 'a worthy friend and neighbour, now in the decline of life, who was once an active politician, and who yet retains so much judgment as to tell me, almost every time I converse with him, that Congress "have not power enough allowed them by the Confederation to preserve the Union, and make it respectable"'.[6]

Belknap ended his letter but not without an odd postscript reminding the Postmaster 'to seal the letter which you put into a bundle, for sometimes the outside cover is torn or opened when I receive it'.[7]

Hazard was indebted to Belknap many times over when he at last took time to respond to his friend during two days in mid-January. One matter that greatly concerned him was that his friend Belknap should have a negative – not to mention erroneous – impression about Hazard's fellow Presbyterians. In one of

Belknap's December letters he had castigated the apparent narrow mindedness of Presbyterians, assuming that their structure and governance necessarily produced rigidity in thinking. Hazard tried to explain that 'there are *several kinds* of Presbyterians, who all agree in the *mode of church government*, though they differ in some of their *tenets*'. Presbyterians in Scotland and America differ greatly as well. In America 'there are ... two parties among them, the *Old side* (or Old Light) and the *New*. The Old admit all to communion with them whom they can charitably suppose to be good men'. Belknap, a so-called Old Light Protestant himself, could identify with them. 'The *New* expect some account of the religious experiences of the candidates for admission. However, both unite in one Synod'. Hazard wrote that he hoped this account would, he joked, 'at least afford you New Light' on the subject. He added that 'a spirit of moderation and catholicism has been amazingly diffused of late; but there is too much bigotry and intolerance amongst Christians yet'.[8]

Hazard, in a wonderful act of friendship, had talked extensively with Robert Aitken, who agreed to share the risk of printing Belknap's manuscript, as long as 'the work would sell. I gave it as my opinion that it would'. Hazard offered to 'correct the press' should Belknap select Aitken as the printer. To 'correct the press' was Hazard's laconic statement for what would be a tremendous amount of labour for a mere 'interested friend'. It would involve checking the handwritten manuscript for errors, helping the printer make decisions regarding unclear passages, deciding upon stylistic matters such as the format of the title page, reading chapter by chapter as it came off the press and suggesting amendments, and generally overseeing the creation of the finished project.[9]

'It is now 8 o'clock at night; and, as I have not been out of the house since last night (nor even had my shoes on), I must go and take some exercise'. Hazard promised to write the next day, 19 January, which he did. Hazard wondered whether or not 'the *Plain* gentleman', Dr Gordon, laughed 'heartily when he told you the story' about his 'clever' '*trick*' to conceal the identity of the author of the 'Parson's Wife' poem. Belknap had asked who was the 'Skunk Association and the priest of Cloacina?' – names used in Philadelphia newspapers. Hazard tried to explain the best he could the reflection in newspaper essays and performances on stage of the petty politics involving Loyalists and Patriots in Pennsylvania, New Jersey and New York. Much of it degenerated into 'smutty, filthy' works. The complete antithesis of which, and a work of the utmost sublimity, was 'the doctrine you mention' – universal salvation. 'I confess I am not unfriendly to it', Hazard wrote,

> because reason certainly approves of it, and I do not think that Revelation contradicts it. The other hypothesis (an eternity of punishment) is utterly subversive of every idea of *mercy* in the Deity, and degrades his *justice* into revengeful cruelty. Are these the thoughts we ought to have of God? By no means. He surely could not punish thus without *delighting* in the death of sinners. However, although I believe the doctrine of

> general restitution, I would wish to see all men live as if the other were true; and, after all, it is of little moment what *our* sentiments may be. The councel of God will stand,

Hazard pronounced, echoing *Ecclesiastes*, 'and our duty is to *fear* Him, and keep his commandments'.[10]

Hazard enclosed for his friend newspapers and a play about 'an old maid, who has been soured by disappointment', which he assumed 'Mrs. B's confidence in you will lead her to excuse my sending you', 'especially as such an one cannot be remarkably tempting'. The newspapers described the British 'evacuation of Charlestown', South Carolina, 'which is now certified by Charles Thomson', with whom Hazard would one day collaborate in producing an English edition of the New Testament – Thomson was currently the Secretary to the Congress of the Confederation.[11]

Ten days later Hazard 'hastily scrawled' an additional note, with enclosed the comments of his friend Dr Geraldus Clarkson, a Philadelphia physician to whom Hazard cryptically referred as 'the father of my Telemachus' – in other words Belknap and Hazard would subsequently call him *Ulysses*. Hazard had told Clarkson about Belknap's ideas on universal salvation, which yielded an 'affectionate', sympathetic response from the doctor. Clarkson also discussed the death of General Charles Lee, the infamous court-martialled Major General, alone in a tavern. Hazard wrote,

> He lies buried in Christ's Church yard. No stone marks his bed. Indeed, those who saw his open grave can scarcely mark the site, as it is continually trodden by persons going into and coming out of the church. Behold the honour of the great![12]

Belknap himself hurriedly responded to Hazard's of 1 January (since lost), noting that the letter 'has relieved my mind of an anxiety respecting a letter I wrote in December' – a letter detailing Belknap's beliefs in universal salvation, a doctrine sufficiently despised among Protestants to demand caution – 'which I was afraid had miscarried'.[13]

On 12 February, Hazard took 'a *large* half-sheet' of paper 'more for the sake of enclosing the papers than because I have time or materials for a long letter; and, indeed, was not yours of the 8th ult. of such a nature as to require an immediate answer, I should postpone it 'til next post'. Hazard enclosed a literary piece from his clerk, *Telemachus* (Philip Freneau). He guessed that peace would come 'before spring'; then 'the quiet of the world will be undisturbed'. And more to the point, prices would fall. Hence it was best for Belknap to wait until the war's end to print his *History of New-Hampshire*, to avoid paying 'the *war* price for every thing'. Hazard responded to Belknap's questions about the costs and manner of printing. 'Binding, if well done ... will amount to near, if not double, the [cost of] paper and print'. The standard 'octavo is a good size' of page, but if the

'English letter' were used, it 'will make it too thick a volume. For this reason, were there no other, I would reject the *English* [14 point] letter; but it will make the work *look heavy*, and, if you will consult the ladies, they will tell you of how much importance a *good appearance* is'. 'The most expensive part of printing is the *composing*, or setting the types, the cost of which will be as much for one sheet as for ten thousand printed from the same types'. Hence Belknap must agree with the printer to a limited number of copies – say, one thousand; otherwise the printer could produce copies ad infinitum, and undersell the author.[14]

'Now, my dear sir, let me tell you that I am anxious for your reputation, which will be connected with the *appearance* as well as the *contents* of the History'. Hazard did not like the work of New England printers, having never seen 'a book printed there which was well done'. Hence the following 'offer': should Belknap send his manuscript to Philadelphia:

> I will undertake to get it printed, and will correct the press. You shall have the whole profits of the sales, without being charged any commissions for my trouble, or interest for my money. I shall expect that the expences of paper, printing, and stitching will be repaid out of the earliest sales; and that, I may take the liberty of making the edition elegant.[15]

However, 'I have been so engaged about the History that I have trespassed upon the time allotted to other business, and must abruptly bid you adieu. Eben. Hazard'.[16]

'My dear Sir', Belknap wrote in mid-February,

> Your favours of the 17th and 29th ult. are arrived with the enclosed papers and books, for which I beg you to accept my thanks and those of my children. Your very kind attention to me and my concerns keeps a constant stream of gratitude and respect flowing from my heart.

Hazard's delineation of Aitken's 'moral character' and his outstanding 'workmanship' as well as Hazard's offer to correct 'the press' almost ensured Belknap's choice to print in Philadelphia. The next step was to print 'subscription papers' and to 'circulate them through this and the neighbouring State' of Massachusetts; Hazard could distribute them in the Middle States. This was the only sure way to determine the prospective sales and the number, therefore, to print.[17]

The debate was bubbling up over universalism throughout New England. The Reverend Joseph Eckley had written a pamphlet defending the 'Divine Glory displayed in the Condemnation', to which an adequate response from the other side, in favour of universal salvation, was not yet forthcoming. Dr Charles Chauncy's manuscript could not be printed until it was sent to England, as no 'Greek types' are 'to be had in the country'. 'The *Plain* gentleman [Dr Gordon] I hear is about writing in the controversy'. One object of controversy centred on the word *eternal*: one side could fathom an eternal punishment; the other side thought it was limited in duration. Belknap thought it was everlasting *in time*; the agent of such punishment was fire, which 'was kindled at the creation, and is now subsisting within the globe, frequent ebullitions of it being seen in volcanoes'. Said fire 'will produce an universal conflagration' during which time the ungodly will be severely punished in another life from which they will die again, this time in purity to eternal salvation. Some contemporary scholars thought the description of eternal fire, like the description of the flood, metaphorical – but Belknap thought such descriptions were literally true because scientific evidence supported their existence. Descriptions of Mt Etna and Mt Vesuvius sounded very much like the description of God's cleansing fire in the Bible. Good people, the 'Saints', would be preserved from the raging fire of the end of time. Belknap asked, 'Is there any thing unnatural, unphilosophical in this interpretation? Is not the globe the proper habitation of man? Was it not, at first, a Paradise?' 'And is it not capable of reverting to its ancient primitive, paradisaic state, and then to be an "habitation of righteousness"?' How? By means of 'material agents, already in being under the direction of the great Author, the moral purpose of which is to advance his glory and the full establishment of his Son's kingdom'. Taking his cue from traditional theology, Belknap distinguished the Earthly from the Heavenly City.

> Temporal kingdoms are set up ... by way of experiment; but, as they do not answer the moral ends of government, but degenerate into tyranny, cruelty, &c., they are destroyed and come to nought. But the kingdom of Christ will answer these ends, will overcome all evil and advance all good in a moral sense, therefore it will end in a different manner, *i.e.* will end in complete perfection; for, when 'all enemies are subdued', the object will be attained, and universal rectitude, peace, and happiness be the final result.

Belknap confessed these were 'some of my present thoughts' and asked for Hazard's opinion – and disagreements if he had any.[18]

Upon additional consideration of the matter, Belknap added that besides the fire of volcanoes to punish the sinful there exists 'the electric fluid, which is known to be a most powerful as well as universal principle of dissolution to terrestrial bodies'. The Second Letter of Peter in the New Testament describes 'the day of the Lord', Christ's return, as being accompanied by 'a loud noise'. Is this not the product of 'the electric fluid'?[19]

Assuming that human selfishness overwhelms all customs and institutions, even religion, Belknap concluded:

> Notwithstanding what the opposers of restitution say, I think the most rational conclusion of all is in favor of practical religion. 'What manner of persons ought we to be?' is the argument which Peter draws from it. Surely no one who considers the

dreadful nature, the unknown degree and duration of the punishment of the future state, with its horrid end, the second death, the terror of which will as much exceed that of the first, as the guilt of rejecting the Gospel exceeds the guilt of Adam's eating of the forbidden fruit, – no one, I say, can reconcile himself to the thought of passing through it (for the sake of a little paltry gratification here), even though there be a prospect of his rising, when the 'last enemy is destroyed', to a state of happiness![20]

Peace was certain and close at hand – such was Hazard's take on the current situation. His evidence was anecdotal, reports from peace negotiations across the Atlantic, and circumstantial, the gathering of former New Yorkers – like that of the 'dispersed of Israel' – to return to their city upon evacuation by the enemy.[21]

Two weeks later in early March Hazard wrote again, telling Belknap of his disinterest in his own ancestry and his viewing of a circumcision: 'I have thought so little about my ancestors that I cannot tell of what country my grandfather was a native, and I am very uncertain about the birthplace of even my father' – whom Hazard lost when he was but thirteen years old.

> I never thought it worth while to attempt to particularize all the links in the chain from Adam to me (many of which would probably be found to have been very *rusty*), any more than to prove an 'uninterrupted succession' in the Church, from the Apostles to the present day; because, however great the merits of my ancestors may have been, it could have little effect as to me, except in attracting attention to my conduct, which might prove a disadvantage or otherwise, according to circumstances.

As for his own descendants, Hazard joked with Belknap that notwithstanding his intentions he would probably die *'conjugii nescius'*; that he might be a bachelor for life was given slight support by his attending a 'circumcision' for the first time: '*Curiosity* occasioned it, but I think *Humanity* will prevent my ever seeing a second exhibition of the same kind'. The ceremony was Jewish, performed upon an eight-day-old infant. 'The Apostle's declaration, that 'the *law* was *given* by Moses, but *grace* and truth *came* by Jesus Christ', never struck me so forcibly before', Hazard wrote, implying that circumcision reflected Jewish inflexibility and impiety. 'If it had not been for the singing, which drowned the cries of the child ... I should have thought of little more than a company of farmers assembled for the purpose of marking hogs'.[22]

Belknap's letter of 17 March, besides a subtle prayer for peace from the negotiations in Paris, was largely a gracious acceptance of Hazard's offer to oversee the printing of Belknap's book in Philadelphia: 'Yes, my dear sir, you shall be paid out of the earliest sales, and sooner, if I can procure the money, or any part of it, by the assistance of other friends'. Belknap enclosed a sample subscription form for Hazard's consideration and comments. 'I suppose three months will be long enough to collect subscriptions, or, at least, to see whether enough will be wanted to make it worth while to begin to print'. Meanwhile Belknap would prepare the final copy of the work and distribute subscription papers to his close friends and relatives, who would do their best to drum up business and subscription money to pay (partially) the cost of printing. Belknap liked a work by Hazard's clerk, Philip Freneau – *Telemachus* – that Hazard sent him. Of Freneau Belknap added, 'He has a good practical genius ... but there is one thing which, perhaps, it would be a kindness to mention to him. I think he plays rather too freely with Scripture in some of his allusions and comparisons'.

Belknap hoped to see Hazard in New Hampshire again, suggesting that the Postmaster General leave his assistant James Bryson in charge so that the former could engage in 'a Northern excursion' for the sake of, among other things, his health. Belknap added, by postscript: 'Mrs. B. wishes to see you, and tell you how much she respects you'.[23]

Hazard, writing with the onset of spring at the end of March, added little to his offer of assistance with the *History* except to add: 'It will always add to my happiness if I can contribute to yours, for I know no person for whom I entertain a more sincere friendship'. Hazard, contemplating religion of late more than history (or even, perhaps, postal business), agreed with Belknap's sentiments respecting the ultimate restitution, or salvation, of *all* sinners with God. Hazard found a passage from 1 Timothy 4:10 that clearly spoke of salvation in terms of inclusion rather than exclusion. Even so, he believed that this was the Apostle Paul's *opinion*, as expressed to Timothy, that all men will be saved. One cannot assume that Paul's opinion and the literal truth of '*the Lord*' are the same. Paul's epistles, though divinely inspired, may still be less than absolute truth. Hence debate over specific passages of Scripture must be balanced by common sense and piety. 'But I find I am commencing a critic, instead of a friendly correspondent'.[24]

Moving from religion to politics, Hazard mentioned a pamphlet that condemned the states for withholding 'their quotas of supplies' for the Continental Army during the war, and lamented the weakness of Congress to do anything about it. Controversy was now turning from international to domestic squabbling. The war was over: 'The *official* account has not arrived, but there can be no doubt of the *fact* ... The humiliation of Great Britain is evident, and the generosity and magnanimity of France equally conspicuous'.[25]

On the last day of March, Belknap wrote to Hazard concerned about the prospects of republicanism, at least in New Hampshire. 'The inattention of the people' of Dover during a town assembly to discuss the 'very important matter' of the state constitution was 'so great that I thought it my duty yesterday to preach from those words, Judges 19, 30: *Consider of it, take advice, and speak your minds*'.[26]

Of most importance to Belknap were the works of the Creator. Few advantages came from living on the New Hampshire frontier, and Belknap did his share of complaining about the rusticity of his situation. But standing before the wonders of God, he was a dutiful child again, silent until spoken to – in New Hampshire, there was much to hear. In particular, Belknap enjoyed observing the aurora borealis, which is not very frequent to New Hampshire observers, but is sometimes there to witness. Belknap had such a chance one Saturday evening towards the end of March. The day was mild, for a March in New England: some rain in the afternoon, accompanied by a rainbow. 'About 10 o'clock the hemisphere was all in a glow; the vapor ascended from all points, and met in a central one at the zenith'. There was a light wind. In the silence of the evening Belknap could distinguish a sound, 'like the brushing of silk'. Once he had assumed that the theory of a sound accompanying the aurora borealis was the product of 'credulous' and uninformed minds. But on several occasions, including this one, Belknap distinctly heard it. Still thinking about the *end time*, Belknap wondered whether or not the aurora borealis was 'among the number of those instruments which the Creator has prepared to bring the heavens and earth into' a 'volcanic state'.[27]

Hazard wrote in early April, when spring was in the air – and so, too, was peace. Hazard knew only of the 'preliminaries between France, Spain, [and] England'; rumour had it that the official 'peace has been proclaimed in New York'. Hazard promised to handle printing the subscription papers for Belknap; he hoped to twist Aitken's arm to do them without cost. 'I fear Bryson [Hazard's assistant] will not return before June; but, if he should, other engagements will prevent my visiting New England soon. Should I live, this will probably be a busy year with me'. 'Our *Plain* friend [Dr Gordon] has sent me one of his pamphlets against universal salvation, but I have not yet had time to read it'. Hazard allotted himself 'but a few minutes' for the letter, so quickly closed.[28]

Later that afternoon, at '5 o'clock, p.m.', Hazard scribbled a quick note to Belknap: 'The King of England's Proclamation, announcing peace between England, France, Spain, the United Provinces, and the United States of North America, and that hostilities were to cease in America the 3rd inst., has just been read at the Coffee House'.[29]

When Belknap wrote to Hazard in mid-April from Portsmouth, his mind was not on peace and victory but on the fate of the victims of war. He agreed with Hazard that one must deal carefully with New Testament passages that do not directly come from Christ. The passage from Paul's Letter to Timothy that Hazard mentioned was discussed at large in Dr Charles Chauncy's book, still unpublished, but which Belknap had read in manuscript form. Chauncy referred to the theory of universal salvation as 'the *Pudding*' – and so, henceforth, would Belknap and Hazard. Belknap had not yet seen Dr Gordon's attack on the pudding; he hoped proponents and opponents alike would calmly wait in expectation of Dr Chauncy's profound study of the problem.[30]

Ruth Belknap, who had recently been ill, was 'better than when I wrote before, and I apprehend her cough will go off like that of the children, which is abated'. A close call, no doubt – many times, as Belknap well knew, such throat distempers yielded death in great numbers. Speaking of sorrow, Belknap lamented the death in childbirth of the firstborn of the Metropolitan, Reverend Buckminster, and his wife. Hazard's former amour Eliza 'was ill a long time'. Belknap wrote the letter from their house, and reported it to Hazard as it was told him. Amid sickness, death, and peace Belknap was busy copying 'the first chapter of my history'; 'the rest will be as soon as I can get time, and it shall be sent whenever or in what proportion you shall think best'.[31]

Belknap wrote again ten days later, in part to laud 'that illustrious chief whom Providence has raised up and supported to add a peculiar dignity to the noble struggle in which America has been obliged to engage in support of her rights and liberties' – George Washington. Belknap thought him as good as the great Roman heroes of ages past, such as Cincinnatus, Fabius and Scipio. Washington had the same '*heroic virtue*'.

> What a contrast to Cromwell, who, placed in the same circumstances, made use of his vast ascendency over the army to overturn the constitution which they had taken up arms to preserve! How happy to be born and live in an age which has produced so excellent a man![32]

After this brief paean, Belknap went on to his three favourite subjects: religion, history and politics. Natural history, was another, of course, but Belknap often considered it as a subset of the first, religion, as this letter revealed. Belknap had by now seen 'the Plain Doctor's piece' attacking universal salvation, which he found was well argued and much better than his historical writing. Of this Belknap wrote,

> But, in my humble opinion, the point is not to be settled by criticism. It requires a large, generous, candid examination of those 2 great works of the same author, the Book of Nature and the Book of Revelation. They are the best comments on each other, and must not be studied separately.

The benevolence of God that Belknap thought he detected from reading scripture he found absolutely confirmed when examining the Creator's work, writ large and wonderfully in America.[33]

The Creator's canvas included, of course, human affairs; the mark of God upon which Belknap could clearly detect when studying the past years of conflict. He compared the Tories to 'true sons of Cain', condemned to 'wander forlorn, exposed to the hatred and contempt of mankind'. And England herself was, as Scripture teaches, 'one of the broken toes of Nebuchadnezzar's image' – as Daniel of the Old Testament described it, 'an incoherent mixture of iron and clay'.

> I assure you the thought of this has been for several years a great support to my mind, and even in the height of our distresses, in the spring of 1777, I ventured a sermon on

the subject, which was intended to comfort the sorrowful and confirm the doubting. I was then persuaded that, however the war should end, we, once disunited, should never be again restored to our connexion with her.[34]

Belknap was less confident about his thoughts on the 'population of America', and decided it was best not to include them in his *History*, or in any other way publish them at this time. He did not think his ideas altogether original, and had discovered that there was great controversy surrounding the question of the origins of the Indians – a 'figure' in said controversy he had no desire to be. Belknap was busy, nevertheless, transcribing his *History* for the press. As the business proceeded, he added,

> I must beg the favor of you to let me know the exact amount of every article of expence as it arises, and if you think it proper to have any formal obligation from me, please to dictate the form, and it shall be executed immediately.[35]

A titbit from 'the treaty with Spain' amused Belknap: 'to see the et ceteras annexed to the Count D'Aranda's name'. Belknap 'could not but recollect an anecdote' about

> one of those Castilian grandees who, being benighted on a journey, called late at a French inn for a lodging. The host enquired who was there, upon which he began to tell over his names and titles, but before he had done the Frenchman shut his window, telling him that he had not room enough in his house to accommodate *so many* gentlemen.

Belknap asked Hazard 'how long do you intend to remain "*conjugii nescius*", and signed himself 'unfeignedly and largely yours'.[36]

Hazard responded on the last day of April to Belknap's, 'favors of 31st ult. and 15th inst'. He expressed thanks for Belknap's 'remarks upon the Aurora Borealis, and shall take the liberty of communicating them to the American Philosophical Society', of which Hazard was a member, 'at the next meeting'. He added, 'I never observed or heard of the *sound* you mention'. Tired of the unending 'controversy' regarding universal versus particular salvation, Hazard wondered who could be the winner of such a contest. 'If it would not be derogating from their Apostolical dignity, I would say that they remind me of dogs which I have sometimes seen worrying each other almost to death for a *picked bone*, which the victor found *non opera pretium*', worthless.

Hazard was 'glad to hear that Mrs. B. is better', but felt sorry for the Metropolitan Buckminster: 'Poor fellow! he has soon had reason to hang his harp upon the willows'. 'Did the Metropolitan ever tell you of some curious letters I wrote him? Don't ask him about them'.[37]

Belknap wrote Hazard the same day from Dover to report that he had already sent chapter one of his manuscript. He hoped Hazard could 'contrive it so that the subscription papers may be at Boston by the day of their annual election, viz., 28th May, which will afford a good opportunity to distribute them'. During the following week the New Hampshire 'General Court and Convention will sit' – a perfect time for their distribution to gentlemen taking subscriptions for the book. Belknap had already been at Portsmouth when they celebrated the peace; Dover was planning one on 1 May. 'So the *feu de joie*', the bonfire of liberty, 'runs through the country'. Contrasting the joy of liberty was George III, 'the connecting link between the glory and disgrace of Brittain [*sic*]'. Belknap once, twenty years before, respected, even lauded the King at the beginning of his reign. But time had intervened. He now wrote,

> Intoxicated with former successes, he has ventured an experiment which none of his predecessors dared to make; and, after throwing away thousands of lives and millions of treasure, he has lost the brightest jewel from his crown.[38]

Hazard, doubly hurried, spun off two letters in two weeks, neither one more than a brief paragraph. The one of 7 May was a brief note to Belknap stipulating that 'Congress have resolved to recommend it to the several States to pass laws for the security of literary property'. A week later he acknowledged 'the receipt of [Belknap's] favour of 25th ult. with No. 1 of your MS'; but his clerk 'being sick' he was unable to write at large.[39]

Belknap, inspired by a reading of Thomas Paine's *Crisis*, wrote on 19 May to discuss politics. It troubled Belknap that Americans could not quite agree upon, nor understand, the meaning of *sovereignty*. The notion of a divided sovereignty of thirteen independent powers (states) loosely united by a weak Congress – the essence of the Confederation – was absurd. 'I remember, in the beginning of the controversy, we were put in mind of the necessity of union, by the figure . . . of a serpent cut into twelve or thirteen pieces, and the motto was, "By uniting we stand, by dividing we fall"'. Belknap considered the Confederation a division. A better analogy, 'because it is of an higher origin', is that from the Book of Daniel:

> the iron and clay of Nebuchadnezzar's image is in some degree the composition of our unwieldy republic; and, if there be not something more done to perfect our constitution, we 'shall not cleave one to another, even as iron is not mixed with clay'. We have a congress who have the sole power of the sword, but cannot command a shilling out of the purse of any man in America.

Belknap also disliked the lack of a common treasury and of a common economic and trade programme. He wrote, 'I could pursue these thoughts further, but I have said so much already that I am afraid you will think I have got a fit of the hypochondria. So I'll leap from the political into the natural world'. At least in the 'natural world' one can find order rather than chaos, stability rather than change. All is sameness according to an everlasting decree.[40]

Belknap saw 'another vivid aurora; the evening serene, with only a gentle zephyr from the S. W., but no flaws'. Amid the silence he heard 'the *sound*', notwithstanding the gentle hum of a 'distant waterfall' and the 'croaking of frogs'.

> I heard distinctly the sound of the flash. It was not a continued noise, but seemed like the ascent of a distant rocket, which, you know, begins with a degree of fierceness, and which grows fainter the higher it rises, till it gets beyond our hearing. I do not know whether this comparison be not worth pursuing, but I am not philosopher enough to dare it.

It worried Belknap that Hazard intended to communicate 'it to the American [Philosophical] Society', for it 'cannot be corroborated without a peculiarly favorable concurrence of circumstances'. Besides, 'I am not ambitious of being noticed as the author or communicator of discoveries, the truth of which will depend on my observation alone'. Should Hazard proceed with his intention, Belknap asked him:

> do it with caution, and with an introductory apology, – so as that I may not be exposed to ridicule; for when I first heard the thing mentioned, I own I laughed at it, and I suppose, according to the law of retaliation, I shall be laughed at in my turn by some no wiser than myself.[41]

For fun, Belknap enclosed a seventeenth-century '*Witch Law*', which included an assumption of 'the *feeding* of evil spirits' by 'supernatural *teats*' on the bodies of witches, by 'which they *suckled* the young devils' – 'some women were searched to find them'. 'A flea bite would be sufficient to convict them. What surprizing power has nonsense over the minds of men, not only individuals, but collective, legislative, and judicial bodies!'[42]

Regarding Hazard's allusion to the *Metropolitan*, he answered: 'The Metropolitan never gave me any account of the letters you mention; but you said something about them, and I should be glad to know what they are, but am not eager to pry'.[43]

At the end of May Hazard responded to Belknap's letter of the end of April, indicating the receipt of his chapter. The printing of the subscription papers 'Mr. Aitken makes you a compliment of, and he defies America to produce better'. The paper used was expensive, but they hoped to get cheaper paper 'at 20s. *Pennsylvania* [currency] per ream' for the printing of the book. Hazard agreed that Belknap's '*Conjectures*' about the population of America would work best as a magazine essay rather than as the preface to his book. There was some talk of a '*literary* paper' to be 'set up' in Philadelphia, which would make a good outlet for Belknap's ideas. 'Indeed', Hazard agreed, 'the poor Tories are in a dreadful plight. They deserve it'.[44]

Hazard's life was '*marvellously* hurried' – he joked, 'O for a sight of Bryson!' (his assistant); and he would soon be even more hurried. 'Not long', was his response to Belknap's question about the length of his bachelorhood.

> I have fixed upon a partner and *preliminaries* are settled; but no time is yet fixed for signing the *definitive treaty*. Some time since I bought a small lot in a delightful part of the city, and the workmen are now busy in erecting a back-building, which is intended for a kitchen and wash-house. Should I live til next year, *and be able*, I intend to build a decent, snug dwelling-house; and, if you and Mrs. B. will pay me a visit, I will shew you both the house and its mistress. In the mean time, I expect to live in my own hired house, as St. Paul did, to which you will be equally welcome.

And like St Paul, Hazard answered Christ's call to spread the Gospel and to promote the Kingdom of God, *in his own way*.[45]

Hazard, about to begin a family, wondered as Belknap did about the order and security of his society. His concern turned to beliefs and morals: 'Pray, does Deism begin to infest your part of the country? It has made some hasty strides here'. Hazard enclosed for Belknap a literary piece attacking their (from his standpoint) pernicious doctrine based on science and natural law, accepting God's presence but not His will, erecting a passive God the existence or non-existence of which is inconsequential. All of Hazard's life and belief stood in opposition to such nonsense.[46]

Belknap's letter of 26 May enclosed a copy of a romantic epistle from his old friend, just deceased, the Reverend Joseph Adams, the *Bishop of Newington* (in Belknap's parlance), to a lady friend, the mother of Belknap and Hazard's mutual friend, Dr Joshua Brackett of Portsmouth. Belknap obtained the copy from the Bishop years ago 'under an engagement never to disclose it during his life'. Belknap shared it but begged Hazard to breathe not a word of it to anyone, for 'some of your intimates at Portsmouth ... would be wounded sensibly if it were known'.

Additionally, Belknap was on his way to Connecticut by way of Boston, where he planned a brief stop for a solemn occasion, to help bury 'an excellent wife' of his friend Samuel Eliot, Ruth's brother.[47]

Belknap wrote again a fortnight later after his return to Boston from his southern 'excursion'. He 'found a bundle containing 25 subscription papers', 'the beauty and elegance of' which 'I need not say is extremely pleasing to *me*. It excites the admiration of the best judges, who feel a pride in the thought of its being "American workmanship"'. Belknap wondered what the current estimate of expenses was, and expressed concern that half payment be demanded from those subscribing to the work. 'However, relying on your judgment, I shall make no objection to it'. Samuel Eliot, recently widowed, a new acquaintance of Hazard, apologized by means of Belknap for neglecting Hazard, for he was going to England, from where 'he wishes to correspond with you'.[48]

Belknap was suitably impressed both by Robert Aitken's printing abilities and moral character. 'Does he want an apprentice? I have a lively boy in his 14th year whom I would wish to put under such a master as I think he is'. Belknap asked Hazard to talk to Aitken about it, then at the first opportunity write at large (and secretly, on another sheet of paper). He added, 'You will not perhaps see the reason of this at once; but after you have been married sixteen years, if you need it, I will tell you'. Belknap was happy that Hazard 'found your rib at last'; he continued,

> You did not tell me her name. That is to *me* at present immaterial, as I positively should not know her if you did. You did not tell me her character, nor need you; for, if she is a lady of *your* choice, I can judge by a former specimen [Mrs Buckminster] what her character is. All I fear is, that I shall never see her, unless you will please to bring her within such a distance of your humble servant as that I may shew her that respect which is due to the wife of my friend. Your very kind invitation [to visit Philadelphia] I should gladly accept, were it possible for me to annihilate time and space.

Belknap wanted to 'chatter a little more' but had to journey home to Dover to '*visit* Mrs. B., from whom I have been absent above a fortnight'.[49]

Belknap did not close the letter before his departure, so took a last minute opportunity to tell Hazard of his 'grand acquisition', the 'Letterbooks from 1732 to 1735' of Massachusetts Governor Jonathan Belcher. 'The rest have been (here you will join me in a sigh) torn up for waste paper. These are but "scarcely saved"'. How appropriate is the 'motto', *time destroys all things*. 'Having written out my paper, I must conclude. Ever yours, J. B'.[50]

Having penned a quick note a week earlier, Hazard sat to write a proper letter on 11 June. He was reluctant to discuss his letters to the *Metropolitan* and added, 'therefore I must beg you to excuse me'. Hazard, apparently quite overcome by Buckminster's marriage to his amour, wrote letters 'intended only to rally him soon after marrying; and I don't know whether the joke was not carried a little too far. However, we now go on decently'. 'So the old Bishop [Joseph Adams] is dead'. The letter written by Adams to his lady friend, the mother of Dr Joshua Brackett, 'was highly entertaining ... Is the lady living?'

Hazard hoped that at some point Belknap could visit Philadelphia; 'then I shall probably have an house of my own to entertain you at. I am sorry to hear of your brother Eliot's loss'. Hazard had a mind, but not the time, to send Belknap a treatise on 'dephlogisticated air'. He requested Belknap to pass around the treatise against Deism that he had sent him.[51]

A week later Hazard had 'rummaged up' the time to transcribe a piece from 'Dr. John Ingen House's [Ingenhousz] Experiments upon Vegetables' on the principles and qualities of air. Respecting the Confederation, Hazard agreed with

Belknap about the absurdity of thirteen separate sovereignties. 'It is certainly for the common good that the hands of Congress should be more effectually strengthened. If they are not, we shall appear ridiculous in the eyes of the world, notwithstanding all that we have done'. The American Philosophical Society 'agreeably received' Belknap's observations regarding the aurora borealis. Hazard enjoyed reading the *Witch Law*, which 'discovers a great deal of zeal and very little knowledge ... It is a great happiness to live in a day when such ignorance and delusion are unknown'. In response to the Tories he wrote, 'the rage now seems to be to banish' them so that 'they will never be allowed to return. This ought to be the case. They chose their side, let them take the consequence'.[52]

Belknap returned from his journey – 'an absence of about three weeks, which is a very long one for me' – in mid-June to find that Portsmouth Postmaster Jeremiah Libbey had distributed the subscription papers for the *History* throughout the region. One part of the subscription proposal perplexed some of Belknap's Dover neighbours. The subscription read: 'The price to the subscribers will not exceed [blank], stitched in blue boards'. He continued, that the difficulty, 'would never have existed but in *such* a place. You must know, sir, that in this lumber country it is common to pay debts and give obligations to pay them in boards. When the phrase "in boards" came to be read', some interested parties

> were at a loss where the boards should be delivered, and who should receive them. Accordingly, I was gravely made acquainted with the difficulty; and you may guess how I received their information. I was obliged to shew them a book stitched and covered in the form I expected this would be, and tell them, as I would a child, that the boards mentioned were pasteboard with which the book was to be covered, and not pine boards received for the pay. Thus you have a specimen ... of this ignorant wooden world.[53]

Oh, to be in Boston again! An example of the kind of man for whom Belknap intended his book was his brother-in-law Samuel Eliot, who was taking passage to England after becoming a widower, and who 'is *earnestly* desirous of being acquainted' with Hazard. Belknap described Eliot as 'a man of good sense, quick perception, high sensibility, pretty largely acquainted with modern authors, among whom Dr. Johnson is a great favourite'. That choice alone counted quite a bit with Belknap. 'He is a person of strict integrity' with 'a pretty considerable fortune'. Belknap continued that he

> has an only daughter of 7 years old, who is a sweet, engaging child, and in whom his whole soul is wrapped up, having lost two before her birth. He is a bitter enemy to all quackery in religion or politics, and zealously attached to the West Church, of which he is a member, being initiated by the late Dr. [Jonathan] Mayhew.

Additionally, 'Our friend the Freemason [John Eliot] is another of his intimates, so that you see you are like to be in good company, if you are numbered among his friends'. While in London, Samuel Eliot was representing Belknap, hoping to convince a publisher to put out a London edition of his *History*.[54]

Belknap wrote again on 28 June after receiving Hazard's of 11 June, *in statu quo*. Regarding the Bishop of Newington and his love interest, she had long been dead. 'He lived with her' out of wedlock 'but a very short time'. 'He was obliged to make her a visit of a week long at her own [house], with the interval of about a fortnight, so that they were together about one-third of their time. The distance of their habitations was about 6 or 7 miles', the distance of Newington to Portsmouth, where she lived. Belknap wrote, 'I suppose the reason of this singularity was the disagreeableness of the match to the children on both sides'.[55]

Belknap was enthusiastic about copyright laws in the various states; it was talked about in New Hampshire. He asked: what about Pennsylvania? Jeremiah Libbey had been busy collecting subscriptions, as had Joshua Brackett of Portsmouth, the son of the woman hitherto discussed. Belknap had a dozen questions about the subscriptions, mode of payment, collection of money, contract with the printer, and so on. Jeremiah Libbey, 'an obliging, clever fellow', wondered when Hazard would journey north again. 'I answered that I had heard nothing of such a design, but that there was *another* in hand (you did not enjoin secrecy). He replied that you were consistent with yourself, because you had often said you would not marry while the war lasted'.[56]

Belknap mentioned a writer about American relations with Indians, which set him thinking. Although Belknap had involved himself in missionary activities for years, he believed that: 'Our policy with regard to the Indians must undergo a change; we must let them see that we are not afraid of them. We must not purchase their friendship with guns and rum ... as heretofore; and, as to the plan of civilizing or converting them, it is indeed highly benevolent' but 'totally impracticable in any methods that have yet been adopted here. Those of them who have been partly civilized and educated prove the worse rogues for it'. A case in point was the violent Tory Joseph Brant, a Mohawk leader during the war who had been 'one of [Eleazar] Wheelock's scholars' at Dartmouth College. Belknap believed Jesuit Catholic missionaries had the most success in their relations with the Indians, but 'we have no *such* Jesuits among us. Our Jesuits are all for serving *themselves*, not for benefiting mankind'.[57]

Charles Leslie's *Short and Easy Method with the Deists*, which Belknap received from Hazard, would be promptly served to the only one in Dover. The *Metropolitan* could use 'a dozen' copies, so many were the Deists of Portsmouth. Belknap wrote that Buckminster 'is much worried by having so many young *cubs* of that litter, or *puppies* I might have said, under his nose; and I dare say would be glad of an opportunity to put into their hands so clever a *bone to pick*'. Having sufficiently mixed his metaphors Belknap proceeded to combine religion, prophecy and science into one mess.

> What tremendous accounts we have from Sicily and Italy! Vesuvius, too, has ceased burning, which is a presage of convulsions! We have had no earthquakes in this part of the world for a long time. The last, I think, was in September, 1774, which was, like most others for 19 years before, a slight one. Is it not time to expect a repetition?

Belknap enclosed the latest 'Egg' from New Hampshire, which contained much 'nonsense', about which 'you will not wonder when you cast your eye on the Hibernian signature'.[58]

Belknap's 'favour of 23d ult'. brought about a spell of 'laughing' in Hazard when he confronted the 'simplicity' of the Dover farmers 'about the *boards*'. Hazard, hurried, had time only to complain about his hurry and to mention advertisements in local newspapers about Belknap's book. He added: 'The Metropolitan has wrote to me lately in such a way as shews he is deeply interested in your favour. He hopes the work will be made as profitable to you as possible. Respects to Mrs. B'.[59]

Matters in Philadelphia would increasingly engross Belknap's attention in the coming years, in part because of the printing of his book there, in part because, as always, Philadelphia was the intellectual capital of the United States of America, and in part, as well as more immediately, because Belknap intended to apprentice his son Joseph to printer Robert Aiken. There were three 'difficulties to be encountered' in accomplishing this endeavour. First and most important was '*maternal* fondness'. Belknap tried to convince his wife Ruth with the same arguments he used to convince himself. As a poor pastor with neither title nor fortune, and without the funds to send Josey (as he was affectionately called) to Harvard, Belknap's *Alma Mater*, the father had little choice but to apprentice the son to a craftsman. That such training especially in the printing trade could eventually lead to success was shown in the life of one of Belknap's heroes, Benjamin Franklin. He wanted, of course, to make sure that the printer was a fair man who would adopt Josey into his family like a son – Hazard's characterization of Aitken convinced Belknap that he was the man. Mrs Belknap reluctantly relented. Now, if only Belknap could convince Aitken that should the parents provide the clothes the master should provide the shoes! Also, what about schooling the boy? Dover had afforded him few opportunities in that regard. Belknap had done his best as a tutor to his son, but Philadelphia offered the chance for better education. The second difficulty was the passage to Philadelphia. Josey could hardly go the way of Franklin sixty years before with neither friend nor funds. So Belknap was on the lookout for a good ship with a kind master whose generosity matched his gentleness. Third on the list of problems was the reports Belknap had that Philadelphia 'generally, if not always', has the smallpox. In the eighteenth century, cautious people who had faith in science and medicine inoculated themselves and their children. The process of inoculation was a primitive form of vaccination: it led to the illness in a less virulent, usually non-fatal form, and it required several weeks of quarantine. There were no facilities for such a process in New Hampshire nor, surprisingly, in Boston – where inoculation in America had begun sixty years before because of the work of Cotton Mather. Belknap hesitated to send the fourteen year old to Philadelphia unprotected against the smallpox. Belknap discussed these issues at length in his letter of 14 July to Hazard, 'for I consider you and [Aitken] as one person in this matter'.[60]

The letter finished and signed, all sorts of additions followed:

> Mrs. B. here puts in a word about the long absence from home, which must be the consequence of his going to such a distance, and wishes to know *how often* during his apprenticeship she may expect the pleasure of a visit from him? Which may also conduce to the convenience of fitting him with clothing, linen, &c.[61]

Belknap followed with a series of questions: 'Do you expect your office will follow Congress in their peregrinations from one State to another? O that the 5 per cent impost [on trade] had been seasonably *agreed to*! Have you a Cromwell' or other such corrupt republican 'in the Pennsylvania line? What should you think of admitting some of the less obnoxious' Tories 'upon their paying a handsome capitation, to be applied towards discharging the public debt? Had not nations better be governed by their interest than their passions?' 'You see I can't suppress some ebullitions of things that I have been thinking on, though I meant to confine this letter to one thing only'.[62]

Belknap followed up four days later with a letter replying to Hazard's June letters, one of which, subsequently lost, apparently described in detail the character of Hazard's new love, Abigail Arthur, originally from Nantucket, and now living with her family in New Jersey. She was twenty-three years old, the only daughter of a sea captain, Joseph Arthur, and his wife, Jane Chevalier. Hazard, appropriately, referred to her as Miranda (*wonderful*) in his letters to Belknap, who was 'pleased ... with the account you have given me of her ... I think it is most prudent to do as the Vicar of Wakefield, who chose his wife, as she chose her wedding gown, for such qualities as would *wear well*'. Belknap knew from personal experience. He enclosed 'for your edification and encouragement' an excerpt from one of Governor Jonathan Belcher's letters of advice to his son. The letters were providing Belknap with a new appreciation of the difficulties of being, and the character of, 'a Plantation [Colonial] Governour':

> They were a set of dependent creatures, – dependent on the breath of a favourite, or the smile of a minister, or the avarice of a clerk. At home [in London] they kept spies in the public offices to watch the words and looks of their superiors, and the motions of their enemies; and here they were plagued with cross assemblies, their support

withheld, their views obstructed, their temper (unless like Job) always in a fret; and to steer between the Scylla and Charybdis of offending their master and the people whom they governed, was a laborious task.[63]

Belknap was 'glad' that the American Philosophical Society accepted without ridicule and laughter Belknap's observations on the sound of the aurora borealis. 'Were it necessary', he wrote with renewed confidence,

> I could produce a great number of persons, and some of superior characters for judgment, critical observation, and veracity, who have been witnesses of the fact, of which indeed I have no more doubt than of the luminous appearance. Pray, were these observations, or rather the thing observed, as *new* to the Society as to yourself?[64]

Belknap had little more to add, save his whereabouts in transcribing his book, a question about subscriptions, a request for information about the high quality letter-paper Hazard used, and a wish to 'you all the blessings and happiness that you can wish for yourself, and in particular that your union with the amiable Miranda may be the source of mutual felicity'. He added the postscript: 'Mrs. B. joins in the most cordial congratulations and wishes, especially on that account.'[65]

One assumes that Belknap's work transcribing his book and his worry over the impending journey of his firstborn son filled him with anxiety, because the man who normally stored Hazard's epistles away like a squirrel preparing for winter was unexpectedly absent-minded during the late summer months of 1783. One letter that did survive was Hazard's of 23 July, which, as he was 'preparing to leave the city for about ten days on a visit to my female friend' in New Jersey, quickly and methodically responded to Belknap's 'of 28th ult'. Hazard and Aitken thought the number of subscriptions received for Belknap's book were sufficient 'to give orders for the paper to be made immediately, that it may be finished before rains come on and muddy the waters, when it would not be so white. I think we shall determine to print; but, if we should not, the paper may be sold again'. Hazard agreed that 'something in writing by way of contract' would be useful to formalize the agreement between the two friends, 'that, in case of mortality (as my uncle used to say), those who come after us may know upon what plan we acted'. Hazard expected 'we shall get a good profit, if we find a ready sale'. Unfortunately Hazard could be and was often wrong about such matters. Hazard thought the latest '*Egg*' Belknap had sent 'should have been signed "Major General"', in reference to the Hibernian John Sullivan. He ended, 'P. S. We are told that the Definitive Treaty has arrived at New York.'[66]

Belknap sent a short letter in early August in which he expressed satisfaction that the Metropolitan Buckminster wished him well. 'Indeed, he is a friendly man, and a very good neighbour, and it adds not a little to his worth that he chose so good a partner for himself'.

Additionally, Belknap sent the second chapter, and was beginning the third. He intended 'as soon as the weather grows cooler, to ride round and collect' completed subscriptions for the forthcoming book. Belknap wondered whether or not the formalities had been signed with Hazard's prospective 'rib'. 'Must you move after Congress, or shall you keep your station' in Philadelphia? 'Will the late offer from N. Jersey to [host] Congress be accepted?'[67]

Two days later, for fun and edification, Belknap transcribed for Hazard a 'curious and remarkable' occurrence made *'more marvellous'* by rumour and gossip. One Mehetabel Whiddon was an eighteen year old 'struck blind with lightning' on a clear day:

> She had just been stooping to a cradle, and was raising herself up with her face towards a west window, and not nearer to it than five or six feet, the sash being down, when a sharp flash of lightning met her eye, which, as she says, caused the sensation of heat in her face, and immediately deprived her of sight.

She was blind for 'three weeks', then 'dreamed' that in two days, precisely, 'she should recover her sight' – which happened. Belknap, who distrusted though was fascinated by reports of prophecy and miracle, interviewed the girl himself. He wrote to Hazard that, 'She seems to be a modest, sensible girl, and has a grateful sense of the Divine goodness in her recovery'.[68]

Belknap wrote again and again in short order during August: 'I hope this will find you returned from your excursion to your "female friend", and the negotiation so far advanced as to promise a speedy conclusion, much to your mutual satisfaction and to that of all persons concerned'. Regarding Belknap's *History*, the subscriptions were coming in slowly – at most there were about 250 pledges to buy the book. Most refused to advance half upon subscription. Some refused to subscribe at all because it was to be printed in Philadelphia rather than Boston. Belknap wondered whether or not it was advisable to print 1,000, as Hazard planned. Yet, he concluded: 'But, as you are a much better judge than I can be of the proportion which the subscription may bear to the probable sales, I shall leave it to you to limit the number'. In Mid-August he wrote to send the third chapter of the manuscript. 'This will doubtless find you returned from your rural excursion, the bargain pinn'd, and all ready for the knot.' Ten days later Belknap optimistically reported that over 300 were subscribed for, and twenty pounds currency collected. Belknap yearned to hear from Hazard, and sent Josey to Portsmouth to see if any letters were waiting. He noted, 'I would go myself, but am not well: the heat yesterday overcame me'.[69]

Hazard, ever hurried, finally wrote at the end of August, urging Belknap to finish transcribing the *History* as soon as possible – 'For when the press once begins we shall go on rapidly, and it will not do for the workmen to be stopped for want of copy'. Additionally, Congress would not decide where to locate 'before October'.

Hazard was incredulous about Mehetabel Whitten's story, especially 'her *dreaming*' about the return of sight. He wrote, 'Yours of the 11th found me returned from my "excursion to my female friend"; and the negotiation is so far advanced that I expect to revisit her' in a week, 'and the definitive treaty is to be signed on the 11th September'. Subscriptions might be slow in coming, but 'many will *purchase* who will not *subscribe*, and I feel no doubt but we shall be able to pay all expences out of the books'. True, Bostonians might object to a book printed in Philadelphia, for 'you know they have a strong attachment to "town-born children"' – of which Belknap was one. Hazard, buying paper, needed the subscription money as soon as possible. He added, 'It will not answer to print less than 1000 copies; because the smaller the number, the greater in proportion is the cost. Besides, 500 disposed of (or perhaps a few more) will pay the whole expence'.[70]

Belknap, assuming that Hazard was preoccupied with love, excused his friend not writing, but himself kept the pen going. He wrote two letters in succession at the beginning of September, one as a cover to his fourth chapter, the other to discuss the forthcoming apprenticeship of Josey to Robert Aiken. Belknap 'determined' on 'a trial' and wrote, '[I] shall now do the best I can to prepare him for his voyage, and desire my friends in the sea-port towns to look out for him a good opportunity of conveyance, and some careful person with whom I may trust him'. Belknap relied on Hazard to help Josey once he reached Philadelphia; already Hazard had contacted Dr Geraldus Clarkson – *Ulysses* – to arrange to inoculate the boy upon arrival. Belknap emphasized that 'the child will need friends, being so far removed from home'. Jeremy and Ruth worried that Hazard might be forced to relocate. In turn Belknap promised to help promote, by writing and soliciting writers, Robert Aitken's weekly 'literary paper'. The poetess 'Mrs. B. is reserved, but an application from *you* might educe something' by way of contribution.

As the wedding day approached, 'I shall bear in mind the *11th of September* as a memorable æra in the life of my friend; and, when it comes, shall fancy myself at the nuptials, and wish you *joy of the day*. You must be my proxy to administer the salutation', or kiss, 'of your friend to Mrs. Bride'. 'Mrs. B.', the husband added in a postscript, 'is exceedingly obliged by your care of her child, and wishes you a thousand blessings'.[71]

True to his word, on the evening of 11 September Jeremy and Ruth 'did not forget ... to drink, or, to speak in the Johnsonian style, to "bibulate to the salubrity" of [their] friend and his bride'. He added, 'By this time, I conclude you have taken leave of your bachelorship, and are initiated into the science of matrimony'. And in a mood for hilarity, Belknap wrote:

You must accept of this wish, "warm from the heart", instead of an epithalamium [nuptial song] which I am [in] no capacity for composing; and, if I was, it would be needless, for no more than this fairly implies could be said, though the sentiment be drawn out into a Pindaric of a yard long. They say gaping [yawning] is catching; perhaps marrying is. Our friend, the freemason [John Eliot] had kept up his heart "in an ivory box" till he heard of your manœuvres in the hymeneal field; and now he has let it fairly be catched up by a girl of 17, a daughter of Mr. [Jacob] Treadwell, of Portsmouth; and so, as good brother Harvey says, 'the world is peopled', and so it ought to be, say I; and there's an end of my discourse on the subject.[72]

Respecting other matters: regarding the *History* Belknap sent along further chapters of his manuscript, and more subscription papers; regarding Josey, 'Mrs. B. is preparing her son for his expedition' to Philadelphia; 'I have not yet heard of an opportunity to send him, but am on the enquiry'. Regarding Hazard's work: 'Pray, my friend, how goes on your collection of papers? When do you intend to begin the printing of them? I have heard nothing of the work for a long time'. Hazard's letter 'of 27th ult' arrived the next day, so Belknap added numerous postscripts, including Ruth's continued 'congratulations on the (supposed) nuptials'.[73]

Belknap, in the mood to talk to his friend, soon wrote again: 'I have no letter from you this week', he told Hazard on 20 September, 'nor did I expect it, as you told me in your last that you was likely to be engaged in business that required your *personal* attendance out of town' – namely, in New Jersey, where Hazard and Abigail Arthur were married. Belknap was happy to hear that Congress expected to remain in Philadelphia – hence so, too, would Hazard. He wished to support the idea by holding 'up both hands', 'as an old Representative said about burying [Massachusetts] Governour Shirley'. Belknap wrote that he had 'been very industrious this week, for me, in the copying way'. But he did have one question, regarding a seventeenth-century affidavit that, he thought, would enlighten the reader about the politics of the time; it was coarse and crude, and he wondered 'whether it will suit the gravity and decency of an History or not'. Should Hazard decide not, would he please add it as 'a marginal note'. Belknap wanted to send Hazard money to cover the costs of paper, but could find neither 'bank-bills' nor 'bills of exchange' among Portsmouth financiers – he would have to write to Boston to this end. Meanwhile, 'I cannot hear of a passage for Jo. The tailors are fitting him up for his voyage'.[74]

Hazard eventually wrote at the end of September, telling his friend that with all the subscriptions it was safe to print, but 'as Mr. Aitken has an unfinished job in hand ... we shall not begin the History 'til about a month hence'. Hazard wrote that he would 'take the same liberties with your History, as to correcting, pointing, &c., as if it was my own'. As for the nuptials, 'your friend was married the 11th September: he has administered your salutations to the bride. He was married on *Thursday*: on *Friday* his wife's sister lost a child, which was buried on *Saturday*. You may guess at his situation, obliged to rejoice and mourn at the same time: it was singular. We came to town last Thursday evening, since which we have been very busy receiving congratulations and compliments. This ceremony will continue 'til the end of this week, and after that we shall begin to settle a little'.[75]

Belknap sent a brief note at the end of the month, indicating that a 'bank note to the value of £20, our lawful money', was on the way. Josey was not yet. Belknap was seeking a passage, yet was hesitant at the same time. 'The seaport towns are very sickly, and we hear Philadelphia is remarkably so, which makes us concerned about Jo'.[76]

On 1 October Hazard wrote reporting on his marital bliss, anticipating the like experience in his friend the *Freemason*. 'The youth, the inexperience, and the feelings of 17', the age of Eliot's intended, 'may assist him in carrying on the siege; but, perhaps, they may produce inconveniences afterwards. So young a person can hardly have sufficient acquaintance with the management of family affairs; pray, what is *his* age?' Hazard congratulated Belknap on the number of subscriptions to his book in New England.

> We have not been successful here, though we published our design in three different papers. The country of which you write is so far from hence, that people this way seem to feel no interest in it: they have, moreover, an aversion to subscriptions, having been frequently cheated either by the book not being published at all, or done in so slovenly a manner as not to be worth half the money.

As for Hazard's historical collection,

> it goes on very slowly; indeed, no addition has been made to it for a long time, except the last volume of the Pennsylvania Assembly's Minutes, which I petitioned for, and obtained a present of from the House. Between courting, marrying, building, and a thousand other things, I have been too much hurried to think of the collection: if the cares of the world don't encrease [*sic*] too fast upon me, I may perhaps find leisure to resume it.[77]

Belknap, slightly exasperated, wrote in the first week of October chiding his friend for not writing; he figured, however, that

> the old excuse, 'I have married a wife', is good in this case; and I am willing to deny myself so far as to wait one revolution of the moon, from the 11th of September. I am happy all this time in thinking that you have much superior enjoyment.

Meanwhile, Josey remained home. 'There is a prospect of a vessel's going from this river [the Piscataqua] soon, when I shall endeavour to get him a passage', notwithstanding the incoming reports 'of a great sickness in Philadelphia'.

> If this be so, it may be best for Mr. Aitken not to have an addition to his family, nor for Jo to be absent from home, till it is abated. We are as healthy here as ever; but most of the seaport towns have been visited with mortal sickness, in a great degree.[78]

Hazard, having received Belknap's seventh and eighth chapters, and the request to consider the seventeenth-century affidavit, gave as his opinion that it would not 'be inconsistent with the gravity and decency of an History', which involved giving 'a true picture of the temper and language of the people at that time'. Aitken expected Josey soon, indeed needed him, having 'lately refused an apprentice'. *Ulysses*, Dr Clarkson, was willing to inoculate Jo upon arrival, '*gratis*'.[79]

Rumour regularly feeds upon crisis, as Hazard discovered during the Revolution, and as Belknap, in more modest circumstances, discovered during the autumn of 1783. 'We have had truly formidable and alarming news of an epidemical sickness in your city', he wrote to his friend.

> Last week, I was told by a gentleman of character, whose information seemed direct, that it was a yellow spotted fever, and that great numbers had died. The papers mention ... that the stages were stopped by reason of it. These accounts, you may well think, have affected the minds of parents concerned for a son whom they are about sending thither.

Fortunately, Belknap had not yet found for his son a passage by ship from the Piscataqua Valley to Philadelphia, though there was a faint promise of one in preparation at Portsmouth. He wrote that Hazard's letters

> relieve me in some measure, for in the first place you say nothing of the sickness: then you write that you have moved your wife into town so lately as the 18th ult., which you would not have done if the infection had been alarming; another comforting circumstance is, that Mr. A. mentions nothing of it; and surely, if the pestilence were raging to the degree we have heard, he could not desire an addition to his family.

Philadelphia had its share of sickness and epidemics, but not this year.[80]

Hazard responded mid-month with good news. *Ulysses* was busy getting subscriptions for Belknap's *History* among his patients. Sickness was present in Pennsylvania,

> but has not proved mortal: indeed, considering the number of inhabitants, I believe few places are more healthy than Philadelphia; and, when you recollect that the same Providence takes care of the Philadelphians and Dover people, and that we have the advantage of you in point of medical abilities, I think you need not make yourself uneasy about Josey.

There had been a few deaths; 'a woman died here in child-bed yesterday'. 'But', Hazard joked, 'I think it probable he will be safe enough on that score'.[81]

At the same time Belknap wrote from Dover, having heard from Thomas Longman, publisher of London. Longman had no interest in publishing Belknap's book, but would willingly sell however many (which he expected to be quite few) he could. Belknap wondered whether or not this would change the print order of one thousand copies. It concerned him enough that 'if I was within *one* hundred miles of Philadelphia, I would certainly take my horse and hold a council with you and Mr. Aitken on the subject'. On second thought Belknap, ever watchful over his own prose, wrote: 'you will not think that I mean that my *horse* should be *of the council*'. The issue of Josey's passage, along with 'violent' weather, preoccupied Belknap such that he had been amiss about copying his manuscript. 'With respects to your other half, in which mine joins, I am your sincere and obliged friend'.[82]

Hazard sent a brief note at the end of October, requesting that Belknap send Josey as soon as possible. He added, 'You seem to hear more of sickness in Philadelphia than we do who live here'. 'Adieu'.[83]

The issue of Josey's passage and other family concerns so overwhelmed Belknap that he sent Hazard seven letters in one month. Hazard having asked about Eliot's intended, Belknap gave the details. 'The Freemason's age is 29. Miss, in her teens, is rather solid than gay, and is said by those who are best acquainted with her to have an excellent mind. He follows on very closely, having made three journies' from Boston to Portsmouth 'since the middle of July'. Like Hazard, Belknap's own scientific and historical researches had taken a backseat to family matters.

> I have long felt that the concerns of a family are a great hindrance to scientific labours, and especially during the late reign of war, paper money, regulation-acts, beggars on horseback, &c., &c., &c., when the most of my attention was engaged in keeping the belly and back from grumbling, and the kitchen-fire from going out. There is now a dawn of what we have often wished over a glass of wine; viz., 'better times'. I mean in a family way, for as to public matters I am afraid that the end of one revolution will be the beginning of another. But I won't teaze you with my 'closet conjectures'.[84]

Belknap wanted Hazard to 'expunge' one section of his third chapter, regarding the Quakers. The passage appeared disapproving, which Belknap was, but he did not want to appear that way in the public performance of a book.

> Poets lose half the praise they would have got,
> Were it but known what they discreetly blot.[85]

Belknap gained a clear understanding of the practices of 'merchants and shipmasters' during the end of October and early November, when he was 'led to expect' a vessel departing Portsmouth for Philadelphia, was put off, the hope renewed, then put off again. He journeyed with Josey, bags packed, from Dover to Portsmouth, back to Dover, back to Portsmouth, and then in exasperation on to Boston where a ship was found and passage to Philadelphia accomplished. All the while Belknap's nervousness about Philadelphia plagues lessened, so that he could write Hazard with the confidence and courage gained with hindsight: 'We are now assured that the reports of plagues and pestilences at Philadelphia are without foundation. For my part, I never gave so much heed to it as to relax or delay in the least; but Mrs. B. was something afraid'. Josey sailed the first week of November in

> the sloop 'Caroline', Moses Killsa master ... She is a fine new large vessel, laden with rum and flax-seed; and I had the very great pleasure of finding that there was a young gentleman named Myrick, a passenger on board, who was so very kind as to let Josey have part of his cabbin [*sic*] and mattress on the voyage.

The cost of the voyage was 'eight dollars', which Belknap requested Hazard to pay upon the ship's arrival at Philadelphia; Josey would reimburse him with gold stored in his chest. Belknap continued,

> If I hear of his safe arrival at Philadelphia, my desires will be crowned. I must beg you, my dear friend, to let me know every circumstance that you can learn relative to his voyage, his treatment on board, &c., and with the watchful eye of a father to observe his conduct while with Mr. A., and let me know impartially every circumstance that you think I ought or would wish to know concerning him and his connexion there.[86]

Josey sailed on 10 November; 'the weather ... was fine for a fortnight or more after', hence the voyage no doubt went without a hitch. Belknap was confident that all would be well with Josey.

> His conduct during the parting scene was so firm and manly, and he shewed such an attention to his interest in the whole affair, that I own it left an impression on my mind much to his advantage, and greatly helped my feelings on the occasion.

Belknap sent with Jo several letters to Hazard and others. One letter to Hazard contained an extract of a letter from Samuel Eliot, in London trying to drum up interest in Belknap's book, without success. But no matter – 'When I have done what I can toward the accomplishment of a favourite plan, and I find all my efforts ineffectual, I am satisfied that it is not best that my desires should be gratified, and there leave it'. To Hazard he sent a request for a list of books to purchase for Dover's social library, as well as several titles for Jo's personal use, the payment for which could be found in 'Jo's chest' which had 'two English guineas, one French one, and ten crowns'.[87]

It is possible that Hazard wrote around 1 November but that the letter never reached Belknap because of a robbery of the mail. He briefly wrote again on 12

November to inform Belknap that he had yet to receive one of his letters and to comment on their friend John Eliot.

> For a man of 29 the Freemason is one of the most outrageous *lovyers* I ever met with. From the stile of his letters, it is clear to me that if a windmill stood in his way when he was going to Portsmouth he certainly would ride over it.[88]

Belknap realized 22 November, upon his return from Boston and Jo's send-off, that letters were missing. He soon read in a newspapers that 'the mail had been robbed at Princeton'. 'I hope', he told Hazard, 'the rogue will be detected'. In the same letter he informed Hazard, and hence Aitken, that 'people are impatient for the publication of my History. I tell them that I suppose it is now in hand, and that it will go on rapidly. Mr. A. having advertized [Dr. Hugh] Blair's Lectures', his current project, 'I imagine mine will go into the press next'. 'I see in some of your papers a piece advertised against the [Society of] Cincinnati, supposing it dangerous to republicanism. Is it so or not?' After many years of gestation, New Hampshire's 'Egg is perfected at length, and is to be hatched next June'. Belknap enclosed some information about it for Hazard's perusal.[89]

Belknap wrote a week later on 30 November, 'surprized to find by yours of the 12th inst. that my letter containing a copy of Mr. Longman's has miscarried. It is, I think, the first instance of the kind since our correspondence begun; and I cannot easily account for it'. Belknap wrote of business matters respecting the impossibility of a London, 'transmarine edition', and the price of 'pasteboards at Boston' in response to a query from Aitken. Of John Eliot he wrote,

> The Freemason continues making his approaches. Even the rugged influence of *Capricorn* does not deter him from attempting to enjoy the softening smiles of *Virgo*! I know not how he would do with a windmill, if it stood in his way; but I am persuaded, if a land journey was impracticable, he would brave the blasts of *Boreas* and the raging of *Neptune* rather than miss his object.[90]

November ushered December into 1783 with a violent storm, 'of snow and hail'. Belknap decided to add to his letter, begun the day before, as he could not send it until the storm 'abated', for 'crossing the ferry is impracticable'. The storm was such as to sink 'a Dutch man-of-war' off of 'Cape Ann: 40 men out of about 350 were saved in the boats'. Notwithstanding the 'melancholy' productions of nature, Belknap enjoyed keeping track of it by means of daily measurements and almanacs. He kept a daily journal in his interleaved almanac. He asked Hazard, '[do] you keep a journal of the weather?' Perhaps they could share notes to ascertain the causes, extent and course of weather systems and patterns. Belknap would begin: 'Wednesday, Nov. 12, at Boston. Morning wind at W. and S. W. Before noon veers to N. E'. Mid-afternoon it 'begins to snow; continues all night; but not a heavy gale. (N. B. this, I hope was a fair wind for Jo, as the westerly breezes of the two preceeding [*sic*] days were judged sufficient to carry the vessel clear of the cape and islands.)' For whatever reason, 'we have had no remarkable Aurora Borealis this autumn'. Would Hazard 'be so kind as to send me one of Bradford's Almanacks for 1784' to aid in meteorological observations?[91]

Other news and commentary included that New Hampshire had passed 'an act for the encouragement of literature' – has Pennsylvania?, asked Belknap. Additionally, newspapers hinted that

> Congress ... are preparing a seat at or near Trenton. Pray how wide is the river at those falls? I hope, in some of the buildings, they will have an apartment for the trophies taken from the enemy at various times in the late war. The Cantons of Switzerland are extremely careful to preserve such monuments of the valour and victories of their ancestors, the sight of which serves to fan the flame of liberty and independence.[92]

Regarding war, it astonished Belknap how events the explanation for which long eluded human understanding, the fulfilment of which long eluded human action, could simply *occur*. A case in point was the settling of Nova Scotia. Belknap's old friend, former New Hampshire Governor John Wentworth, was the new royal governor of the British province, which 'bids fair to be peopled now (if the poor wretches can struggle through this winter)'. It would then follow the example of New England, which promised to be peopled long before it was. Likewise, Nova Scotia's promise was based on fishing, particularly because of the nearness of the Gorges Banks. Great Britain clearly intended Nova Scotia to rival, perhaps surpass, New England fishing, which, wrote Belknap, had led some 'to regret the vengeful policy which forbad the readmission of the refugees among us'. Belknap himself 'reprobated the manner of our conduct' in refusing to allow the Tories readmission to the United States of America. 'Had we not been so rash, they would have been glad to have come among us on the same terms that the Gibeonites were spared, in the days of Joshua'. He asked whether they should have feared their retribution. 'Many of those who fled from us and took refuge in the British posts were not, and never could be, one hundredth part so dangerous enemies as some who have lived unmolested among us all the time; and yet we fear nothing from them'. Some of Belknap's New England neighbours who were 'Toretically inclined' now wished to move to Nova Scotia. But Belknap knew Hazard's sentiments were quite different, so halted his diatribe.[93]

A week later Belknap wrote again, having received Hazard's letter 'of November 19, in which I was in *some* hope of hearing of Josey's arrival, but find I must wait another week. The rogue who stole the mail at Princeton was the cause of a whole fortnight's anxiety to me'. Yet Belknap had 'no other wish for the fellow than what [the Apostle] Paul wished to Alexander the coppersmith' – God would deal with the sinner. Belknap's lost letter of 19 October continued to perplex him; he advised the Postmaster of the British attempts to guarantee 'the security of mails'. 'It was that it be enclosed in a strong iron box, fastened with staples and locks to an iron axle-tree; the post-boy to be seated on it, and the post-masters of the several offices to keep the keys'. Hopefully Hazard had candour enough to withstand such unsolicited advice. Would he have sufficient patience to meet another of Belknap's comments? 'For the sake of a number of warm and sanguine subscribers whose patience is on the stretch, I wish the printing may be speedily begun'.[94]

The winter was sufficiently severe that Belknap spent much of his time at the writing desk. He tossed off letter after letter to Hazard, who was more thrifty with his correspondence. In mid-December Belknap told Hazard of a hip ailment he had which put him in mind of his *'punning* uncle, Dr. Byles'. Mather Byles had become quite infamous in Boston both for his refusal to side with the Patriots, his refusal to leave Boston, and his refusal to refrain from making light of his situation. Belknap could hardly forgive him for his politics, but was so attracted to his wit to continue to love him. He visited the old man of seventy-eight when in Boston during the autumn. He found Byles

> in an easy chair which has a back hung on hinges. In such a chair I found him sitting, and as I approached him he held out his hand. 'You must excuse my not getting up to receive you, cousin [Belknap was his grandnephew]; for I am not one of the *rising* generation'.[95]

Was the harsh winter the cause of Belknap misplacing so many of Hazard's letters? Hazard's letter of 26 November and 3 December do not survive. Hazard informed Belknap of the arrival of Josey at Philadelphia and his wandering about the city instead of going immediately to Aitken's shop as instructed. Belknap supposed 'he had some reason' for truancy. As if Hazard did not have enough to do, Belknap wondered why 'you and Mr. Aitken' cannot 'cook ... up' an 'American Gazetteer'. It was clearly needed. 'The destruction of men by shipwrecks, on the North American coast, the year past, is immense. I have heard it computed at 1500, including the Dutch man-of-war ... Five vessels were wrecked on Plumb Island, near Newbury' – notorious for its dangers to shipping – 'in the last storm, and all the people lost. The clouds are now gathering thick for another, Thursday, A. M.', that is, the following day.[96]

Hazard's letter of 3 December was difficult for Belknap to read, because it contained the comment: 'Mr. A. laments exceedingly Josey's want of education'. Belknap responded:

> How much more exquisite must be my sensations! Especially when I have five more children to lament over! I have long thought, and do still think it one of the greatest misfortunes of my life to be obliged to rear a family of children in a place and among a people where insensibility to the interests of the rising generation, and an inveterate antipathy to literature, are to be reckoned among the prevailing vices; where there

is not so much public spirit as to build a school-house; where men of the first rank let their children grow up uncultivated as weeds in the highway; where grand jurors pay no regard to their oaths ... You may think, perhaps, that this picture is too highly coloured. But it is literally and exactly true.

Belknap suggested, should Hazard doubt him, to ask General John Sullivan, whose character Belknap's pen had often scathed, but whom was now generally respected by Belknap. Sullivan was 'a friend to literature, as men who have emerged from nothing through the force of their own genius commonly are.'[97]

Belknap's diatribe against Dover and its want of civilization, education and concern, its preponderance towards ignorance, apathy and savagery, went on for the next hour or so until lack of paper forced him to halt. Belknap's loneliness was never more apparent than in this letter, wherein his soul cried out for compassion and friendship, for help and empathy. He wrote to his friend,

> The scenes we have passed through have extinguished every sentiment that was favourable to education in the minds of the people at large, and all the attempts which a poor lonely individual or two in a town can do to revive or rekindle the flame are totally ineffectual. I have preached, talked, convened special meetings for the purpose, offered my services in person, all to no purpose.

Forced to tutor his own children, he was largely unsuccessful. Belknap continued,

> A sense of duty to [Josey], and a regard to his interest, in conjunction with my other children, have led me to a determination, as soon as ever they are of sufficient age, to put them out of this place. It is not in my power to place them at public schools where their board must be paid for; but if I can get them into some good family in the rank of apprentices, in places where they may have some opportunities of profiting by evening schools, and at the same time be learning some trade to get their future living in the world, it is all that I can do for them; and I must, in the use of these means, commit them to the care of Divine Providence.

Josey had sufficient common sense and self-interest to see that his future depended on himself rather than his father. Hopefully he would, like Franklin, find success and happiness in life.[98]

Belknap followed up with another letter a week later, at the end of December. Aware that 'my last to you was rather of a melancholy complexion', he continued in the same vein, explaining Josey's apparent ignorance according to the season – he arrived in Philadelphia after the summer and autumn farming and harvesting seasons, when little schooling was done.

> Since I wrote that letter, another subscription has been started to build a school-house in this town, and I have laboured the point with a number of the most wealthy people in this place. Next week will shew the effect; but I am afraid it will turn out like the rest.

Father and mother remained worried about smallpox, and Josey's inoculation. Yet, Belknap wrote, 'God be praised that appearances, when you wrote were so favourable, and that he has fallen into so good hands as Dr. C.', Geraldus Clarkson.[99]

The year ended in Philadelphia with Hazard trying to balance his duties as postmaster general with his new responsibilities as a husband, as well as the significant tasks he had taken upon himself on Belknap's behalf: overseeing the publication of Belknap's *History of New Hampshire* and overseeing the relationships and feelings of a fourteen-year-old boy alone in a big city. The year ended in Dover with Belknap calming his own fears (and those of his wife) regarding their son, and trying to stay warm as a big storm blew in to welcome the new year. 'Do they make cast iron stoves in Philadelphia?' Belknap wrote to Hazard as the snow fell. 'I have seen some at Boston, with an upper story that serves for an oven. If such are to be had in your city, be so kind as to let me know the price'.[100]

9 THE MYSTERIES OF LUCINA

A heavy New Hampshire snowstorm ushered in the new year of 1784. 'Snowdrifts are six feet deep', wrote Belknap, 'and 'tis at least three feet on a level. Our people are now turning out to break the paths'. The air was bitter cold, the sky grey – a lonely, forbidding environment, yet peaceful all the same. 'We have had scarce any Aurora Boreales this autumn and winter'. The Shakers, a peculiar New England religious sect given to extravagant claims, incorporated eschatology into astronomy, claiming that the aurora 'are entirely ceased'. Belknap wondered: 'Have you any of those creatures in Pennsylvania?'[1]

Meanwhile Hazard was cold and ill with rheumatism. 'I believe I caught cold in consequence of changing my cloaths', which would seem to be, nevertheless, an utter necessity. Belknap's letter describing his punning uncle Mather Byles and his wit 'made me laugh very heartily'. Hazard, like Belknap fascinated by the weather, reported that 'we have had, a few days past, a deep snow; on Monday and Tuesday, a remarkable thaw, accompanied with a thick fog; yesterday it was clear and cold; to-day, *very* cold, and the [Delaware] river fast'. Reporting news of the son for the father, Hazard reassured Belknap that 'Josey is well'. Aitken, crotchety, 'says "he does not know what is in him, but the folks downstairs (the workmen) like him, and the folks upstairs (the family) like him"'.[2]

The best day Belknap had in a long time was 13 January. Five letters arrived: two from Hazard, and one each from Dr Geraldus Clarkson, Aitken and Joseph Belknap, Jr. All this news and love 'produced a flood of gratitude to our Divine Benefactor, and to the worthy instruments which he has been pleased to make use of in conferring benefits on me and mine': said instruments, of course, were Hazard, taking care of Josey, Aitken, the 'careful master' to the apprentice and surrogate father 'who seems to have the interest of my son so much at heart', and Dr Clarkson, the 'beloved physician' who inoculated the boy.[3]

Hazard having asked whether or not volume two of the *History of New Hampshire* would follow soon upon volume one, Belknap responded, 'I fully intend it, and have already begun to collect and compile'. But how long it would take him he could not say, 'considering the situation I am in, and the many duties that are required of me as a son, a husband, a father, a pastor, and a friend'. The first volume 'cost me off and on nine or ten years' – the second would be similarly costly. Belknap refused to throw something together like 'a Grub Street Gazetteer', whom, no doubt, 'Doctor [Samuel] Johnson had in view' when he pronounced that 'no writer has a more *easy* task than the historian'. One remark in Johnson's *Rambler* series infuriated Belknap, who spent the next thirty minutes in an epistolary chewing out of the great critic, poet and lexicographer. Belknap assumed that Dr Johnson had never written a true history, at least the type that Belknap had; hence he would not know what it is to spend hours rummaging through 'private papers' found 'in the garrets and rat-holes of old houses', and all the other forms of 'drudgery' a historian has to endure to recreate the past. In short and contrary to Dr Johnson, respecting a second volume, 'I must know a great deal more than I do now, and must take a great deal of pains to obtain that knowledge'.[4]

Moving on to science: 'You know I have made a practice of communicating to you every observation, occurrence, discovery, or improvement that has fallen within my sphere of knowledge since our acquaintance, and which might either gratify curiosity or be useful'. Belknap having heard of a device to help the deaf hear, and having an uncle in Connecticut with a hearing problem, he tried an experiment. He attempted to communicate with a deaf person by holding a strong stick of wood between their respective teeth. He discovered that the person experienced an auditory sensation, *hearing*. On this he wrote, 'These, my dear sir, are *facts*. I shall not presume to examine them theoretically' – though he wondered whether or not there was 'a communication between the dental and auditory nerves before they reach the sensorium', that part of the brain that registered such physical sensations.[5]

Hazard had sent Belknap an almanac, for which he thanked him. Belknap 'wanted it for the place of the planets, which our N.E. almanac-makers have for some years omitted'. Belknap hoped Hazard would 'act in my stead to bind' Josey as an apprentice to Aitken. He noted that there were 'More shipwrecks daily', and ended with the postscript: Dover once again defeated 'another projection' to build a 'school-house', as he had predicted.[6]

The literati of Philadelphia with whom Hazard had discussed Belknap's experiences at Dover, Hazard reported to his friend on 16 January, 'were astonished and as much hurt as myself at the thought that a man of your genius and education should be doomed to drag out a miserable existence among such savages'. Dr Clarkson wanted Belknap to relocate to Philadelphia to take a Presbyterian parish. Hazard agreed that Philadelphia would fit Belknap and his whole family, including the children, quite well. He had good news to report about Josey: Aitken, along with his wife and their children were all delighted with the newcomer; 'If one of' the Aitken children 'comes to get but a piece of apple-pye, there must be a piece for Jo too'. Hazard knew his comments were 'trifling', but not to an anxious father and mother. Mr and Mrs Aitken were always ready to praise the boy, who was learning how to bind books. Hazard added that the Delaware River was hard frozen; otherwise he would send the books Belknap ordered for the Dover social library.[7]

Besides the cold, Pennsylvania had recently experienced an earthquake, upon which Hazard reported:

> I felt the first shock of the earthquake very sensibly, and so did all my family. The noise was like that made by rolling a full barrel over a floor. Our maid-servant, who had gone to her bed-chamber in the third story of the house, came running down stairs in a great fright. She said her chamber door was burst open, and the house reeled so that she expected it would have fallen.

Hazard, who was unperturbed by the commotion, 'slept too soundly to feel the other shocks'. Like an earthquake was the heart of the *Freemason*, Hazard joked, who vibrates 'between *Sagittarius* and *Virgo* ... Pray when is he to become *stationary?*'[8]

Congress, in debate over 'their *permanent* residence' generated the comments of various 'wags' who 'take great liberties'. One, for example, suggested that the Congress locate in 'a *moving town* ... to which the equestrian statue of General Washington was to be attached'. Philadelphia, doing everything it could to keep the Congress, planned 'a grand exhibition ... in honour of General Washington' that included 'a triumphal arch' and various other 'elegant' forms of art. But 'Mrs. H. hurries me so much to come to supper that I have only time to send our joint respects to Mrs. B., and assure you that I am unalterably yours'.[9]

Hazard wrote again a week later to inform Belknap of various scientific matters, including Belknap's election to the American Philosophical Society, of which Hazard (who nominated Belknap) was a member. Hazard hoped Belknap would send periodic communications from the north on scientific and historical matters. He asked, 'Have you ever enlarged and methodised your "Conjectures about the Population of America?" Do you make any meteorological observations? Can't you sketch out a short Natural History of N. Hampshire?' The natural history of Pennsylvania included a comet, seen recently and studied by the premier American scientist and astronomer David Rittenhouse. But cloud cover kept it from Hazard's view. 'Our weather of late has been remarkable, – one day intensely cold, the next a thorough thaw. The Delaware has been so frozen that it has been crossed with horses and sleighs', but the recent weather now made this dangerous. Firewood was scarce and very expensive.[10]

The 'elegant exhibition' was a thorough failure.

> Through some mismanagement, the paintings caught fire; the flames communicated to the rockets, which were not fixed up; they flew horizontally among an amazing

concourse of people, killed some, wounded others; hats, caps, bonnets, cloaks, handkerchiefs, shoes, canes, were lost; all was uproar and confusion.

Another fiasco was the Bank of North America, in existence for several years, directed by Robert Morris, but ultimately a failure. The conservative Hazard had supported it and hoped a replacement would soon appear. He admitted that the bank benefited mostly the rich to the detriment of the poor.[11]

Of his friend's son, Hazard wrote,

> Josey called upon me to-day with a book to send you, as a specimen of his abilities as a bookbinder. He gave it to me in the sheet, wrapped up in paper. I told him I would send it. "Please to look at it, sir", said Jo. He said this in a way that shewed he was pleased with the work himself, and wished me to admire it. I did not disappoint him. It so exceeded my expectations that I could [not] help addressing him with, "Now, Jo, tell me if you did all this honestly and fairly yourself". He said he did, except stretching the leather over it.

Hazard, an expert on the subject, sent it to the father with the comment that Josey 'knows more about the business already than one-half the bookbinders in New England'.[12]

Hazard's letter of 7 January, *ultimo*, arrived at Dover on Valentine's Day; the letter was tardy, Belknap supposed, owing to 'the weather and roads'. Hazard sent Belknap a pamphlet attacking the institution of the Society of the Cincinnati, a military organization, which 'set' Belknap thinking; 'I have already had some thoughts, but they are not mature enough to commit to paper'.[13]

Hazard meanwhile informed Belknap in a brief letter that 'the paper-maker has disappointed us' by raising the price, which so angered Hazard that 'if it was not that he lives in another county, and I have not time to attend courts, I would prosecute him for breach of contract, and am clear I should recover damages'. Hazard would search for paper at a better price, and quickly, as Mr Aitken was almost ready to begin printing.[14]

Three of Hazard's letters arrived at Dover on 26 February – a good day for Belknap. 'Reading them took up almost the whole day'. Belknap was pleased with Hazard's anecdotes about Josey: 'your mentioning them shews that you have an insight into human nature, and know how to touch its tender springs'. Belknap was impressed with Josey's 'workmanship', and was happy that Mr Aitken showed such 'fatherly feelings' towards his son. In response to Hazard's sympathy, Belknap wrote: 'To live in a warmer climate and among a more polished people would be very agreeable'. But to serve in a Presbyterian church? 'Would not a prospective clergyman,' Belknap asked, 'have to subscribe to a dogmatic formula?'. Belknap's election into the American Philosophical Society at once satisfied and frustrated him.

> Though I am conscious of being a passionate lover of nature in all her forms, yet I am unfurnished with any kind of instruments but a sun-dial and a burning-glass. I can make no meteorological observations but such as every child can make.

Hazard's suggestion to write a 'natural history of New Hampshire' was a good one; 'I have made some beginning, which I intend as a part of my second volume, together with some other observations in the form of our geographical grammars'. The comet Hazard mentioned he 'never could get sight of'. He 'did not know of it' until some of his parishioners asked him about 'the strange star'. 'You may judge from hence that I can derive no great advantage from my neighbours in point of speculation'.[15]

Hazard responded to Belknap's query about Philadelphia stoves, for which Belknap thanked him. Belknap had wanted one for use in his study, but he had since found an appropriate one, made of 'plated iron, and at about half the price of a cast one', that would answer the purpose. The winter, which 'has been very severe', required good stoves. 'A long spell of cold, dry weather and deep snows have rendered travelling, for a great part of the time, impracticable'. Once again several aurora boreales had appeared, proving the Shakers to be *'false prophets'* Belknap wrote,

> They have come within six miles of us, and perform their agitations with a volatility and flexibility which the ignorant observers can account for only by witchcraft. It is confidently said, and I believe it is true, that one of their late meetings was introduced by handing round a bottle of rum; of which each taking a large draught became *inspired*.[16]

Belknap spent the cold days worrying about the Confederation, a 'democratic government' that the conservative republican Belknap thought 'was extremely inconvenient in itself, and very inadequate to the purpose' of governing a large territory, growing ever larger. Belknap, testing friendship, wondered: 'What is the reason that the printing of my work is so long delayed? I am at a loss how to answer the enquiries that are frequently made on this subject'. Betraying friendship, he added, 'Mrs. B. says no cordial revives her like your letters'.[17]

Hazard reassured his friend on 1 March that the printing of the *History* had begun once paper at a good price was discovered, which put Hazard in 'better humour' than his previous state of 'great wrath'. Hazard excused his hurry and lack of attention to Belknap's interests as being out of his hands: 'indeed, I can hardly ever call an hour my own: it is but seldom that I get home to dine with my family', his new wife and their servants.[18]

Belknap, long in contemplation over the threat to civil order posed by the Confederation government, spent the better part of a day, 3 March 1784, exploring his social and political views in a long epistle to Hazard. Belknap typically began by quoting Benjamin Franklin, who wrote in 1760 that it was impossible for the thirteen colonies to unite into one government except in response to an outside danger. This happened in 1776, when the threat to their common liberty forced the American colonies into a temporary union that became the Confederation government. Belknap wondered: 'If an union could not be formed until we were driven to it by external oppression and tyranny, is it likely that such an union will hold when that pressure is removed?' Belknap found it absurd that there should be thirteen *sovereign* states joined together into one; the Congress had little power, and could scarcely enforce its decisions or raise a revenue. The States alone decided the issue of taxation, raising a revenue for the use of the whole; self-interest usually overwhelmed public support of the united government. Added to this were divisions between the states over issues of representation, taxation, jurisdiction over western territories and trade. Belknap scoffed at pure democracy based on pure equality, arguing that inequality is 'the natural tendency of things', both in nature and among humans. 'Is not this noble creature, man, necessarily subject to lords of his own species in almost every stage of his existence?' Man is 'a miserable creature' without the artificially-imposed order of government. Living in Dover had taught Belknap a harsh lesson that humans, as long as they are generally content with their lives, are apathetic about the nature and structure of government. Taking his cue from the geography of New Hampshire, where such apathy reigned, he wrote: 'If Providence has placed us in a mountainous country, why should we reduce it to a plain? Let it stand as a principle that government originates from the people; but let the people be taught ... that they are not able to govern themselves'. With that Belknap declared, 'but I have done, and I believe you will think it is time'.[19]

Hazard wrote on the Ides of March in response to Belknap's query about the required testimonials for the Presbyterian faith. A Presbyterian minister 'would be expected' to 'declare his assent to the doctrines contained in the 'Westminster Confession of Faith', drawn up the century before by devout British Presbyterians. He reassured Belknap that membership in the American Philosophical Society should neither be taxing or daunting, for the society was young and its transactions few. The Delaware was beginning to thaw, which would allow Hazard to forward to Belknap by ship the books meant for the Dover social library. Aitken included a gift for Belknap's social library of his recent labour, Hugh Blair's *Lectures on Rhetoric*. Hazard warned Belknap that although '*plated* iron stoves cost *less* money', the '*sheet iron*' will 'soon *burn out*'; hence he recommended that Belknap spend more for the cast iron stove. Hazard was glad to report that notwithstanding the problems with the previous 'grand exhibition' in honour of George Washington, like the 'Phœnix ... a new one is to rise from the ashes'. Hazard agreed that the Shakers were absurd enough to be dangerous, but counselled: 'Let them alone. Opposition will serve only to encrease [*sic*] their numbers'. Aitken was sending Josey to school, and was finally ready to begin printing Belknap's *History*. There was one problem: no paper: 'Mr. A. was obliged to use your paper [to print Blair's *Lectures*], as the severity of the season was such as to prevent any being made ... This will not finally delay your work, because he could not begin upon it before' the other 'was finished'. More paper was to arrive within the week. Hazard, already busy and hurried, spent his 'evenings now in revising your manuscript'.[20]

Three days later he appended further news: Josey was attending school kept by a 'famous' teacher, Mr Lesley, for whom parents of young scholars waited in line. Thawing ice had caused quite a problem in Philadelphia:

> The ice in Schuykill [River] broke up a few days ago: it formed a dam below what we call the *middle ferry*, which occasioned a flood, and strewed the bank with a great number of congeries of ice. These now form a very romantic scene. They appear like huge rocks irregularly placed upon the shore, and are in form something like haystacks. One of them which was measured is 15 feet in height. Much damage has been done upon the banks of the river.[21]

Hazard, who knew about patience in matters of love, was duly impressed by the *Freemason* John Eliot: 'so long engaged, his bliss so long delayed, and he alive! Who would have thought it possible? Is not Mrs. B. surprised at it?' Speaking of whom, would it not be nice to visit Philadelphia in the spring and 'gratify Mrs. Belknap's wishes by bringing her with you?' 'I am glad that my letters afford Mrs. B. amusement. Tell her that I shall watch opportunities of communicating agreeable information, and from the goodness of her son's character and conduct I am persuaded she will receive it frequently'.[22]

The same day Belknap wrote, enclosing the 'power of attorney' for Hazard to bind Josey as apprentice to Aitken. Belknap thanked Hazard again for his help, assuring his friend of his complete confidence not only in Hazard but in the entire decision and process to convey Josey to Philadelphia and to apprentice him to Aitken. Upon committing Josey 'to the care of a gracious Providence', Belknap's faith, unable to repress anxiety, did vanquish regret. Belknap wished to visit Philadelphia, but could only do it in June, and he refused 'to interrupt the mysteries of Lucina', who oversees fertility and childbirth. Should Mrs Hazard have the child on the fifteenth of Juno's month, 'it will coincide with the *dies natalis* [New Style dating] of your humble servant, who will then complete his 40th year'. Belknap nevertheless wished to see Hazard, as, he wrote, 'I have not one of the right sort with a dozen miles of me: I mean a sympathetic and congenial soul, with whom I can *mix essences*, and talk upon *every subject* with equal ease and pleasure'.[23]

March in New England is forever muddied, hence so affected were the roads that few of Belknap's epistles could clear Dover: one 'waited here at a tavern, a whole week, for a conveyance. I then took it up and covered it again, but it lay several days longer, and finally, having an opportunity' of a friend bound for the south, Belknap 'sent it to the post-office in Boston'.[24]

Belknap followed with another letter at the end of March, patiently awaiting the printing of his book, still hoping that copies would arrive in time for Election Day in Massachusetts, at which Belknap, as well as many of his subscribers, would be in attendance. Belknap, in considering the amount of new mail occasioned by expanding foreign trade, could think of no one to compare with Hazard's industry than he whom Solomon had in mind when he wrote: 'Seest thou a man diligent in his business? He shall stand before kings; he shall not stand before mean men'. That Hazard could also spend so much time on Belknap's concerns (of book and child) amazed Belknap further; he thought Hazard's 'benevolence' easily equalled his industry.[25]

On 11 April Belknap received Hazard's letter of 18 March, *ultimo*, the several attachments of which yielded quite a bit of laughter. One, a '*Dialogue of the Dead Dog and Cat*', was a biting satire about the filth of Philadelphia's streets. The treatise describing 'the experiment to prove the inflammability of *bowel-air*' was particularly humourous; it 'served to dissipate the stagnating vapours of a week's confinement'. Belknap, in the mood for hilarity, responded to Hazard's request that his friend visit Philadelphia with the comment that like a Quaker '[I] feel a drawing' to go; if his parish would furnish him with 'a viaticum', he, like a Roman on assignment, would take leave of them for 'six or eight Sabbaths' – alas he was neither a Quaker nor a Roman![26]

Nor was he a Presbyterian. Notwithstanding his friend's best wishes that he relocate to Philadelphia, Belknap was a Congregational minister who believed literally in the Protestant tradition in the right of each individual to examine the Word, as well as his own conscience, to determine the fiat of Jesus. He engaged in a long, vehement denunciation of the contrary, which sounded a lot like Hazard's Presbyterian beliefs! Belknap vicariously placed himself before the Presbyterian elders who would demand his conformity to dogmatic catechisms, to which he would eloquently dissent. Likewise, Belknap wondered whether science would have made such strides during the past two centuries if science societies such as the Royal Society demanded that prospective members assent to a systematic 'scheme of Philosophy'. Belknap believed that theology as well as science demands an open and free inquiry, for 'the book of Nature and the book of Scripture, being works of the same Author, are open to the inspection of all men, and our business is to search them, and learn what we can of them'. Hence, it matters little whether the searcher is a philosopher, a scientist or a clergyman – the search and the object of inquiry are the same. 'Creeds, either in philosophy or divinity, should never be imposed, because they tend to fetter the mind and stop its genuine excursions into the field of truth'. Only once, in 1767 upon accepting the call of the Dover Parish, had Belknap 'subscribed' to a 'confession', which merely reflected his sentiments at that time; he had gone through quite an alteration of belief during the intervening years. The singular guide to Christianity is the New Testament, the interpretation of which varies with each individual over time. As for Church government, Belknap agreed with Alexander Pope: 'That which is best administered is best'. Belknap loved 'to *breathe a free air*' in political as well as religious matters, and was thankful that the brotherhood of ministers in his 'neighborhood' sought not to impose standards and catechisms.[27]

Aware of the length of his letter, Belknap laughed with 'the good apostle Paul' who 'once said' 'bear with me a little in my folly'. Belknap asked Hazard to 'let me have *my own* way' and 'I will, another time, consult *your* ease, and be shorter'. Belknap, whose opinion respecting General John Sullivan had gone through quite a change, 'had the honour of his being one of my auditory to-day, when I preached an *Easter* sermon'. Belknap wondered whether or not Sullivan was a member of the American Philosophical Society. New Hampshire's natural history interested Sullivan, as it did Belknap, who planned a 'circuitous journey' northward to acquire observations with which to form a long chapter for the second volume of his *History*. He found that the second volume progressed faster than the first, 'for the same reason that a man who has built one house knows better how to go about a second'. Which was why Belknap was growing irritated with Aitken, who should know his craft well enough not to delay the printing of a book much desired by its subscribers (as well as by its author).[28]

Less irritating were the Shakers, who did not know any better. 'There are a few of them at Barrington, about 6 or 7 miles from here, and another parcel at a place called Loudon, which is near the confluence of the Pemigewasset and Winnipiseoge [Winnipesaukee] Rivers, and some at Massabesick [Massabesic], in the county of York', in Maine. 'They have strange postures and actions; the common opinion is that they are under the power of *witchcraft*. This is the usual way (among ignorant people) of solving every uncommon appearance'. One Shaker belief fascinated Belknap: 'that they are judges of the world, and that the dead are daily rising, and coming before them to be judged'. Many sinners had appeared before them, such as George Fox and George Whitefield, both of whom were 'absolved from their errors, and are now at rest'.[29]

The *Freemason* John Eliot was, however, never at rest, because of love. Belknap wrote of his friend's trials,

> To persevere for six or eight months in such a line of conduct requires as much skill as to regulate the movement of an air-balloon. He appears to have a sufficient quantum of *gas* in his composition; but he keeps it so well counterpoised and tempered that it does not carry him beyond the force of gravitation, so that I hope his flight will be steady, and his return gradual and safe.[30]

Belknap, unwilling to release the pen and close the letter, the next morning looked outside and reported to his friend: 'This morning we have one sure indication of the breaking up of winter, viz., the flight of pigeons; but there is a great quantity of snow yet on the earth, in spots. We have had an extremely long, severe winter'. He added the postscript: 'Just as I am closing this, I have a letter from the Freemason, by which I expect to see him at Portsmouth next week. I shall then, perhaps, be able to tell you whether his amour is near consummation'.[31]

Hazard, up to his ears in postal affairs, domestic duties, checking on Josey, correcting the press for Belknap's book and attending Philosophical Society meetings, could scrawl but a hasty line in the third week of April. He informed his friend that a brief piece Belknap had sent to the American Philosophical Society on the efficacy of parsnips at sea as nutritious food for sailors was read, 'and proved very satisfactory'. Hazard enclosed the first sheets of the printed *History* for Belknap's inspection, commenting on its 'elegance'.[32]

Belknap, in similar 'haste' because the state 'legislature have appointed a fast this week', wrote to tell Hazard that 'the Freemason's eternity is to end in June. He is by this time tête-à-tête with his dearest'. He added that Portsmouth Postmaster Jeremiah Libbey was very busy as a 'committee man to build a meeting-house' for the town.[33]

Belknap wrote again a week later, thanking Hazard for information (in a lost letter) about 'Josey's illness: he was subject to sudden ill turns on occasion of any irregularity in his diet, but they are soon over'. Belknap apologized for his bad spelling, which he blamed on his 'polyglot' sermons, which are 'composed of long hand, short hand, clipped words, hieroglyphics, mathematical figures, and arbitrary marks'. Particularly in the wake of Jo's sickness, Belknap wished to go to Philadelphia, 'but an empty purse is a poor travelling companion'. Meanwhile Belknap wondered whether the Congress has 'the art of necromancy', such were the many names they 'conjured up' for ten proposed western states. 'Such a mixture of Greek, Latin, English, and Indian, perhaps, never was seen before'. The Freemason 'goes on swimmingly', as does the Metropolitan Buckminster, though his wife, once dear to Hazard, 'has had an ill turn lately'. Likewise, Ruth Belknap's 'nerves are weak'; she intended journeying to Boston as a cordial. She and Mrs Aitken were exchanging letters, as were the Belknap and Aitken children.[34]

Hazard sent more printed 'sheets of your History' with his letter of the first week of May, in which he earnestly wished that Belknap could journey to Philadelphia soon, perhaps in the autumn, when 'it is a pleasant season for travelling, and the heat will not be so troublesome and oppressive as in summer'. 'My reasons for wanting to see you are particular, and I do not choose to commit them to writing'. Hazard, concerned for his friend's welfare, hoped to convince Belknap that a move to Philadelphia would suit Belknap as well as his family. But these were private matters, not fit for the post. 'The distance between us is too great to admit of asking questions and communicating information. More may be done *here* in half an hour than in three months in our present situations'.[35]

Belknap's letter of the same day, 3 May, contained a not so subtle criticism of Aitken's decisions and work. 'The paper' used for Belknap's book 'is not so good as that on which Blair's Lectures is printed', which was the paper originally intended for Belknap's book! 'I am sorry it so happened', Belknap claimed, 'more for Mr. Aitken's sake than my own'. To add insult to injury, 'I wish I had seen and read Blair's Lectures [on writing style] before I sent my copy to the press. I should certainly have corrected the style in many places; but it is now too late'. At least the quality of Aitken's print was good.[36]

In early May Hazard at last found time to write Belknap a proper letter. 'Yes', he replied, 'the dialogue between the cat and dog, and the experiment upon Bowel Air, were funny enough'. True, Philadelphia streets were disgusting, but he maintained that in all fairness to the 'commissioners' in charge of cleaning, when the dialogue was written during winter 'the frost was not out of the ground, and they had prepared materials for collecting and removing the dirt as soon as it was practicable'. Hazard continued to twist Belknap's arm to visit the city, notwithstanding the filth. 'Some particular friends (say Ulysses and his brother) to whom I communicated your political letter' of March 3rd, *ultimo*, attacking the Confederation, 'are very anxious to see you: they think you could be useful among us without any injury to yourself. You know *my* partiality. Compare this with my last letter'. *Ulysses*, Dr Clarkson, apparently was talking quite a bit about Belknap, with the result that he had sold subscriptions to Belknap's book among political conservatives.[37]

Hazard was anxious to dispel Belknap's apparent negative view towards the Presbyterians. 'I find we are upon the same plan as to creeds and confessions' – that is, neither man liked them. Hazard chose to live under the mode of Presbyterian church government, just as he chose to live under the American Republic. He thought for himself as a citizen of both governments, civil and religious. He wrote,

> I am neither of Paul ... Luther, Calvin, nor anybody else, but will think for myself, in spite of all the popes, councils, kings, bishops, general assemblies, synods, prebyteries, and church sessions in the universe; so that you see I am as much of a latitudinarian as yourself, notwithstanding the Presbyterians have lately chosen me one of the trustees of their temporalities [modes of church government].[38]

On other matters Hazard wrote that General Sullivan 'is a member of the [American Philosophical] Society'. He joked that the Shakers, by acquitting 'Fox and Whitefield', 'may gain friends by their civility'. He had just seen Josey, who 'is well'. The '*exhibition* is to be this evening: *it is said* that an air balloon', recently successfully flown in France, 'will form a part of it. We now have beautiful spring weather'. The *Freemason*'s coming nuptials excited Hazard: 'As he contains such a quantity of gas, it will be well if he does not become ignited in consequence of the heat; and then, woe betide him, he'll never live to top another chimney'. Jeremiah Libbey's 'sectarian zeal' in helping to start a universalist religious society in Portsmouth surprised Hazard, who wondered what the Metropolitan, who was a more traditional Calvinist, thought of the 'schism'. Another of Hazard's clerical friends, Dr Gordon, had been visiting but was now on his way south to visit Mount Vernon for the sake of examining General Washington's papers as part of his research to write a history of the War.[39]

Belknap's love and respect for Hazard continued to grow. 'How you spare time', he wrote to his friend in May, 'from your necessary business to attend so much to me and my concerns, I can judge only from my heart, which tells me that I would gladly do as much for you, were it in my power, though I should redeem time from sleep'. How much Belknap wished to relocate to Philadelphia: 'I think on coming to Philadelphia with as much earnestness as the crew of Æneas's ship did on Italy'. Yet it would never be so, as Belknap no doubt suspected. 'But if I should never see you there, yet there is a place where, I trust, we shall meet, and all our social affections find full and uninterrupted indulgence'. One must wait upon death.[40]

Belknap, in from Portsmouth, knew of a dozen or more serious 'readers' who would love a copy of Blair's *Lectures*, if Aitken would send copies to sell. Speaking of Portsmouth, Belknap's friend the 'Metropolitan (who, though nervous to a high degree, has an excellent heart) ... was observing that a very good use might be made of these air-balloons which are so much talked of, without endangering anybody's life or limbs'. Perhaps they could propel carriages, serving as a replacement for horses. Buckminster was 'an excellent husband' to Hazard's former amour, 'though sometimes [he is] rather too gloomy, which he cannot help'. His situation in Portsmouth as a preacher who was far removed from the intellectual centres of the new nation, as well as his wife's constant health problems associated with pregnancy and childbirth, led to melancholia. Belknap feared for Eliza, his wife, whose 'mother died young'; her father, the Reverend Benjamin Stevens, of Kittery, Maine, downstream from Portsmouth, was similarly in 'the dull business of preaching to a few sleepy fishermen'; 'paddling up and down to Portsmouth every week' was his only 'amusement'.[41]

Belknap, this spring of 1784, was 'at present in a kind of widowed state, Mrs. B. having taken a ride to Boston ... to try the effect of change of air, and the motion of a carriage on her nervous system, which from many concurring causes' – war, finances, loneliness, boredom, worry over children – 'seems to be giving way. If this journey should not mend it, I shall begin to expect the worst; but I beg you would not mention a syllable of this in any of your letters, for she constantly reads them, and is always highly delighted with them'.[42]

Belknap's comment in his letter of the '30th ult', respecting his strange hieroglyphic notes reminded Hazard of Dr Ezra Stiles and his attempt to translate the mesmerizing inscription of Dighton Rock, found at Massachusetts. As confusing were names proposed by Congress for new states (such as Sylvania, Michigania, Cheronesus, Illinoia, Saratoga), at which Belknap rightly laughed – but Hazard as postmaster general 'must say nothing'. Ah, the trials and tribulations of love! 'The poor Freemason! Why don't you instruct him how to shorten his eternity?' The Metropolitan, already married, was no better off – 'his expectations were raised high indeed' for a wonderful son or daughter. The tragedy of the miscarriage would possibly be repeated, for 'such mishaps tend to produce more'. Hazard added that his own 'prospects are at present fair'.[43]

Belknap wrote three letters in short order at the end of May. One was merely to lament the sluggishness of the post:

> I generally receive your letters on Saturday or Sabbath day; and though I often write in the Sabbath evening, or Monday morning, yet if Monday be foul weather, or there be an high wind, I cannot get any letters down[river] so as to go by the post on Tuesday

Hence they would sit in Portsmouth for several days before being sent south to Boston. Mrs. Belknap had just returned from Boston; her spirits were 'bettered by the journey'. Belknap wondered in his letter of 24 May who '*Ulysses's brother*' was, whom he hoped to someday meet, along with Hazard's other Philadelphia friends. On this subject he added,

> I wish, however, that when the time shall come for me to see them they may not have cause to alter that opinion which you say they have formed of me. It was always my unhappiness not to be able to express myself so well in conversation as in writing; at least not so much to my own satisfaction, for which reason my friends must always be in the exercise of candour towards me.[44]

Belknap, feeling loquacious, continued, asking Hazard about the origins of 'St. Tammany's day' in the Middle States, and informing him of the death of Anthony Benezet, a Philadelphia Quaker who gave 'his estate for the purpose of educating negro children'. Belknap, who opposed slavery and the oppression of other people according to race and background, wished 'we had more such good men. Let them appear in what garb or belong to what denomination soever, my heart will always love them'. Belknap, who felt a special affinity to Hugh Blair (Aitken being the printer of Blair's book), continued his study of the *Lectures*. He discovered that his own teacher of rhetoric at Harvard, William Dugard, taught like one master carpenter did his apprentice: he gave him tools with their names, but never taught him how to use them. Belknap yearned to have a master like Blair examine his *History* and either pass it or 'censure' it. 'By the way, what think you of my sending a copy to General Washington? I have had such a thought, but submit it to your advice: you know the high esteem I have for his character'.[45]

Hazard's employee Portsmouth Postmaster Jeremiah Libbey 'is a clever, candid, obliging man', whom had unnecessarily gained the ire of Joseph Buckminster because of his efforts to establish a universalist society in Portsmouth. Buckminster and Belknap did not see eye to eye on this issue. Buckminster took the old Calvinist stance of enduring torment for sinners; Belknap could not conceive of a *just* God allowing his children eternal pain. Belknap anxiously awaited Dr Charles Chauncy's new book on the topic, which was on its way from London, where it had been printed. 'When it arrives, and begins to be read', wrote Belknap, 'I intend to be more open and explicit on the subject than I have yet been'. One opponent with whom Chauncy (and Belknap) would have to contend was Hazard's good friend William Gordon, currently engaged in research at Mount Vernon. Belknap, clearly a bit jealous, demanded of Hazard: 'What mean these frequent long peregrinations?' Belknap, intending at some point to peregrinate southward to Hazard's neighbourhood, had until then to rely on the written word to form the images of the activities and growth of his son Josey. Belknap wondered about the 'account of his expences for schooling and clothing', and hoped Aitken would forward it soon, 'for I love to keep the sounding line a-going, that I may know whereabouts I am'. Belknap wanted to talk long into the night with Hazard about personal and family matters: 'let me suspend them till we can confer *viva voce*'.[46]

'The May storm is now upon us' – Belknap, knowing that his letter would not go out for another week, sat on it, adding whatever he could think of. May in New Hampshire is an awkward month of hints of summer and memories of winter. The north wind reminded people such as Belknap of the latter: 'it has continued three days',

> Our apple-trees are now but just beginning to shew the blossom unfolded: the usual time for full bloom is the 20th of May. I have not yet done planting my corn at the parsonage, which Josey can tell you I used to do 12 days sooner than this.

Belknap was as anxious as an expectant father for news of Mrs Hazard's travail and Mr Hazard's joy.[47]

'Tuesday, May 25th. N.E. wind and rain; the fourth day of the May storm' – and Belknap, indoors and restless, wrote to Hazard again to tell him of his deaf uncle's successful experiment contriving a chestnut rod with notches at both ends for the teeth of speaker and listener. Belknap transcribed the letter at large for Hazard, adding: 'If I lived where artists were handy, I would certainly interest myself in the affair from a principle of benevolence, as well as for the sake of improving natural knowledge'.[48]

Hazard wrote on the last day of May to inform Belknap that he was a new father: 'last Wednesday evening', the 26 May, 'Mrs. H. was safely delivered of a son' – 'both she and the child are as well as can be expected'. He followed up a week later, telling his friend:

> my most sanguine wishes have been gratified. Mrs. H. continues remarkably well for the time, and the young gentleman thrives cleverly. We intend to call him *Samuel*, which was my father's name. If he discovers as good an *ear* as he does a *voice*, I think he will be fit for a professor of vocal music, should he live.

Hazard was becoming 'quite a domestic character', unlike his old bachelor days, which at least taught him how to be '*methodical* in my business', the only way he could simultaneously look after the post office, his family, and Belknap's concerns. Notwithstanding his constant attention to detail, some errors crept into Belknap's *History*, which reminded Hazard of the story

> of a man in Europe who printed a Bible, and determined there should not be an error in it. For this purpose, when he had very carefully corrected a sheet himself, he hung it up at his door, with an offer of a guinea to any person passing by for each erratum he should discover. He soon disliked his plan, for he found his guineas went much faster than he expected, and at length concluded to be contented with his own corrections.[49]

Responding to Belknap's letter of two months earlier, Hazard thought that Belknap's reasons for not wanting to subscribe to Presbyterian 'formularies' were 'perfectly just, and I cannot help hoping the time will come, and that before long, when men will dare to assert their Christian as well as natural liberties'. Hazard had more to say on this topic regarding the comparison of church and state, but 'a *woman* has come to my house, and she keeps such a talking that I can write no more'. He promised to write again soon.[50]

The May storm had departed in the wake of warm weather and sunshine which drove fruit trees to blossom and black flies to bite incessantly when Belknap sat to pen a long epistle on one of his favourite topics, the discovery of America. Hazard had mentioned in passing Dr Ezra Stiles, and his investigations into the strange hieroglyphics of Dighton Rock. Belknap supposed Hazard 'had never seen' Stiles's 'Election sermon, wherein, among a thousand pretty stories, he tells us that a copy of the inscription had been sent to a learned professor in France, who has discovered the characters to be *Phenician*, and that they are a proof that America was visited by some of the Canaanites' fleeing the attacks of Hebrew marauders three millennia earlier. This was an odd twist to an idea more current among eighteenth-century investigators, that the American Indians could have been one of the lost tribes of Israel. Belknap disagreed with such notions in particular because they contradicted his theory that America was without inhabitants for at least another thousand years, until after the birth of Christ. He continued making fun of Stiles: 'The Doctor has given the whole detail of the population of America, which was certainly the work of these Phenician navigators, who having set up a pillar at Tangier', Morocco, 'passed the straits [of Gibraltar], got into the trade wind, and were wafted to America. How the trade-wind blew them to *Dighton*', in Massachusetts, 'I know not: its natural course would have carried them to the West Indian islands; but perhaps they could sail close upon a wind', tacking, 'or perhaps they might coast the continent northward; or – or – or – there is no end of conjectures when one's imagination is warmed, as the Doctor's apparently is with his system'. Belknap laughed at Stiles's theory that some of the Canaanites made their way, in a purposeful manner, to the north-west coast of America. He wrote:

> When I came to read this, I could not forbear bursting out into a great laugh, and repeating part of a little song, which I remember was part of a childish play:
> Some go east, and some go west,
> And some go over the crow's nest.

Belknap assumed that Dr Stiles's speculations would find their way to 'Mother Goose', and be remembered in 'song'. 'If I was acquainted with the Doctor, I would suggest to him that the Sachem Madockawando, of Penobscot, was probably a descendant from Madoc, the Welsh prince, who is said to have been blown over to America in the 12th century!'[51]

Love continued to overflow from Boston to Maine in the persons of John Eliot and Joseph and Eliza Buckminster. Eliot, the *Freemason*, must continue to lie 'diagonally in his bed ... for three months longer' because 'the old folks have, I know not for what reason, concluded to defer his conjunctions [marriage] till after the dog-day heats are over, so that you need not so much fear an ignition'. Meanwhile 'the Metropolitan's "home" can "now salute him with a father's honoured name". He had a son born the week before last, and I heard last week that all was well'.[52]

Hazard, in a lost letter, vehemently disagreed with Belknap's assertion that the paper used for his book was substandard. Aitken huffed that he was 'willing to risque his reputation on the goodness of the paper'. Belknap had to relent, and apologize. He went out of his way as well to thank Hazard over and over for his efforts on his behalf.[53]

Belknap also admitted that his enthusiasm of several years earlier for the talc, *isinglass*, was overdone, that it was not so wonderful a discovery, and scarcely useful for anything save 'lanthorns [lanterns]'. Its use as window glass was very limited, as Belknap saw on a small house in Summersworth [Somersworth, New Hampshire] that was glazed with it 3 or 4 years ago, and the windows now look very dirty and shabby. They tell me also that the wind shatters it. It did well enough in the time of war, when glass was not to be had; but it is now not much used.

Ruth Belknap joined her husband in wishing Mrs Hazard 'a good – what shall I say? – *parturition* is the Johnsonian word'.[54]

The parturition was successful, as Hazard informed his friend in a mid-June letter. 'The young postmaster,' three weeks old, 'has paid the *Lower House* a visit' in the care of his nurse; 'his *mother* flatters us with the hopes of a similar honour from her'. Hazard, a father now, tended to reflect on his own boyhood; Belknap's question about Tammany gave him a perfect excuse. He reflected,

> When I was a boy, I used to wear in my hat upon that day [St Tammany's Day] a buck's tail, gilded, and a picture of an Indian (Tammany, no doubt) shooting a deer with a bow and arrow. We used to talk of *King* Tammany then; but it seems he has been canonized since the Declaration of Independence, and has now become a *saint*. He will make as good an one as any in the Calender; though I have not heard that he has been approved by *his Holiness* [the Pope]. However, as he is, I suppose, to be the tutelar saint of Pennsylvania, and Pennsylvania is one of the United States, Congress ought to have been consulted about it. Should the 'balance of power' between the States be destroyed by this accession of weight to the Pennsylvanian scale, it would be a sad affair.

Such was the extent of the Postmaster's political satire.[55]

Hazard thought that 'it will be quite polite to present General Washington with a copy of your History, and it will produce a letter from him in *his own handwriting*, which will be worth preserving. I have several, which I intend to hand down carefully to posterity as highly valuable'. Their mutual antiquarian friend Dr Gordon was 'indefatigable' in his search for the past. Having been denied access 'to the secret papers of Congress' once before, he finally 'succeeded' – not only with Congress but with General Washington as well in gaining admittance to his 'archives'.[56]

Hazard, considering Belknap's comments about universalism, had several questions:

> Why do you consider repentance and holiness as necessary to complete the work of redemption upon the universal plan? Does not suffering the penalty compensate the transgression? Are repentance and holiness, upon your plan, to be considered as *meritorious* of salvation, or only as *evidences* of a change of heart?[57]

Belknap, still very much the Bostonian, made the annual pilgrimage in the spring to Boston to experience Election Day. From Boston he wrote Hazard that his letters had arrived at Portsmouth, but through 'the forgetfulness of the messenger did not reach me before I left home; so I must have the mortification of not seeing them till my return, which will be next week'. One of the advantages of visiting Boston in June was to sit in on the town meeting. Here, Belknap had the 'opportunity of seeing *democracy* exhibited in perfection'. Belknap barely found room in the crowded hall; he felt adrift in a sea of faces, most of whom were from the 'inferior orders of people'. Not surprisingly they voted against alterations in the town government that they took to be against their hard-won freedoms. 'No debate was allowed' and those who tried to vote conservatively were shouted down by a 'great ... clamour' followed by a vote against the proposals: 'the shew of hands put me in mind of Milton's description of the flaming swords drawn and flourished in Pandemonium; for with the hands up went the hats, and three loud cheers, succeeded by shouts and whistlings'. Belknap, himself of humble roots but augmented by a Harvard education, sneered that 'the persons who composed this majority ... do not pay one fiftieth part of the taxes laid on the town'. Like most conservatives, Belknap believed that the maintenance of order necessitated the republican subjugation of the common people. Belknap ended his letter in grand rhetorical flourish: The Bostonians 'are as disorderly as any people on earth; and, if I wanted to see an orderly meeting, I would look for it in the council hut of any tribe of Indians on this continent, rather than in the town-hall of my native place'.[58]

Hazard, responding to Belknap's criticisms of Dr Stiles's theories on Dighton Rock, jested,

> Madockawando [the Penobscot chief] would be a good subject of antiquarian discussion, and if it could be found out that *kawando* signifies *descended from* (like the Welch *Ap*, the Irish *O*, and the Scotch *Mc*.) the grand desideratum would be obtained. Perhaps it is best that we should remain in ignorance upon this subject, otherwise we should have to fight the *Welch* [Welsh] as well as the English.

Hazard rejoiced in the simultaneous birth of his son and the Metropolitan's. The *Freemason* wrote that rather than being consumed in the heat of love 'he is as cool as a philosopher'.[59]

Charles Chauncy's (and Belknap's) friend, Boston minister John Clarke, preached at Hazard's church on a tour of the Middle States, 'but was not approved of'. Hazard wrote,

> His subject was the story of the young man who had kept the [Old Testament] law from his youth up. He said so much about politeness and complaisance, that a lady told me she expected he would have recommended *dancing schools* next. Plain, blunt preaching suits our congregation best; and the more the preacher says about human depravity and the absolute necessity of holiness, the better we like him.

Clarke 'said nothing about universal redemption, which', though Hazard believed in it, his fellow parishioners did not, hence Hazard 'was glad of, as he would have given great offence, had he mentioned it'.[60]

In a brief letter at the end of June, Hazard told Belknap,

> Mrs. H. was abroad yesterday for the first time. She has graced my table for some time past, but we thought it not prudent for her to venture out of the house: it is more easy to prevent disorders than to cure them. She has grown very fat, and her son increases in stature. Remember us to Mrs. Belknap. Josey is well.[61]

Belknap, returned from Boston in early July, wrote of the 'late heats' and the drought of 'three weeks' running. 'I am concerned how Josey bears the heat of your climate?' But to the religious issue at hand: 'Now, my dear sir, I must attend to the very important question which you put to me' regarding 'repentance and holiness as necessary in the universal plan'. Belknap disagreed with contemporary antinomians who believed that each human has an 'antecedent' union with Christ, from which they receive the holiness that they experience in life. Belknap believed holiness required personal merit, and was necessary for the happiness of salvation. One cannot live an evil life and expect eternal happiness – at least not yet. Christ frees us from sin by his own act of holiness; we free ourselves from sin, likewise, through trying to conform to Christ and His teachings. Belknap wrote of this as the path to

> eternal life, which is a state of perpetually growing conformity to God. 'Tis begun in the world, and though seemingly is not really interrupted by death, but will be carried on by more rapid degrees in the resurrexion state. Holiness, then, is the direct, essential, and indispensable qualification for happiness: indeed, happiness may be considered as a consequential effect of salvation, rather than as the thing itself. To be righteous, to be conformed to God, is the substance or essence of salvation, and the direct end and tendency of all the instructions, operations, promises, threatenings, trials, sufferings, and discipline which God uses or exercises towards moral beings.

God imposes suffering as a means to bring us to Himself; otherwise, 'I do no see how they could be inflicted by a being of infinite benevolence'. Some universalists believed that God threatens the sinner such that 'at the resurrexion [*sic*]' they 'will rise in a state of horror and distress; but their case will be only like that of a criminal going to the gallows, who receives a pardon by the way, and thus escapes the dreaded execution'. Belknap, on the other hand, believed that the sinner will live again a life of utter torture, followed by a 'second death', wherein the purified sinner, now experiencing holiness, will be meet for God's love in eternal life. 'An immortality in sin or in misery is an idea which the Scripture does not countenance, if its expressions be genuinely and fairly examined. On the contrary, *death* is the wages of sin, and by *death* cannot be understood *immortality*'.[62]

These were Belknap's ideas 'at present ... at least so far as the Scripture gives me light, and beyond that I do not wish to be wise'. No one can presently *know*. Total understanding awaits death. But 'in this general thought my mind rests, that He who is perfectly holy, wise, and good, would never have permitted sin nor misery to have entered into his world, if He had not designed to bring good out of these evils'. Here Belknap halted his pen for the night, picking it up again the following afternoon to finish the letter. He was sorry his fellow universalist John Clarke 'sped no better' at Hazard's parish. 'Clarke is a valuable man; rather too volatile, but a true genius and good at heart. The Freemason, however, is his superior in many respects'.[63]

'I hope this will find Mrs. Hazard on the recovery'. Belknap looked forward to someday visiting Hazard to 'kiss *your little image*'.[64]

Meanwhile the printing dragged on. The appendix of Belknap's book swelled; Aitken ran low on paper – and cash. His Bible did not sell well, nor did Blair's *Lectures*; and Belknap's *History* did not bring in enough subscription money – but the journeymen had to be paid. 'If you have any subscription money on hand, I wish you could contrive to send it on, as Mr. A. is very much pressed'. Bankruptcy and debtor's prison always threatened independent businessmen, even in this 'enlightened' age.

> We have had a very capital bankruptcy here: one Sluyter, a Dutchman of no property, found means to get credit to a very large amount, and has failed (some say for £160,000) to the ruin of several others. I expect this is only the beginning of sorrows, and that this week will reveal more distressing secrets.[65]

Belknap wondered in a June letter whether or not Hazard knew William Haslett, who was making himself known throughout Boston as a critic of good books (like Blair's *Lectures*) as well as of sound Christian doctrine. Hazard responded that he had heard of him, but disliked him too much to want to know him. 'I have been informed, and that by his friends, that he is a *Socinian*', – meaning that he denied Christ's divinity. 'I can have no pleasure or satisfaction in the company of a man who wishes to deprive me of my only foundation of hope for eternity'. The belief in the divinity of Christ and an honest attempt to imitate His virtues were necessary in all times, at all places, especially eighteenth-century America. An example was Belknap's description of Boston democracy, which 'would be a good form of government, could virtue be preserved immaculate, and property be always equally distributed'. Fortunately the monstrous errors and misfortunes of democracy in America are 'controlled by the sovereign power of the Universal Monarch'.[66]

The printing of the book nearly finished, now the binding of books would begin. Hazard was glad that Belknap still thought of someday journeying to Philadelphia. 'Least I should forget it hereafter, I tell you now that I live in Arch Street, between 4th and 5th streets, and nearly opposite the Church Burial-ground Gate'. What often seemed a pleasant spot was currently ugly beyond words, for tragedy beckoned: 'Our little boy is very unwell: I fear dangerously so; and his mother is not a little deranged by her anxiety on his account'.[67]

Belknap wrote on Independence Day, 1784, complaining to Hazard of a 'stiff-necked' Quaker who had withheld one of Hazard's letters to Belknap for an inordinate number of days before reluctantly delivering it as per the request of Postmaster Jeremiah Libbey. 'The communication between here [Dover] and Portsmouth is irregular and accidental', Belknap wrote. Befitting the day (4 July *and* Sunday) Beklnap preached 'on the duty of grand jurors', at which he knew that Hazard would wonder. 'But , if you recollect some of my accounts of this part of the country, you will not judge it impertinent. But, like many other sermons, I suppose it will be disregarded; and I am too much used to this to be mortified about it'.[68]

Belknap finally received a copy of his book, the highest 'value' of which, he wrote his friend Hazard, was the 'back side of the title-page, where *your* name appears' – Hazard registered the book with the 'prothonotary' of Philadelphia. This reminded Belknap of Alexander Pope's friendship with Lord Bolingbroke:

> Shall, then, this verse to future age pretend?
> *Thou* wert my guide, philosopher, and *friend*!

Belknap thought of Pope as well when he noticed the title page, wherein his name as author included his Harvard degrees. 'To be, as Pope says, "stuck o'er with titles", is not my ambition'. But since it was obviously Hazard's wish – '"of his special grace and meer motion" (to use the royal style)' – to include 'the humble A.M.', Belknap was glad to acquiesce.[69]

The rage in Philadelphia, as the cultural capital of the new nation, was air balloons. 'Pray do you intend to take an aerial voyage in the new balloon?' wrote Belknap, 'The proprietors have invited the assistance of everybody to forward their project. If I was acquainted with them, I would write them a letter of recommendation to the Man in the Moon, if they should happen to make a port there in their cruise'.[70]

Belknap was not going so far as the moon, but he was intent on a journey north into the wilderness. 'I expect, next week, to set out on a *land* tour to the White Mountains, in company with several gentlemen of a scientific turn'. Belknap had planned the journey for almost twenty years – something always had prevented before now. No war, no expectant wives, no sickness, nor any other crisis existed at Dover or in the Belknap household; hence it was time to act on what Belknap considered a dangerous mission from which he might not return. 'If I live to come back', he told Hazard, 'you may depend on such a description as I may be able to give. I shall wish you one of the party'. But of course Hazard could not go, weighed down as he was with domestic and official responsibilities.[71]

Yet not even without the burden of responsibility could Hazard have gone, he wrote to his friend on 18 July, because,

> this is the ninth day, my dear sir, that I have been confined by the gout. My pain has been great enough part of the time, but I believe the severity of the fit is over. My feet and ancles [*sic*] are yet sore and stiff, and extremely feeble, so that it is uncertain when I shall be able to visit the office.

In no other way but sickness did Hazard take a *vacation* from his duties as postmaster. At least the gout allowed Hazard the chance to catch up on his correspondence as well as watch from his 'chamber window' when

> a large balloon was sent up, which was intended to carry up a man; but by an accident the ropes by which his chair was suspended were broken, and the balloon ascended alone ... It rose, as near as I could judge, about a mile perpendicularly, when it took fire and was consumed. It is said that, had the man gone up with it, he would have regulated the fire, prevented its being burned, and have raised it much higher, which I think probable.

Hazard, fascinated by the remarkable, declared it 'was a grand and pleasing sight'. He also had some good news: 'Our child is better'. Belknap's child, Josey, Hazard thought was also well, though gout had prevented him from seeing the boy.[72]

Belknap found Hazard to be a most punctual correspondent whenever his friend had gout. Hazard, confined to his bed and no doubt bored, wrote Belknap an atypical long and wordy letter on the last day of July.

> Dear Sir, – This will probably find you returned from the White Mountains, to which yours of 11th and 19th inst. told me this morning you intended a visit. O that I could have gone with you! It was once my expectation. But I have no right to expect to visit *every* place in the world, and I can fully rely upon the testimony of your senses. Should you not have been disappointed, I dare say I shall have a very accurate description of those famous hills; and, probably, such an account of them as may make a suitable memoir to be laid before the Society.[73]

Belknap having pointed out, the month before, a 'capital' error in the printing of a page in his book, Hazard explained that Aitken, who 'stands very much upon his P's and Q's', reprinted the entire page rather than simply let it be noticed on the list of *errata* appended to the book. Hazard had wanted very much to include Belknap's titles, considering that 'they have a prodigious influence upon men, both learned and unlearned'. Many would buy Belknap's book simply because his degrees indicated his learnedness. 'We must take mankind as we find them, and there is no harm in taking an innocent advantage of their weakness'. It flattered Hazard to see his name in Belknap's book, 'because it placed me in a very respectable point of view, as the friend of merit and the patron of science'. Hazard thought 'an aerial voyage in the new balloon ... may be safely done'. Yet money was so scarce because of financial panics and bankruptcies that the 'proprietors' would be unable to pursue their project further. Hazard directed Aitken to forward a 'neatly' bound copy of the *History* for 'General W.', as well as one for the Philosophical Society, who 'have a kind of claim to the literary productions of their members, whom they honour in return by giving their works a place among their archives'. The grapevine indicated that New Englanders were critical of the place of printing of the *History*; Aitken planned to send Belknap a copy to 'shew them' to see whether or not 'they ever saw a book printed and bound in that manner in New England'.⁷⁴

Hazard ended his letter,

> Mrs. H. is well, and sends respects to Mrs. B. She wishes to see her. Our little boy is much better than he was. Within these last four days I have made out to go abroad twice with my flannels on and my feet *upon* my shoes ... Adieu.⁷⁵

Still suffering, 'an invalid', 'attacked with the intermitting fever', Hazard continued writing as August progressed. 'By this time I suppose you have returned from the White Mountains. What are they like? Tell me all about them'. Hazard sent the hundreds of copies of Belknap's book to Boston by ship. 'You gave no directions about insuring the books: perhaps you did not think of it?' Hazard, conservative and cautious, *had*, of course. Anticipating a profession he would embrace in coming years, Hazard figured out the cost of the books, how much Belknap should lose if the ship were lost, and since it was August, a time when storms were prevalent, he insured the books 'for £6 or £7. It will be better to deduct this sum from the profits than to risque the whole'.⁷⁶

During the following week, Belknap learned from his friend in a 23 August letter that Hazard with his wife and child went to the docks to take a short coastal voyage down the Delaware River, round Delaware Bay, then up the coast of New Jersey to Shrewsbury, to visit Abigail's parents. But before embarking, 'I was suddenly taken ill with a giddiness in my head and a fever, and a violent storm arose, which would have prevented our going, had I not been indisposed'. Hazard was impatient to be well. 'For upwards of six weeks I have been unable to go to the office, – a very extraordinary confinement for me!' But then, Hazard had never been a new father before! He wrote,

> My gout seems to be gone, but my feet are swelled yet, and very weak. So long confinement has brought on an universal debility and languor ... My child is much better. Had he died, I should have had no uneasiness about his future state, as I have long been satisfied that subjection to mortality, the cares, pains, troubles, and sorrows of life, and finally the death of the body, are all the punishment ever threatened for *original* sin. You will say this is a curious sentiment for a Presbyterian elder to entertain; but I must judge Scripture for myself.⁷⁷

Belknap, like Hazard a universalist, had the same sentiments, lately strengthened not by disease, as in Hazard's case, rather by a journey to the north and failure to climb the highest point in New England, which forced Belknap to consider the weight of the flesh in general, and the transience of life.

10 PATIENCE AND FLANNEL

Exhilaration mixed with disappointment upon Belknap's return to Dover in the first week of August, 1784. The images and experiences of the White Mountains continued to engage his mind and occupy his emotions. The recollection of failure continually replayed in his thoughts. He wrote to his friend Hazard almost by way of confession:

> My very dear Friend, – Last Saturday I returned from my journey, in which I encompassed the White Mountains and partly ascended the highest, which, being in an angle of 45°, proved rather too fatiguing for my thorax, and, after labouring for 2 hours, I was obliged to leave my company to pursue the ascent, which they accomplished in about 3 hours more.[1]

Belknap, writing from Portsmouth, where he had gone to pick up his mail, among other things, promised to write about the journey at large when he returned to Dover and felt settled. In the meantime he sympathized with his friend's sufferings with gout. He had himself likewise suffered on the journey to the White Mountains. The pains of the temporal state taught Belknap not to have 'such an opinion of long life in this world as some people are fond of entertaining'. According to Belknap, the best remedy for life in general and for gout in particular was 'patience and flannel, my good friend' – as well as, perhaps, 'a piece of lean raw beef applied to the hands and feet when hard swelled, and shifted every 12 hours', which 'will soften the skin and help the exudation of the morbific matter'. And why contemplate the length of life when God holds out for us the promise of eternal life? Hence Belknap wrote to console his friend: 'May Heaven spare your child, or, if taken away, grant you the comfort of believing that the promise of salvation extends to it, – notwithstanding all that Adam and Eve did'.[2]

Ten days later, settled and life back to normal, Belknap sat for the day to pen for Hazard a narrative of adventure in the White Mountains. 'To proceed methodically, I must discharge myself of arrears, or, in the sea phrase, make up lee way, before I give you an account of my late tour. I am four letters in debt'. Hazard had condemned the Rev. William Haslett's 'Socinian' beliefs, to which Belknap concurred. He wrote,

> I think I never met with a person who was really a man of sense, and a scholar, whose company was so disgusting to me. I heard him preach once, and he performed very well. His subject ... was a vindication of the ways of Providence, in suffering the wicked to prosper and the righteous to be afflicted in this world.

Hazard hoped that Belknap, now the able and experienced traveller, would journey next to Philadelphia to see family and friends. Belknap wrote,

> 'Tis true I did indulge the pleasing thought, but, within these few days since my return, my mother has been taken ill, and her disorder threatens to be lingering and distressing. I must not therefore think of being absent while such a material revolution in the family as will be occasioned by her sickness, and (if it should please God so to order) death, is expected.

Meanwhile Hazard's letters revealed his fear of losing a cherished loved-one. 'I am much afflicted with the fears you express of losing your child', Belknap wrote.

> 'Tis an event which, through Heaven's mercy, never yet happened in my family; but I have several times come so near it as to feel the distress in a very high degree; yet it was always mixed with such 'strong consolation' concerning the future state of dying infants, and the mercy of the Supreme Disposer, as I believe would have induced a patient resignation to the divine will, and an increase of love to the divine character and ways.

This would precisely be the case when disaster struck the Belknap family five years hence, and his son Sam died. 'Should you be called to "give up your comfort to the Lord", may he grant you the *superior blessing* of an assurance that "the promise is to your children as well as to you", and that *this promise* is not merely, according to some expositors, a covenant of outward privileges', such as church membership, communion and baptism, 'but a promise of eternal salvation, – such a promise as is worthy of a God to give'.[3]

Belknap, ever on the look-out, as were most eighteenth-century clergymen, not only for remedies of the soul but also for empirically-tested remedies for physical ailments, 'recommended ... a beefstake poultice', which 'seems to sooth and soften the dry skin, and helps perspiration in the swelled part; but I hope by this time you have laid aside your wooden legs, and are restored to health and business'.[4]

'Now for the *White Mountains*'. As the most important adventure of his life, Belknap wrote at length, creating an observant travel narrative of his experiences. The twelve-day journey was 'a genuine tour in the wilderness'. For three days they travelled amid the unknown peaks of the mountains; on 24 July some of his companions ascended the highest peak in New England, Mount Washington, then known simply as the Great Mountain. Accompanying Belknap, who organized the journey, were his fellow clergymen Manasseh Cutler of Massachusetts and Daniel Little of Maine, the physician Joshua Fisher, adventurers John Heard and Enoch Wingate, guide George Place, merchant and land-speculator Joseph Whipple, two Harvard students, John Bartlett and Dudley Hubbard, and the frontiersman and *pilot* Captain John Evans. They set out from Dover on 20 July, taking three days to reach Conway, which lies in the shadow of the White Mountains. The route from Conway to the Great Mountain covered

> 18 miles, the greater part of the way through an old road; *i.e.*, one that was cut 10 years ago, and has been disused for several years; and 'tis now grown up with bushes as high as a man's head on horseback, full of wind-fallen trees, deep mires, and broken bridges; and in one place a tornado had so torn up the trees that we laboured with excessive difficulty to get through with our horses.

They learned from local observers that snow had only recently vanished from the side of the Great Mountain; 'and yet at Conway we had full-grown *cucumbers*. This may sound like a traveller's story, but you may depend on the truth of it. But why, you will say, does the snow lie so long on the south side?' Belknap, who had spent some time investigating the question, concluded that the north wind drives the snow from the summit into deep gullies, where it accumulates, the sun's rays scarcely being able to melt it. These high peaks chill the wind as it scours their tops, so that it arrives brisk and cold at settlements, such as Dover, to the south and east.[5]

The *pilot*, John Evans, an experienced hunter, axe-man and guide, led the men paralleling the course of the descending Ellis River, along the east side of the mountains, to a grassy meadow, high above sea level, that sat in the shadow of the Great Mountain. Here are the origins of several important New England rivers. The axe-man Evans constructed a sturdy hut of evergreen poles and branches, under which they slept in expectation of the next day's journey.[6]

'Saturday, July 24, at 6 ¼ A.M., we began our ascent'. The scientists (or rather, the guides) carried with them barometers, thermometers, a telescope and a sextant, with which to perform a variety of laudable scientific experiments, in particular to calculate the latitude and elevation of the Great Mountain, so to show without a doubt that America, too, produces grand and wonderful phenomena. But by the time they reached the summit, many of the instruments were broken. Not everyone reached the summit. Joshua Fisher experienced a terrible pain in his side soon after they began the ascent. Shortly after he descended Belknap, who had been huffing and puffing all the way, finally found his 'breath', legs and overall strength give out – and they were not even half way up! Should he continue and reach the top, 'I should be fit for nothing but to lie down and sleep'. Belknap 'consented to come down alone, comforting [him]self with that old adage', *To be willing is noble enough*. Making the best of his lonely and depressing circumstances, Belknap did a bit of exploring on his own, and found a beautiful and awesome wall of black, 'square-faced stones, laid as fair and regular as a piece of masonry, the water trickling out from between them'.[7]

He reached the base camp by mid-morning. After a meal and a nap, he and Fisher, partners in failure, wandered about the meadow, discovering an abandoned beaver dam. 'It was old and firm, and overgrown with alders; we could see no trace of their cabbin [*sic*]'. To their own 'cabin' the men repaired at dusk; they put additional hemlock branches on the roof to protect it from the rain, which was falling. 'Notwithstanding all our precautions', the hut leaked and the fire threatened to go out. They spent a long, wet, dismal night, constantly wondering where their friends were.[8]

The others, meanwhile, continued the ascent with great fatigue, reaching the summit by early afternoon. There they found themselves in an inhospitable situation. The wind was piercing and cold. Clouds surrounded them, obscured the view, prevented scientific measurements, then brought an icy fog that so enveloped the men that they realized their desperate condition and the necessity to descend – quickly. The guides, unfortunately, had lost their way, and were unsure how to proceed. Their compasses behaved erratically. Their hands numb, their bodies exhausted, their minds uneasy, they guessed the trail. Their guess proved to be the correct direction, but one so precarious that their chief guide, Captain Evans, took a wrong step and slid 300 ft, fortunately without serious injury. The others, forced to seek an alternative route, did so successfully, rejoining the Captain at the tree line at about dusk. They built a hasty 'fire, and by the side of it stood or lay during the night, parboiled and smoke-dried'. The next day they found their way back to camp. Belknap continued, 'Soon after daybreak, Sunday, July 25, we heard the report of a gun, which we answered; then voices, which we likewise answered; and by six o'clock our friends arrived safe, and not so wet as I expected to find them'.[9]

After a brief rest, they proceeded north and then west of the mountains on overgrown paths towards Joseph Whipple's *plantation* at Dartmouth (now Jefferson), New Hampshire.

> The road was worse than what we had travelled on Friday. The greatest expedition we could make was two miles in an hour, and in some parts not so much. We kept *one man before* [Captain Evans] *with an ax, to cut away windfalls*, or limbs of windfalls, over many of which we leaped our horses, and under many crawled, and went round the tops or roots of many more, and over many broken or rotten bridges, and through many deep sloughs; and, to *aid* the difficulty, we met with an heavy shower, of two hours' continuance, which wet us every one to the skin, and after all were obliged, by the approach to night, to stop eight miles short of our object, and encamp on the wet ground under a bark tent hastily constructed by the side of a large fire made to windward of our tabernacle, so that, if we raised our heads a foot from the ground, we were suffocated.

Belknap kept up his 'spirits' the best he could with healthy doses of chocolate.[10]

The next day, Monday, they arrived at Whipple's home, which often masqueraded as a stockade and a tavern, depending upon the intentions of travellers who knocked at his door. The men arrived wet and tired. 'However, a dry house, a good fire (ay, a *good fire* in the middle of July), and a change of linen, which I had preserved dry in my saddle-bags, was a grand refreshment'. Dr Fisher, 'a delicate, hyp'd gentleman, who, when at home, cannot go into his garden till the dew is off ... was amazed at himself when he found he got through' the adventure 'alive'. Belknap noted that Fisher had 'every symptom of a pulmonic consumption', except that he was '*growing fat*!'[11]

Belknap added finally, 'By this note you may judge that I am very far gone in the same way. How is it with you and Mrs. Hazard?'[12]

Three days later Belknap sat to continue the story. First he responded to Hazard's 'favor of the 31st ult'. Belknap agreed with Hazard's wish that he could have gone on the journey. 'But what signifies wishing, 'tis the most ineffectual work a man can do, and often an excuse for the omission of work and neglect of duty?' He knew that some printers and others in Boston criticized him for having the *History* printed in Philadelphia. Belknap's response was to pay them no heed: 'They are', he wrote of the printers, 'in general, a set of clumsy, selfish fellows'. Belknap promised to set his narrative in the style of a report for the American Philosophical Society – but first he must finish the tale for Hazard, recording the adventure 'just as it rises in my mind, from an inspection of my journal, and *my* own recollection'.[13]

'Whipple's plantation' was situated

> in the midst of a vast amphitheatre, surrounded on all sides but the N.W. by cloudcapt mountains. The view was grand. The vapours were rising in innumerable columns from the sides of the mountains, and converging toward their summits, forming into clouds, and then descending in showers, after a while reascending as before, and thus keeping up a constant circulation.

For a brief moment, the mountains were partially free of cloud cover; Belknap sketched them so to recover the image of them more efficiently later, when home.[14]

'Tuesday, July 27. Cloudy morning'. Storms threatened, then arrived during a hasty church service in a barn where thirty-eight people heard Belknap preach on the first book of Corinthians. It was the first sermon ever given at Dartmouth. 'Eight of their children were baptized'. Other, corporeal pleasures consisted of the joys of maple sugar, wandering about the fertile intervales of the Israel River, and hearing moose-hunting stories.[15]

The next morning they departed Dartmouth on the route south through the Western (Crawford) Notch, a narrow defile between the Mountains, which rise perpendicularly on the eastern side, and on the other sides *in an angle of* 45°, forming a bason, in which is an open meadow, a most *sublimely* picturesque and romantic scene! This is the only practicable passage through the White Mountains.

Belknap advised Hazard that, should a postal route ever be established in this country, this route would be the most efficient. A road, built upon 'the proceeds of a confiscated estate', was under construction. 'The narrowest part' 'of the defile' was '22 feet'. Here was the source of the Saco River, which the men planned to parallel on their return journey.

> These beauties of Nature gave me inexpressible delight. The *most romantic imagination here finds itself surprized and stagnated! Every thing which it had formed an idea of as sublime and beautiful is here realized. Stupendous mountains, hanging rocks, chrystal streams, verdant woods, the cascade above, the torrent below, all conspire to amaze, to delight, to soothe, to enrapture; in short, to fill the mind with such ideas as every lover of Nature, and every devout worshipper of its Author, would wish to have*.[16]

'It was with regret that I left this place and descended toward the south'. The Saco 'is rapid, and full of falls'. Immense heights of rocks surrounded them. 'These,' Belknap wrote,

> when incrusted with ice, being open toward the S. and W., reflect the moon and starbeams in the night, and are sufficient to give rise to the fiction of *carbuncles*, which the Indians and their captives used to report, and which have swelled into marvellous and incredible stories among the vulgar.

The locals as well believed that 'these mountains were possessed by genii, or invisible beings, and therefore never ventured to ascend them'. At Conway, for example,

> the good women were glad there were three *clergymen* in the company, because they hoped we should 'lay the spirits' (this was their own expression). Our pilot [Captain Evans], who was a man of humour, assured them, at our return, that we had done it. So, my good friend, you see I have arrived at the reputation of a *conjuror*. I have been asked, since I came home, whether I did not hear *terrible noises* among the mountains. O the power of nonsense, superstition, and folly! When will mankind make use of their senses and be wise![17]

Even in the mountains Belknap could not stop thinking of books: 'On the side of one mountain was a *projection resembling a shelf, on which appeared four large square rocks, set up edgeways, like four huge folio volumes*'. The circumference of the mountains, they judged, was about seventy miles. They guessed the number of summits to be ten, 'but it is impossible to tell the exact number, unless we should make an aerial voyage, in a balloon'. Here was the source of the great rivers of northern New England. '*If the roads were clear on the back of the Mountains, you might in the same day drink of waters of Saco, Amariscogin [Androscoggin], and Connecticut*.[18]

The expedition split up at Conway; Belknap and his friend Daniel Little accompanied Captain Evans to his home at Fryeburg, the site of the infamous battle in 1725 between the Massachusetts militia, led by Captain John Lovewell, and the local Pequawket Indians. The last day of the journey he returned through Maine to New Hampshire in company with a man from Saco who was, according to Belknap,

> going in pursuit of his wife, who had run away with a company of Shakers, taking with her a borrowed horse, and 25 dollars out of her husband's desk, in his absence. The poor man, if he cannot find her, must lose his *money*, and pay for the *horse*, which some men would be glad to do for the sake of getting rid of *such* a wife.[19]

The scientists had hoped to judge the height of the Great Mountain, but with bad weather conditions and uncertain calculations, they could only guess. Belknap thought it over 9,000 ft. But he knew how 'deceptive' mountainous territory can be to an inexperienced observer. What was most significant about the journey, Belknap told his friend, was not what the 'sons of science' saw, but what they did *not see*.[20]

The culture of early New England and the legends of the White Mountains were inseparable. Here was the great hypothetical treasure-trove of New England, where fabulous crystals and gems shimmered and glowed, and treasure of gold and silver, or more modestly, limestone and lead, could be found a spade's depth away. Here the doomed Rangers of Rogers' company brought their cursed booty, the silver statue of the Virgin Mary and silver candlesticks, only to abandon them to the mountains and their jealous spirits of the dead. Here were amazing summits of white moss and glimmering stone. Here were hobgoblins, angry spirits of the dead, a host of satanic forces, storming and booming and frightening countless generations of intervale dwellers. Here were stories of treachery, deception and death.

Belknap, incredulous before the journey and doubly so afterward, sallied forth with a list of negative discoveries: 'To begin as high as possible, then, I saw no *silver mines*', nor lead – at least 'no person knows where to find it', nor 'limestone, which would have been of more service to the country than silver or gold mines'; no snakes nor any other serpentine creatures, physical or spiritual: 'we saw no hobgoblins, demons, nor cacodemons, no wandering ghosts, nor the least appearance of *Hobamoke*, though I suppose Dr. [Cotton] Mather would have said we had invaded his territories, being "Prince of the Power of the *Air*"'.

> Should you ask what is the cause of the *white* appearance of these Mountains, I would tell you in one word, – *snow*, which lies on them, commonly, from September or

October till July, There is no white moss, nor white flint, nor white rocks, which can give any such reflection as is caused by the *snow*.[21]

Belknap hoped his letter would 'be able to correct one which I think I formerly sent you a copy of, written by G[eneral] S[ullivan] to [Monsieur] Marbois', which was filled with second-hand, erroneous if romantic speculations about the White Mountains'. Hazard was free to share with his friends titbits about Belknap's trip; meanwhile Belknap planned to write a 'memoir' in 'a form suited to the gravity of a philosophical body'. Belknap meant to use the story of the journey for the edification of as many people as possible; hence he asked Hazard to take the letter with him the next time he visited Aitken's, and 'read such parts of it as you may think fit in the hearing of my son ... for I always endeavor to acquaint my children (as they are able) with matters of *curiosity*, and Jo has a large share of it'.[22]

'For your further gratification', Belknap enclosed a rough map of the mountain regions, including a detail of the explorers' circuitous journey and a sketch of the mountains as they appeared on several occasions.[23] He ended with the postscript: 'please to tell Josey that his grandmama is in a declining way. The rest of the family are well, and send their love to him'.[24]

Belknap followed up his long narrative a week later with a brief letter enclosing his *grave* report to the Philosophical Society. Belknap strongly suggested that his mountaineering companion, Manasseh Cutler, be nominated for membership, as he 'merits highly in the literary way'. Belknap, impressed not only with Hazard's prose but the paper upon which he penned as well, asked: 'I wish you would let me know the exact name or quality of the paper on which you write your letters, that I may get some of the same'.[25]

Making up for lost time, Belknap wrote again four days later to respond to Hazard's letter of 16 August, *in statu quo*. He was particularly worried by Hazard's concern that Belknap insure the shipment of books, on their way currently from Philadelphia to Boston. Hazard's letter was 'ambiguous', and Belknap was not sure if Hazard had taken the liberty to insure them or not. If not, it would unfortunately 'have an odd look for me to insure now. It will look as if I thought the vessell [*sic*] was lost, and wanted to save myself at the expense of the under*takers*' ... 'I mean under*writers*'. Belknap attributed 'the ambiguity of your expression to the ill state of your health, of which I am informed by the 1st sentence in your letter'. Belknap's own (current) messy handwriting was caused not by a return of his old enemy, 'the rheumatic fever', rather the loss of his 'penknife' with which to trim the quill, which he 'lent ... to Mrs. B. about 3 hours ago, and she has gone on a visit to Rochester, and I suppose has carried it with her, for I cannot find it'. Belknap had a momentary friendly-evil thought that his friend should continue sick, which would force him to take a journey for his health, which Belknap, his host, would gladly nurse back to normal. Meanwhile Belknap expected that by this time his first letter describing the White Mountains had arrived at Philadelphia, 'in which you will have as much of the White Mountains as a sick man can bear'.[26]

He ended with the postscript:

> I rejoice most sincerely to hear that your son is recovered. When you have recovered too, as I trust you will after the dog-day heats are over, my joy will be complete. 'T is good, however, my friend, to have these cuffs and rubs; they make us more sensible of the value of health. This, as well as all our enjoyments, are heightened by contrasts.[27]

Hazard, continuing a slow recovery, still 'fatigued and fluttered' by such activities as a 'walk that I can hardly write', forced a short epistle to acknowledge Belknap's first narrative account of his journey, 'which has afforded me much entertainment', and to reassure Belknap that his books were insured, so rest easy. 'We have no news. Mrs. H. is well: the child grows better fast. Josey is well: I saw him this morning and gave him your letter. Will talk with Mr. A. about binding him. Love to Mrs. B'.[28]

The concerns of the flesh and the attempts of the spirit and the will to overcome illness and death continued to haunt the two men during the autumn of 1784. Belknap wondered that Hazard could 'write at all, considering your sickness, for which I do most sincerely pity you'. Illness was easier to endure because of *Miranda*. Belknap knew from personal experience. 'Mrs. B ... knows what it is to tend a flannelled pair of legs and hands, and even to *lift* 180 or 190 lbs. of mortality from a bed to a chair, and back again'. With such experiences to recommend her, Mrs B. lamented her husband's tragedy, but had expected it all along. 'The spirit was willing, but the flesh (*i.e.* the lungs) weak', Belknap continued to tell himself, explaining to Hazard it is no 'wonder that such a quantity of matter could not ascend the White Mountains farther than *it* did'.[29]

Belknap consoled himself that Hazard, normally strong and virile, would have failed in the ascent of the Great Mountain as well. 'I hope by this time you will have recovered your health; at least, so far as to make an excursion into the country'. Perhaps bathing would help Hazard exit the sickroom.

> I have a high opinion of the efficacy of *cold water*, internally and externally used; and have been frequently benefited by it. I do not wish you to undergo the operation of such a *shower-bath* as we had in the woods on the north side of the White Mountains.[30]

On 14 September 1784, upon reading Belknap's description of his journey to the White Mountains, Hazard declared:

> Alas, alas! pray end what you began,
> And write next winter more Essays on Man.

Hazard's admiration for Belknap's ability to describe the White Mountains suggested to him the idea that, based on Belknap's obvious talent for understanding the geography of New Hampshire, he should contrive a map of the state and append it to his second volume of the *History*, whenever it should be completed. Intending to write more, Hazard could not, because the 'eastern post' rider, who delivered the letter, 'stays but 2 hours (from his arrival) in this city'. Hazard abruptly closed the letter.[31]

Sabbath evening, 12 September, Belknap responded to Hazard's 'of 30th ultimo'. One friend empathized with the illness and weakness of the other: 'Your inward man is strong enough, though your hand flutters when you write. You will gather strength by degrees, and you must husband it well'. Belknap, assuming a paternal, pastoral figure – but one with much wit, rather like his Uncle Byles – advised the young husband of the risks of approaching the temple of Venus too often when the body is so weak. 'I write as Solomon did his Book of Ecclesiastes, – ab Experientia'. A hitherto unknown experience for Belknap was the illness and death of a loved-one. 'My mother's illness increases, which prevents my enlarging, as I have several letters to write this evening and must visit her too. Love to you all'.[32]

On 19 September, Belknap penned a short epistle to note the storminess of the weather and a visit from the *Freemason* Eliot, who had journeyed to Dover to 'preach for' his friend Belknap, but who could not stay, 'for reasons best known to people newly married'.[33]

Hazard, writing at the end of the month, sent his letter 'at a venture', for, he wrote, 'I have lately ordered a new regulation of the post between this city [Philadelphia] and New York, and cannot yet determine by which day's mail to send letters for you'. 'So the Freemason is *initiated* at last. His next letter, I suppose will be a curious one'. Hazard enclosed something in French for his friend's perusal, then as a postscript asked, 'Can you read French?'[34]

Belknap's letter of 2 October had two purposes, the first was to congratulate Hazard on his recovery, and to express continued concern for Samuel, the newborn of Ebenezer and Abigail, who had been ill: 'may gracious heaven spare its life, and make it a rich blessing to you'. Belknap's son Joseph, much older and in Philadelphia, was chiefly on Belknap's mind. The father drew 'a new power of attorney' to allow his friend Hazard to bind Josey as an apprentice to Aitken. Belknap hoped his son would learn not only to print and bind books but to learn the art of bookselling as well. He asked Hazard to read the entire indenture to Josey, commenting on it when appropriate, inquiring if the boy understood his responsibilities.[35]

If all that Hazard had hitherto done for his friend were not enough, he now informed Belknap, 12 October, that he had written to a London publisher, Thomas Longman, encouraging him to publish an English edition of Belknap's

History, informing Longman of the quality of the research and the writing, that a second volume was forthcoming, and that the author 'was a clergyman with a very small living and a very large family'. Hazard on the other hand had a very small family, but a lively one all the same: 'if our little boy could entertain us with his words as he now does with his gestures, he would give a ... hint' of his love for Belknap and family, akin to the affection felt by his father and mother.[36]

Belknap wrote briefly on 17 October to inform his friend of the death of Sarah Byles Belknap, who 'is at length released from her confinement by the hand of Death, having patiently and quietly resigned her spirit to the Father of Spirits on the 12th instant'. Her surviving husband Joseph Belknap, Sr, would outlive her by thirteen years, dying in 1797.[37]

Hazard, meanwhile, attended the recent meeting of the American Philosophical Society to deliver a copy of Belknap's *History* as well as a 'Memoir about the White Mountains', which particularly caused excitement among the scientists. 'The Secretary' of the Society 'has orders to acknowledge the receipt of them. I hope soon to forward you a letter from him'. Alas, sickness again prevailed in the Hazard family. 'Mrs. Hazard has something of a fever, and her head is much disordered. Our son is well. We all send hearty salutations to your fireside'.[38]

Cool autumn winds on 1 November gave Belknap the needed excuse to spend a quantity of time at the writing desk. He lamented Abigail Hazard's illness, but noted a bright spot:

> How happy is it that you are not all down at once! To have so much sickness at your first setting out in a family way is a severe tryal [*sic*]; but tryals [*sic*] are always accompanied with some alleviating and consoling circumstances, and among others, you may reckon my *not* coming to Philadelphia this fall, for as things have happened with you this would have been an additional burden. Providence often disposes of us and provides better for us than we are aware. I shall anxiously expect to hear by the next that your dear partner is recovered. May gracious Heaven bless you both and make your little son a peculiar blessing to you.[39]

The *Freemason* Eliot, wrote Belknap, likewise newly married, was ill as well, 'and now looks very poorly'. 'He is a most worthy character; but it is rather unfortunate that he went out of Boston for a wife!' This entailed constant travel from Boston to Portsmouth and back, fatigue and illness.[40]

Belknap lamented that his book was not selling 'in these parts ... so great as I wished'. He blamed the price, which he thought Aitken and Hazard had set too high, as well as grumbles about a homegrown author having it printed in Philadelphia, as well as competition from Charles Chauncy's *pudding* finally finding its way in print from a London publisher.[41]

Hazard wrote on 6 November to tell his friend the latest news. The Marquis de Lafayette made a special presentation on 'new discoveries in magnetism' at a recent Philosophical Society meeting. This cheered men who were otherwise worried: trade was languishing as it often does in the wake of war, and Hazard expected hearing of 'many bankruptcies soon' – debtor's prison loomed for many. Hazard added in a letter written a week later that it was 'distressing' to have so much illness in the family, 'but', he continued, 'I have no promise of exemption from the common lot of mankind, nor any right to expect it. If our afflictions work for us the peaceable fruits of righteousness, we shall have reason to rejoice, and glory in them. May this be their effect'. Hazard, having read Chauncy's new treatise on universal salvation (which Belknap had sent him), believed that the 'common lot of mankind' extended to heavenly bliss. Eternal happiness notwithstanding, we live in a world of the passing of time – who knows what the immediate future will bring. Hence, 'great caution will be necessary to keep our little son from proving a snare to us; he gains upon us daily; your experience must long since have taught you the meaning of this'.[42]

A limitation of the Articles of Confederation was that Congress could not form national banking policy, nor issue a standard, national currency. Instead each state issued its own currency and devised financial policies peculiar to itself. Belknap found this created quite a problem when he heard from Hazard that Aitken urgently needed money from the sale of his book, then tried to send bills of payment drawn on New England banks – Philadelphia financiers would not accept them. It required personal intervention from friends and neighbours. Hence Belknap got John Eliot to send a bill to General Mifflin of Philadelphia requesting payment of an old debt; fortunately Mifflin had the money; the bill requested that he remit it to Hazard, which he did. Even so, Belknap had no cash, the book sold poorly, and Aitken needed money. Belknap decided to help the best he could, so wrote a poem, entitled *Jack Frost*, and sent it to Aitken to print and sell in the coming winter season.

Speaking of winter, Belknap wrote that 'the season is now approaching when my correspondence with you will be very much interrupted; but I desire you would write, though my letters may not come regularly. I am now denned like the bears till next April, but have taken care to lay in a stock of literary fodder', which included Dr Samuel Johnson's *Lives of the Poets* as well as '16 volumes of [Charles] Rollin's Roman History'. These, he wrote, 'will enable me to chew the cud through a great part of the ensuing winter'. One might say of Belknap that inactivity begat wit.

> Mrs. B. desires her best regards to your *self*, including both parts of it. Why may not you and I use the regal style, and say *ourself*. I wish no greater impropriety had ever come from the throne. What a miserable figure will *the puppet* who now sits there [King George III] make in history!
>
> I'd rather be a dog and bay the moon
> Than *such* a Briton![43]

Writing at the end of November, particularly in response to Hazard's mixed feelings of the past months of fear for his son's life, tremendous love for the boy, and a sense that a more distant attachment to children is best, Belknap had to disagree. Speaking as a friend and pastor, he counselled:

> I have no fondness for encouraging parents in making themselves uneasy because they love their children, as if they were in danger of idolizing them. It is natural to love them, it is necessary we should. Reason, prudence, and time will teach us how to set bounds to this fondness; but where is the harm of indulging it, especially at first, when the thing is new? How much more rational to play with a darling child than with a lapdog, or parrot, or squirrel! Let Nature have vent.
>
> Enjoy the present, nor with needless cares
> Of what may spring from blind misfortune's womb
> Appal the surest hour that life bestows.
>
> I have administered the same wholesome advice to our good friend the Metropolitan, who has the same fears respecting his child. For my part, I think it is an exercise of gratitude to Heaven for its blessings, to *enjoy* them. As they are sent to sweeten the bitter cup of life, let us taste the sweet, and thank the Giver.[44]

Hazard, unconvinced, responded laconically three weeks later: 'Your advice about loving children is *natural*, but not *prudent*; for, in case of their being taken away, the pangs of separation must be in proportion to the strength of the attachment, and that must be very, very, very great'.[45]

Such was the variable impact of the War for Independence upon Americans of the 1780s. The suffering and violence of war taught Belknap to put himself completely in the hands of God, to receive all experiences, even those of pain and suffering, with piety and gladness, to allow love for God to extend to love for family and friends – if said love for God is unlimited, why should it be any less for those closest to himself? But Hazard had seen too much suffering as he travelled on post roads during the years of war. He saw too many orphans, too many widows. Such sorrow was too much to bear. One can enjoy love, but a little distance is best in a world where one never knows 'if I shall live' from one moment to the next. Indeed, his insecurity during the war years would haunt Hazard for the rest of his life.

EPILOGUE: LET *PASSION* BE RESTRAIN'D WITHIN THY SOUL

In the coming years, for the remainder of the decade of the 1780s and into the 1790s, Hazard and Belknap continued to participate in, and watch and comment about, public political, social, cultural and religious events as they simultaneously tried to order their personal lives and activities in accord with changes in the new American republic. Both men believed that the Articles of Confederation saddled the thirteen states with too much freedom and not enough order, which they believed to be unhealthy for the individual much less a republic of millions of people.

Hazard was enthusiastic about the Constitution drawn up in Philadelphia in 1787 without realizing that a change of government might mean a change in political officers. Although he had hitherto been ardently attached to George Washington's reputation and character, Hazard was taken off guard, disappointed and hurt, when President Washington chose to replace him as postmaster general under the new Constitution. Once again, in 1789 in his mid-forties with a growing family, Hazard was at loose-ends, uncertain and searching. He spent several anxious years trying to manage a sufficient income, eventually involving himself in the burgeoning insurance industry. Meanwhile he edited and published the documents that he had spent so much time and energy searching for and transcribing, although the sales of his *Historical Collections* were lacklustre.

While public political changes caused quite a revolution in Hazard's life, the growth of the American republic brought Belknap increasing security and a growing public reputation as a historian and writer. Lack of support from his Dover parish eventually forced pastor and people to separate; Belknap found a new parish in Boston, and he, Ruth, and their children happily relocated to the city of the parents' birth. Secure in continuing a profession that he had for many years been tempted to leave, Belknap unleashed a flurry of writings to trace and contribute to the American national identity. Belknap finished work on the second volume of his *History of New-Hampshire* in 1791; although he had long planned to include a section on natural history in volume two, he so took to the subject that he penned an entirely separate volume, published in 1792, on the natural history of the state. Meanwhile he published in short-lived American serials a series of biographies on the first explorers and colonizers of America. Belknap used the pen name 'American Plutarch'. After years of acquiring material for a biographical dictionary, the American Plutarch finally published a collective biography, the *American Biography*, in 1794. Meanwhile he wrote a satire of America's colonization and growth towards independence, *The Foresters*; a historical analysis of the validity of the New Testament, the *Dissertations on the Character, Death, & Resurrection of Jesus Christ*, responding to the attacks on the Gospels of Thomas Paine's *Age of Reason*; and a volume of poems and hymns, *Sacred Poetry*. All of these works brought Belknap financial success and literary accolades, cut short by his death in 1798.[1]

The inner experience of revolution during the 1770s and 1780s and the changes in the hearts and minds of these two Americans, Hazard and Belknap, involved personal conflict and private doubts over public events. The Belknap–Hazard correspondence during the 1780s reveals the struggles of two men to juxtapose the personal and emotional freedoms of revolution with the demands of order and security. They found examples in their own personal lives that illustrated the larger American debate concerning freedom versus order. For Hazard and Belknap, the personal freedoms consequent upon the American Revolution were akin to the freedom of the will that God allows the sinner. Free will is a blessing as well as a curse, however. Too much freedom leads one away from the sanctions of God, just as unrestrained license in public affairs results in disorder and threatens anarchy. Shays's Rebellion, and similar events in other states during the 1780s, taught political conservatives such as Hazard and Belknap that order must be imposed upon freedom; otherwise the revolution would disintegrate into never-ending private conflicts. A just God allows His children freedom, but never at the expense of divine order. However, divine order does not mean divine wrath, as God is love, just as public order over private passion can be done with justice and humanity. A minister over his congregation leads with benevolence not tyranny; a government develops flexible laws not rigid rules. God grants humans freedom to act, does not impose a controlling will, but still saves them even after they have fallen short of His commandments. Likewise, Hazard and Belknap believed that the blessings of American freedom must be extended to all Americans, not just whites but blacks and Indians; the order of government, of the Constitution, protects the rights of all Americans, universally. The Presbyterian Hazard and the Puritan Belknap broadened their concept of Christianity to make it more ecumenical, just as they broadened their idea of God, making God so benevolent as to accept all sinners, even non-Christians. But these universalists, Hazard and Belknap, believed that God chastises with the Second Death, bringing sinners in line with His will. Likewise, during the war and afterward, liberty-loving, inherently anarchic Americans must be restrained and chastised by a strong central government; freedom must be constrained by the artificially-imposed order of the Constitution. Belknap gave vent to this personal as well as public conflict, the personal and public consequences of revolution, in 1791, when he wrote an admonition to himself: 'Let *Passion* be restrain'd within thy Soul'. The public events of revolution and the struggle for order within the context of freedom mirrored the private events of the soul, God's truth versus personal temptation, doubt and error. The personal struggle of one's life is brought to a close with death, though the public struggle continues throughout the life of the American Republic.[2]

The go-between of the personal and public is the close friendship of two individuals who bare their souls to each other and mutually gauge the progress of society in the ways of order and freedom. Hazard and Belknap developed this kind of friendship, in which letter-writing along with journal-keeping and other forms of writing – history, memoranda, transcribing documents, sermons, poetry – helped to maintain normalcy during contrary times. These pious scientists and historians used thought and writing as a means to discover truth in chaos, and order in disorder, to explain God's love and constant will amid the multitude of contradictory public events. Hazard and Belknap's mutual faith, love and piety drove them not to despair, but to hope, and to action. Science, history, politics and religion were the means of constant reassessment of their own beliefs – of duty, piety and love – in light of what they understood about God's providence.

When the War for Independence began in 1775 Hazard was postmaster of New York; when it ended in 1783 he was postmaster general of the United States of America. He was a determined bachelor during the war, considering marriage only at war's end. By then he was in his upper thirties, tired of the travelling life, of which he had had much during the previous half dozen years. His travels now were because of changes in government. When Congress moved to New York in 1785, Hazard, of course, followed. Business constantly preoccupied him: When surveyor of post roads from 1776 to 1782, his continual journeys from Philadelphia north to Maine and south to Georgia took him to fascinating places that peaked his interest in natural and human history. His antiquarian interests resulted in a collection of natural and historical items – his *museum,* as he called it. The end of his travels in 1782 and the adoption of a settled lifestyle of home and family meant that Hazard's subsequent journeys were professional and domestic. Perhaps because he had lost his father when he was fourteen, Hazard was reluctant to give his heart unreservedly to others for fear that sudden death would result in the horrible feelings of loss that he had once felt. The destruction and deaths of the war encouraged these feelings of reluctance to love. But in the end he surrendered. Having risked his life so many times during the war,

Hazard took on a new risk in 1784, when he and his wife had a child, his firstborn, Samuel.

If Hazard's experience of revolution was one of movement towards rest, acceptance of the domestic consequences of peace, Belknap's experience was quite the opposite. Before the war Belknap had accepted the responsibilities of being a husband and father, and during the war he found these responsibilities growing in size and changing according to circumstances. He yearned, however, for the kind of adventures Hazard was having, travelling from place to place, seeing first-hand the evidence of historical transactions, experiencing natural wonders of rivers and mountains. Whenever Belknap had a chance to travel, he took it, though his journeys were typically short, going down the Piscataqua to Portsmouth, or ascending the Salmon Falls River to Berwick, or journeying inland to explore the forest and ascend small hills. In 1780, he climbed Mt Agamenticus, a small hill along the Maine coast, from which he could see the Piscataqua valley, which whetted his appetite for more such excursions. In 1782, he journeyed to a larger hill, north of Dover, called Moose Mountain. Such adventures were necessarily restricted because of the war, and the threat of enemy troops, especially in the mountain regions to the north. War's end brought new opportunities for the would-be explorer. The White Mountains had been, since New England was first colonized, the great object of scientific endeavour for explorers. Peace and the achievement of an independent American Republic inspired nationalists such as Belknap to journey to make known the natural curiosities and potential productions of America, which was still a largely unknown continent. His modest endeavours were part of a long line of explorers who took it upon themselves in the coming decades to discover the mysteries of America. The end of the war brought independence to America in general and Belknap in particular – the sense of independence to search for knowledge and share it by means of his many writings. His three-week journey to the White Mountains in July and August, 1784, for example, became the basis for the third volume of his *History of New-Hampshire*. Belknap followed his journey to the White Mountains in 1784 with a journey to Philadelphia in 1785 and, in the 1790s, journeys to upstate New York with scientist and missionary Jedidiah Morse and a journey in search of Bartholomew Gosnold's 1602 failed colony with Noah Webster. Peace unleashed the physical and literary energies of Belknap.

It was, in the end, quite appropriate that Hazard chose Mercury as the symbol of the American postal service. Hazard and his friend Belknap had during the war been messengers of the word in its many forms: science, literature, politics, history, public and private matters. The Belknap–Hazard correspondence was a counter to disorder, passivity and fear. Their many letters and literary attachments uplifted, enlightened and inspired the two men. Their correspondence provided continuity, a mode of certainty, which forms the basis of hope. It is no wonder that both men believed that Providence ordered their own lives and guided the Americans at war, when their letters registered a chronicle of the best of human experience, of seeking, understanding and love, even during, in Paine's words, 'the times that tried men's souls.'

NOTES

The following abbreviations have been used throughout the notes:

AA	American Archives
AE	Andrew Eliot
CMHS	Collections of the Massachusetts History Society
EH	Ebenezer Hazard
JE	John Eliot
JB	Jeremy Belknap
JW	John Wentworth
MHS	Massachusetts Historical Society
RB	Ruth Belknap

Prologue

1. 'History of the United States Postal Service, 1775–1993', online at http://www.usps.gov/history [accessed 16 September 1999].
2. The majority of the Belknap–Hazard correspondence, as well as their respective letters to and from John Eliot, is found in the Belknap Papers, MHS. Most of these letters are published in the *CMHS*, series 5, vols 2 and 3 (with appendix), and series 6, vol. 4 (Boston, MA: MHS, 1882, 1887, 1891). JE to JB, 4 July 1776, *CMHS*, series 6, vol. 4, p. 97.
3. EH to JB, 4 August 1779, JB to EH, 16 August 1779, *CMHS*, series 5, vol. 2, pp. 7–10; JE to JB, February 1781, *CMHS*, series 6, vol. 4, p. 207. Chauncy's book was published as *The Mystery Hid from Ages and Generations* (London: C. Dilly, 1784); see also C. H. Lippy, *Seasonable Revolutionary: The Mind of Charles Chauncy* (Chicago, IL: Nelson-Hall, 1981).
4. See R. M. Lawson, 'Essays on Man: The Belknap Hazard Correspondence', *Historical New Hampshire*, 52 (1997), pp. 19–27.
5. Hazard has not received sufficient attention from historians and biographers. Published accounts of his life include F. Shelley, 'Ebenezer Hazard: America's First Historical Editor', *William and Mary Quarterly*, 13 (1955), pp. 44–73; T. R. Hazard, *Recollection of Olden Times* (Newport, RI: John P. Sanborn, 1879); and A. E. Vermilye, 'The Early New York Post-Office: Ebenezer Hazard, Postmaster and Postmaster-General', *Magazine of American History*, 13 (1885), pp. 113–30. These can be supplemented by R. E. Blodgett, 'Ebenezer Hazard: The Post Office, the Insurance Company of North America, and the Editing of Historical Documents' (PhD dissertation, University of Colorado, 1971). Additionally, the American Philosophical Society has a small collection of Hazard's papers.

6. Belknap has had numerous biographers, including C. K. Shipton, *Biographical Sketches of Those Who Attended Harvard College*, 17 vols (Boston, MA: Massachusetts Historical Society, 1933–75), vol. 15, pp. 175–95; G. B. Kirsch, *Jeremy Belknap: A Biography* (New York: Arno Press, 1982); L. L. Tucker, *Clio's Consort: Jeremy Belknap and the Founding of the Massachusetts Historical Society* (Boston, MA: Massachusetts Historical Society, 1990); and R. M. Lawson, *The American Plutarch: Jeremy Belknap and the Historian's Dialogue with the Past* (Westport, CT: Praeger, 1998). Another good, if dated, source is J. B. Marcou, *Life of Jeremy Belknap, D. D. The Historian of New Hampshire* (New York: Harper & Brothers, 1847). The majority of the Belknap Papers are at the MHS.
7. EH to JB, 15 September 1784, *CMHS*, series 5, vol. 2, p. 385. My understanding of the epistle as essay derives in part from reading the great letter-writers and essayists of the past, such as St Paul's epistles in the New Testament; the epistles of Pliny the Younger and the Roman philosopher Seneca's wonderful *Letters from a Stoic*, trans. R. Campbell (London: Penguin Books, 1969); M. de Montaigne, *The Complete Essays*, trans. D. Frame (Stanford, CA: Stanford University Press, 1958); and Plutarch, *Essays*, trans. R. Waterfield (London: Penguin Books, 1992).
8. Walpole's comment is quoted in the frontispiece of *The Letters of the Younger Pliny*, trans. B. Radice (Harmondsworth, Middlesex, England: Penguin Books, 1969). N. Webster, *An American Dictionary of the English Language* (New York: Converse, 1830), p. 526.

1 Commencement of a Civil War

1. G. Wadleigh, *Notable Events in the History of Dover, New Hampshire* (Dover, NH: by the author, 1913), p. 109.
2. JW to JB, 10 March 1774, 23 September 1774, 18 November 1774, JW to Thomas Waldron, 30 December 1774, and JB to JW, 15 March 1774, *CMHS*, series 6, vol. 4, pp. 48, 54, 64, 71; 'Deposition in Favor of Governor Wentworth', 1 January 1773, *CMHS*, series 6, vol. 4, p. 43.
3. J. Belknap, Interleaved Almanac (Diary), A.1.10., 1774, Belknap Papers, MHS. The beginnings of the conflict in 1774 in Portsmouth are discussed in R. M. Lawson, *The Piscataqua Valley in the Age of Sail: A Brief History* (Charleston, SC: History Press, 2007), pp. 61–4.
4. JE to JB, 9 November 1774, 18 November 1774 and 30 January 1775; JW to JB, 18 November 1774, *CMHS*, series 6, vol. 4, pp. 61–2, 65, 76; J. Belknap, *The History of New-Hampshire*, 2 vols (Dover, NH: Stevens and Ela & Wadleigh, 1831), vol. 1, p. 355.
5. JW to Waldron, 20 January 1775; JE to JB, 30 January 1775, 28 February 1775, 11 April 1775, *CMHS*, series 6, vol. 4, pp. 72, 76, 84–6.
6. JE to JB, 11 April 1775, *CMHS*, series 6, vol. 4, p. 86. The debate between Novanglus and Massachusettensis is reproduced in G. A. Peek, Jr (ed.), *The Political Writings of John Adams* (Indianapolis, IN: Bobbs-Merril, 1954).
7. JB to AE, 26 June 1774, 161.A.76, Belknap Papers, MHS. For Andrew Eliot, see B. Bailyn, 'Religion and Revolution: Three Biographical Studies', in *Perspectives in American History*, (Cambridge, MA: Harvard University Press, 1970), vol. 4, pp. 85–169.
8. Kirsch, *Jeremy Belknap*, p. 59; Marcou, *Life of Belknap*, p. 89; Belknap, Interleaved Almanac, 1775, MHS.
9. JB to RB, 20 April 1775, in Marcou, *Life of Belknap*, p. 89.
10. Marcou, *Life of Belknap*, pp. 89–90; Kirsch, *Jeremy Belknap*, p. 59; Belknap, Interleaved Almanac, 1775, 1778, MHS.

11. Marcou, *Life of Belknap*, pp. 36–7; Kirsch, *Jeremy Belknap*, p. 59; D. P. Corey, *The History of Malden Massachusetts, 1633–1785* (Malden, MA: by the author, 1899), pp. 653–4, 742–3, 748.
12. Marcou, *Life of Belknap*, pp. 9–10; S. Sewall to Joseph Belknap, 28 September 1778, *CMHS*, series 6, vol. 4, pp.128–9.
13. Henry Pelman to Charles Startin, 3 May 1775, Henry Pelman to John Singleton Copley, 16 May 1775, *Letters & Papers of John Singleton Copley and Henry Pelman, 1739–1776* (Boston, MA: MHS, 1914), pp. 314, 318–21.
14. AE to Thomas Brand Hollis, 25 April 1775, *Proceedings of the Massachusetts Historical Society*, 1878 (Boston, MA: MHS, 1879), pp. 281–2.
15. Belknap, Interleaved Almanac, 1775, MHS.
16. T. Gage, 'Permit to Pass through British Lines, May 1775', Miscellaneous Bound Collection, MHS; D. Rutman, *Winthrop's Boston: A Portrait of a Puritan Town* (New York: Norton, 1965), p. 24; E. Forbes, *Paul Revere and the World He Lived In* (Boston, MA: Houghton Mifflin Co., 1942); AE to Samuel Eliot, 28 April 1775, *Proceedings of the MHS*, 1878, pp. 182, 288; H. A. Hill, *History of the Old South Church (third Church) Boston, 1669–1884*, 2 vols (Boston, MA: Houghton, Mifflin & Co., 1890), vol. 2; R. Frothingham, *History of the Siege of Boston* (Boston, MA: Little, Brown & Co., 1903), pp. 94–5, 97–8.
17. S. Sewall to Joseph Belknap, Sr, May 1775, 28 September 1778, *CHMS*, series 6, vol. 4, pp. 87–8, 128–9; John Phillips to JB, 23 March 1775, *CMHS*, series 6, vol. 4, pp. 94–5; Belknap, Interleaved Almanac, 1775, MHS.
18. JE to JB, 26 May 75, *CMHS*, series 6, vol. 4, p. 89; Marcou, *Life of Belknap*, p. 99; Belknap, Interleaved Almanac, 1775, MHS. For a contemporary account of the Battle of Bunker Hill see W. Gordon, *The History of the Rise, Progress, and Establishment of the Independence of the United States of America* (New York: Samuel Campbell, 1801), pp. 350–8.
19. AE to JB, 3 August 1775; Samuel Webster to JB, 6 July 1775, *CMHS*, series 6, vol. 4, pp. 90, 91; G. B. Spaulding, *The Dover Pulpit during the Revolutionary War* (Dover, NH: Morning Star Steam Job Printing House, 1876), p. 22; Belknap, Interleaved Almanac, 1775, MHS.
20. Belknap, Interleaved Almanac, 1775, MHS.
21. Marcou, *Life of Belknap*, pp. 91–3; J. Belknap, 'A Draught of the Harbour of Boston and the adjacent Towns & Roads', 1775, 161.A, volume of tippin-in manuscripts, 1637-1784, part 1, Belknap Papers, MHS; JB to RB, 18 October 1775, *CMHS*, series 6, vol. 4, p. 92; Belknap, Interleaved Almanac, 1775, MHS.
22. Marcou, *Life of Belknap*, pp. 92–4.
23. Ibid., pp. 94–6; JB to RB, 18 October 1775, *CMHS*, series 6, vol. 4, p. 92.
24. J. Belknap, *Sermon on Military Duty, Preached at Dover, Nov. 10, 1772* (Salem, MA: Hall, 1773), p. 7; Marcou, *Life of Belknap*, pp. 96–7; Belknap, Interleaved Almanac, 1775, MHS.
25. Marcou, *Life of Belknap*, p. 97; Belknap, 'Draught of the Harbour of Boston'; JB to RB, 10/18/1775, *CMHS*, series 6, vol. 4, p. 92.
26. Marcou, *Life of Belknap*, p. 97; Belknap, 'Draught of the Harbour of Boston'; 'Roads to the principal Towns on the Continent, &c. from Boston', Interleaved Almanac, 1778, MHS; Belknap, Interleaved Almanac, 1775, MHS.

2 Melted Majesty

1. 'The New-York Post Office', *New York Times*, 27 August 1875; Vermilye, 'Early New York Post-Office', pp. 113, 120; T. Jones, *History of New York during the Revolutionary War*, 2 vols (New York: New York Historical Society, 1879), vol. 1, pp. 39–40; 'Records of the New York Committee of Safety', 3 May 1775, 'NY Congress to NY Delegates in Cont Congress', 26 July 1775, AA: Documents of the American Revolution, 1774–6, online at http://lincoln.lib.niu.edu/ [accessed 18 March 2010].
2. Blodgett, 'Ebenezer Hazard', pp. 3–5; Vermilye, 'Early New York Post-Office', p. 117; The Forum at The Online Library of Liberty, online at http://oll.libertyfund.org/index.php?option=com_content&task=view&id=592&Itemid=259#c_lf0009_footnote_nt_636 [accessed 24 January 2011].
3. Blodgett, 'Ebenezer Hazard', pp. 4–5.
4. EH to [Horatio] Gates, 5 July 1776, 12 July 1776, 9 August 1776, AA; R. K. Wright, Jr, *The Continental Army* (Washington, DC: Center of Military History, 1983), pp. 61–2.
5. EH to Robert Livingston, 29 August 1776 and Minutes of the NY Committee of Safety, 30 August 1776, AA; Shelley, 'Ebenezer Hazard', p. 52; H. S. Commager and R. B. Morris, (eds.), *The Spirit of '76: The Story of the American Revolution as Told by Participants* (New York: Harper & Row, 1976), pp. 428–48.
6. Minutes of the NY Committee of Safety, 30 August 1776, EH to John McKesson, 1 September 1776 and 6 September 1776, EH to NY Committee of Safety, 25 September 1776, NY Committee of Safety to EH, 25 October 1776, AA.
7. EH to General [Horatio] Gates, 11 October 1776, AA; J. R. Alden, *The American Revolution: 1775–1783* (New York: Harper & Row, 1954), pp. 103–7.
8. 'Memorial of EH', 14 November 1776, EH to Rev. John Witherspoon, 14 November 1776, AA; Shelley, 'Ebenezer Hazard', pp. 52–3.
9. S. Bayne-Jones, *The Evolution of Preventive Medicine in the U. S. Army, 1607–1939* (Washington, DC: Department of the Army, 1968), pp. 65–6.
10. 'Roads to the principal Towns on the Continent, &c. from Boston', Interleaved Almanac, 1778, MHS.
11. Letters of Gordon respecting the British occupation of Boston are found at the American Archives: Documents of the American Revolution, 1774–1776, http://lincoln.lib.niu.edu/.
12. For Newburyport in the late eighteenth century, see B. W. Labaree, *Patriots and Partisans: The Merchants of Newburyport, 1764–1815* (New York: Norton, 1975).
13. R. M. Lawson, *Portsmouth: An Old Town by the Sea* (Charleston, SC: Arcadia Publishing, 2003).
14. JB to EH, 30 January 1790, *CMHS*, series 5, vol. 3, p. 211.
15. Information on Daniel Little is scattered throughout forgotten contemporary periodicals and manuscript sources. For a brief synopsis, see Shipton, *Biographical Sketches of Those Who Attended Harvard College*, vol. 12. I have recreated Hazard's route and stops with the help of 'Roads to the principal Towns on the Continent, &c. from Boston', Interleaved Almanac, 1778, Belknap Papers, MHS.

16. P. Force, *American Archives*, 4th series (Washington: Clarke and Force, 1837–1846) vol. 3, p. 154; Commager and Morris, *The Spirit of '76*, pp. 172–3; 'Roads to the principal Towns on the Continent', Interleaved Almanac, 1778, Belknap Papers, MHS.
17. Shelley, 'Ebenezer Hazard', pp. 53–4.
18. F. Shelley (ed.), 'Ebenezer Hazard's Travels through Maryland in 1777', *Maryland Historical Magazine*, 46 (1951), pp. 46–7.
19. Ibid., p. 47.
20. Ibid., p. 48. S. Foster and J. A. Duke (eds), *A Field Guide to Medicinal Plants and Herbs of Eastern and Central North America*, 2nd edn (Boston, MA: Houghton Mifflin Co., 2000).
21. Shelley (ed.), 'Ebenezer Hazard's Travels through Maryland', pp. 48–9.
22. Ibid., pp. 49–50.
23. Ibid., p. 50.
24. Ibid.
25. Ibid., p. 51; F. Shelley, (ed.), 'The Journal of Ebenezer Hazard in Virginia, 1777', *Virginia Magazine of History and Biography*, 62 (1954), pp. 401–2.
26. Ibid., pp. 402–3.
27. Ibid., pp. 403–4.
28. Ibid., p. 404.
29. Ibid., pp. 404–5.
30. Ibid., pp. 405–6.
31. Ibid., pp. 406–10.
32. Ibid., pp. 409–11.
33. Ibid., pp. 411–12, 414.
34. Ibid., p. 414.
35. H. B. Johnston, 'The Journal of Ebenezer Hazard in North Carolina, 1777–1778', *North Carolina Historical Review*, 39 (1959), pp. 359–61.
36. Ibid., pp. 362–5.
37. Shelley (ed.), 'The Journal of Ebenezer Hazard in Virginia', pp. 418–19.
38. Ibid., p. 418; F. Shelley (ed.), 'Ebenezer Hazard's Diary: New Jersey during the Revolution', *New Jersey History*, 90 (1972), pp. 171–4.
39. Shelley (ed.), 'Ebenezer Hazard's Diary: New Jersey during the Revolution', p. 174.
40. Ibid., pp. 174–9.
41. Alden, *American Revolution*, pp. 121–4; J. McClure, 'The Continental Congress in York Town', Historical Society of Pennsylvania, online at http://www.hsp.org/default.aspx?id=491 [accessed 24 January 2011]; F. Shelley (ed.), 'Ebenezer Hazard in Pennsylvania, 1777', *Pennsylvania Magazine of History and Biography*, 81 (1957), pp. 84–6. Congress composed the Articles of Confederation during its stay at York.
42. Shelley (ed.), 'Ebenezer Hazard Travels through Maryland', p. 54; Shelley (ed.), 'Journal of Ebenezer Hazard in Virginia', pp. 419–23; Johnston (ed.), 'Journal of Ebenezer Hazard in North Carolina', pp. 366–76.
43. Johnston (ed.), 'Journal of Ebenezer Hazard in North Carolina', pp. 376–81.
44. H. R. Merrens (ed.), 'A View of Coastal South Carolina in 1778: The Journal of Ebenezer Hazard', *South Carolina Historical Magazine*, 73 (1972), pp. 179–93; F. Shelley (ed.), 'The Journal of Ebenezer Hazard in Georgia, 1778', *Collections of the Georgia Historical Society*, 41 (1957), pp. 317–19; Alden, *American Revolution*, p. 229.

3 Barren as a Pitch-Pine Plain

1. Belknap, Interleaved Almanac, 1776, Belknap Papers, MHS; JE to JB, 4 July 1776, *CMHS*, series 6, vol. 4, pp. 97–8.
2. JB to Mr J. Clarke, 13 January 1777 and JB to Dr Cooper, 14 January 1777, Letterbook 1768–88, Belknap Papers, MHS.
3. JE to JB, 12 January 1777 and 19 March 1777, *CMHS*, series 6, vol. 4, pp. 99–107.
4. JB to Parish Selectmen of Dover, 7 March 1777 and n.d., *CMHS*, series 6, vol. 4, pp. 153, 155.
5. JE to JB, 9 May 1777 and 12 June 1777, *CMHS*, series 6, vol. 4, pp. 108–112, 119. Andrew Eliot died 13 September 1778.
6. JE to JB, 17 June 1777, *CMHS*, series 6, vol. 4, pp. 122–25.
7. JB to JE, 17 September 1777 and 5 October 1777, Letterbook, 1768–88, Belknap Papers, MHS. Belknap, Interleaved Almanac, 1777, MHS.
8. Belknap, Interleaved Almanac, 1777, MHS.
9. J. Brackett to JB, 21 December 1778, *CMHS*, series 6, vol. 4, pp. 134–5; J. Belknap, *A Sermon Delivered on the 9th of May, 1798, the Day of the National Fast* (Boston, MA: Samuel Hall, 1798).
10. Belknap, Interleaved Almanac, 1778, 1779, Belknap Papers, MHS.

4 Life of a Cabbage

1. EH to JB, 29 January 1779, *CMHS*, series 5, vol. 2, p. 1. The book was T. Gorges, *America Painted to the Life* (London: N. Brook, 1658).
2. EH to JB, 29 January 1779, *CMHS*, series 5, vol. 2, p. 1.
3. JB to EH, 2 February 1779, *CMHS*, series 5, vol. 2, pp. 1–3.
4. A few surviving letters written by Ruth Eliot Belknap, as well as many more written to her by her husband and children, are preserved at the MHS and, particularly, at the New Hampshire Historical Society.
5. There are several extant drawings and a portrait of Belknap; the latter, painted by Winthrop Sargent in 1794, is found at the MHS.
6. JB to EH, 2 February 1779, *CMHS*, series 5, vol. 2, pp. 2–3.
7. EH to JB, 19 April 1779, *CMHS*, series 5, vol. 2, pp. 4–5.
8. JB to EH, 12 May 1779, *CMHS*, series 5, vol. 2, pp. 5–7.
9. J. Belknap, *Jesus Christ, the Only Foundation* (Portsmouth, NH: Daniel Fowle, 1779); D. Macclure to JB, 9 July 1779, *CMHS*, series 6, vol. 4, p. 142.
10. EH to JB, 4 August 1779, *CMHS*, series 5, vol. 2, pp. 7–8.
11. Ibid., pp. 8–9.
12. JB to EH, 16 August 1779, *CMHS*, series 5, vol. 2, p. 9.
13. JE to JB, 31 July 1779, *CMHS*, series 6, vol. 4, pp. 146–7.
14. JB to EH, 16 August 1779, *CMHS*, series 5, vol. 2, pp. 9–10.
15. Ibid., pp. 10–11.
16. EH to JB, 31 August 1779, *CMHS*, series 5, vol. 2, pp. 11–12.
17. Ibid., pp. 12–13.
18. JB to EH, 5 October 1779, *CMHS*, series 5, vol. 2, pp. 13–14.
19. Ibid., pp. 14–15.
20. Ibid., pp. 15–16. Pope's *Art of Sinking* was a condemnation of mediocre poetry.
21. Ibid., p. 16. Joseph Caryl published twelve volumes on the Book of Job.

22. EH to JB, 20 October 1779, *CMHS*, series 5, vol. 2, pp. 16–18.
23. Ibid., pp. 18–19.
24. JE to JB, 29 March 1777, 9 May 1777, 20 May 1777, *CMHS*, series 6, vol. 4, pp. 107, 111–12, 114–15. For background on the strategic importance of the Hudson River during the Revolution and American attempts to control it, see L. Diamant, *Chaining the Hudson: The Fight for the River in the American Revolution* (New York: Fordham University Press, 2004).
25. EH to JB, 20 October 1779, *CMHS*, series 5, vol. 2, p. 20.
26. EH to JB, 30 October 1779, *CMHS*, series 5, vol. 2, pp. 20–1. Alden, *American Revolution*, pp. 228–38.
27. EH to JB, 30 November 1779, *CMHS*, series 5, vol. 2, p. 22.
28. EH to JB, 15 December 1779, *CMHS*, series 5, vol. 2, pp. 22–4.
29. EH to JB, 28 December 1779, *CMHS*, series 5, vol. 2, p. 24.
30. JB to EH, 28 December 1779, *CMHS*, series 5, vol. 2, pp. 24–6.
31. Ibid., pp. 26–7.

5 Hurried through Life on Horseback

1. EH to JB, 4 January 1780, *CMHS*, series 5, vol. 2, p. 27.
2. Ibid., pp. 27–9. Ethan Allen published *Deism, the Only Oracle of Man*, in 1784. For his life, see C. Jellison, *Ethan Allen: Frontier Rebel* (Syracuse, NY: Syracuse University Press, 1983).
3. EH to JB, 4 January 1780, *CMHS*, series 5, vol. 2, pp. 28–9.
4. Ibid., p. 29.
5. Ibid., p. 30.
6. JB to EH, 1 February 1780, *CMHS*, series 5, vol. 2, p. 30.
7. Ibid., pp. 30–1.
8. JB to EH, 4 February 1780, *CMHS*, series 5, vol. 2, pp. 253–4.
9. Ibid., p. 255.
10. EH to JB, 18 February 1780, *CMHS*, series 5, vol. 2, p. 31.
11. Ibid., p. 32.
12. Ibid., pp. 32–4.
13. Ibid., p. 34.
14. Ibid., p. 35.
15. EH to JB, 10 March 1780, *CMHS*, series 5, vol. 2, pp. 35–6.
16. Ibid., pp. 36–7; EH to JB, 11 March 1780, *CMHS*, series 5, vol. 2, pp. 37–8.
17. EH to JB, March 11, 1780, *CMHS*, series 5, vol. 2, p. 39.
18. JB to EH, March 13, 1780, *CMHS*, series 5, vol. 2, pp. 39–43.
19. Ibid., pp. 43–4.
20. EH to JB, 1 April 1780, *CMHS*, series 5, vol. 2, pp. 44–7.
21. Ibid., pp. 47–8.
22. JB to EH, 1 April 1780, *CMHS*, series 5, vol. 2, pp. 48–9.
23. Ibid., p. 50.
24. Ibid., pp. 50–1.
25. EH to JB, 5 May 1780, *CMHS*, series 5, vol. 2, pp. 51–2.
26. JB to EH, 5 June 1780, *CMHS*, series 5, vol. 2, pp. 52–3.
27. Ibid., p. 53.
28. Ibid., pp. 53–4.

29. Ibid., pp. 54–5.
30. Ibid., pp. 55–7.
31. Ibid., pp. 57–8.
32. EH to JB, 27 June 1780, *CMHS*, series 5, vol. 2, pp. 58–9.
33. Ibid., pp. 59–60.
34. Ibid., p. 60.
35. Ibid., pp. 60–2.
36. Ibid., pp. 62–3.
37. Ibid., p. 63.
38. EH to JB, 11 July 1780, *CMHS*, series 5, vol. 2, pp. 63–4.
39. JB to EH, 5 August 1780, *CMHS*, series 5, vol. 2, pp. 64–6.
40. EH to JB, 9 August 1780, *CMHS*, series 5, vol. 2, pp. 66–8.
41. Ibid., p. 68.
42. JB to EH, 28 August 1780, *CMHS*, series 5, vol. 2, pp. 69–70.
43. Ibid., pp. 70–1.
44. Ibid., pp. 71–2.
45. Ibid., p. 74.
46. EH to JB, 2 October 1780, *CMHS*, series 5, vol. 2, pp. 75–6.
47. Ibid., pp. 76–7.
48. Ibid., pp. 77–8.
49. JB to EH, 25 October 1780, *CMHS*, series 5, vol. 2, pp. 78–81.
50. EH to JB, 2 December 1780, *CMHS*, series 5, vol. 2, pp. 81–2.
51. JB to EH, 18 December 1780, *CMHS*, series 5, vol. 2, pp. 82–3.
52. EH to JB, 5 December 1781, *CMHS*, series 5, vol. 2, pp. 83–4.

6 Touch and Go is a Good Pilot

1. EH to JB, 5 February 1781, *CMHS*, series 5, vol. 2, pp. 83–4.
2. Ibid., p. 84.
3. EH to JB, 1 March 1781, *CMHS*, series 5, vol. 2, pp. 84–5.
4. JB to EH, 8 March 1781, *CMHS*, series 5, vol. 2, pp. 85–6.
5. Ibid., p. 87.
6. Ibid., pp. 88–9.
7. EH to JB, 8 March 1781, *CMHS*, series 5, vol. 2, pp. 89–91.
8. Ibid., pp. 91–2.
9. Ibid., pp. 93–4.
10. JB to EH, 23 April 1781, *CMHS*, series 5, vol. 2, pp. 94–5.
11. Ibid., pp. 95–7.
12. Ibid., p. 97.
13. EH to JB, 14 May 1781, *CMHS*, series 5, vol. 2, pp. 97–8.
14. Ibid., pp. 98–9.
15. JB to EH, 28 May 1781, *CMHS*, series 5, vol. 2, p. 482.
16. JB to EH, 7 June 1781, *CMHS*, series 5, vol. 2, pp. 99–100.
17. Ibid., pp. 100–1.
18. EH to JB, 2 July 1781, *CMHS*, series 5, vol. 2, pp. 101–2.
19. JB to EH, July 1781, *CMHS*, series 5, vol. 2, pp. 102–3.
20. Ibid., p. 104. Mount Washington was ascended half a dozen times during the seventeenth and eighteenth centuries. General Sullivan's account of the White Mountains is

found in Belknap's 'Several Accounts of the White Mountains', Belknap Papers, MHS. See R. M. Lawson, *Passaconaway's Realm: Captain John Evans and the Exploration of Mount Washington* (Hanover, NH: University Press of New England, 2002), p. 64.
21. EH to JB, 7 August 1781, *CMHS*, series 5, vol. 2, pp. 104–5.
22. EH to JB, 5 September 1781, *CMHS*, series 5, vol. 2, pp. 105–6.
23. Ibid., p. 107.
24. Ibid., pp. 107–8.
25. Ibid., p. 108.
26. Ibid., p. 109.
27. JB to EH, 16 November 1781, *CMHS*, series 5, vol. 2, pp. 110–12.
28. Ibid., p. 111; EH to JB, 4 December 1781, *CMHS*, series 5, vol. 2, pp. 112–13.
29. EH to JB, 18 December 1781, *CMHS*, series 5, vol. 2, pp. 113–14.
30. EH to JB, 11 February 1782, *CMHS*, series 5, vol. 2, pp. 114–15.
31. JB to EH, 17 February 1782, *CMHS*, series 5, vol. 2, pp. 115–17.
32. EH to JB, 26 February 1782, *CMHS*, series 5, vol. 2, p. 117.
33. EH to JB, 15 March 1782, *CMHS*, series 5, vol. 2, p. 118.
34. Ibid.
35. JB to EH, 20 March 1782, *CMHS*, series 5, vol. 2, pp. 119–20.
36. Ibid., p. 120.
37. Ibid., pp. 120–1.
38. Ibid., pp. 121–2.
39. Ibid., p. 122.
40. Ibid., pp. 122–3.
41. Ibid., p. 123.

7 War and *GREET Brittain*

1. EH to JB, 10 April 1782, *CMHS*, series 5, vol. 2, pp. 123–6.
2. Ibid., pp. 124, 126.
3. JB to EH, 10 May 1782, *CMHS*, series 5, vol. 2, pp. 126–8.
4. Ibid., p. 128. The poem, 'The Pleasures of a Country Life', is reproduced in *CMHS*, series 6, vol. 4, pp. 228–9.
5. Ibid., p. 128.
6. EH to JB, 14 May 1782, *CMHS*, series 5, vol. 2, p. 129.
7. Ibid.
8. EH to JB, 5 June 1782, *CMHS*, series 5, vol. 2, pp. 130–1.
9. JB to EH, 19 June 1782, *CMHS*, series 5, vol. 2, p. 132.
10. Ibid., pp. 132–3.
11. JB to EH, 27 June 1782, *CMHS*, series 5, vol. 2, p. 134.
12. EH to JB, 1 July 1782, *CMHS*, series 5, vol. 2, pp. 135–6.
13. Ibid., pp. 136–7.
14. JB to EH, 26 July 1782, *CMHS*, series 5, vol. 2, pp. 138–42.
15. Ibid., pp. 142–3.
16. Ibid., p. 143.
17. Ibid., pp. 143–4.
18. EH to JB, 7 August 1782, *CMHS*, series 5, vol. 2, pp. 144–6.
19. Ibid., p. 146.

20. EH to JB, 28 August 1782, *CMHS*, series 5, vol. 2, pp. 146–7. Jonathan Trumball's *M'Fingal* was a form of literary burlesque poking fun at Gage's occupation of Boston.
21. JB to EH, 2 September 1782, *CMHS*, series 5, vol. 2, p. 147.
22. Ibid.
23. Ibid., p. 148.
24. Ibid.
25. Ibid.
26. Ibid., pp. 148–9.
27. EH to JB, 3 September 1782, *CMHS*, series 5, vol. 2, pp. 149–50.
28. Ibid., p. 151.
29. Ibid.
30. JB to EH, 10 September 1782, *CMHS*, series 5, vol. 2, pp. 151–2.
31. Ibid., p. 152.
32. Ibid.
33. JB to EH, 23 September 1782, *CMHS*, series 5, vol. 2, pp. 152–3.
34. Ibid., p. 153.
35. Ibid., p. 154.
36. Ibid., pp. 154–5.
37. Ibid., pp. 156–7.
38. JB to EH, 27 September 1782, *CMHS*, series 5, vol. 2, pp. 157–8.
39. EH to JB, 2 October 1782, *CMHS*, series 5, vol. 2, p. 158.
40. Ibid., p. 159.
41. EH to JB, 29 October 1782, *CMHS*, series 5, vol. 2, pp. 159–60.
42. Ibid., p. 160.
43. JB to EH, 10 November 1782, *CMHS*, series 5, vol. 2, p. 161.
44. Ibid., pp. 161–2.
45. Ibid., p. 162.
46. EH to JB, 20 November 1782, *CMHS*, series 5, vol. 2, pp. 162–3.
47. EH to JB, 27 November 1782, *CMHS*, series 5, vol. 2, pp. 163–4.
48. JB to EH, 2 December 1782, *CMHS*, series 5, vol. 2, pp. 164–5.
49. Ibid., pp. 165–6.
50. Ibid., pp. 166–7.
51. Ibid., p. 167.
52. EH to JB, 11 December 1782, *CMHS*, series 5, vol. 2, p. 167; 18 December 1782, *CMHS*, series 5, vol. 2, pp. 167–8.
53. EH to JB, 18 December 1782, *CMHS*, series 5, vol. 2, p. 168.
54. JB to EH, 19 December 1782, *CMHS*, series 5, vol. 2, p. 169.
55. Ibid., p. 170.
56. Ibid.
57. Ibid., pp. 170–1.
58. Ibid., pp. 171–2.
59. Ibid., pp. 172–4.

8 Keeping the Belly and Back from Grumbling, and the Kitchen-Fire from Going Out

1. JB to EH, 8 January 1783, *CMHS*, series 5, vol. 2, p. 174.

2. Ibid., pp. 174–6.
3. Ibid., p. 176.
4. Ibid., p. 177.
5. Ibid., pp. 177–8.
6. Ibid., pp. 178–9.
7. Ibid., p. 179.
8. EH to JB, 17 January 1783, *CMHS*, series 5, vol. 2, pp. 179–81.
9. Ibid., p. 181.
10. Ibid., pp. 181–3.
11. Ibid., pp. 183–4.
12. EH to JB, 29 January 1783, *CMHS*, series 5, vol. 2, p. 184.
13. JB to EH, 7 February 1783, *CMHS*, series 5, vol. 2, p. 185.
14. EH to JB, 12 February 1783, *CMHS*, series 5, vol. 2, pp. 186–7.
15. Ibid., p. 188.
16. Ibid.
17. JB to EH, 19 February 1783, *CMHS*, series 5, vol. 2, pp. 189–90.
18. Ibid., pp. 190–3.
19. Ibid., p. 193.
20. Ibid., p. 194.
21. EH to JB, 19 February 1783, *CMHS*, series 5, vol. 2, pp. 194–5.
22. EH to JB, 8 March 1783, *CMHS*, series 5, vol. 2, pp. 195–7.
23. JB to EH, 17 March 1783, *CMHS*, series 5, vol. 2, 198–9.
24. EH to JB, 26 March 1783, *CMHS*, series 5, vol. 2, pp. 200–1.
25. Ibid., pp. 201–2.
26. JB to EH, 31 March 1783, *CMHS*, series 5, vol. 3 (with appendix), p. 373^5.
27. Ibid., p. 373$^{3-4}$.
28. EH to JB, 9 April 1783, *CMHS*, series 5, vol. 2, pp. 202–3.
29. Ibid., p. 203.
30. JB to EH, 15 April 1783, *CMHS*, series 5, vol. 3 (with appendix), p. 373$^{5-6}$.
31. Ibid., p. 373^6.
32. JB to EH, 25 April 1783, *CMHS*, series 5, vol. 3 (with appendix), p. 373^7.
33. Ibid., p. 373^8.
34. Ibid., p. 373^9.
35. Ibid., p. 373$^{8-9}$.
36. Ibid., p. 373^{10}.
37. EH to JB, 30 April 1783, *CMHS*, series 5, vol. 2, p. 204.
38. JB to EH, 30 April 1783, *CMHS*, series 5, vol. 2, p. 205.
39. EH to JB, 7 May 1783 and 14 May 1783, *CMHS*, series 5, vol. 2, p. 206.
40. JB to EH, 19 May 1783, *CMHS*, series 5, vol. 2, pp. 206–7.
41. Ibid., p. 208.
42. Ibid., pp. 208–10.
43. Ibid., p. 373.
44. EH to JB, 21 May 1783, *CMHS*, series 5, vol. 2, p. 211.
45. Ibid., pp. 211–12.
46. Ibid., p. 212.
47. JB to EH, 26 May 1783, *CMHS*, series 5, vol. 2, pp. 212–13.
48. JB to EH, 10 June 1783, *CMHS*, series 5, vol. 2, pp. 214–15.
49. Ibid., pp. 215–16.

50. Ibid., pp. 216–17.
51. EH to JB, 11 June 1783, *CMHS*, series 5, vol. 2, pp. 217–18.
52. EH to JB, 18 June 1783, *CMHS*, series 5, vol. 2, pp. 218–19.
53. JB to EH, 23 June 1783, *CMHS*, series 5, vol. 2, pp. 221–2.
54. Ibid., pp. 222–3.
55. JB to EH, 28 June 1783, *CMHS*, series 5, vol. 2, pp. 224–5.
56. Ibid., p. 225.
57. Ibid., pp. 227–8.
58. Ibid., pp. 228–9.
59. EH to JB, 9 July 1783, *CMHS*, series 5, vol. 2, pp. 229–30.
60. JB to EH, 14 July 1783, *CMHS*, series 5, vol. 2, pp. 230–1.
61. Ibid., p. 232.
62. Ibid.
63. JB to EH, 18 July 1783, *CMHS*, series 5, vol. 2, pp. 233–4.
64. Ibid., p. 234.
65. Ibid., p. 235.
66. EH to JB, 23 July 1783, *CMHS*, series 5, vol. 2, pp. 235–7.
67. JB to EH, 2 August 1783, *CMHS*, series 5, vol. 2, p. 237.
68. JB to EH, 4 August 1783, *CMHS*, series 5, vol. 2, pp. 238–9.
69. JB to EH, 11 August 1783, 17 August 1783, 25 August 1783, *CMHS*, series 5, vol. 2, pp. 239–42.
70. EH to JB, 27 August 1783, *CMHS*, series 5, vol. 2, pp. 243–4.
71. JB to EH, 30 August 1783 and 1 September 1783, *CMHS*, series 5, vol. 2, pp. 244–6.
72. JB to EH, 12 September 1783, *CMHS*, series 5, vol. 2, p. 247.
73. Ibid., pp. 248–9.
74. JB to EH, 20 September 1783, *CMHS*, series 5, vol. 2, pp. 249–50.
75. EH to JB, 24 September 1783, *CMHS*, series 5, vol. 2, p. 256.
76. JB to EH, 29 September 1783, *CMHS*, series 5, vol. 2, p. 257.
77. EH to JB, 1 October 1783, *CMHS*, series 5, vol. 2, pp. 257–8.
78. JB to EH, 4 October 1783, *CMHS*, series 5, vol. 2, p. 259.
79. EH to JB, 8 October 1783, *CMHS*, series 5, vol. 2, pp. 260–1.
80. JB to EH, 12 October 1783, *CMHS*, series 5, vol. 2, pp. 261–2.
81. EH to JB, 15 October 1783, *CMHS*, series 5, vol. 2, p. 263.
82. JB to EH, 17 October 1783, *CMHS*, series 5, vol. 2, pp. 264–6.
83. EH to JB, 22 October 1783, *CMHS*, series 5, vol. 2, p. 266.
84. JB to EH, 23 October 1783, *CMHS*, series 5, vol. 2, pp. 266–7.
85. Ibid., pp. 267–8.
86. JB to EH, 27 October 1783, 21 October 1783, 7 November 1783 and 11 November 1783, *CMHS*, series 5, vol. 2, pp. 269–75.
87. JB to EH, 7 November 1783 and 30 November 1783, *CMHS*, series 5, vol. 2, pp. 271–4, 279.
88. EH to JB, 12 November 1783, *CMHS*, series 5, vol. 2, p. 275.
89. JB to EH, 22 November 1783, *CMHS*, series 5, vol. 2, pp. 276–7.
90. JB to EH, 30 November 1783, *CMHS*, series 5, vol. 2, pp. 277–9.
91. JB to EH, 1 December 1783, *CMHS*, series 5, vol. 2, pp. 280–1.
92. Ibid., p. 281.
93. Ibid., pp. 281–3.
94. JB to EH, 8 December 1783, *CMHS*, series 5, vol. 2, pp. 284–5.

95. JB to EH, 13 December 1783, *CMHS*, series 5, vol. 2, p. 285.
96. JB to EH, 17 December 1783, *CMHS*, series 5, vol. 2, pp. 286–7.
97. JB to EH, 21 December 1783, *CMHS*, series 5, vol. 2, pp. 287–8.
98. Ibid., pp. 288–90.
99. JB to EH, 30 December 1783, *CMHS*, series 5, vol. 2, p. 290–1.
100. Ibid., p. 291.

9 The Mysteries of Lucina

1. JB to EH, 2 January 1784, *CMHS*, series 5, vol. 2, p. 291.
2. EH to JB, 7 January 1784, *CMHS*, series 5, vol. 2, pp. 292–3.
3. JB to EH, 13 January 1784, *CMHS*, series 5, vol. 2, p. 293.
4. Ibid, pp. 294–5.
5. Ibid., pp. 295–7.
6. Ibid., pp. 297–8.
7. EH to JB, 16 January 1784, *CMHS*, series 5, vol. 2, pp. 298–9.
8. Ibid., pp. 299–300.
9. Ibid., p. 300.
10. EH to JB, 24 January 1784, *CMHS*, series 5, vol. 2, pp. 300–1.
11. Ibid., pp. 301–2.
12. Ibid., p. 302.
13. JB to EH, 14 February 1784, *CMHS*, series 5, vol. 2, p. 303.
14. EH to JB, 23 February 1784, *CMHS*, series 5, vol. 2, pp. 303–4.
15. JB to EH, 27 February 1784, *CMHS*, series 5, vol. 2, pp. 304–6.
16. Ibid., pp. 306–7.
17. Ibid., pp. 307–8.
18. EH to JB, 1 March 1784, *CMHS*, series 5, vol. 2, p. 308.
19. JB to EH, 3 March 1784, *CMHS*, series 5, vol. 2, pp. 308–15.
20. EH to JB, 15 March 1784, *CMHS*, series 5, vol. 2, pp. 315–17.
21. EH to JB, 18 March 1784, *CMHS*, series 5, vol. 2, p. 318.
22. Ibid., pp. 318–19.
23. JB to EH, 18 March 1784, *CMHS*, series 5, vol. 2, pp. 319–20.
24. Ibid., p. 321.
25. JB to EH, 28 March 1784, *CMHS*, series 5, vol. 2, pp. 321–2.
26. JB to EH, 11 April 1784, *CMHS*, series 5, vol. 2, pp. 322–3.
27. Ibid., pp. 323–6.
28. Ibid., pp. 326–7.
29. Ibid., pp. 327–8.
30. Ibid., pp. 329.
31. Ibid.
32. EH to JB, 19 April 1784, *CMHS*, series 5, vol. 2, p. 332.
33. JB to EH, 20 April 1784, *CMHS*, series 5, vol. 2, pp. 332–3.
34. JB to EH, 30 April 1784, *CMHS*, series 5, vol. 2, pp. 333–5.
35. EH to JB, 3 May 1784, *CMHS*, series 5, vol. 2, p. 336.
36. JB to EH, 3 May 1784, *CMHS*, series 5, vol. 2, p. 337.
37. EH to JB, 10 May 1784, *CMHS*, series 5, vol. 2, pp. 337–8.
38. Ibid., p. 339.
39. Ibid., pp. 339–40.

40. JB to EH, 11 May 1784, *CMHS*, series 5, vol. 2, pp. 340–1.
41. Ibid., pp. 341–2.
42. Ibid., p. 342.
43. EH to JB, 17 May 1784, *CMHS*, series 5, vol. 2, p. 343.
44. JB to EH, 17 May 1784 and 24 May 1784, *CMHS*, series 5, vol. 2, pp. 344–5.
45. JB to EH, 24 May 1784, *CMHS*, series 5, vol. 2, pp. 345–6.
46. Ibid., pp. 347–8.
47. Ibid., pp. 348–9.
48. Ibid., p. 349; JB to EH, 25 May 1784, *CMHS*, series 5, vol. 2, pp. 349–50.
49. EH to JB, 6/5/1784, *CMHS*, series 5, vol. 2, pp. 351–2.
50. Ibid., p. 352.
51. JB to EH, 6 June 1784, *CMHS*, series 5, vol. 2, pp. 353–4.
52. Ibid., p. 354.
53. Ibid., pp. 354–5.
54. Ibid., p. 355.
55. EH to JB, 14 June 1784, *CMHS*, series 5, vol. 2, pp. 355–6.
56. Ibid., pp. 356–7.
57. Ibid.
58. JB to EH, 19 June 1784, *CMHS*, series 5, vol. 2, pp. 358–61.
59. EH to JB, 21 June 1784, *CMHS*, series 5, vol. 2, p. 361.
60. Ibid., p. 362.
61. EH to JB, 28 June 1784, *CMHS*, series 5, vol. 2, p. 363.
62. JB to EH, 2 July 1784, *CMHS*, series 5, vol. 2, pp. 363–7.
63. Ibid., pp. 367–9.
64. Ibid., p. 369.
65. EH to JB, 5 July 1784, *CMHS*, series 5, vol. 2, pp. 369–70.
66. EH to JB, 10 July 1784, *CMHS*, series 5, vol. 2, pp. 370–1.
67. Ibid., pp. 372–3.
68. JB to EH, 4 July 1784, *CMHS*, series 5, vol. 2, pp. 374–5.
69. Ibid., p. 375.
70. Ibid.
71. Ibid., pp. 375–6.
72. EH to JB, 18 July 1784, *CMHS*, series 5, vol. 2, pp. 376–7.
73. EH to JB, 31 July 1784, *CMHS*, series 5, vol. 2, p. 377.
74. Ibid., pp. 378–9.
75. Ibid., pp. 379–80.
76. EH to JB, 16 August 1784, *CMHS*, series 5, vol. 2, p. 380–1.
77. EH to JB, 23 August 1784, *CMHS*, series 5, vol. 2, pp. 381–2.

10 Patience and Flannel

1. JB to EH, 6 August 1784, *CMHS*, series 5, vol. 3 (with appendix), p. 373[12].
2. Ibid., p. 373[12–13].
3. JB to EH, 16 August 1784, *CMHS*, series 5, vol. 3, pp. 168–70. Belknap would journey to Philadelphia the following year, 1785.
4. Ibid., p. 170.
5. Ibid., p. 171.

6. Ibid., pp. 172–3. For an extensive account of the journey, see Lawson, *Passaconaway's Realm*.
7. Ibid., pp. 173–4.
8. Ibid., p. 175.
9. Ibid., pp. 175–7.
10. Ibid., pp. 177–8.
11. Ibid., p. 178.
12. Ibid.
13. JB to EH, 19 August 1784, *CMHS*, series 5, vol. 3, pp. 179–80.
14. Ibid., p. 180.
15. Ibid., p. 181.
16. Ibid., pp. 181–3.
17. Ibid., pp. 183–4.
18. Ibid., pp. 184–5.
19. Ibid., pp. 185–6.
20. Ibid., pp. 186–7.
21. JB to EH, 19 August 1784, *CMHS*, series 5, vol. 3, pp. 187–9.
22. Ibid., pp. 188–9.
23. JB to EH, 19 August 1784, *CMHS*, series 5, vol. 3, p. 189.
24. Ibid.
25. JB to EH, 26 August 1784, *CMHS*, series 5, vol. 3 (with appendix), p. 373[13].
26. JB to EH, 30 August 1784, *CMHS*, series 5, vol. 3 (with appendix), p. 373[14–15].
27. Ibid., p. 373[15].
28. EH to JB, 30 August 1784, *CMHS*, series 5, vol. 2, p. 382.
29. JB to EH, 4 September 1784, *CMHS*, series 5, vol. 2, p. 383.
30. Ibid., p. 384.
31. EH to JB, 14 September 1784, *CMHS*, series 5, vol. 2, pp. 385–6.
32. JB to EH, 12 September 1784, *CMHS*, series 5, vol. 3 (with appendix), p. 373[16].
33. JB to EH, 19 September 1784, *CMHS*, series 5, vol. 3 (with appendix), 373[17].
34. EH to JB, 28 September 1784, *CMHS*, series 5, vol. 2, pp. 401–2.
35. JB to EH, 2 October 1784, *CMHS*, series 5, vol. 3 (with appendix), 373[17–18].
36. EH to JB, 12 October 1784, *CMHS*, series 5, vol. 2, pp. 402–3.
37. JB to EH, 17 October 1784, *CMHS*, series 5, vol. 3 (with appendix), p. 373[19].
38. EH to JB, 23 October 1784, *CMHS*, series 5, vol. 2, pp. 403–4.
39. JB to EH, 1 November 1784, *CMHS*, series 5, vol. 3 (with appendix), p. 373[20].
40. Ibid., p. 373[22].
41. Ibid., p. 373[20–1].
42. EH to JB, 6 November 1784 and 13 November 1784, *CMHS*, series 5, vol. 2, pp. 404–6.
43. JB to EH, 16 November 1784, *CMHS*, series 5, vol. 3 (with appendix), p. 373[25].
44. JB to EH, 27 November 1784, *CMHS*, series 5, vol. 2, p. 409.
45. EH to JB, 18 December 1784, *CMHS*, series 5, vol. 2, p. 411.

Epilogue

1. The personal crisis involving Hazard's replacement as postmaster general is traced in his letters to Belknap in *CMHS*, series 5, vol. 3. For his subsequent business career see Blodgett, 'Ebenezer Hazard', and M. James, *Biography of a Business, 1792–1942, Insur-*

ance Company of North America (Indianapolis: Bobbs-Merrill, 1942). Belknap's life and writings from 1784 until his death in 1798 are discussed in Lawson, *American Plutarch*.
2. J. Belknap, 'Motto for My Family Arms', 1791, 161.J.105, loose manuscripts, 1682–1858, Belknap Papers, MHS.

WORKS CITED

Manuscript Sources

Massachusetts History Society.

Belknap, J., Interleaved Almanac (Diary), 1774, 1775, 1776, 1777, 1778, 1779, A.1.10, Belknap Papers.

—, 'A Draught of the Harbour of Boston and the adjacent Towns & Roads', 1775, 161.A, volume of tipped-in manuscripts, 1637–1784, part 1, Belknap Papers.

—, 'Roads to the principal Towns on the Continent, &c. from Boston', Interleaved Almanac, 1778.

—, 'Motto for My Family Arms', 1791, 161.J.105, loose manuscripts, 1682–1858, Belknap Papers.

—, 'Several Accounts of the White Mountains', Belknap Papers.

Jeremy Belknap to Mr J. Clarke, 13 January 1777, Letterbook, 1768–88, Belknap Papers.

Jeremy Belknap to Dr Cooper, 14 January 1777, Letterbook, 1768–88, Belknap Papers.

Jeremy Belknap to John Eliot, 17 September 1777 and 5 October 1777, Letterbook, 1768–88, Belknap Papers.

Jeremy Belknap to Andrew Eliot, 26 June 1774, 161.A.76, Belknap Papers.

Primary Sources

American Archives: Documents of the American Revolution, 1774–6, online at http://lincoln.lib.niu.edu/ [accessed 24 January 2011].

Belknap, J., *A Sermon on Military Duty, Preached at Dover, Nov. 10, 1772* (Salem, MA: Hall, 1773).

—, *Jesus Christ, the Only Foundation* (Portsmouth, NH: Daniel Fowle, 1779).

—, *Dissertations on the Character, Death & Resurrection of Jesus Christ* (Boston, MA: Apollo Press, 1795).

—, *Sacred Poetry, Consisting of Psalms and Hymns* (Boston, MA: Apollo Press, 1795).

—, *American Biography,* 2 vols (1794; Boston, MA: Thomas & Andrews 1798).

—, *A Sermon Delivered on the 9th of May, 1798, the Day of the National Fast* (Boston, MA: Samuel Hall, 1798).

—, *The History of New-Hampshire*, 2 vols (Dover, NH: Stevens & Ela & Wadleigh, 1831), vol. 1.

Belknap Papers, *Collections of the Massachusetts Historical Society*, series 5, vols 2 and 3 (with appendix) and series 6, vol. 4 (Boston, MA: Massachusetts Historical Society, 1882, 1887, 1891).

Chauncy, C., *The Mystery Hid from Ages and Generations* (London: C. Dilly, 1784).

Force, P., *American Archives*, 4th series (Washington, DC: Clarke & Force, 1837–46).

Gordon, W., *The History of the Rise, Progress, and Establishment of the Independence of the United States of America* (New York: Samuel Campbell, 1801).

Gorges, T., *America Painted to the Life* (London: N. Brook, 1658).

Hazard, E., *Historical Collections: Consisting of State Papers, and Other Authentic Documents; Intended as Materials for an History of the United States of America*, 2 vols (1792; Philadelphia, PA: Dobson, 1792).

Johnston, H. B., (ed.), 'The Journal of Ebenezer Hazard in North Carolina, 1777–1778', *North Carolina Historical Review*, 39 (1959), pp. 358–81.

Jones, T., *History of New York during the Revolutionary War*, 2 vols (New York: New York Historical Society, 1879), vol. 1.

Letters and Papers of John Singleton Copley and Henry Pelman, 1739–1776 (Boston, MA: Massachusetts Historical Society, 1914).

Massachusetts Historical Society Online Collection, http://www.masshist.org [accessed 24 January 11].

Merrens, H. R. (ed.), 'A View of Coastal South Carolina in 1778: The Journal of Ebenezer Hazard', *South Carolina Historical Magazine*, 73 (1972), pp. 177–93.

Proceedings of the Massachusetts Historical Society (1878; Boston, MA: Massachusetts Historical Society, 1879).

Shelley, F. (ed.), 'Ebenezer Hazard's Travels through Maryland in 1777', *Maryland Historical Magazine*, 46 (1951), pp. 44–54.

—, (ed.), 'The Journal of Ebenezer Hazard in Virginia, 1777', *Virginia Magazine of History and Biography*, 62 (1954), pp. 400–23.

—, (ed.), 'Ebenezer Hazard in Pennsylvania, 1777', *Pennsylvania Magazine of History and Biography*, 81 (1957), pp. 83–6.

—, (ed.), 'The Journal of Ebenezer Hazard in Georgia, 1778', *Collections of the Georgia Historical Society*, 41 (1957), pp. 316–19.

—, (ed.), 'Ebenezer Hazard's Diary: New Jersey during the Revolution', *New Jersey History*, 90 (1972), pp. 169–79.

The Forum at The Online Library of Liberty, online at

http://oll.libertyfund.org/index.php?option=com_content&task=view&id=592&Itemid=259#c_lf0009_footnote_nt_636 [accessed 24 January 2011].

Webster, N., *An American Dictionary of the English Language* (New York: Converse, 1830).

Secondary Sources

Alden, J. R., *The American Revolution: 1775–1783* (New York: Harper & Row, 1954).

Anon., 'The New-York Post Office', *New York Times*, 27 August 1875.

Bailyn, B., 'Religion and Revolution: Three Biographical Studies' in *Perspectives in American History* (Cambridge, MA: Harvard University Press, 1970), vol. 4, pp. 85–169.

Bayne-Jones, S., *The Evolution of Preventive Medicine in the U. S. Army, 1607–1939* (Washington, DC: Department of the Army, 1968).

Blodgett, R. E., 'Ebenezer Hazard: The Post Office, the Insurance Company of North America, and the Editing of Historical Documents' (PhD dissertation, University of Colorado, 1971).

Commager, H. S., and R. B. Morris, *The Spirit of 'Seventy-Six: The Story of the American Revolution as Told by Participants* (New York: Harper & Row, 1975).

Corey, D. P., *The History of Malden Massachusetts, 1633–1785* (Malden, MA: by the author, 1899).

Diamant, L., *Chaining the Hudson: The Fight for the River in the American Revolution* (New York: Fordham University Press, 2004).

Forbes, E., *Paul Revere and the World He Lived In* (Boston, MA: Houghton Mifflin Co., 1942).

Foster, S., and J. A. Duke (eds), *A Field Guide to Medicinal Plants and Herbs of Eastern and Central North America*, 2nd edn (Boston, MA: Houghton Mifflin Co., 2000).

Frothingham, R., *History of the Siege of Boston* (Boston: Little, Brown & Co., 1903).

Hazard, T. R., *Recollections of Olden Times* (Newport, RI: John P. Sanborn, 1879).

Hill, H. A., *History of the Old South Church (third Church) Boston, 1669–1884*, 2 vols (Boston, MA: Houghton, Mifflin & Co., 1890), vol. 2.

'History of the United States Postal Service, 1775–1993', online at http://www.usps.gov/history [accessed 16 September 1999].

James, M., *Biography of a Business, 1792–1942, Insurance Company of North America* (Indianapolis, IN: Bobbs-Merrill, 1942).

Jellison, C., *Ethan Allen: Frontier Rebel* (Syracuse, NY: Syracuse University Press, 1983).

Kirsch, G. B., *Jeremy Belknap: A Biography* (New York: Arno Press, 1982).

Labaree, B. W., *Patriots and Partisans: The Merchants of Newburyport, 1764–1815* (New York: Norton, 1975).

Lawson, R. M., 'Essays on Man: The Belknap Hazard Correspondence', *Historical New Hampshire*, 52 (1997), pp. 19–27.

—, *The American Plutarch: Jeremy Belknap and the Historian's Dialogue with the Past* (Westport, CT: Praeger, 1998).

—, *Passaconaway's Realm: Captain John Evans and the Exploration of Mount Washington* (Hanover, NH: University Press of New England, 2002).

—, *Portsmouth: An Old Town by the Sea* (Charleston, SC: Arcadia Publishing, 2003).

—, *The Piscataqua Valley in the Age of Sail: A Brief History* (Charleston, SC: History Press, 2007).

Lippy, C. H., *Seasonable Revolutionary: The Mind of Charles Chauncy* (Chicago, IL: Nelson-Hall, 1981).

McClure, J., 'The Continental Congress in York Town', Historical Society of Pennsylvania, online at http://www.hsp.org/default.aspx?id=491 [accessed 24 January 2011].

Marcou, J. B., *Life of Jeremy Belknap, D. D. The Historian of New Hampshire* (New York: Harper & Brothers, 1847).

Montaigne, M. de., *The Complete Essays*, trans. D. Frame (Stanford, CA: Stanford University Press, 1958).

Peek, Jr, G. A., (ed.), *The Political Writings of John Adams* (Indianapolis, IN: Bobbs-Merrill, 1954).

Pliny, *The Letters of the Younger Pliny*, trans. B. Radice (Harmondsworth: Penguin Books, 1969).

Plutarch, *Essays*, trans. R. Waterfield (London: Penguin Books, 1992).

Rutman, D. B., *Winthrop's Boston: A Portrait of a Puritan Town* (New York: Norton, 1965).

Seneca, *Letters from a Stoic*, trans. R. Campbell (London: Penguin Books, 1969).

Shelley, F., 'Ebenezer Hazard: America's First Historical Editor', *William and Mary Quarterly*, 13 (1955), pp. 44–73.

Shipton, C. K., *Biographical Sketches of Those Who Attended Harvard College*, 17 vols (Boston, MA: Massachusetts Historical Society, 1933–75).

Spaulding, G. B., *The Dover Pulpit during the Revolutionary War* (Dover, NH: Morning Star Steam Job Printing House, 1876).

Tucker, L. L., *Clio's Consort: Jeremy Belknap and the Founding of the Massachusetts Historical Society* (Boston, MA: Massachusetts Historical Society, 1990).

Vermilye, A. E., 'The Early New York Post-Office: Ebenezer Hazard, Postmaster and Postmaster-General', *Magazine of American History*, 13 (1885), pp. 113–30.

Wadleigh, C., *Notable Events in the History of Dover, New Hampshire* (Dover, NH: by the author, 1913).

Wright, Jr, R. K., *The Continental Army* (Washington, DC: Center of Military History, 1983).

INDEX

Abenaki Indians, 38
Acapulco, 126
Adams, John, 39
Adams, Joseph, 3, 12, 150–1, 153
Aitken, Robert, 117, 127, 130–3, 138–9, 141, 145, 149, 151, 154, 156, 159, 160–4, 166, 169–72, 174–5, 177–82, 184, 188, 190–1, 200–4
Albemarle Sound, 46, 50
Alexander the Coppersmith, 165
Alexander (the Great), 61
Alexandria (Virginia), 40–1
Algonquian Indians, 12, 49, 111
Allen, Ethan, 76, 79
Allen, Moses, 53
Amboy (New Jersey), 47
America, 67, 130–1, 133
American Academy of Arts and Sciences, 93, 103, 105
American colonies, 9–10, 174
American Enlightenment, 4, 6
American independence, 6, 9–11, 22, 55–6, 61, 210
American Indians, 12, 34, 40, 43, 66, 68, 75–6, 85–7, 98, 108, 112–14, 128, 147, 153, 183, 185–6, 198
American Philosophical Society, 85, 89, 92, 98, 147, 152, 156, 171–2, 174, 177–9, 190–1, 197, 200, 203
Amesbury (Massachusetts), 88
Andover (Massachusetts), 25
Andover Road, 25
André, Major (John), 97
Androscoggin River, 111, 199
Anglican Church, 45, 50, 85, 122, 124–5
Annapolis (Maryland), 40–1

Ann Street (Boston) 15, 17
Annunciation, 115
Antilles, 128
antinomian, 64, 187
Apostles, 123, 128, 130, 147
Appalachian Mountains, 84
Articles of Confederation, 5–6, 52, 105, 113–14, 116, 138, 140, 148, 151, 173–4, 179, 204, 207
Aristotelian logic, 130
Arnold, Benedict, 97
Arthur, Joseph, 155
Arundel (Maine), 38
Ashford (Connecticut), 35
Atkinson, Theodore, 7
Atlantis, 128
Augustus Caesar, 123
aurora borealis, 49, 145, 147, 149, 156, 165, 169, 173
azalea (*Rhododenron nudiflorum*), 40

Bache, Richard, 33, 113
Bacon, Francis, 84
　Essays, 83
　Novum Organum, 83
Back River, 7
Baltimore (Maryland), 40
Bank of North America, 172
Baptists, 88, 113
Barefoote, Walter, 71–2
Barnard, Thomas, 38
Barrington (New Hampshire), 129
Barry, Henry, 9–10
Bartlett, John, 195
Batchellor, Stephen, 12
Bath (North Carolina), 50
Battle of Brandywine, 48

Battle of Bunker Hill, 20, 22, 30, 36
Battle of Long Island, 30
Battle of Saratoga, 50, 60
Baylor, George, 23
Bear Mountain, 33–4
Belcher, Jonathan, 47, 96, 151, 155
Belknap, Abigail (Nabby), 8, 11, 14, 17–19
Belknap, Andrew Eliot, 67
Belknap, Jeremy
   American Biography, 4, 208
   American Plutarch, 208
   A Sermon on Military Duty, 24
   antiquarian, 4, 61
   biographer, 4, 65–6, 68–70, 73, 77, 88, 134, 208
   chaplain, 20, 22–24
   character, 3, 65, 106–8
   conservative, 6, 8, 62, 88, 128, 131, 173, 186
   crisis in belief, 4, 56, 58–61
   critic, 6
   death, 3, 208
   Dissertations on the Character, Death, & Resurrection of Jesus Christ, 208
   family, 3–4, 8, 11–19, 21, 25, 56–7, 59, 64, 67, 94–5, 111, 141, 145, 154, 169, 182, 194, 203
   Foresters, 4, 208
   friendship, 4–5, 8, 14, 61–6, 82, 85, 90, 95–6, 99–100, 106, 112, 167, 175, 189, 200–1, 205, 209
   historian, 4–6, 8, 56, 60–2, 64–6, 71, 74, 76–7, 81, 101, 106, 113–14, 116–17, 151, 155, 162, 170, 209–10
   History of New-Hampshire, 4, 8, 36, 64, 67, 70, 106, 138–41, 143–4, 146–7, 152, 154, 156–62, 168–9, 173, 175–9, 181, 185, 188–91, 197, 202–4, 207–8, 210
   Jack Frost, 204
   Jesus Christ, the Only Foundation, 80, 83, 88
   journey to the White Mountains, 191, 193–201, 210
   letters of, 1–3, 5–6, 12, 13–14, 21, 24, 38, 56, 59, 65, 67, 69–72, 74–7, 80–1, 83, 85–91, 93–6, 98–9, 102–116, 118–35, 137–89, 193–205, 209–10
   marriage, 17, 64
   minister, 7, 21, 55–7, 66–7, 80, 88, 95, 102, 154, 205, 207
   patriot, 3, 6, 81
   political views, 6, 8–11, 24, 62, 115, 122, 126, 131, 137–8, 144, 148, 155, 173–4, 186, 210
   religion, 3, 5–6, 11, 20, 23–4, 60–2, 71, 81, 85, 88, 90–1, 102–3, 105–6, 113, 134–5, 141–7, 154, 176, 182, 185, 187–8, 191, 194, 205, 209–10
   Sacred Poetry, 4, 208
   scientist, 4–5, 65, 77, 79, 81, 85, 89–90, 96, 98–9, 103, 123, 128–30, 145–6, 148–9, 154, 162, 164, 170–1, 173, 176–7, 182, 195–200, 202–3, 209–10
   sickness, 58–9, 101–2, 104
   struggles during the war, 3–4, 56–61, 66, 162, 166–7, 205
   teacher, 7, 12, 14
   'Thoughts on the Original Population of America', 118, 121–3, 127–8, 133, 138, 147, 149, 171
   travels, 6–7, 11–14, 16–19, 21–5, 55, 59–60, 65, 150, 152, 191, 193–201, 210
   troubles with parish, 4, 56–7, 66, 80, 88–9
Belknap, John, 56
Belknap, Joseph, Sr, 14–17, 19, 58–9, 203
Belknap, Joseph, Jr, 151, 154, 158–63, 165–72, 174–5, 178–9, 182, 187, 190, 200–2
Belknap, Ruth Eliot, 2, 4, 12–13, 17, 21–2, 24, 56, 63–7, 70–1, 83, 86, 88, 94, 101–2, 112–14, 127, 130, 132, 135, 140, 144–5, 150–1, 154, 156, 158–9, 163, 168, 173–5, 178, 180–1, 187, 191, 200–1, 207
   'The Pleasures of a Country Life', 118–22, 131, 139
Belknap, Samuel, 194
Belknap, Sarah Byles, 14, 17–19, 21, 194, 200, 202–3

Index

Belknap–Hazard correspondence, 1–6, 126, 208, 210
Belknap's Lane, 15
Benedict & Hazard, Booksellers, 28
Benezet, Anthony, 181
Bennett Street (Boston), 17
Berwick (Maine), 61, 210
Beverly (Massachusetts), 13
Big Elk Creek, 39
Bishop of Newington *see* Joseph Adams
Bishop of Rochester *see* Joseph Haven
Blackstone River, 35
Blair, Hugh, 164
    Lectures on Rhetoric, 174–5, 179–81, 188
Bladensburg (Maryland), 41
bloodroot *(Sanguinaria canadensis)*, 40
Bloody Point, 7, 12, 25, 62
blue phlox (Wild Sweet William, *Phlox divaricata*), 40
Bondfield, Charles, 50
Boscawen (New Hampshire), 81
Boston, 3–4, 18, 27, 29, 37–8, 55–9, 61, 63, 65, 69, 71–2, 75–6, 80, 83–4, 86–7, 89, 94, 99, 102, 108–9, 111–13, 115, 121–2, 127, 133–5, 138, 148, 150, 152, 155, 158–9, 162–4, 166, 176, 178, 180–1, 185–7, 191, 197, 200, 203, 207
    occupation of, 2, 8–26, 36,
Boston Common, 22
Boston Harbor, 19–20, 26, 36
Boston Massacre, 15
Boston Neck, 9, 13, 17, 22–3, 25
Bowling Green (New York), 29
Brackett, Joshua, 38, 60–1, 150–1, 153
Bradford (Massachusetts), 25
Bradford's Almanack, 165
Brant, Joseph, 153
Brattle Street Church, 118
Breeds Hill, 18, 36
British Constitution, 10
British Navy (fleet), 27–8, 30, 33, 39, 46, 55, 67, 73–4, 84, 111, 125
Brooklyn, 29–30
Broom, Samuel, 30
Brown, William, 50
Bryson, James, 144–5, 150
Buckminster, Elizabeth Stevens, 38, 110, 146, 151, 184

Buckminster, Joseph, 2, 94, 101, 110, 112, 116, 120–2, 125, 129, 132, 146–7, 149, 151, 153–4, 156, 178, 180–2, 184, 186, 205
Buffon, Count de (Georges-Louis Leclerc), 123–4, 126
    Natural History, 123
Bunker Hill, 18–19, 23, 36
Burgoyne, John, 20, 60, 86
Burnaby, Andrew, *Travels*, 71–2, 75, 80
Bush River, 40
Byles, Mather, 59, 95–6, 166, 169, 202
    Poems on Several Occasions, 96

Caldwell, James, 112
Calvin, John, 179
Calvinism, 28, 62, 102, 134, 180, 182
Cambridge (Massachusetts), 9, 13–14, 20–5, 55
Canada, 29, 55–6, 112, 124
Canceau, 23, 25, 39
Canaanites, 183–4
Cape Ann, 13, 96, 164
Carleton, Guy, 120
Caroline, Queen, 44
Caribbean, 115
Caryl (Joseph), 72
Cartwright's Tavern, 43
Casco Bay, 38
Cephas *see* Peter Thacher
Ceres Street (Portsmouth) 37
Chadborne, William, 61
Chaldean Empire, 61
Charles River, 9, 17–18, 22, 24, 35
Charleston (Massachusetts), 13–14, 17–20, 23–6
Charleston (South Carolina), 52–3, 74, 89, 93, 125–6, 140
Charlestown (Maryland), 39
Chatham (New Jersey), 33, 47
Chauncy, Charles, 3, 60, 127, 134–5, 141, 145, 182, 186, 203–4
Cherokee Indians, 43
Cheronesus, 181
Chesapeake Bay, 39, 42, 48, 111
Chester (Pennsylvania), 39
Chevalier, Jane, 155

Chittenden, Thomas, 137
Chowan River, 46, 50
Christian, William, 43
Christianity, 16, 73, 128, 132, 139, 177, 183, 187–8
Church of England *see* Anglican Church
civil war, 11–12, 15–16
Clark Tavern, 35
Clarke, John, 58, 131, 134, 186, 188
Clarkson, Geraldus, 2, 140, 158, 161, 168–71, 179, 181
Clement of Alexandria, 123
Clinton, Henry, 20
Cobham (Virginia), 44
Cocheco Falls, 7, 62, 65
Cocheco River, 7, 62, 65, 67, 132, 137
Coercive Acts, 8, 13, 36, 87
Colchester (Virginia), 42
College of New Jersey *see* Princeton College
College of William and Mary, 43, 50
columbine (*Aquilegia canadensis*), 40
Coke, Edward, 126
committees of correspondence, 10, 14, 57
Committee of Safety (Massachusetts), 14, 22
Concord (Massachusetts), 11–12, 14, 27, 36, 58
Concord (New Hampshire), 69, 71, 81, 90
Congress (Continental), 9, 22–4, 27–9, 31–3, 43, 49, 55, 94–5, 98, 108, 111, 113, 117, 130, 138, 140, 144, 148, 152, 155, 157–9, 165, 171, 174, 178, 181, 185, 204
Connecticut, 20, 27, 33, 35, 45, 68, 73–4, 84, 93, 115, 124, 150
Connecticut militia, 22
Connecticut River, 35, 99, 111–12, 114, 124, 199
Constitution (US), 5–6, 207, 209
Constitution Island, 74
Continental Army, 27, 31–2, 47, 90, 144
Conway (New Hampshire), 195, 198–9
Cornwallis, Lord, 99, 108–9, 126
Cook, James, 128, 130
Cooper, Samuel, 56
Copp's Hill (Boston), 18
Cotton, John, 72, 103
Cowpens, Battle of, 101, 103
Crawford Notch, 197

Crevecoeur, Hector St John de, *Letters from an American Farmer*, 5
Cromwell (Oliver), 146, 155
Cronk, Hercules, 31
Croton River, 34
Crown, 9–11, 116
Cuba, 114, 138
Cutler, Manasseh, 5, 194, 200

Danbury (Connecticut), 35, 73
Daniel, Book of, 60–1, 146, 148
Danvers (Massachusetts), 36
Dark Day, 89–91
Dartmouth (Jefferson, New Hampshire), 111, 196–7
Dartmouth College, 43, 87, 98, 153
Declaration of Independence, 28–9, 33, 185
Dedham (Massachusetts), 35
Deism, 79, 150–1, 153
Delaware, 39, 47
Delaware Bay, 191
Delaware River, 33, 39, 48, 169, 171, 174, 191
Democritus *see* Isaac Mansfield
Derby (Connecticut), 35
Dick, Charles, 42
Dighton Rock, 181, 183–4, 186
disease, 22, 34
Dobb's Ferry, 31–2, 34
Doddridge, Philip, 71
Dorchester (Massachusetts), 73
Dorchester Heights, 26, 55
Dorchester Neck, 20
Dover (New Hampshire), 4, 10–12, 17–22, 25–6, 55–7, 60, 63–9, 71–2, 76, 81, 87–8, 94–5, 101, 105–6, 111, 118, 120, 128, 144, 147–8, 152–4, 161–3, 167–8, 170–2, 174–6, 189, 193, 195, 202, 210
Dover Point, 7, 25, 62, 94
Druid, 109–10
Dudleian Lecture, 60
Dugard, William, 181
Dumfries (Virginia), 42
Du Pratz, Page, 77
Durham (New Hampshire), 23
Dutch Reformed Church (Fishkill), 34

earthquakes, 81
East India, 126, 130
East River, 29–30, 32
Ebeling, Christopher, 5
Ecclesiastes, Book of, 140
Eckley, Joseph, 'Divine Glory displayed in the Condemnation', 141
Edenton (North Carolina), 45–6, 50
egg *see* state constitution
Election Day, 55
Eliot, Andrew, Sr, 9, 11, 16–19, 21, 25, 55, 57–8, 60, 67
Eliot, Andrew, Jr, 16, 58, 73
Eliot, John, 1, 14, 19, 21, 55–56, 60, 69, 71–3, 75, 77, 79–80, 120–1, 131, 133, 152, 159–60, 162, 164, 171, 175, 177–8, 180–1, 184, 186, 188, 202–4
  and occupation of Boston, 9–11
  letters of, 1–3, 9, 55–9
  universalist, 3
Eliot, Samuel, 132, 150–3, 163
Elizabeth (New Jersey) 33, 47–8, 93
Elizabeth, Queen, 68
Ellis River, 195
Elysian Fields, 128
Episcopal, 40, 43, 45
epistles, 1–6, 29, 58, 65, 75, 79, 100, 107, 131, 138, 144, 156, 175, 201, 210–11
Essay on the Agitations of the Sea, 77, 81–2
Eusebius of Caesarea, 123
Evans, John, 195–6, 198
Evans, Rev. John, 84
Evans, Israel, 114
Exeter (New Hampshire), 2, 8, 17, 22, 86, 98

Fabius, 146
Fairfield (Connecticut), 16, 57–8, 73
Falmouth (Portland, Maine), 23, 25, 37–9, 61–2, 93
Faneuil Hall, 14
Fell's Point, 40
Field, Mr, 117
Finley, Samuel, 28, 68, 69
First Parish of Dover, 7
First Parish of Exeter, 22
First Parish of Kennebunkport, 38
First Parish of Malden, 14
First Presbyterian Church, Elizabeth, 48

First Presbyterian Church, Morristown, 47
First Presbyterian Church, Newark, 48
First Presbyterian Church, Newburport, 36
Fisher, Joshua, 195–7
Fishkill (New York), 34–5, 73, 75
Fish Street (Boston), 15, 17
Folsom's Tavern, 12
Fort Clinton, 34
Fort Hill, 55
Fort Lee, 32, 34
Fort Montgomery, 34
Fort Ticonderoga, 29, 31
Fort Washington, 32, 34
Fort William and Mary, 8, 10, 21, 37, 55
Foster, Hannah Webster, 5
Fountain Inn, 40
Fox, George, 177
Fowle, Daniel, 67, 80
France (French), 8, 38, 56, 60, 75, 89, 99, 108, 111, 115, 120–1, 125, 130, 144–5, 147, 179, 202
Franciscans, 85
Franklin, Benjamin, 5, 23, 27, 31, 154, 167, 173
Fredericksburg (Virginia), 42
Freeman, Samuel, 38, 62
Freemason *see* John Eliot
French-Indian War, 10
French Rococo, 120
Freneau, Philip, 2, 110, 117, 120–1, 140, 144
Fryeburg (Maine), 199

Gabriel, 115
Gage, Thomas, 8, 10, 14, 16–18
Gates, Horatio, 23, 29–31
Gay Head, 81–2
George II, King, 44, 47
George III, King, 9, 11, 22, 24, 29–30, 115, 148, 204
Georgetown (South Carolina), 51–2
Georgia, 52–53, 74–5, 209
Globe Tavern, 37
Glorious Revolution, 10
Goddard, William, 27
Godsgrace, 40
Goldsmith, Oliver, 123, 126
  A Deserted Village, 48

Gordon, William, 2, 29, 35, 63, 67, 70, 73–5, 80, 86, 92, 101, 109–10, 117, 125, 133, 139, 141, 145–6, 180, 182, 185
  History of the Rise, Progress, and Establishment of the Independence of the United States, 2
Gorges Banks, 165
Gorges, Thomas, *History*, 63–4
Gosnold, Bartholomew, 210
Gospels, 122–3, 127, 130, 143
Goths, 128
Gove, Edward, 116
Grafton (New Hampshire), 98–9
Grayson, William, 42
Great Bay, 7, 12, 67
Great Britain (England), 1, 3, 8–11, 15, 46, 56, 61, 72–5, 87, 89, 98, 111, 115–17, 122, 130, 144–6, 151–2, 165
Great Commission, 122
Great Dismal Swamp, 45
Great Island, 37
Great Lakes, 85
great laurel *(Rhododendron maximum)*, 42
Great Migration, 15
Great Mountain *see* Mount Washington
Greene, Joseph, 95–6
Greene, Nathaniel, 108
Greenland (New Hampshire), 7, 12, 37
Gregory, John, 95
  A Father's Legacy to his Daughters, 94
Gregorian calendar, 115
Grenada, 115
Griswold, Matthew, 23
Gyles, John, 66

Halifax (North Carolina), 46
Halifax, Nova Scotia, 27
Hall, Samuel, 121
Hampshire County (Massachusetts), 122
Hampton (New Hampshire), 12, 37
Hampton Falls (New Hampshire), 12, 36–7, 63, 67, 88
Hanover Street (Boston), 17
Harford (Maryland), 40
Harlem Heights, 31–2
Harrison, Benjamin, 23
Hartford (Connecticut), 35

Harvard College, 4, 7, 9, 13–15, 19, 36, 60, 87, 103, 154, 181, 195
Haslett, William, 188, 193–4
Hastings, Jonathan, 13, 36, 83, 99, 121
Haven, Joseph, 2
Haven, Samuel, 7
Haverhill (Massachusetts), 21, 25
Havre de Grace (Maryland), 40
Hazard, Abigail Arthur, 2, 155–6, 158–9, 171, 175, 182, 185, 187–8, 191, 197, 201–3, 210
Hazard, Catherine Clarkson, 28
Hazard, Ebenezer
  antiquarian, 4, 61, 68, 209
  biographer, 66, 68–70
  bookseller, 4, 27, 116
  character of, 3, 28, 73, 205
  chronologist, 84, 88, 114–15
  conservative, 6, 62, 172, 191
  critic, 6
  editor, 4, 43, 67–8, 70, 84, 95, 104–5, 106–8, 114, 139–41, 143–4, 157–8, 168, 178, 207, 209
  family, 183, 185, 187–8, 190, 191, 194, 201, 203–5, 207, 209
  friendship, 4–5, 61–6, 82, 85, 95–6, 99–101, 110, 114, 139, 182, 189, 209
  geographer, 66, 72, 77, 79, 82, 84, 88
  historian, 6, 35–6, 61–4, 77, 114, 210
  Historical Collections: Consisting of State Papers, and Other Authentic Documents; Intended as Materials for an History of the United States of America, 4, 159–60, 207
  in Manhattan, 27–31
  letters of, 1–3, 5–6, 29–31, 63, 65–6, 68, 70–6, 79–80, 82–7, 89, 91–9, 101–18, 121–35, 138–41, 143–6, 147–52, 157–63, 165–6, 169–76, 178–81, 183–91, 194, 197, 200–5, 209–10
  life, 28, 185
  marriage, 150–1, 153, 155–60, 168, 209
  museum, 3, 61, 72, 80, 82, 209
  patriot, 3, 30, 36, 46, 93
  political views, 6, 62, 152, 188, 210
  postmaster general, 1, 4, 113, 117, 120, 138, 144, 165, 168, 185, 189, 207, 209

postmaster of New York, 1, 27, 29–32, 48, 116, 209
Presbyterian, 4, 36, 44, 47–8, 52–3, 92, 113, 135, 138–9, 174, 176, 179, 208
religion, 5–6, 28, 48, 53, 62, 72–3, 75, 82–3, 96, 104, 113, 139–40, 144, 150, 185, 188, 191, 209
scientist, 5, 82–6, 91–2, 98, 101, 104, 117, 147, 149, 190, 209–10
sickness, 190–1, 193, 200–4
surveyor of post roads, 1–4, 28, 32–53, 61–4, 73, 75, 79, 84, 86, 94, 209
translator, 4
travels, 6–7, 33–53, 61–67, 71, 73–5, 82–3, 86, 92–6, 98–9, 101–2, 112, 205, 209
Hazard, Samuel, Jr, 183, 185, 188, 190–1, 201–5, 210
Hazard, Samuel, Sr, 28
Hazzen, Colonel, 89
Head of Elk (Elkton, Maryland), 39, 48
Hebrew, 128, 183
Hellenistic Empire, 61
Hemmingway, Moses, 135
hen *see* state convention
Hennepin, Louis (Father), 77, 85
  Description of Louisiana, 85–6
Henry II, King, 133
Henry, Patrick, 43
Hessians, 42, 48
Hobamoke, 199
Holland, 75
Hollis, Thomas, 17
Holt, John, 27
Holy Bible, 4, 24, 60, 71, 73, 82–3, 85, 90, 127, 130–1, 140, 142, 144–6, 177, 183, 186–8
Holy Land, 71–2
Homer, 110
Horace, 68
Hornby, William, 53
Housatonic River, 35
House of Burgesses, 44
Howe, Richard, 27, 29–30
Howe, William, 20, 26–7, 29–32, 39, 48, 53
Howel's Tavern, 44
Hudson River, 29, 31–5, 74–5, 111
Hume, David, 65, 71
Hutchinson, Thomas, 17

Illinoia, 181
Independent Company of Free Citizens, 30
Independent Ledger, 68–9
Ingenhousz, John, 151
Inglis, Charles, 125
inoculation, 39, 41, 155
Ipswich (Massachusetts), 13
Iroquois Indians, 75
ising-glass, 81, 86–7, 89, 91, 94–5, 98–9, 112, 184
Ising-glass River, 81–2, 85–6
Isle of Wight County (Virginia), 44
Isles of Shoals, 21
Israel, lost tribes of, 183
Israel River, 197
Italy, 154, 183

Jackson, Hall, 21
Jacobs, John, 35
Jaffrey, George, 107
Jamaica Plain *see* Roxbury
James River, 43–4, 50
Jamestown, 43–4
Jefferson, Thomas, 5, 39
Jeffries, David, 107–8
Jesuits, 108, 153
Jesus of Nazareth, 122–3, 143
Job, Book of, 156
Johnson, Samuel, 152
  Lives of the Poets, 204
  Rambler, 170
Jonah, 114
Jones, John Paul, 125–6, 130
Josephus, 90
Joshua, 118, 165
Josselyn, John, 115
Joy Street *see* Belknap's Lane
Julian calendar, 115

Kennebunkport (Maine), 38
Killsa, Moses, 163
Kimball, Nathaniel, 38
King George's War, 107
King William county, 42–3
King William's War, 115, 118
Kingston (New Hampshire), 25
Kingston (New Jersey), 33
Kittery (Maine), 7, 38, 94, 110, 180

Kittery Point, 32, 38
Knight, John, 7
Knight, Mr, 12
Knight's Ferry, 7, 11–12, 62, 94

Lady Day, 115
Lafayette, Marquis de, 203
Lake Champlain, 29, 124
Lake George, 29
Lamprey River, 7
Lancaster (Pennsylvania), 48–9
Langdon, John, 8, 60
Langdon, Samuel, 7, 13, 94
Langdon, Woodbury, 60
Langston's, 45
Lapis specularis *see* ising-glass
L'Auguste, 131
Lebanon (Maine), 98
Lee, Charles, 23, 32, 47, 134, 140
Lent's Tavern, 13
Leonard, Abiel, 23
Lesesne, Peter, 52
Leslie, Charles, *Short and Easy Method with the Deists*, 153
Leslie, Mr, 175
letters *see* epistles
Lexington (Massachusetts), 11, 14, 27, 36
Libbey, Jeremiah, 37–8, 63, 152–3, 178, 180, 182, 189
Lincoln, Benjamin, 52, 74
Linnæus (Carolus), 124
Little, Daniel, 38, 95, 98, 195
Little Bay, 7
Little Carpenter, 43
Little Harbor, 106
Livingston, Robert, 30
Locke, John, 5, 65
London, 116–17, 132, 153, 155, 162–4, 202–3
Long Bay, 51
Long Island, 28, 30, 82
Longman, Thomas, 162, 164, 202–3
Long Wharf, 15
Lord Bolingbroke, 189
Lord Chesterfield, Earl, 97, 107
    Principles of Politeness, 67, 91, 94–5
Lord North, 120
Loudon (New Hampshire), 177

Louisbourg, 107, 115, 118
Louisiana Territory, 77, 85
Lovewell, John, 199
Loyalists *see* Tories
Lucina, 175
Lunan, Patrick, 45
Luther, Martin, 179
Lynch, Thomas, Jr, 23
Lynn (Massachusetts), 13

MacClintock, Samuel, 7
McWhorter, Alexander, 48
Madoc, 184
Madockawando, 184, 186
Magnifique, 126
Maidenhead (New Jersey), 47
Maine, 7, 37–8, 63, 75, 82, 96, 98–99, 128, 177, 180, 195, 199, 209–10
Malden (Massachusetts), 2, 13–14, 16–19, 21–2, 118
Malden River, 14
Malta, 129
Manco Capac, 133
Manhattan *see* New York
Mansfield, Isaac, 2, 22, 86–7, 137
Marbois, François, 108–9, 111, 130, 200
Marcus Aurelius, 29
Market Square (Portsmouth), 37
Martha's Vineyard, 81
Mary (Virgin), 115, 199
Maryland, 39–41, 46, 49, 83, 113–14
Mashamoquet River, 35
Mason, George, 42
Mason, Robert, 71–2, 113–14
Massachusettensis, 10
Massachusetts, 8, 11, 13, 17, 20, 27, 29, 35–6, 73, 82, 85–7, 90–2, 95, 104, 110, 112–13, 141, 151, 159, 176, 194, 199
Massachusetts Bay, 68
Massachusetts Historical Society, 4
Massabesic (Maine), 177
Mather, Cotton, 17, 84, 155, 199
Mather, Increase, 17
Mattaponi River, 42
Mayhew, Jonathan, 152
Medford (Massachusetts), 21, 25
Mendon (Massachusetts), 35
Mentor *see* Ebenezer Hazard

Mercer, James, 42
Mercury, 1–2, 6, 210
Merrimack River, 13, 25, 36, 81, 114
Metropolitan *see* Joseph Buckminster
Michigania, 181
Middletown (Connecticut), 35
Mifflin, Thomas, 23–4, 204
Middletown (Connecticut), 91
militia, 8, 11–14, 20–4, 39–40, 43, 199
Mill Cove (Boston), 17
Milton (John), 185
Miranda *see* Abigail Arthur Hazard
Mississippi River, 77, 82, 85, 114
Mohawk Indians, 153
Monarch *see* Noah Webster
Montreal, 112
Moose Mountain, 80, 129, 210
Morgan, Daniel, 103–4
Morris, Robert, 172
Morristown (New Jersey), 33, 47
Morse, Jedidiah, 5, 210
Moses, 143
Mount Agamenticus, 38, 210
Mount Etna, 142
Mount Vernon, 41, 180, 182
Mount Vesuvius, 142, 154
Mount Washington, 194–6, 199, 201
mountain laurel *(Kalmia latifolia)*, 42
Mowat, Henry, 23, 25, 39
Mrs Bleeker's, 47
Mrs White's Tavern, 47
Muddy River, 22
Murray, John, 127
Myrick, 163
Myrtle Beach, 51
Mystic River, 13, 18, 25

Nantucket (Massachusetts), 155
Narragansett Indians, 35
Narrow, 28
natural theology, 77, 81, 91–2, 145–6, 176, 198
Naugatuck River, 35
Nebuchadnazzar, 60–1, 146, 148
Negroes, 41, 44, 51–2, 181
Nelson's Ordinary, 44
Neuse River, 51
Newark (Delaware), 39

Newark (New Jersey), 33, 48
Newark Mountains, 48
New Bern (North Carolina), 51
Newbury (Massachusetts), 13–14, 166
Newburyport (Massachusetts), 13, 17, 36, 95
New Brunswick (New Jersey), 33
Newburgh (New York), 34
Newcastle Island, 8, 21, 37, 55
New England, 2–4, 9, 15, 20–1, 23, 27,
    33–5, 37, 52, 67–8, 71, 75–7, 80, 89–90,
    99, 108, 113–14, 127, 134, 141, 145,
    160, 165, 170, 172, 175, 191, 194–5,
    198–9, 204, 210
New England Confederation, 67, 104–5
New Hampshire, 2, 7–9, 14, 17–18, 20–1,
    24–5, 27, 36–7, 59–60, 63, 66–7, 71,
    77, 81–2, 84, 86, 91–4, 98–9, 108–9,
    111–16, 124, 126, 128–9, 132, 137,
    144–5, 148, 153, 165, 169, 173–4, 182,
    199
New Hampshire Association of Ministers,
    134
New Hampshire Committee of Safety, 20
New Haven (Connecticut), 35, 68, 104
Newington (New Hampshire), 2, 7, 12, 25,
    62, 153
New Jersey, 29, 33–4, 46–7, 71–2, 74, 92–3,
    112, 139, 155–7, 159, 191
New Light Protestants *see* Protestants
New-North Church (Boston), 11, 15, 17
Newport (Rhode Island), 75
New Rochelle (New York), 32
New Style, 115, 175
Newton (Massachusetts), 14
Newtown (Connecticut), 35
New Windsor (New York), 34, 73
New York, 1, 3, 34–6, 48, 50, 73–5, 76, 79,
    90, 93, 111, 115–16, 122, 124, 126, 139,
    143, 145, 156, 202, 209–10
    British occupation of, 33, 73
    fall of, 1, 28, 31–2
    fight over, 27–32
New York Committee of Safety, 27, 30–1
New York Gazetteer, 28
New York Harbor, 29
New York Provincial Congress, 27, 30–1, 34
Niagara Falls, 77, 85
Ninevah, 114

Nipmuck Indians, 35
Noddle's Island, 19
Noel, Garret, 28, 47–8, 116
Noel and Hazard, 28
North Carolina, 41, 45–6, 50–1, 82
North Castle (New York), 32
Northeast River, 39
North End (Boston), 17–18
North Hampton (New Hampshire), 12, 37
North Parish (Portsmouth), 7, 13
North Santee River, 52
North Square (Boston), 17
Norway, 127, 130
Novanglus, 10
Nova Scotia, 27–28, 165

Occaquam River, 42
Ohio River, 82
Old Light Protestants *see* Protestants
Old North Church (Boston), 18
Old South *see* South Church
Old Style, 67, 115
Old Testament *see* Holy Bible
Old York, 38
Orange (New Jersey), 48
Oyster River, 7, 57, 76

Paine, Thomas, 127–8, 130, 211
   Age of Reason, 208
   Common Sense, 116
   Crisis, 125, 128, 148
Palisades, 33
Pamlico River, 50–1
Pandemonium, 185
Papist (Popish) *see* Roman Catholicism
Paris, 143
Parker Ford, 49
Parliament, 9–11
Passaic Falls, 33, 92
Passaic River, 47
Patapsco River, 40
Patriots, 10, 15, 24, 36, 50, 58, 79, 93, 97, 101, 103, 122, 124, 139, 166
Patuxent River, 40–1
Paul (Apostle), 134, 143–5, 150, 165, 177, 179
Peale, Charles Wilson, 40, 92
Peekskill (New York), 34

Pelham, Henry, 15–16
Pemigewasset River, 177
Pennsylvania, 39, 43, 49, 52, 81, 87, 91–3, 127, 130, 139, 149, 153, 155, 160–1, 165, 169, 171, 185
Pennycook, 68–9
Penny Ferry, 13–14, 18–19
Penobscot Valley, 38, 75, 184
Pepperrell, William, 115, 118
Pequawket Indians, 199
Persian Empire, 61
Peter (Apostle), 142
Philadelphia, 2, 28, 33, 39–40, 46–9, 52–3, 63–5, 67, 72, 74–5, 85–6, 90–9, 107–8, 110, 113, 116–18, 120–1, 123, 126–7, 131, 133, 138–41, 143, 149, 151, 154–5, 157–63, 166–8, 170–1, 173, 175–6, 178–81, 188–9, 194, 197, 200–4, 209–10
Philipsburg (New York), 34
Phillips, John, 19
Phillips–Exeter Academy, 98
Phoenician, 183–4
Pierpoint, Robert, 22
Pidgeon, 43
Piscataqua Bridge, 7
Piscataqua River, 7–8, 10–11, 21, 25, 37–8, 60–2, 67, 94, 106, 112, 125, 160–1, 210
pitch pine (*Pinus rigida*), 45
Pitt, William, 40
physicians, 34
Place, George, 195
Plain Doctor *see* William Gordon
Plaistow (New Hampshire), 25
Plumb Island, 166
Plutarch, 65, 71, 112
Plymouth (Massachusetts), 68, 72, 102–5
Pomfret (Connecticut), 35
Pompton (New Jersey), 33
Pope, Alexander, 5–6, 65–6, 177, 189
   Art of Sinking, 72
Port Bill *see* Coercive Acts
Port Royal, 42
Portsmouth Harbor, 8, 37, 125, 130, 133
Portsmouth (New Hampshire), 2, 7–8, 11, 13, 21, 23, 25, 37–8, 55, 58, 60–4, 73, 83–4, 94, 101, 105–7, 111–12, 115, 121, 124–5, 127, 131, 148, 150, 152–3, 157,

159, 163–4, 178, 180–2, 185, 189, 193, 203, 210
Potomac River, 41–2, 46
Presbyterians, 28, 32, 36, 44, 47–8, 52–3, 92, 113, 132, 135, 138–9, 170, 172, 174, 176, 179, 183, 208
Prevost, Augustine, 52
Prince, Thomas, 15, 71, 84
Princeton College, 28, 32, 47, 52, 68
Princeton (New Jersey), 33, 47, 56, 164
Prince William County, 42
Prospect Hill, 24
Protestant Reformation, 88, 106
Protestants, 3, 28, 36, 38, 50, 88, 92, 113, 118, 137, 139–40, 176
Providence (Rhode Island), 115
Pudding *see* universal salvation
Puddle Dock (Portsmouth), 37
Puritan, 102, 208

Quakers, 46–7, 64, 113, 137, 162, 176, 181, 189
Quantico River, 42
Quincy, Elizabeth, 18
Quinebaug River, 35
Quinnipiac River, 35

Raleigh, 55
Ramapo River, 33
Ramsay, David, 52
Rappahannoc River, 42
Rawling's Tavern, 40
Records of the United Colonies of New England, 67, 102, 104, 107–10
Redcoats, 9–11, 13, 16, 22–3, 25, 30
Red Lion Inn, 40
Reed, Joseph, 23
Regulators, 51
Revelation, 139
Revere, Paul, 18
Revolution *see* War for American Independence
Rhode Island, 20, 27, 33, 35, 74–5
Richardson, Samuel, 5
Riddick, Wills, 45
Rittenhouse, David, 89, 92, 171
Rivington, James, 28, 131, 133
Roanoke River, 46

Rochester (New Hampshire), 2, 200
Rodgers' Tavern, 40
Rodney, George, 125
Rogers, Robert, 199
Rollins, Charles, 204
Roman Catholicism, 38, 85, 87, 92, 113, 137–8, 153
Roman Empire, 61, 85, 122–3, 128, 146, 176, 204
Rowley (Massachusetts), 13
Roxbury (Massachusetts), 2, 20, 22–3, 29, 35–6, 55, 67, 73–5, 85, 92, 94, 99, 101, 104, 106, 109–10, 112, 125, 133, 139
Royal Society, 176
Royalton (Vermont), 99
Rush, Benjamin, 5, 34
Russia, 85, 127

Saco (Maine), 38, 98
Saco River (Valley), 61, 198–9
Sagamore of Agawam, 108
St Francis Indians, 112
Salem (Massachusetts), 13, 121
Salisbury (Massachusetts), 36
Salmon Falls River, 7, 61, 128–9, 210
Saratoga *see* Battle of Saratoga
Saratoga, 181
Savannah (Georgia), 48, 52–3, 74, 125
Savannah River, 53
Scandinavia, 128, 130
Scarborough, 8, 21
Scarborough (Maine), 38
Schuykill River, 48–9, 175
Scipio, 146
Scotland, 139
Seabrook (New Hampshire), 12, 36
Second Death, 143, 208
Second Presbyterian Church of Philadelphia, 28
Seneca Indians, 114
Severn River, 40
Sewall, Joseph, 15, 18
Sewall, Samuel, 18–19
Sewall, Samuel (Deacon), 18
Shakers, 169, 173–5, 177, 179, 199
Shays's Rebellion, 208
Shawmut, 17
Shirley, William, 115, 118, 159

Shrewsbury (New Jersey), 191
Sicily, 154
slaves, 41, 44–6, 50–3
smallpox, 39, 41, 154–5
Smith, John, 39
Smithfield (Virginia), 44
Smith's Tavern, 42
Society for the Propagation of the Gospel, 122, 125
Society of Cincinnati, 164, 172
Society of Friends *see* Quakers
Socinian, 188, 193
Solomon, 176, 202
Somerset, 18
Somerset (Millsborough, New Jersey), 47
Somersworth (New Hampshire), 185
Sons of Liberty, 115–17
sons of science, 5, 79, 137, 199
South Carolina, 51–3, 89, 93, 101, 110, 140
South Church (Boston), 15, 18, 71
South River, 40
South Santee River, 52
Spanish (Spain), 77, 111, 130, 138, 145, 147
Sparhawk, John, 130
Springfield (New Jersey), 33, 47, 112
Squamscot River, 7–8
Stamp Act, 8, 29, 115–16
state constitution, 2, 5–6, 68–71, 73, 112, 131, 154, 156, 164
state convention, 2, 68–9, 71–3, 81, 108–9, 114, 131, 137
Staten Island, 28–30, 47
Stephens, Richard, 50–1
Stevens, Benjamin, 38, 61, 94, 180
Stiles, Ezra, 59, 70, 181, 183–4, 186
Stirling, Lord, 30
Storm, Abraham, 31
Stratham (New Hampshire), 25
Strawbery Banke, 37
Suffolk (Virginia), 44–5
Sullivan, John, 8, 23, 30, 75–6, 108–10, 114, 130, 156, 167, 177, 179, 200
Sumner's Tavern, 45
Surry County (Virginia), 44
Surveyor of the Post Office in the Southern District, 50
Susquehanna River, 39, 49
Sweden, 127, 130

Swift, Jonathan, 72, 128
Sylvania, 181

Tammany, 185
Tappan Sea, 33
Tarrytown (New York), 34
Tea Act, 8–9
Telemachus *see* Philip Freneau
Tennent, Gilbert, 28
Tennent, William, 84
Thacher, Peter, 2, 13–14, 16, 21–2, 118, 121–2, 126
Thames River, 35
Thayer, Ebenezer, 12–13
Third Parish (Roxbury), 35
Thomas, John, 22
Thompson (Connecticut), 35
Thomson, Charles, 4, 140
Throg's Neck (New York), 32
Tillotson, Archbishop, 85
Timothy, 144–5
Titcomb, Benjamin, 20
Topsfield (Massachusetts), 36
Tories, 14–15, 22–3, 27, 30–1, 33, 41, 46–7, 50, 56, 58–9, 72–3, 79, 99, 125, 131, 139, 149, 152–3, 155, 165
Treadwell, Jacob, 159
Trenton (New Jersey), 33, 42, 47, 165
Trinity Church (Fishkill), 34
trout lily (*Erythronium americanum*), 40
Trumball, Jonathan, *McFingal*, 125
Tryon, William, 51, 73
Tuckahoe Creek, 42

Ulysses *see* Geraldus Clarkson
United Provinces, 145
United States of America, 3, 34, 114, 117, 145, 154, 165
United States Navy, 126, 130
universal salvation, 3, 5, 126–7, 131, 134–5, 139–47, 186–7, 203–4
universalist, 3, 5, 180, 182, 185, 187–8, 191, 208
Upper Marlboro, 41

Vandals, 128
Vega, Garcilasso de la, 129, 133, 137
Venus, 5, 57, 202

Vera Cruz, 126
Vermont, 76, 79, 111–14, 116, 124, 137
Verrazano Bridge, 28
Vicar of Wakefield, 155
Virgil, 65, 71
Virginia, 40–1, 43–6, 50, 82–3, 108–9, 113–14
Virginia, 40

Waldron, Thomas, 7
Walpole, Horace, 6
War for American Independence, 1, 3–4, 8–11, 20, 22–3, 25–6, 29–36, 39, 46–9, 52–3, 60, 63, 65, 67, 70–1, 73–7, 84, 89, 93, 99, 107–9, 111, 113, 125–6, 132, 140, 144–5, 161–2, 180, 205, 208–10
Ward, Artemas, 22–3
Ward, Joshua, 22
Wardsessing, 48
Warren, Joseph, 14, 23, 36
Washington, George, 5, 23, 25, 29–34, 36, 41, 48–9, 53, 67, 74, 102–4, 124, 126, 146, 171, 174, 180, 182, 185, 190, 207
Watchung Range, 47
Waters, Josiah, 109
Watts, Isaac, 4, 65, 71
Webster, Noah, 2, 5–6, 210
Webster, Samuel, 20
Wells (Maine), 95, 98, 135
Wells's Tavern, 37, 63
Welsh, 184, 186
Wentworth, John, 7–9, 21, 24, 165
Wentworth, Michael, 105
West India (Indies), 126, 184
Westminster Confession of Faith, 174
West Nottingham Academy, 28

West Point, 34, 74, 97
West, Stephen, 41
Wheelock, Eleazar, 153
Whiddon, Mehetabel, 157–8
Whigs, 11, 27, 29, 31
Whipple, Joseph, 111, 195–7
White Mountains (White Hills), 4, 25, 81, 108–11, 115, 117, 123, 189–90, 193–201, 210
White Plains (New York), 32
Whitefield, George, 28, 50, 177, 179
Widow Noel's, 48
Williamsburg (Virginia), 43–4, 49
Wilmington (Delaware), 39
Wilmington (Massachusetts), 25
Wilmington (North Carolina), 51
Wingate, Enoch, 195
Winnacunnet, 12
Winnipesaukee River, 177
Winslow, Edward, 105
Winter Hill, 21, 25
Winthrop, John, 17, 59
Winthrop, John, IV, 103
Witherspoon, John, 32
Woburn (Massachusetts), 25
Woodbridge's Tavern, 38
Woodyard, 41
Wynne, John, *A General History of the British Empire in America*, 59

Yale College, 35, 70
York Harbor, 38
York (Maine), 38, 177
York (Pennsylvania), 49
York (Virginia), 44, 49
Yorktown, 120, 126

For Product Safety Concerns and Information please contact our EU representative GPSR@taylorandfrancis.com
Taylor & Francis Verlag GmbH, Kaufingerstraße 24, 80331 München, Germany

www.ingramcontent.com/pod-product-compliance
Lightning Source LLC
Chambersburg PA
CBHW070600300426
44113CB00010B/1334